HEARING MU

AN INTRODUCTION

HEARING MUSIC
AN INTRODUCTION

NICK ROSSI
LaGuardia Community College
The City University of New York

HARCOURT BRACE JOVANOVICH, INC.
New York / San Diego / Chicago / San Francisco / Atlanta / London / Sydney / Toronto

Requests for permission to make copies of any part of the work should be mailed to: Permissions, Harcourt Brace Jovanovich, Inc., 757 Third Avenue, New York, N.Y. 10017.

ISBN: 0-15-535597-X
Library of Congress Catalog Card Number: 80-82051

Printed in the United States of America

Cover Painting by Alice Brickner

Dedicated to
Geraldine Smith Healy
whose friendship, help, and encouragement
have inspired my life in music

All art aspires
toward the condition of music.
Walter Pater

PREFACE

The world is filled with the sounds of music of all kinds. Some of this music today we label rock, soul, and salsa. Much of it we call classical. Another popular form is jazz. Virtually every nation or region has its own folk music, that wonderful body of generally anonymous music that often has given inspiration to classical composers. Still another type of music, which we tend hardly to be aware of, serves as background for movies, television, and commercials. It is amazing to stop and realize how much music and how many types of music are available to us every day. Actually, we live in an age that seems almost afraid of silence. We hear Muzak in stores, airports, and elevators. Portable radios and cassette players go with us on picnics, to the beach, and even, with some of us, as we walk down the street. Hardly a car exists that does not have a radio. The very walls of discos vibrate from the pounding beat of the music.

In spite of having all this music around, few people ever really *hear* it—if we define *hearing,* as Webster does, as "the act or instance of actively or carefully listening." Rather, most people let the music engulf them like a tone bath, without ever "actively or carefully" listening to it.

Hearing Music: An Introduction is designed to give students a working knowledge of the constituent elements of music so that they can actively and carefully listen to a wide variety of music with appreciation and understanding. This text also tries to make familiar the basic concepts of that rather elusive characteristic we term *style,* enabling students to discern the changing nature and forms of music over various historical periods. For illustration, this book utilizes music literature that is a pervasive and enduring part of Western culture: instrumental, symphonic, ballet, vocal, and operatic music; jazz; and electronic music. A deeper awareness and understanding of such music literature for its own intrinsic worth is thus provided.

The book is in two parts. The first part is concerned with the constituent elements of music—tone (including timbre), rhythm, melody, texture, dynamics, tempo, and form or design. The second part is concerned with the principal stylistic periods of music, with discussion of representative composers from each period.

Attached to the inside back cover of the book is an envelope containing records for the student—four eight-inch records with complete selections or movements from fifteen masterpieces used to illustrate the two parts of the text. These records give students material for individual listening. At the end of the text are tear-out worksheets with which students can evaluate their learning accomplishments after reading the chapter and listening to the records.

Part I, "The Elements of Music," presents each component of music through three complete selections or movements from well-chosen major works. With the exception of Britten's *Young Person's Guide to the Orchestra,* of which the longer portion is on the student records, two movements of each work are included on six twelve-inch records provided for classroom use by the instructor. The third part or movement of each work is on the student records.

Part II, "Concepts of Style," first moves through the styles most easily understood by students: Romantic, Nationalistic, Impressionistic, twentieth-century, electronic, and jazz. It then goes back to Renaissance music, followed by Baroque (Bach and Handel) and finally Classical (Haydn and Mozart). Again, each chapter is illustrated by three-part recordings—two parts for classroom use and one for the student. The book is thus arranged for maximum flexibility, adaptable to the interests of the students and the preferences of the instructor. The Instructor's Manual contains answers to the worksheet questions along with sample lessons for class listening activities.

It will be noted that students are not required to purchase a separate workbook and that the records for the instructor have been kept to six. The text is well illustrated, and in Chapter 2, before any musical examples are shown, students learn some of the basics of reading music. Listening outlines specially set off in the text describe each musical selection step by step and include the important themes in staff notation. Part I introduces students to a variety of composers whose music is used to exemplify the constituent elements of music: Britten, Bizet, Copland, Handel, Mussorgsky, Castelnuovo-Tedesco, and Dvořák. Part II presents the leading composers of the periods and styles represented.

The text provides a basic course aimed at getting students to actively listen and think about the music they hear. It allows the instructor to add such other selections as he or she may choose to supplement the classroom experience. Once they have experienced the nature and structure of music, students truly will be hearing music with perception and understanding.

NICK ROSSI

CONTENTS

FOURTEEN/THE RENAISSANCE   330

HEARING MUSIC

AN INTRODUCTION

PART I

THE ELEMENTS
OF MUSIC

There's music in the sighing of the reed;
There's music in the gushing of a rill;
There's music in all things, if man had ears;
The earth is but an echo of the spheres.
Lord Byron

ONE/
TONE

THE world around us is filled with sounds. Some are loud, others soft; some are pleasing to the ear, others harsh and discordant. Some sounds are planned, others accidental. Surprisingly few people ever listen to sounds in all their variety. The next time you find yourself waiting for a bus or walking down the street, notice the many different sounds that surround you—the honking horns of cars and trucks, the wailing sirens of police cars and ambulances, the high-pitched squeal of brakes, the babble of the crowd, the chirps of birds in the trees, the songs of children at play, the whistle of wind as it whips around the corner of a building.

According to physicists, all sound consists of vibrations. Irregular, random vibrations are generally called *noise.* Regular, symmetrical vibrations are called *tones,* and these are the special sounds of music.

Scream   Musical tone

Tones exist only in time. In contrast, a painting or statue is static; it can be perceived as a whole or its parts can be observed in relation to the whole. Music—which is a collection of tones—moves in time, so that if a listening experience is to be more than intriguingly kaleidoscopic in nature, you must remember at later points in a composition patterns of tones that you have heard earlier.

Tones are to music what vowels and consonants are to the spoken language—the stuff out of which the art is created. And, in both language and music, these sounds may not always have a meaning when they are put together. For example, you might understand vowels and consonants when they are used to form words and sentences in English, but you might not recognize them if they were put together to form words and sentences in Greek, Czech, or Chinese. Similarly, you might understand tones when they are put together to form melodies and harmonies in rock, disco, or jazz, but you might not comprehend them if they were put together to form the melodies and harmonies of symphonies, operas, or string quartets. But the human mind can learn and understand many languages; similarly, it is capable of learning and understanding a wide variety of music. If you learn the constituent elements of music, then, with practice and experience, you can learn to understand music's many varied types.

TONE IN MUSIC

Let's begin our examination of the elements of music by learning to recognize the characteristics of tone: pitch, duration, dynamics, and timbre.

Pitch *Pitch* is the highness or lowness of a tone. There are high-pitched tones in the songs of birds and low-pitched tones in the rumble of a foghorn. We can also discover comparative highness or lowness of pitch by experimenting with a piano. After striking one key, the tone sounded by striking any other key to the right of the first one will be higher in pitch. By striking a key to the left of the first one, a lower pitch will be sounded. The greater the distance between the two keys, the more obvious the contrast in pitch. Whether a pitch is high or low is determined by the frequency of its vibrations. (Each pitch has a certain frequency of vibrations per second.) For example, the pitch A used when the orchestra tunes up is 440 cycles or vibrations per second. The greater the frequency of vibrations per second, the higher the pitch. Thus a pitch that vibrates at 30 cycles per second is a very low pitch.

Duration Another characteristic of tone is *duration,* or longness or shortness in time. For example, a driver taps lightly on the car horn to alert the person in front that the traffic light has turned green—a quick short beep. Then another driver honks in anger, leaning on the horn—a long blast. We also can demonstrate duration in music: hum a pitch for a second, then hum the same pitch again, extending its length or duration ten, twenty, or even thirty seconds.

Dynamics How loud is a tone? How soft is it? These questions concern *dynamics,* the volume or intensity of a tone. Imagine that you are walking down a street and you hear a church bell ringing softly in the distance. As you come closer to the church the sound becomes stronger and stronger. As you pass directly in front of the church, the bell's tones become loud and clangorous. You have just heard the dynamic level of the bell's tones grow from soft to loud. A similar effect can be achieved on the piano. Strike a key lightly to produce a soft tone. Then strike the same key again, but with considerable force, to produce a louder tone. Keep your finger on the key and listen to the sound die away. You have just heard the dynamic level of the tone decrease from loud to soft. (See Chapter 5 for a more detailed discussion of dynamics.)

Timbre *Timbre* refers to the color or quality of a tone. It is the element that distinguishes a tone played on one instrument from a tone of equal pitch and intensity played on another instrument. As an example, let's take the pitch A, which is 440 cycles per second. It doesn't matter whether a clarinet or violin plays the pitch A, or even if we sing it; 440 vibrations per second are still produced. How are we able to distinguish the timbre of a clarinet, violin, or trumpet if they all play the same pitch? It's something like the way in which we recognize a voice on the telephone saying just the word "hello" without seeing who is speaking, a characteristic quality that enables us to distinguish the voice of our mother from that of a sister, an aunt, or a grandmother.

The tone color of an instrument results not only from the frequency at which it resonates (the number of vibrations per second) when blown, bowed, plucked, or

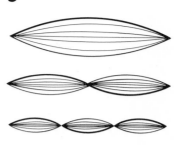

struck, but from the *harmonics* it sets up—frequencies two, three, or ten times that of the original tone. A violin string, for example, doesn't just vibrate in its entirety (which produces the *fundamental tone*), it also vibrates simultaneously in halves and thirds and many smaller segments, all of which produce tones much higher in pitch than the fundamental. The vibrations caused by the string dividing itself simultaneously into smaller segments create the *harmonics* (also called *overtones.*) Because these secondary vibrations are quite soft compared to that of the fundamental tone, our ears do not perceive them as separate pitches but regard them as part of the fundamental tone. The relative intensity or dynamic level of each harmonic differs according to the instrument that produces it. It is the blending of these overtones, the intensity of each of which varies according to the instrument that produces it, that gives the specific timbre or tone quality to each instrument we hear.

INSTRUMENTS OF THE ORCHESTRA

The instruments of the orchestra are divided into families or sections, depending in part on what material vibrates to produce the tone (strings, for example) or what the instrument is made of (brass, for example). There are four families in the symphony orchestra: strings, woodwinds, brass, and percussion. The instruments in a family can be subdivided according to the range of pitches each instrument produces. These subdivisions are usually the same as those used to classify the four major ranges of the human voice: *soprano,* the high female voice; *alto,* the low female voice; *tenor,* the high male voice; and *bass,* the low male voice.

One of the principal ways the pitches of an instrument are changed is by the shortening or lengthening of that which vibrates to produce the tone, be it a string or a column of air. With the exception of the harp, the pitches of stringed instruments are changed by moving a fingertip up or down the vibrating string to shorten or lengthen the portion that vibrates. Woodwind instruments have round holes that are covered or uncovered to lengthen or shorten the column of vibrating air, while brass instruments add tubing to increase the length of the vibrating column of air.

Strings The strings make up the largest family in the symphony orchestra in terms of number of instruments. In an average orchestra of about one hundred players, some sixty-five play stringed instruments. Why are there so many string players when there are perhaps only eight to ten brass players? A stringed instrument produces a relatively small quantity of sound compared to the sound produced by a brass instrument. And, contrary to expectation, two violins do not produce twice as much sound as one violin. In order to achieve the same volume, it is necessary to use a large number of stringed instruments and to put them in front of louder instruments such as the brass.

Violin (left) and viola (right)

Bass viol (left) and cello (right)

The four principal instruments of the string family are

violin (soprano)

viola (alto)

cello (tenor)

bass viol (bass)

These instruments look very much alike—each has four strings—and produce sound in the same way—by scraping the strings while drawing a horsehair bow across them, or by plucking them with the index finger of the right hand (called *pizzicato*). In each instrument the strings are stretched over a hollow wooden body that resonates and amplifies the tone. There are two f-shaped holes or scrolls on the upper side from which the sound emerges. Pegs attached to the neck of the instrument increase or decrease the tension of the strings as they are tuned. A small, thin piece of wood called a *bridge* supports the strings, which are spaced across the arc-shaped top so that one string can be played at a time. (It is possible to play two strings simultaneously—called *double stopping*—when it is so desired.) A tailpiece firmly anchors the other end of the strings. The four strings are tuned to a prearranged standard of pitches, and the player can change these pitches by pressing the strings down against the wooden neck with the fingers of the left hand so that only a portion of the entire string vibrates. By varying the length of the vibrating portion, the player produces the desired pitch.

The *violin* is the highest-pitched stringed instrument, the most frequently used instrument of the orchestra, and usually the most prominent in orchestral music. A skillful violinist can shade tones from soft to loud, and from the lush, romantic sound of a gypsy violin to the stark, brittle, and sometimes brutal sound of a modern symphonic work by Penderecki or Takemitsu. More common, however, is the lyrical, singing quality used in the Mendelssohn and Tchaikovsky violin concertos.

The violins in a symphony orchestra are divided into two sections: the *first* and *second violins.* There are about sixteen to eighteen of each, all of identical construction. The first violins usually play the higher, more important melodic line in compositions; the second violins usually play either in harmony with the first violins, or a melody of secondary importance to that of the first violins. The first violins are always seated to the conductor's left. The player closest to the conductor is the leader of the section and is called the *concertmaster.* All other string players take their cues from the concertmaster regarding movement of the bow and other points of playing.

The *viola* is identical in design to the violin, but is one seventh larger in size. This amounts to something less that a three-inch difference in length, making it somewhat difficult to distinguish the violin from the viola by sight unless the two are placed side by side. Because its strings are slightly longer and thicker and its body slightly larger, the viola can play five tones lower than the violin. The timbre of the viola is darker and more somber than that of the violin. There are usually about twelve to fourteen violas in a symphony orchestra.

The *cello* or *violoncello,* identical in design to the violin and viola, is twice the size of the viola and an octave lower in pitch. Because of its size, the cello rests on the floor when played, supported by a peg that protrudes from the lower part of its body. The cello's tonal and dynamic range are the greatest in the string family, being able to produce both extremely soft tones as well as extremely loud ones. The quality can vary from a lyrical tone similar to the human voice to a very gruff, rasping sound. There are usually about ten to twelve cellos in a symphony orchestra.

The *bass viol* (also known as the *string bass, contrabass, and double bass*) is about six feet tall. Because of its height, players have to stand up to play it, or sit on a high stool. The bass viol is not a member of the violin family as are the violin, viola, and cello but rather is descended from the family of instruments, known as *viol* or *vielle,* which was the forerunner of the modern violin family. The difference in construction of the bass viol can be most easily seen in the sloping shoulders (at the point where the neck melds into the body), and in the narrowness of the upper bout (the outward curve of the upper third of the body) compared to the broader sweep of the lower bout. Because of its more primitive design, the bass viol has a coarser and less refined timbre than the other members of the string family. The bass viols provide the bass or underpinning to the string section. Most orchestras have about ten bass viols.

The *harp* appeals to the eye as well as to the ear because of the beauty of its functional design. Although the harp's origins can be traced back 4,000 years to Mesopotamia, the orchestral harp in use today, the *double-action* or *pedal harp,* was introduced by Sébastien Érard about 1810. The pedals enable the length of the strings to be altered, thus providing a change in pitch. The Érard harp has seven pedals and forty-seven strings. So that the player has a point of reference, some strings are colored blue and some red. The harp usually plays the notes of a chord in rapid and even succession (an *arpeggio*), but it can also play isolated notes and complete melodic lines. There are usually two harps in most symphony orchestras, but they are used primarily in compositions written since the late nineteenth century, when the harp first joined the orchestra as a regular member. The tone of the harp is quite delicate and soft, usually suggesting a rippling effect when arpeggios are played.

Harp

Woodwinds The four principal members of the woodwind family are

> flute (soprano)
> oboe (alto)
> clarinet (tenor)
> bassoon (bass)

Each of the four woodwind instruments listed above has a close relative that is also a member of the woodwind family: piccolo (a half-sized flute), English horn (an alto oboe), bass clarinet, and contrabassoon. There are usually three each of flutes, oboes, clarinets, and bassoons in a 100-piece symphony orchestra. Customarily one player in each group plays not only the principal instrument but also the closely related one. This is called *doubling* on a second instrument.

Before the twentieth century, all the instruments in the woodwind family were made of wood. Today piccolos and flutes are usually made of silver or platinum. This

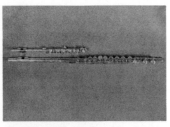

Piccolo (top) and flute (bottom)

Oboe

English horn

metal construction gives them a somewhat brighter, larger tone that blends better with the sound of the modern symphony orchestra. Oboes, clarinets, and related instruments are made of grenadilla or African blackwood. Bassoons are made of rosewood.

There are three methods of tone production in the woodwind family: blowing across a mouth hole, vibrating a single reed, and vibrating a double reed. The *flute* and *piccolo* depend on blowing across a mouth hole to set up the vibrating column of air for their sound. This method is roughly equivalent to blowing across the top of a bottle or jug to produce a sound. The flute is two feet in length; the piccolo, about half the size in length and diameter, plays one octave higher in pitch. The highest notes of the piccolo are quite shrill and piercing, and they can be heard easily above the sound of all the other instruments in the orchestra. On the other hand, the low tones of the flute are quite breathy and can be heard only in solo passages. Both flute and piccolo are agile instruments and can play extremely fast, complicated passages.

The *oboe* is usually the first instrument heard at a concert, because the A the first oboist plays before the concert begins is used by the other musicians to tune their instruments. The oboe is used because its pitch is fairly constant, and also because its pitch is difficult to adjust. The oboe, similar to other double-reeded instruments (such as English horn, bassoon, contrabassoon), is considered difficult to play. Unlike all the other brass and woodwind players, the double-reed player has to force the breath through a narrow opening between two cane reeds that are a quarter to a half inch wide. Because of its somewhat reedy tone quality and its Middle Eastern origins, the oboe is frequently used to play melodies of an exotic nature.

Playing approximately five notes below the oboe, the *English horn*—technically neither English nor a horn—is an alto or lower-voiced oboe. The English horn is wider and longer than the oboe and can be easily recognized by the angled tube connecting the reed to the body of the instrument as well as by a pear-shaped bell at the other end. The penetrating tone of the English horn is akin to the oboe's, but richer and deeper.

The *clarinet* is a single-reeded instrument. The clarinet reed is roughly a half inch wide and is attached to the underside of a black mouthpiece by a metal band called a *ligature*. Actually, a clarinet player may bring two instruments to a concert. One is pitched in A, the other in B-flat. The clarinetist may switch from one to the other, depending on the key of the work or musical passage being played. Although either instrument is capable of playing any melody, it is easier to finger certain scales and passages on one than on the other. A versatile instrument, the clarinet can play highly florid and fast-moving passages as well as slow, sustained melodic lines.

The *bass clarinet* is twice the size of a clarinet and sounds one octave lower in pitch. Because of its greater size, it is angled at the mouthpiece and has a curve at its bell end. Although at first glance you might assume from its shape that it is a saxophone, closer inspection will show that the bass clarinet has a black body because of its construction from wood. A saxophone is always made of brass. The sound of the bass clarinet is rich and somber.

Clarinet

Bass Clarinet

Bassoon

Contrabassoon

The *bassoon* and its relative the *contrabassoon* are the lowest-pitched instruments in the woodwind family. The contrabassoon is the lowest-voiced instrument in the orchestra, capable of playing down to a thirty-cycle tone.

The tubing of the bassoon is eight feet long and is doubled back against itself once. The contrabassoon, with tubing sixteen feet in length, is doubled back against itself four times. Both instruments have double reeds and, because of their depth of pitch and slowness of vibration, a very penetrating and reedy quality is characteristic in the lower range of each instrument. In its upper register or range, the bassoon sounds somewhat similar to the lyrical quality of a saxophone.

Saxophones are not considered regular members of most symphony orchestras, although composers have from time to time made use of them in their orchestral works (Ravel's *Bolero* is a good example). Invented by Adolphe Sax around 1840, they are played with a single reed attached to a mouthpiece resembling that of a clarinet. For this reason, saxophones are considered members of the woodwind family even though the instruments are made of brass. There are four sizes of saxophones in current use: soprano, alto, tenor, and baritone. (*Baritone,* in the singing voice, refers to the middle range of the male voice, between tenor and bass.) The bass saxophone is no longer used because it is large and cumbersome. Saxophones produce a mellow sound which is characterized by a prominent *vibrato,* or wavering of the tone. (See photo, page 309).

Brasses The brass instruments are among the most spectacular and impressive in a symphony orchestra. They produce a tremendous quantity of sound that is both dra-

Cornet (left) and trumpet (right)

French horn

Trombone

matic and penetrating, which is one reason they have been associated with signal calls for armies and marching battalions over the centuries. All four members of the family are descendants of an ancient line that started with animal horns hollowed out and blown by warriors to signal the start of battle. Because of this origin, some musicians call all members of the brass family *horns.*

The four contemporary members of the brass family are
trumpet (soprano)
French horn (alto)
trombone (tenor)
tuba (bass)

Tone is produced in a brass instrument by the vibrating lips of the player. The instrument itself enlarges and enriches the tone. The exact pitch is determined by the tightness of the lips as they vibrate and by the length of the tubing. The tubing in each instrument can be lengthened and shortened. This is most obvious with the trombone, whose slide moves in and out to change the length of the tubing. Valves are used on trumpets, French horns, and tubas to do this: when a valve is depressed, an additional length of tubing is added to the column of vibrating air. Trumpets use a piston valve, so called because it moves up and down like a piston in a gasoline engine. French horns use rotary valves that are actuated by levers connected to them by short lengths of gut. Tubas have either rotary or piston valves.

The *trumpet,* highest-pitched and most brilliant of the brass instruments, has approximately six feet of tubing with three valves to alter the length in order to make it possible to play a scale or melody. There are usually three trumpets in a 100-piece symphony orchestra. Trumpets produce a brassy, military sound.

The *French horn* has seventeen to eighteen feet of tubing, more than twice as much as the trumpet, and plays approximately an octave lower in pitch. There are three rotary valves on every horn, and some types, called *double horns,* have a fourth valve for the thumb that changes the instrument from its fundamental key of F to B-flat. The player may switch to F or B-flat depending on the key of the composition being played. Although either the F or B-flat horn is capable of playing any melody, it is easier to play certain passages in tune on one than on the other. There are usually four horns in an orchestra. The first and third horns play the higher parts, and the second and fourth horns the lower parts. The rich and mellow timbre of the horn blends easily with the sound of either the brass or woodwind sections.

The *trombone* dates back to the fifteenth century. Its use of a movable crook or slide instead of valves and its overall appearance have not changed much since the Renaissance. The sound of the trombone is not quite as bright as that of the trumpet, but it is still brassy and somewhat military in sound when it needs to be.

There are two sizes of trombone, of which the *tenor trombone* is the more common. The *bass trombone* is pitched a fourth lower and has a less brilliant tone quality than the tenor. Most symphony orchestras have three trombones, two tenor and one bass.

Tuba (far left);
timpani or kettle drum

The *tuba* is the true bass voice of the brass family. Like the bass viol and the contrabassoon, it is seldom heard as a solo instrument, and it is used most commonly to reinforce the trombone part an octave lower and to give a solid underpinning to the sound of the brasses. Only one tuba is normally used in an orchestra.

Snare drum or side drum

Percussion The percussion section of the orchestra differs as a family from the brasses and strings, whose instruments look alike and produce a similar kind of sound in similar ways. The percussion instruments have in common only the fact that they must be struck or shaken in order to produce sound. Because the number of instruments in the percussion section exceeds the number of percussion players in an orchestra—usually only three or four—most percussionists play several instruments. The exception is the timpanist, who plays only that group of instruments.

The *timpani* or kettledrums are the most important of the percussion instruments since they are used regularly in almost all orchestral music. Timpani are *tuned* or *pitched* drums; that is, they can play definite tones of the scale rather than producing indefinite pitches, as do other drums. Timpani are used in pairs, usually tuned five tones apart. They are played with pairs of felt-covered mallets. In modern works, sometimes as many as four or six timpani are used.

Timpani are single-headed drums with a calfskin or plastic skin stretched tautly across a huge copper bowl. The pitch is changed by tightening and loosening the tension of the skin by means of screws around the top or by the use of a footpedal at the base.

The other drums in an orchestra are *untuned* or *unpitched*. The *snare drum* and *bass drum* are both two-headed drums. Snare drums have coarsely coiled metal wires called *snares* on the underside (the unseen second head) that vibrate when the drum is played. These vibrating snares give the instrument its name and characteristic sound. The snare

Bass drum

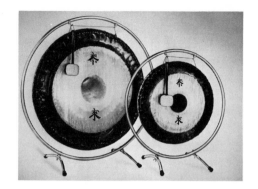

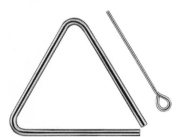

Left, from top: Wood block (or Chinese block), triangle, castanets, whip, tambourine, cymbals. Above, left: xylophone; right: Chinese gong.

drum can also be played without the snares vibrating. Pairs of hardwood sticks called *drumsticks* are used to play the instrument. A large, felt-covered mallet is used to play the bass drum.

The *mallet instruments* are so named because each is played with a pair of mallets (small hammers). All such instruments are tuned percussion and can play melodies. The mallet instruments include the *orchestra bells* (sometimes called *glockenspiel*), the *xylophone* (with wooden bars, under each of which is a metal resonating chamber), the *vibraphone* (with metal bars, under which fanlike rotating blades spin to produce a shimmering effect), and the *tubular chimes*. The *celesta* is a set of orchestra bells fitted with a keyboard so that it can play chords and fast passages.

Percussion of indefinite pitch include a variety of instruments from various parts of the world: *triangle, cymbals, gong* (also known as *tam-tam*), *wood block, whip* (or *slap-stick*), *maracas, castanets, tambourine,* and *sleigh bells.*

The Young Person's Guide to the Orchestra
by BENJAMIN BRITTEN

An easy way to learn to recognize the individual timbres of the instruments of the symphony orchestra is through listening to a composition entitled *The Young Person's Guide to the Orchestra.* This work was commissioned in 1946 to accompany a British educational film that was to demonstrate the instruments of the orchestra. The film company chose a then relatively unknown young English composer named Benjamin Britten to write the score.

The Los Angeles Philharmonic Orchestra, seating arrangement with strings in front, percussion in back left center, woodwinds in front center, brass in rear center.

Britten decided to use a melody by the early English composer Henry Purcell (c. 1659–1695) as the basis or theme for a set of variations, a different instrument or family of instruments playing each variation.

When completed, *The Young Person's Guide to the Orchestra* was so melodious and artistic that the entire composition, without narration, became popular and is now performed in orchestral concerts. The work has even served as the accompaniment for a ballet.

For this composition, Britten uses an orchestra of two flutes, a piccolo, two oboes, two B-flat clarinets, two bassoons, two trumpets, four French horns, two tenor trombones and one bass trombone, a tuba, timpani, percussion (bass drum, cymbals, tambourine, triangle, snare drum, Chinese block, xylophone, castanets, gong, whip), first and second violins, violas, cellos, bass viols, and a harp.

In the score Britten describes the instruments:

There are four teams of players: the strings, the woodwind, the brass, and the percussion. Each of these four teams uses instruments which have a family likeness. They make roughly the same kind of sound in the same way. The strings are all played with a bow or plucked by the fingers. The woodwind are blown by the breath. The brass are blown too. The percussion are banged. First you will hear a Theme by the great English composer, Henry Purcell, played by the whole orchestra and by each of the four groups of instruments.[1]

1. Benjamin Britten, *The Young Person's Guide to the Orchestra,* score (London, 1947).

On the recording, you will hear the voice of a young boy reading (as the composer intended) the narration Britten wrote to explain each instrument and each section of the music.

LISTENING OUTLINE

The Young Person's Guide to the Orchestra begins with the entire orchestra playing Purcell's theme (Example 1). Even though you may not be able to read musical notation—the symbols that represent the sound of music—you can see the contour of the melody, its ups and downs, from the general outline of the notation.

Example 1

Copyright 1946 by Hawkes & Son (London) Ltd. Renewed 1973. Reprinted by permission of Boosey & Hawkes, Inc.

Having presented Purcell's theme, Britten next offers four variations in succession, each introducing the sound of one of the four orchestral families. Variants of the theme (Example 1) are, in turn, played by:
    the woodwinds
    the brass
    the strings
    the percussion
The entire orchestra then restates the original theme (Example 1).

Britten next introduces the members of each family, moving from the highest pitched to the lowest pitched in each section (except in the case of the French horn). Variants of Example 1 are played, in turn, by:
    woodwinds
        2 flutes and a piccolo
        2 oboes
        2 clarinets
        2 bassoons

strings
    first and second violins
    violas
    cellos
    bass viols (double basses)
    harp
brass
    4 French horns
    2 trumpets
    2 tenor trombones, 1 bass trombone, and 1 tuba
percussion
    timpani (kettledrums)
    bass drum and cymbals
    tambourine and triangle
    snare drum (side drum) and wood block (Chinese block)
    xylophone
    castanets and gong
    whip
    all percussion

The closing section of *The Young Person's Guide to the Orchestra* is a *fugue,* a composition (or section of a larger work) in which a melody, called a *subject,* is first stated by one voice or instrument, then by others, each in turn. The subject of Britten's fugue appears as follows in staff notation:

Example 2

If you listen closely, you can hear each of the types of instruments of the orchestra playing the melody of the fugue (Example 2). The statements of the subject are made in turn by:

piccolo	cellos
2 flutes	bass viols
2 oboes	harp
2 clarinets	4 French horns
2 bassoons	2 trumpets
first violins	2 tenor trombones, bass trombone, tuba
second violins	percussion
violas	

Britten ends his *Guide to the Orchestra* in a majestic and thrilling manner— all the brasses play Purcell's theme (Example 1) very slowly while the strings and woodwinds play a variant of the fugal subject (Example 2) against it, bringing the work to a rousing climax.

About the Composer

BENJAMIN BRITTEN

Born: November 22, 1913
Lowestoft, England

Died: December 4, 1976
Aldeburgh, England

The cold, bleak, and often cruel North Sea had a lasting influence on the life and work of Benjamin Britten. Born in the seacoast town of Lowestoft, Britten spent the greater part of his creative career in Aldeburgh, the town on the North Sea where he later established a famous international music festival. Known primarily as a composer of operas, he used the North Sea and its coastal villages as the setting for several of his stage works.

Of his youthful days, Britten once said:

> My mother was a very sweet singer. My father, a dental surgeon, had an open, clear mind and almost a dislike of music. But, as my mother loved music and my father felt that I could do as I wanted, there really was no problem at all. I started to write music when I was five. I just kept putting patterns all over the paper and then asked my mother to play the notes. She couldn't, of course; the music was unplayable. When I was six or seven, the notes became associated with their sound in my mind.[2]

By the time Britten was fourteen, he had composed a number of large works for both piano and voice as well as several instrumental pieces. As a result of these works, Britten received a scholarship to the Royal College of Music in London. By the time he was twenty-one, Britten was earning a good part of his living by composing. He continued to do so until his death, avoiding all teaching positions and other noncompositional music-related endeavors.

In addition to composing more than ten operas, Britten focused much of his attention on children. He wrote to entertain them (*Let's Make an Opera*) and to educate them (*The Young Person's Guide to the Orchestra*). He wrote about them (*The Turn of the Screw*) and in response to their specific requests (a highly demanding *Quartet* for flute, violin, and two pianos for a pair of gifted twelve-year-old Hungarian twins).

Britten was especially gifted in creating settings of texts in English for both solo voice and chorus, providing a melodic line which enhances the text yet leaves it completely comprehensible when sung. One of his finest choral works is *A Ceremony of Carols,* settings of medieval poems. Another outstanding choral work is the *War Requiem,* written in commemoration of those who died in the Second World War.

Benjamin Britten is best known in the world of music for his many operas. *Peter Grimes,* first produced in 1945, is one of Britten's most frequently performed operas.

2. Quoted by Joan Peyser in "Composers Talk Too Much!" *New York Times,* Nov. 16, 1969.

Based on George Crabbe's tragic poem *The Borough,* its story concerns a fisherman, a social misfit named Peter Grimes. Grimes lives in a Suffolk fishing village on the North Sea during the 1830s. The fisherfolk of the village accuse him of the murder of one of his young apprentices. The opera is created around his trial and its tragic aftermath.

Billy Budd (1951), which has been staged with success by the Metropolitan Opera in New York City, was based on the novel *Billy Budd, Foretopman* by Herman Melville. Scored for an all-male cast, the opera presents its story through the eyes of Captain Vere, the man who has the power of life and death over Billy. Its action takes place during the summer of 1797 on board the H.M.S. *Indomitable.* The ship, bound for the Mediterranean, is short of men. When a merchantman is sighted, the sailors board it and Billy Budd is taken from its crew. A handsome boy, Billy—who has a stammer at times—gets on well with everyone on the *Indomitable* except for Claggart, the master-at-arms, who plots Billy's downfall. Captain Vere sees through the plot and brings Claggart and Billy together in his cabin. So shocked by Claggart's scheming that he cannot reply, Billy strikes Claggart, who falls down dead. The captain summons a court at once, and Billy is sentenced to be hanged from the yardarm.

Much of Britten's music was inspired by and written for his close friend Peter Pears. As early as 1939, Britten was writing vocal works for Pears, who had a light tenor voice and could sing extremely difficult, florid passages. Pears not only presented the world premieres of such vocal works as Britten's *Michelangelo Sonnets, Donne Sonnets,* and the famous *Serenade for Tenor, Horn and Strings;* he created major operatic roles in *Peter Grimes, The Rape of Lucretia, Albert Herring, Billy Budd, Gloriana, The Turn of the Screw, A Midsummer Night's Dream, Owen Wingrave* (commissioned by the BBC for television), and, in his old age, *Death in Venice.*

Benjamin Britten was granted a life peerage for his service to music by Queen Elizabeth II in June of 1976. He became Baron Britten of Aldeburgh.

Bibliography

Evans, Peter. *The Music of Benjamin Britten.* Minneapolis: University of Minnesota Press, 1979.

Mitchell, Donald. *Benjamin Britten, 1913–1976: Pictures from a Life.* New York: Charles Scribner's Sons, 1978.

Rhythm is the art
of well-ordered movement.
St. Augustine

TWO/
RHYTHM

HAVE you ever found yourself tapping your foot to the beat of a marching band as it parades by? Or perhaps caught yourself keeping time with a disco tune you are listening to on the radio? If you have, you were physically responding to the element of music we call *rhythm,* the heartbeat of music. The word is derived from the Greek *rhythmos,* "measured motion."

Rhythm is a pervasive part of life. The human body is governed by the rhythm patterns of heart and lungs; we breathe, walk, run, play, talk, and live in rhythmic movement. The universe around us moves rhythmically; the days, months, seasons, and years are controlled by the orderly rotations and orbits of the sun, moon, stars, and planets. In music, rhythm is perceived as a pattern of duration, stress, release, and pause, organized for expressive purposes. The three fundamental aspects of rhythm that we experience can be identified as *beat, meter,* and *rhythm pattern.*

BEAT

Beat, the pulse of music, is the basic unit of rhythm. A beat is one of a series of regularly recurring, equal pulses. Like ticks of a clock, beats mark off equal units in the passage of time. Often you can *hear* these beats. They may be banged out by the bass drum in a march or disco music, or more subtly suggested by the rhythm section of a jazz ensemble. But you can also experience a beat subjectively. Once established, a sense of regular pulses tends to continue in your mind even after the external sound has stopped.

You can easily discover your heartbeat by feeling your pulse; tapping your foot is one of the best ways to discover the underlying beat in a musical composition. A work that depends on a strong rhythmic pattern as a chief element of its design—a disco tune, a march, or a waltz, for example—is the easiest type of music in which to discover the underlying beat. But while it is easy to discover the beat of a disco tune, a march, or a waltz, it may be quite difficult to distinguish the pulse in other forms of music in which rhythm is very subtly treated.

METER

We tend to group any endless series of equal beats into units or sets, accenting some of them so that they are louder than the others. As we listen to the ticking of a clock or the clicking of railroad cars in motion, we start to arrange these equal pulses into understandable sets of two or more. A set of two seems to be both the most basic and the most common in everyday life. We talk about breathing in and out, about day and night, just as we listen to the *tick-tock* of a clock.

The first beat of each set usually receives a little more stress; this is called the natural *accent*. We can illustrate this by tapping a pattern—the thick lines being accented more than the thin lines:

We can also experience a rhythm set of two in these lines from William Blake's poem "The Tiger":

> Tíger! Tíger! búrning bríght
> In the fórests óf the níght

Meter in music is established by the organization of beats into groups through a pattern of recurring accents such as we have just experienced, the accent being a slightly louder beat. We refer to the pattern tapped earlier and experienced in the Blake poem as *duple meter* because the beats were grouped into sets of two.

Through a simple, well-known children's song, we can discover the grouping of musical beats into the sets of two we call duple meter.

Twín - kle	twín - kle	lít - tle	stár——
ONE two	ONE two	ONE two	ONE two

Hów I	wón - der	whát you	áre——
ONE two	ONE two	ONE two	ONE two

The grouping of beats into sets of three is known as *triple meter*. We can experience a rhythm set of three also in poetry; for example, the following lines by John Dryden.

> The trúmpets' loud clángor excítes us to árms,
> With shríll notes of ánger and mórtal alárms.

Notice, as you read the lyrics to the first stanza of the national anthem, *The Star-Spangled Banner,* that, as in the Dryden poem, a natural emphasis or accent falls on every third syllable.

> O sáy can you sée, by the dáwn's early líght,
> What so próudly we háiled at the twílight's last gléaming?
> Whose broad strípes and bright stárs, thru' the périlous fíght,
> O'er the rámparts we wátched, were so gállantly stréaming?
> And the róckets' red gláre, the bombs búrsting in aír,
> Gave próof thru' the níght that our flág was still thére.
> O sáy, does that Stár-Spangled Bánner yet wáve
> O'er the lánd of the frée and the hóme of the bráve?

Now it would be very boring indeed if every syllable of a poem and every tone of its musical setting were of precisely equal duration. Therefore, once having established our underlying pulse or beat, and having decided that our text is in triple meter, we can emphasize certain syllables of the text and tones of the melody by making them longer than others. We can also increase interest and add variety by making some syllables and tones shorter than the basic beat.

If we again take *The Star-Spangled Banner* as our musical example, we could graph its opening in this manner:

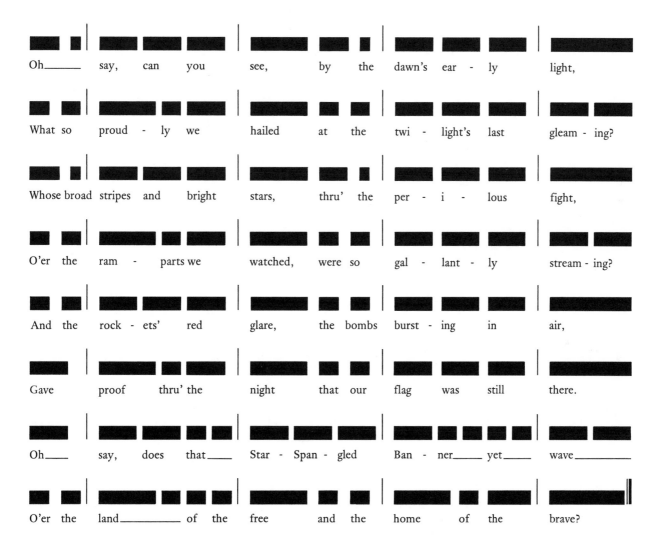

While duple and triple are the basic meters, there are others, called *compound meters* because they are compounded or made up of groupings of two and three. *Quadruple meter,* for example, is simply two sets of two; *sextuple meter* is two sets of three. While a five-beat measure is not very common, it is compounded in a like manner: a set of two and a set of three.

Knowing meter, however, is much more than just being able to tap sets of two, three, or more. As one writer has said, "It is feeling the sense of space, of dimension, related directly to the tempo of those little charges of energy [on the accent], and feeling the rigidity and squareness of duple 'two-ness' that relates directly to our two-sided physical beings and our environment (left–right, front–back, up–down) and the flexibility and roundness of triple meter."[1]

MUSICAL NOTATION

While it is not the purpose of this book to train the reader in the intricacies of musical staff notation, there are some easily recognizable musical symbols that will help the beginning listener to better understand the nature of a composition.

The shape of a note determines the length of time a given sound is to be produced. Starting with the whole note (the largest unit currently in use), each note can be subdivided into smaller units:

1 whole note

= 2 half notes

= 4 quarter notes

= 8 eighth notes

= 16 sixteenth notes

Notice that the note stems that have *flags* (♪) can be joined by a horizontal *beam* in place of the flags; this does not change the name or value of the notes, nor does it make a difference whether the stems go up or down from the notehead.

Any type of note may be followed by a dot (♩.) that gives the note one-and-a-half times its normal value.

Two notes of the same pitch may be connected by a curved line; this is called a *tie*. The tone is sounded only once and is continued for the total time of the notes connected by the curved line. When two notes of different pitch are connected by a curved line, the line is called a *slur*. In this case there is no pause between the notes so connected.

1. Robert M. Boberg, "Ear-Opening Experiences with Rhythm and Pitch," *Music Educators Journal,* December 1975, p. 34.

Occasionally a composer wishes to subdivide a note into units of three instead of two. An inscribed 3 is used to embrace these notes (♪♪♪ or ♩♩♩); such units are called *triplets.* They are sounded for the amount of time ordinarily consumed by two such notes.

When several notes of different pitches are connected by a curved line, the line indicates a phrase, the smallest musical design unit, somewhat similar to the relation of a phrase to a sentence in grammar.

Just as notes may be subdivided, so may rests, which are really timed silence.

1 whole rest	▬
= 2 half rests	▬ ▬
= 4 quarter rests	𝄽 𝄽 𝄽 𝄽
= 8 eighth rests	𝄾 𝄾 𝄾 𝄾 𝄾 𝄾 𝄾 𝄾
= 16 sixteenth rests	𝄿𝄿𝄿𝄿𝄿𝄿𝄿𝄿𝄿𝄿𝄿𝄿𝄿𝄿𝄿𝄿

All these symbols have values relative to each other; a quarter note, for example, could equal a half-beat, a full beat, or even two beats. A *meter signature* (sometimes called a *time signature*) is needed at the beginning of a piece of music or section to indicate the basic unit of the meter. It consists of two numbers, one on top of the other. The lower number indicates the unit of measurement (quarter note, half note, and so on) used in the section or piece. The upper number indicates how many of these units comprise a *measure* or *bar* in the piece. In musical notation, these measures or bars are delineated by vertical lines: | |. The **2** in the meter signature of the following musical example indicates duple meter, a subdivision into units of two with the first beat of each measure receiving a little stronger accent or stress than the others.

Twin - kle,   twin - kle,   lit - tle   star,

The lower numeral in a meter signature, which indicates the *basic unit* (that is, the kind of note that receives the beat), has one of the following values:

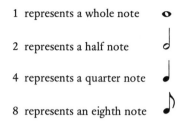

In the foregoing example from the familiar children's song *Twinkle, Twinkle, Little Star,* we used the quarter note as our basic unit. We could have used the half note:

or eighth notes:

or even dotted quarters (representing three eighth notes):

Let us look at another example of a meter signature. The upper number, **3**, indicates that the song is in triple meter. The lower numeral, **4**, indicates that a quarter note occupies each beat.

All time signatures that have numbers higher than **8** as the upper number are compound meters. Thus $\frac{4}{4}$ is made up of two units of two; $\frac{5}{4}$ is made up of a unit of two and one of three; $\frac{6}{8}$ is made up of two units of three. In each case, there is a *secondary accent,* an emphasis of secondary importance. In the following samples, the size of each number indicates its dynamic (loudness) level:

$$\frac{4}{4} \quad 1 \quad 2 \quad 3 \quad 4 \quad 1 \quad 2 \quad 3 \quad 4$$

$$\frac{5}{4} \quad 1 \quad 2 \quad 3 \quad 4 \quad 5 \quad 1 \quad 2 \quad 3 \quad 4 \quad 5$$

$$\frac{6}{8} \quad 1 \quad 2 \quad 3 \quad 4 \quad 5 \quad 6 \quad 1 \quad 2 \quad 3 \quad 4 \quad 5 \quad 6$$

RHYTHM PATTERNS

In addition to beat and meter, there is a third fundamental aspect to rhythm, that of rhythm patterns. *Rhythm pattern* may be defined as a recognizable and memorable short grouping of tones or sounds of equal or varying length. As an example of what we mean by rhythm pattern, tap out the rhythm of *Jingle Bells* for a friend, telling that person only that it is a melody of the Christmas season, and ask your friend to identify the tune from the rhythm you are tapping. Chances are excellent that your friend will guess the tune with ease. The clue, of course, is the organization of rhythm patterns within its melody, thus making it easy to identify.

There are certain basic rhythm patterns that are well known. The following examples illustrate a few of them. The use of the musical symbol ⸺ indicates a stress or accent, the emphasized unit.

Since rhythm in music is created by the relative duration of its tones, we usually come closer to its essential quality when we perceive rhythm patterns in association with tonal patterns rather than in isolation from them. Let us therefore investigate various aspects of rhythm through listening to a masterpiece of the symphonic repertory.

Carmen (center), the Dragoons of Alcalá, and the girls from the cigarette factory. *Carmen,* Act I. New York City Opera Production.

Carmen Suite

by GEORGES BIZET

Carmen, one of the most popular of all operas, is a love story about the fiery passions of a gypsy girl who works in a cigarette factory in Seville. The year is 1820.

Based on the novel by the French essayist and man of letters Prosper Mérimée, the opera by Georges Bizet is built around three principal characters: Carmen, who—

in addition to working in the cigarette factory—belongs to a band of smugglers; Don José, a corporal in the Dragoons, who—as a Basque from Navarre guilty of killing or badly wounding an enemy in a fight—was forced to take refuge in the army; and Escamillo, a handsome toreador (man of the toro, or bullfighter).

In the first scene of the opera, Carmen reveals her philosophy in the lines:

> Love is like a wild bird
>   That no one can tame, . . .
> First it lights here, now there;
>   No one knows why;
> No one knows for how long.

These words prove prophetic and, indeed, become the crux of the plot. José meets Carmen, who flirts with him. The corporal falls in love with her, and she, for a time, returns his love. For the gypsy girl, however, love, the "wild bird," soon moves on, and Carmen next becomes enamored of the handsome toreador, Escamillo. José becomes intensely jealous. Carmen, threatened by José, remains true to her gypsy blood, saying: "Carmen has never lied. . . . This heart is no longer yours, José . . . I know you will kill me, but Carmen will *never* give in! Free she was born, free she will die!"

Carmen was first produced in 1875 at the Opéra-Comique in Paris, where the reception was less than enthusiastic—because audiences at that theater were accustomed to stories with happy endings and quite unaccustomed to plots involving girls who smoked on stage and who had such loose moral standards as Carmen's. Nevertheless, an orchestral suite—consisting of several movements derived from the opera and scored for orchestra without voices—was soon created from the opera. We shall investigate three movements from the *Carmen Suite*.

Les Dragons d'Alcalá

The military group in which Don José serves as a corporal is known as the Dragoons of Alcalá, dragoons being horse-mounted soldiers armed with short muskets. The barracks of the dragoons is located at Alcalá, a small city about fifteen miles southeast of Seville.

Since *Les Dragons d'Alcalá* serves as a march in the opera, it is in duple meter. (This is indicated in the time signature of the following music examples by the upper numeral **2** .)

LISTENING OUTLINE

As the bassoon plays the initial melody (Example 1), plucked strings (*pizzicato*) and a snare drum accent the rhythm:

(a   dum,   dum,   dum - dee - dum rhythm)

The bassoon melody begins:[2]

Example 1

Twelve measures later, the bassoons continue with a second theme (Example 2). This is also accompanied by the same rhythm pattern as Example 1. The second melody begins:[3]

Example 2

In an interlude, short melodic figures played by flute and clarinet are answered by the strings.

The first melody (Example 1) returns in the clarinet, which is joined by the bassoon, now with a countermelody (a second melody that is heard simultaneously with the first) made up of descending and ascending figures. Only the two instruments are heard.

2. The curved line that connects notes of different pitches is called a *phrasing mark* and indicates that the tones so embraced are to be performed in a *legato* fashion—that is, without any break or silence between them. The dot found over certain note heads is called a *staccato mark,* indicating that such tones are to be cut quite short of their total time value, thus, in effect, making a rest part of the time value normally allotted to the note itself.

3. The very small note found in the third measure is called a *grace note.* It is printed in small type to indicate that the time value of this has not been counted in the measure, and that the time to perform such a note must be borrowed from the previous note or rest.

The clarinet continues with the melody of Example 2, the bassoon still playing in counterpoint (literally, "melody against melody"—music of two or more lines played simultaneously). The strings reenter with the rhythm pattern first heard at the beginning. The flute takes up Example 1; that melody is completed by the oboe. Figure A from it is played first by the clarinet, then by the bassoon. Three rhythmic chords bring the march to an end.

Les Toréadors

We are plunged at once into the spirit and excitement of a Spanish holiday in Seville just before a thrilling and colorful *corrida* (bullfight) is to take place. Musically, *Les Toréadors* is based on three melodies, the first being extremely rhythmical and the theme that appears before and after each of the other two tunes. You will probably recognize the latter of these other tunes, since it is the *Toreador's Song,* one of the most famous melodies in all of opera.

LISTENING OUTLINE

Les Toréadors is written in duple meter ($\frac{2}{4}$). The low-pitched instruments immediately establish a marchlike basic beat:

(DUM   dum   DUM   dum)

Over this basic beat, the upper woodwinds and strings start a lively, martial melody characterized by the rhythm pattern:

(DUM dee - dee DEE - dee - dee - dee)

This melody (Example 1) is played by flutes, oboes, clarinets, and violins. Notice the constant use of the rhythm pattern indicated by the brackets over the notes.[4]

Example 3

Flutes, Oboes, Clarinets, Violins

The second half of this 16-measure melody (not quoted) starts like Example 1, but ends differently. The entire 16-measure melody is then repeated.

A quieter, more lyrical theme (Example 2) is introduced by the woodwinds and strings. It is characterized by the rhythm pattern:

(DUM dum dum dum DUM dee - dee dum dum)

Example 4

Flute, Oboes, Clarinet, Violins

After a ten-measure passage in which the rhythm pattern

(dee - dee - dum dee - dee - dum)

is prominent, the melody of Example 1 returns.

---

4. The symbol ⌐⌐⌐⌐⌐ found in this musical example in measures 4 and 8 is used to indicate a *trill,* a fast alternation between the pitch indicated and the next tone higher; it continues for the time value of the note over which it appears.

The famous *Toreador's Song* follows. Trumpets and trombones play a four-measure introduction in which, by emphasizing the basic duple beat, they establish the marchlike nature of this song. Following the rhythmic introduction, the strings play the well-known melody of the *Toreador's Song*:

Example 5

Violins, Violas, Cellos

After a large *crescendo* (increase in the dynamic level), the first melody—Example 1—returns, and brings *Les Toréadors* to a stirring conclusion.

Aragonaise

The *Aragonaise* serves as a prelude to Act IV of the opera, an act that opens with a colorful procession of townspeople and city dignitaries to the arena for the bullfight. Musically, the *Aragonaise* is a *jota,* a lively dance in triple meter from Aragon, a province in northeastern Spain.

LISTENING OUTLINE

A rhythm pattern, introduced at once, becomes a pervasive part of the entire dance.

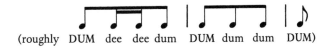

(roughly DUM dee dee dum DUM dum dum DUM)

The entire orchestra plays this rhythmic opening figure:

Example 6

Upper Strings, Woodwinds

Harp, pizzicato strings, and tambourine (which plays the rhythm pattern of Example 1) establish the rhythmic background for a theme (Example 2) played by the oboe:

Example 7

Oboe

A piccolo and clarinet answer with a melodic figure that moves first upward, then downward in pitch.

The oboe repeats the melody of Example 2; piccolo and clarinet answer once again.

The woodwinds boldly announce a new theme (Example 3). The short rhythm pattern ♩♪♪♪ ♪ (dee-dee-dee-dee dum) heard twice at the beginning of this new theme is answered by the strings and brass:

Example 8

Flute (octave higher)[5]

A variant of Example 3 follows, and leads to a section in which the violins play short melodic figures that move first upward, then downward, in alternating patterns.

---

5. In order to avoid music examples that would require the use of many *ledger* (added) lines above the staff, this book frequently quotes themes on the staff and indicates that in performance they are heard an octave higher.

A new theme is announced by the violins, one in which the rhythm pattern [♫♫] indicated under brackets at Figure A is heard three times:

dee - dee dum - dum

Example 9

The oboe responds with a repetition of Example 2. Piccolo and violins play the answering pattern this time. All the strings take up the melody of Example 2 in a forceful yet expressive manner.

The opening rhythm pattern returns as an introduction for the melody of Example 2 played by the oboe; as in the beginning, piccolo and clarinet respond.

After a *ritardando* (gradual slackening in speed), the flute plays the upward and downward melodic figures heard earlier. Harp, strings, and tambourine provide a soft rhythmic background that dies away to silence at the end.

About the Composer

GEORGES BIZET   Born: October 25, 1838
Paris, France

Died: June 3, 1875
Bougival, France

Born Alexandre-César-Léopold Bizet in Paris on October 25, 1838, he was christened about a year and a half later as Georges Bizet, the name that he used for the rest of his life except in legal documents.

Both of Bizet's parents were musical. His father Adolphe Bizet had once been a wigmaker and hairdresser and had given that up to become a voice teacher, specializing in coaching opera singers. Bizet's mother was a Delsarte, a musical family that claimed remote Spanish ancestry.

Showing an early talent for music, Georges Bizet was encouraged by his parents to become a professional musician. His musical training started very early. Although ten was the minimum age at which students were ordinarily accepted for the Paris Conservatory of Music, Bizet's family pulled strings and were able to have Georges take the entrance examination when he was nine. He passed his interviews brilliantly, performed spectacularly on the piano, and demonstrated his gift of absolute pitch and his knowledge of harmony.[6]

Bizet studied piano, organ, and composition at the Conservatory. After winning several routine prizes, he was awarded the coveted Prix de Rome at nineteen. The Prix de Rome is awarded annually by the French Académie des Beaux-Arts. Although it has taken many forms during its long existence, basically it has always been a scholarship awarded each year after competition to outstanding young painters, sculptors, architects, musicians, and sometimes other artists. During the 1850s, winners lived in Rome, staying at the Villa Medici on a government subsidy, spending the third year of their grant in Germany. Bizet spent his third year, by special permission, in Rome.

Returning to the French capital at the end of his tenure in Rome, Bizet considered teaching at the Conservatory or perhaps becoming a concert pianist. He decided against both and resolved to stay in Paris and pursue a career as an opera composer. In order to support himself, he gave private piano lessons, usually to students who only wanted to learn for social reasons. He also arranged orchestral scores of countless operas for the piano. Bizet was even known to have composed some third-rate dance music to help himself financially.

An excellent description of the composer was written by one of his American pupils, who said Bizet was

> very plump and vigorous—a very showy, attractive man without ever thinking that he was, or seeming to care what his effect was on other people. He had light brown hair and a full beard, almost russet or reddish brown. His eyes were dark gray or blue. He dressed with extreme care and for his own personal satisfaction.[7]

In the early 1860s, Bizet started to work on an opera with an Oriental setting, *Les Pêcheurs de perles* (*The Pearl Fishers*). It was introduced at the Théâtre Lyrique on September 30, 1863. Although judged a failure by the music critics of the time, the opera has since been remounted from time to time with moderate success.

In 1869, Bizet married Geneviève Halévy, the daughter of his teacher, Jacques Halévy. Soon Bizet was back at work writing operas: *La Jolie Fille de Perth* (*The Fair Maid of Perth*) in 1866 and *Djamileh*—another opera with an Oriental setting—in 1872. Neither opera enjoyed much success with either music critics or public.

Léon Carvalho, who became the new director of the Théâtre du Vaudeville at about this time, asked Bizet to write some incidental music for a play by Alphonse

6. *Absolute pitch* is the ability to identify correctly the exact pitch of any musical tone without the use of any external referent or basis of comparison.
7. Stuart Henry, *Paris Days and Evenings* (London, 1896).

Daudet that he was producing, *L'Arlésienne (The Girl from Arles)*. Bizet accepted the commission and wrote twenty-seven orchestral numbers for it. While the play itself was a failure, Bizet's music was not. To this day, Suites 1 and 2, made up of separate movements from the twenty-seven original numbers, enjoy frequent performances on orchestral concerts.

In the spring of 1873, Bizet started to work on an opera based on the story of a fiery young gypsy girl named Carmen. Although *Carmen* was not the wildly proclaimed success Bizet had hoped that it would be, the opera did receive thirty-three performances during its first season at the Opéra-Comique (1875).

Suffering most of his life from a chronic throat ailment, Bizet succumbed to it shortly after the curtain had come down on the thirty-first performance of *Carmen*.

Bizet's most successful orchestral work, *Symphony in C,* was given its first performance on February 26, 1935, in Basle, Switzerland, sixty years after the composer's death and eighty years after it had been written. *Symphony in C* was composed in 1855 when Bizet was a student. The score for it had been among a collection of scores, including that of *La Jolie Fille de Perth,* which Geneviève Bizet, the composer's widow, gave to his friend Reynaldo Hahn. Hahn later gave these scores to the library of the Paris Conservatory without, apparently, having looked through them. The first English biographer of Bizet, D. C. Parker, discovered the score of the symphony in 1935 and immediately brought it to the attention of Felix Weingartner, one of the greatest conductors of the era.

Bibliography

Curtiss, Mina. *Bizet and His World.* New York: Vienna House, 1974.
Cooper, Martin. *Georges Bizet.* Westport, Ct.: Greenwood Press, 1971.

The language of tones belongs equally to all mankind, and the melody is the absolute language in which the musician speaks to every heart.

Richard Wagner

THREE/
MELODY

HAVE you ever noticed, when you are alone, that you sometimes find yourself humming or whistling? Perhaps you are puttering around your room, walking down the street, or even driving on a long trip. What you find yourself humming or whistling might be the No. 1 tune from the weekly pop chart or the love theme from a movie recently seen. It could even be a melodic motive from a symphonic program heard on television. No matter its source, most of us would agree on the fact that what you are humming or whistling is that which we call *melody*.

The dictionary tells us that a melody is "a particular succession of notes." But that is a very limited concept of something that many consider to be the very essence of music, the stuff out of which the art is created. It takes more than "a particular succession of notes" to make us want to go out and buy an album or drop a coin in a juke-box to play a record.

Melody is that magical element of music that captures our imagination and remains in our memory to be recalled, hummed, or whistled long after the lyrics and the harmonic setting have been forgotten. For most of us melody is what music is all about.

Aaron Copland, one of America's most famous composers, said that melody is "like a continuous thread which leads the listener through a piece from the very beginning to the very end."[1]

CHARACTERISTICS OF MELODY

Melody is, in the most general sense, a succession of musical tones that has some kind of design or musical meaning, as contrasted with *harmony*, which consists of musical tones sounded simultaneously. Thus melody and harmony represent the horizontal and vertical elements of musical texture.

Since the tones in a melody move in succession, melody may be said to be the *line* or *curve* of music. Which way the contour of a line of melody moves (up or down) depends upon the relative highness or lowness of its pitches.

The relative duration of the tones in a melody determines its *rhythm*. This is frequently as distinguishing a characteristic of the melody as is the contour of the pitches themselves. Whether a melody seems to be smoothly flowing or angular and jerky may be due to differences of pitch, but the rhythm of the melody may contribute equally to this effect. Since rhythm is an essential attribute of melody, the development of melodic concepts requires both tonal and rhythmic imagery.

To develop such concepts of melody, we must understand how tones in a melody move, how they are organized, and how they can be changed. It is equally important for us to realize that a melody is an *organized unit of sound,* usually constructed in phrases and patterns, much as words are organized into clauses and sentences. Not all melodies need to be tuneful. In fact, what one person regards as tuneful may not seem

1. Aaron Copland, *What to Listen For in Music* (New York, 1964).

so to another person. Any succession of tones logically and systematically arranged can be thought of as a melody.

A good melody—whether it be in jazz, rock, folk, soul, or the symphonic literature—has a *sense of continuity:* a beginning, a dramatic or emotional peak, and a definite ending. A melody is usually sung or played in its entirety by the same voice or instrument, and the principal or most important melody in a piece of music is usually the highest-pitched sound in the composition at that point.

DIRECTION AND DISTANCE

In discussing the nature of melody, we must note that a succession of tones indicates both direction and distance. Tones in a melody may move up or down, or momentarily remain the same. When tones in a melody change, they may do it by *conjunct,* or scalewise, movement (*scale* comes from the Italian word *scala* meaning "step").

The opening phrase of the Christmas song *Joy to the World* is a good example of a melody that moves downward by step or conjunct motion. This is easily observed in staff notation because the melody makes use of each adjoining line and space, skipping none.

Joy   to   the   world,   the   Lord   is   come.

Tones in a melody may also change by leaps. This is called *disjunct* movement. The opening of our national anthem is a good example of a melody in which the tones move by disjunct motion. With reference to the direction of the melody, notice that the movement is first downward and then upward. Notice also that, in staff notation, disjunct melodies skip intervening lines and spaces.

Oh__   say   can   you   see

THE CHROMATIC SCALE

Most discussions concerning the tones used in music of Western culture relate them to what we call the *chromatic scale.* It is perhaps easiest for us to understand the nature of and relationships that exist in the chromatic scale if we use the piano keyboard and the grand staff for illustrative purposes. By *staff* we mean a series of five parallel horizontal lines: ▤; musical notes are written on and between these lines. For notating most music, we use two *clef signs;* these are signs written at the beginning of each staff to establish the pitch of notes written in each line and space of that staff. We use the *treble* or *G clef* sign (𝄞) for notating the higher pitches, and the *bass* or *F clef* sign (𝄢) for the lower pitches. These two staffs, together with an imaginary line between them, form the *grand staff:*

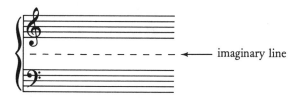

← imaginary line

To show tones above or below the pitches represented by these staffs, we use additional lines that we call *ledger lines.*

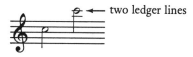

← two ledger lines

Now if we relate the grand staff to the white keys of the piano keyboard, we have the following:

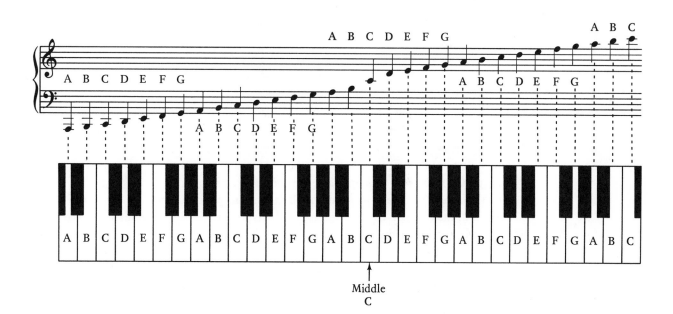

Middle
C

In addition to the white keys, there are recurring patterns of black keys in alternating groups of two and three. Each black key may be called by two names. For example, the black key between C and D may be called either C-sharp or D-flat. In the following illustration, the symbols for sharps ♯ and flats ♭ are used in naming each of the black keys.

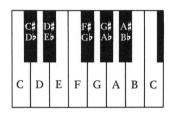

The distance between a black key and its adjacent white key is known as a *half step*. The symbol known as a sharp (♯) raises a note by a half step; the symbol called a flat (♭) lowers a tone by a half step. The following chart relates the black keys to their staff notation.

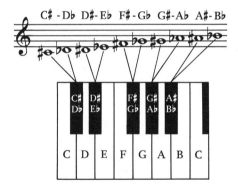

White keys such as E and B also may be sharped, in which case the resulting tone is another white key. Similarly, F and C may be flatted, in which case the resulting tone is also a white key. A *natural sign* (♮) is used to cancel a previous sharp or flat. For cases in which we want to lower further a pitch that has already been flatted, we use the *double flat* sign (♭♭); the *double sharp* sign (×) raises a pitch two half steps.

The *chromatic scale* is made up of all the half steps found on the staff or the piano keyboard; the distance between each pitch—as we have seen—is a half step. Now you will notice that the white keys of the piano are named after the first seven letters of the alphabet: A B C D E F G. That pattern of letters is repeated over and over, up and down the staff and the piano keyboard. There is a good reason for this. The early Greeks, who discovered the principles behind the chromatic scale, found that if the length of a vibrating string is doubled, the string produces only half as many vibrations or cycles per second. We call this *interval*—the distance between two such tones—an *octave.* The sound of this interval is the most perfect consonance to be found, so perfect that unskilled ears frequently cannot tell the difference between the original pitch and the one an octave higher or lower. The tone we call *middle C* (because it is in the middle of the grand staff), vibrates at 256 cycles (vibrations) per second, the next higher C vibrates at 512 cycles, and "high C" at 1,024 cycles. Similarly, the C below middle C vibrates at 128 cycles, and "low C" at 64 cycles.

While some music is based on the chromatic scale, most is based on other scale patterns, as we will see in the following section. It is interesting to know, however, that every scale pattern makes use of the octave interval.

SCALES AND MODES

Until the seventeenth century, music in Western civilization used several different arrangements of intervals called *modes.* Each mode was made up of a different sequence of half and whole steps (that is, units of two half steps) and each, therefore, had its own unique "flavor" (called *ethos* by the Greeks).

During the seventeenth century, two particular patterns—now known as *major* and *minor scales*—began to be used more than the others. And, of the two, the major scale soon became the more frequently used. The pattern for the major scale, and for the half-step and whole-step intervals of which it is made, can be illustrated by C major, the easiest scale to illustrate since it makes use of only the white keys of the piano:

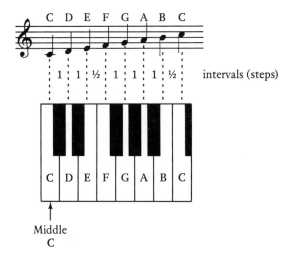

There are three kinds of minor scales illustrated in the following example. You will notice that the common element in all three types of minor scale is the lowered, or flatted, third tone (known as a *minor third*). When you listen to music to try and establish whether a work is based on a major or minor scale—called the *tonality* of the composition—it is easiest to listen for the relationship of the first three tones of the scale. You may have learned the *do-re-mi* system in elementary or junior high school. This makes it easy to discover whether a work is in a major or minor tonality. If you can sing *do-re-mi* and match it to that portion of the scale on which the work is built, it is in a major tonality. If, instead, you can sing *do-re-meh,* it is in a minor tonality.

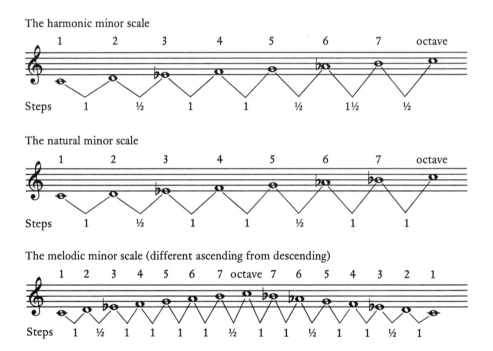

The major and minor scale patterns can be shifted up or down to make any pitch from A to G (including all the black keys) the starting point, or *tonic,* of a scale. This tonic is what we call the *key* or *tonality* of a composition, and this is what we mean when we say that the national anthem is "in" *A major* or the love theme from the movie *The Godfather* is "in" *c minor.*[2]

2. Custom suggests that we capitalize letters identifying major scales (for example, A major) and use lower-case letters for minor scales (a minor).

So that a person reading music does not become confused by a proliferation of sharps, flats, and natural signs throughout a work, we use *key signatures* to indicate which notes are to be sharped or flatted *throughout* a work unless an *accidental* (any additional symbol such as a flat, sharp, or natural sign) is employed. The following chart illustrates the most common key signatures. Notice that each signature represents two tonalities, a major and its relative minor.

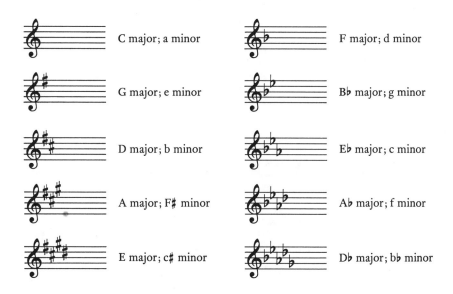

C major; a minor

G major; e minor

D major; b minor

A major; F♯ minor

E major; c♯ minor

F major; d minor

B♭ major; g minor

E♭ major; c minor

A♭ major; f minor

D♭ major; b♭ minor

While the major and minor scale patterns are the most frequently employed in music of Western civilization, other patterns are also used from time to time. The *pentatonic* or five-tone scale corresponds to the sound produced by playing the five black keys of the piano. *Transposed* (changed) to a starting pitch of C so that only white keys of the piano are used in playing it, the pentatonic scale in staff notation would read as follows. Notice that no half-step intervals are used.

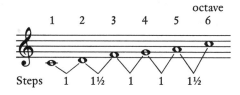

The familiar New Year's Eve song *Auld Lang Syne* is a good example of a pentatonic melody. If you have access to a piano, try playing that melody using only the black keys of the piano.

Another scale pattern is the *whole-tone scale,* so called because it involves only whole-tone or whole-step intervals:

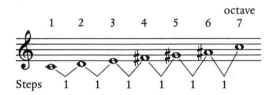

Claude Debussy used the whole-tone scale on occasion to give his music an ethereal effect, one achieved by the *floating* nature of the whole-tone scale, since it does not have a true *tonic,* or starting and ending note. (It can start or end on any tone.)

PHRASES AND CADENCES

Just as longer works in literature are subdivided into chapters, paragraphs, sentences, and clauses, so in music larger works can be subdivided into movements, sections, melodies, and phrases. Since we are discussing melody in this chapter, it is important to learn how melodies are made up from groups of phrases.

When we think of the music of *The Star-Spangled Banner* (p. 45), for example, most of us probably do not perceive it all at once. We grasp the melody in short sections. Such sections, which usually correspond to the lines of the poem, are called *phrases.* There are three phrases (marked A, B, and C) in the stanza or verse, and one in the refrain or chorus (D), each eight measures in length.

Unity is achieved in music by repeating certain design elements. Notice in *The Star-Spangled Banner* how unity is achieved by the use of two phrases that are identical —melodically and rhythmically (phrases A and B). You may also notice that there is a great similarity between the last half of the first two phrases, A and B, and the last half of the third phrase (C). The difference between these phrases, though slight, is of great significance, as we will see in a moment.

Like most melodies, that for *The Star-Spangled Banner* has a beginning, a middle, and an end. You can discover this for yourself by experimentation. Try singing the first three phrases, A, B, and C, and then stopping. When you get to the end of that third phrase, your innate musical sense tells you that the melody is not complete, that something must follow. Similarly, after singing the fourth phrase, D, you instinctively know that you have reached an end or conclusion of the melody.

Most phrases in vocal music and many in instrumental music end with a *cadence,* a

melodic formula that conveys the impression of a conclusion—either momentary or permanent.

As we just observed, there is a difference between the ending of the first three phrases of *The Star-Spangled Banner* and the fourth phrase. The first three phrases end with a cadence that suggests only a momentary pause; this is called an *imperfect cadence.* The fourth phrase concludes with the feeling of a permanent conclusion. Such a cadence is called a *perfect cadence.*

Just as we cannot logically separate a melody from its rhythm, so we find it difficult if not impossible in many instances to separate a melody from the harmony or chords that accompany it. Such is the case when we speak of cadences. For the purposes of this chapter, we will use the word *cadence* to refer to the melodic conclusion of phrases and melodies, but it must be understood that all such cadences provide very strong harmonic implications, which we will consider in the next chapter.

Let us now experience the magic and mystery of good melodies through music by the American composer Aaron Copland.

Above and below: two scenes from *Rodeo*. American Ballet Theatre production.

Rodeo

by **AARON COPLAND**

Rodeo, or *The Courting at Burnt Ranch,* is a ballet based on a story created by choreographer Agnes de Mille, who described it as follows:

> Throughout the American southwest, the Saturday afternoon rodeo is a tradition. On the remote ranches, as well as in the trading centers and towns, the "hands" get together to show off their skill in roping, riding, branding and throwing. Often, on the more isolated ranches, the rodeo is done for an audience that consists of only a handful of fellow-workers, women-folk and those nearest neighbors who can make the eighty or so mile run-over.
>
> The afternoon's exhibition is usually followed by a Saturday night dance at the Ranch House.
>
> The theme of the ballet is basic. It deals with the problem that has confronted all American women, from earliest pioneer times, and which has

3. Aaron Copland, *Four Dance Episodes from Rodeo,* score (London, 1946).

never ceased to occupy them throughout the history of the building of our country: how to get a suitable man.[3]

In the opening scene of the ballet, the cowboys of Burnt Ranch are gathered for their weekly rodeo. The young Cowgirl, a tomboy, becomes aware of men for the first time, for she has developed a crush on the Head Wrangler. In an attempt to show off for him, she gets thrown from a bucking bronco. Everybody laughs at her, including some city girls who have stopped by for the dance that will follow the rodeo. The Cowgirl's heart is broken, for the Head Wrangler goes off with the Rancher's Daughter.

That evening at the Saturday-night dance, the Cowgirl, still dressed in bluejeans and boots, appears lonesome and neglected. Her friend, the Champion Roper, takes pity on this wallflower and shows her how to dance a few steps. As the lesson is progressing, she sees the Head Wrangler waltzing cheek to cheek with the Rancher's Daughter. The Cowgirl runs away in misery.

The ranch hands, who have continued to dance, stop in astonishment when the Cowgirl returns. For the first time she has put on a party dress and done up her hair with a bow. The men discover what a pretty girl she really is. The Head Wrangler now competes with the Champion Roper for her attention. She settles on the Roper, the only man that has ever shown her any attention.

Aaron Copland wrote the music in June and orchestrated it in September of 1942. The composer subsequently extracted an orchestral suite from the ballet score for concert performance under the title *Four Dance Episodes from Rodeo.* The episodes are named *Buckaroo Holiday, Corral Nocturne, Saturday Night Waltz,* and *Hoe-Down.*

A number of American folk songs are woven into the score. Source material was drawn from *Our Singing Country* by John A. and Alan Lomax and from Ira Ford's *Traditional Music of America.* Two songs from the Lomax volume are incorporated into the first episode: *If He'd Be a Buckaroo by His Trade* and *Sis Joe.* According to the composer, "the rhythmic oddities of 'Sis Joe' provided rich material for reworking." A square-dance tune called *Bonyparte* provides the principal theme of the *Hoe-Down.*

Buckaroo Holiday

LISTENING OUTLINE

Buckaroo Holiday opens immediately with an original Copland melody (Example 1), which is bold and forthright. This melody starts with downward, conjunct movement; upper woodwinds and strings play this opening motive. It is answered by the brass and percussion with a phrase that moves upward by disjunct motion.

Example 1

Upper Woodwinds, Strings

Variants of Example 1 are repeated four times.

The music becomes slower and softer. A short melodic figure (based on only three different pitches) is introduced by the flute and horn. This figure is repeated many times.

The oboe introduces a quiet, tranquil theme.

Before long, the music picks up speed, and we hear the low-pitched instruments of the orchestra establish a square-dance rhythm.

Finally, the upper woodwinds and strings introduce the rhythmical melody of this section (Example 2), a theme that includes many repeated tones and one in which the rhythm is a chief characteristic of the melody. Copland adapted this melody from the old railroad work song, *Sis Joe* (*Sis Joe* is the name of a famous old steam engine.)

Example 2

Upper Woodwinds, Piano, Upper Strings

The melody of Example 1 returns and, in an extended section, is heard in several variants.

The strings then take up an "oom-pah-oom-pah" accompaniment. The solo trombone introduces a "perky" and "humorous" theme (to use the composer's words). This theme (Example 3) is a variant of the early American song *If He'd Be a Buckaroo.* It is interrupted by pauses, one of which is indicated by the symbol ⌐2⌐ for two measures of rest.

Example 3

Trombone

Soon a solo trumpet is heard with the melody of Example 3; piccolo and oboe then repeat it. Variants and fragments of it are taken up by the strings.

After a rhythmic section in which the rhythmic element is predominant, the full tune of *If He'd Be a Buckaroo* is then played boldly by the entire orchestra.

As the dynamic level drops, flute and oboe introduce a more sustained melody.

Eventually the rhythmic drive and intensity of the opening section return, and the descending melody of Example 1 reappears, leading to an extended section based on the rhythmic melody of *Sis Joe* (Example 2).

At the climax, Example 3 (*If He'd Be a Buckaroo*) returns and builds to the final climax of this dance episode.

Saturday Night Waltz

LISTENING OUTLINE

The *Saturday Night Waltz* opens with an introduction in which the string instruments sound as if they are tuning. Finally they play a long-held tone as the brass enter.

The tempo changes to a slow waltz. The oboe plays a haunting melody (Example 4) that reminds us of the folk song *Old Paint,* on which it is based. The composer uses the symbol ' to indicate where the soloist should breathe, thus suggesting the correct phrasing for this passage.

Example 4

The violins repeat this beautiful melody, with the oboe joining them in the fourth measure.

The violas respond with a melody of their own in answer to that of the violins and oboe.

Once again the violins and oboe play Example 1; a countermelody in the flute is heard above it.

Eight measures of sustained pitch in the woodwinds and strings lead to the middle section of the waltz. The tempo becomes slower. After a brief passage for the solo clarinet, the violas enter with a new melody:

Example 5

The flute and clarinet carry on a duet above this long viola melody.

The tempo returns to that of the first section. After a five-measure passage reminiscent of the *Old Paint* tune, the violins and oboe repeat the melody of Example 1, which brings the waltz to a close.

Hoe-Down

LISTENING OUTLINE

The *Hoe-Down* is introduced with many repetitions of Figure A from Example 6A quoted below. Then, for nine measures, the strings sound as if they are tuning; in the meantime, the brass instruments play a rhythmic figure. More repetitions of Figure A follow.

An important rhythm pattern is then introduced:

The first section of *Hoe-Down* opens with a melody played by the violins, a quotation—note for note—of the old fiddler's tune *Bonyparte* (sometimes called *Bonaparte's Retreat Across the Rocky Mountains*):

Example 6A

The violins complete the tune:

Example 6B

Violins

Example 6A is repeated by the violins.

The first half of Example 6B is played by the strings; the last half of Example 6B is played by the woodwinds.

The entire orchestra, in a very loud passage, repeats Example 6B.

Violins and clarinets play Example 6A once more in its entirety; then they seem to get stuck on Figure A, which they repeat several times.

The middle section is based on a saucy little trumpet tune that is characterized by a wide leap upward at the end of each segment:

Example 7

Trumpet

As this melody continues, it is played, in turn, by the violins and the oboe.

The violins repeat the melody of Example 7.

In a passage that forms a bridge to the closing section, the piano and brass are heard with a rhythmic figure that alternates with a fast-moving string passage.

After a dynamic climax, the rhythm pattern of the introduction returns in the piano.

The closing section begins with Example 6A played by the violins and clarinet.

Example 6B is started by the woodwinds and finished by the full orchestra.

The melody of Example 6A is heard once more, and leads to the close of this wild hoe-down.

About the Composer

AARON COPLAND   Born: November 14, 1900
Brooklyn, New York

"I was born on a street in Brooklyn that can only be described as drab," Aaron Copland has written. "It had none of the garish color of the ghetto, none of the charm of an old New England thoroughfare, or even the rawness of a pioneer street. It was simply drab. . . . It was there that I spent the first twenty years of my life."[4]

Although there was music in the Copland home—Aaron's eldest brother played the violin to his sister's piano accompaniment, and ragtime sheet music could frequently be found on the piano—it was not the kind of environment out of which, a person would think, one of America's greatest composers would emerge.

The idea of becoming a professional musician first occurred to Copland when he was thirteen. "Music as an art was a discovery I made all by myself," Copland once said. "No one ever talked music to me or took me to a concert."

After two years of piano lessons, Copland decided to become a composer; he was just fifteen. He tried at first to learn the rudiments of harmony by correspondence. When he discovered that this did not work, he secured a private teacher. After graduation from high school, Copland devoted all his energies to the study of music. He traveled to Paris to study at a new school that had just been established for Americans at Fontainebleau. For three years he studied with Nadia Boulanger, the noted teacher of composition and theory who went on to teach several generations of Americans. On completing these studies, Copland returned to the United States. Although he had been requested to compose a work for Nadia Boulanger, who was about to make a concert tour of the United States, Copland found it necessary to play in a hotel trio to earn enough money to live on.

Almost from the day of the premiere of the requested work, *Symphony for Organ and Orchestra,* Copland was able to earn much of his livelihood by composing. Like his close friend Benjamin Britten, Copland has been able to support himself largely without resorting to teaching and other noncompositional activities.

Copland is probably best known for his ballet music, including among others *Billy the Kid* (1938), *Rodeo* (1942), and *Appalachian Spring* (1944). His two operas, *The Second Hurricane* (1937) and *The Tender Land* (1954), have not been as successful as his ballets in terms of audience enthusiasm, primarily because of the lack of dramatic tension in the story line of the operas, and because most of the musical and melodic interest of the operas is centered in the orchestral texture rather than in the vocal lines. Copland's most frequently performed orchestral works include his *Dance Symphony* (1925), *El Salón México* (1936), *Quiet City* (1940), *Fanfare for the Common Man* and the

4. Aaron Copland, "Composer from Brooklyn," *Magazine of Art,* 1939.

Lincoln Portrait (both 1942), and *Connotations for Orchestra* (1962). The composer has also created outstanding scores for several films, including *Our Town* (1940) and *The Red Pony* (1948).

While Copland's early works reflect the jazz idiom of the United States in the late 1920s and early 1930s, most of the works for which he is well known reflect a strong interest in folk music. (He actually quotes folk melodies in his *Applachian Spring, Rodeo,* and *El Salón México.*) His later works, including *Connotations for Orchestra* (which he wrote for the opening of Avery Fisher Hall at New York's Lincoln Center), reflect the more abstract, less tonal music of the contemporary style of composition.

In *Music Today,* Dr. Carleton Sprague Smith wrote: "Aaron Copland is without question North America's leading composer. He has a flavor which is at once personal and American. . . . He can be grand, solemn or gay—bleak or 'juicy.' As a teacher, public lecturer, author, pianist and conductor, Copland has had the greatest influence of any composer now active in the United States." The many tributes made on the occasion of the composer's eightieth birthday in 1980 support Dr. Smith's statement.

Bibliography

Berger, Arthur. *Aaron Copland.* New York: Oxford University Press, 1953.

Dobrin, Arnold. *Aaron Copland: His Life and Times.* New York: Thomas Y. Crowell, 1967.

If only the whole world could feel the power of harmony . . . .

Wolfgang Amadeus Mozart

FOUR/
TEXTURE

HAVE you ever tried strumming chords on a guitar, or pushing buttons on a chord organ? When you were in elementary school, did you ever experiment with the sounds of an autoharp, or, in later years, did you ever blend your voice with others as you tried a bit of harmonizing around a campfire? If you have had any of these experiences, then you have already encountered harmony, one of the important aspects of the texture of music.

We sometimes use the verb *harmonize* in referring to any agreeable combination of tones, as when we say that we are *harmonizing* with a friend who is singing a folk song. The noun *harmony,* however, refers to chords that are related to a key center or tonality. *The New College Encyclopedia of Music* (New York, 1960) says that *harmony* means "the structure, functions and relationships of chords."

Chords consist of three or more different pitches sounded at the same time. Here is an example of a chord in staff notation:

The four tones, reading from bottom to top (the manner in which musicians "read" chords) C–E–G–C, are sounded at the same time.

If we were to play the same tones one after another and add a little rhythm, a melody could be made out of the tones of this chord:

Most melodies can be harmonized in several ways, although melodies, such as the one just quoted, that "outline" a chord are best harmonized with that chord. As a melody moves along, it usually gives the musician clues to ways in which it may be harmonized with different chords. The chords a folk singer might use can be harsh, pleasant, or even surprising. A composer frequently uses a wider variety of chords than a folk singer does.

In many pop, disco, and rock tunes, the composer writes down only the melody and then expects an arranger to create the chordal accompaniment. Jazz is different. The pianist might play a twelve-bar pattern of chords over and over while the other musicians create a changing melody to fit the pattern.

Some of the same chord patterns used by Bach and Beethoven are still used by jazz, rock, symphonic, and folk musicians today. While new chords or patterns are always being sought by the creative composer, the simple chord patterns of long ago are still used in all kinds of music.

THE BIRTH OF HARMONY

Even in the Western world we have not always had harmony. Actually harmony has been around for only about 300 years, starting with the use of major and minor scales. Originally, most Western music was vocal and consisted of just a single melodic line based on Greek modes rather than on major or minor scales. The Church preserved this tradition for centuries with men's voices all singing the same melodic line in unison. We can illustrate such music by a single horizontal line:

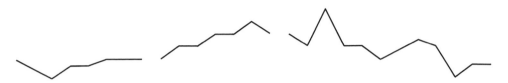

Such music, consisting simply of a single melodic line without any kind of accompaniment, is known as *monophonic* music (*monos* meaning "one"; *phono* meaning "sound" or "voice").

When boys were added to the choir, their unchanged soprano voices sang the melody an octave higher. This did not change the sound very much. The added boys' voices moved above the men's voices in a line that exactly paralleled the original:

Boys' voices

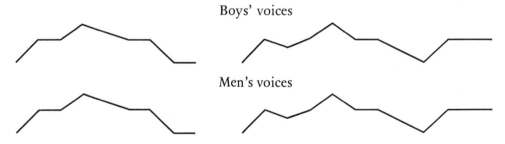

Men's voices

It was eventually discovered that each voice in a composition could sing its own melodic line. In this newly emerging style, each voice would frequently sing the same tune, just as we do nowadays in a round, each voice singing the same melody but starting at a different time:

Third voice

Second voice

First voice

Such music, with more than one concurrent melodic line, is known as *polyphonic music* (*poly* meaning "more than one"). This type of polyphonic writing is frequently called *counterpoint* (or *contrapuntal music*), since *point* originally meant a mark indicating a note or sound; thus, logically, "note against note" or, by extension, "melody against melody."

While rounds are the simplest form of counterpoint, we will later study such involved forms as the *fugues* of Johann Sebastian Bach.

Around the year 1600, a new way of creating musical works began to develop. Instead of basing melodies on the old-fashioned modes, two of those modes were changed slightly and became known as major and minor scales.

By 1700, major and minor scales had become the basis for most music, and chords had developed out of polyphonic music. Another way of saying this is that the melodies of polyphonic music were moving toward the formation of chords. For example, J. S. Bach wrote a work we call *The Little Fugue in G Minor* (to distinguish it from another much larger fugue in the same key). Now if we look at the following portion of that music, we see four places where the notes constitute what we call *chords,* the sounding at the same time of three different tones. Harmony as we know it was in the process of being born.

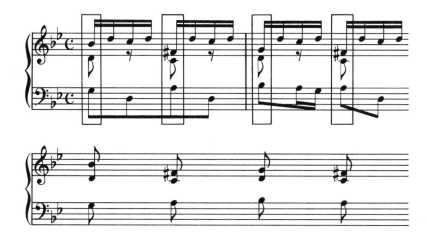

In the *Hallelujah!* chorus by Handel (which we will examine in detail shortly), we can hear this changing back and forth from harmonic writing (in which the melodies move together and sound like a chord pattern) to polyphonic writing (in which concurrent melodies move independently of one another).

The style of composition that emerged, the accompaniment of a single melodic line with a series of appropriate chords, is known as *homophonic music* (*homo* meaning "same"). With the exception of some jazz and some contemporary music, most of the music we hear today is homophonic music, melody accompanied by chords.

SCALES, CHORDS, AND TRIADS

As we have seen, chords are the basis of harmony. And in order for us to have a logical sequence of chords—a chord progression—these chords must be related to a tonal center or *tonic*.

For example, if we take the C-major scale—the scale that makes use of only the white keys of the piano—we can build a chord of three tones beginning with C and using every other key up the keyboard: C–E–G. We call a chord in this position a *triad* because it is made up of three tones spaced in this particular manner.

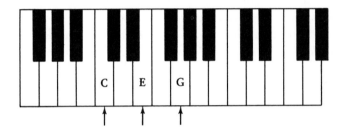

If we were to write a three-tone chord, or triad, built on C, it would look like the following in staff notation, each of the three tones appearing on neighboring lines with C as the lowest tone:

A triad, of course, may be built on any tone; and chords more complex than a triad can also be built on any pitch.

The tones of a chord—C, E, and G in the C triad illustrated—do not always have to appear in the same order. In the second chord in the following example, E is the lowest tone, with G and C above it. The third chord has G as the lowest tone, with C and E above it. These three chords are made up of the same three tones as the original C chord, even though the tones appear in different positions. Since C is the root, or basis, of this chord, the example on the left of the following chart with C as the root or lowest tone is known as a *C chord in root position*. The next two are, in turn, known as a *C chord* in *first inversion* and *second inversion*.

Staff notation is not the only way of writing chords. Guitarists use a special set of symbols known as *tablature,* a system that indicates which frets are to be used to produce a given chord.[1] The tablature on the left is for a C chord, the one on the right for a d minor chord.

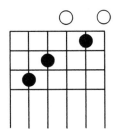 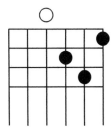

Pop pianists use a *lead sheet* on which chords are indicated above the staff by letters of the alphabet. The small *m* after the D in the following example indicates that the chord built on D is a minor one.

THE SCIENTIFIC ORIGIN OF CHORDS

Theoretically, any chord can move to any other chord, but the progressions we find most pleasing to the ear are the ones based on the physical relationships of tones to a *fundamental.* In order to understand this concept, we must digress for a moment and consider the physical nature of a tone.

The untrained ear tends to perceive or hear a note as a single tone, as if it consisted of a pure sound of a single pitch; but actually when a sound is produced it consists, in addition to the easily detectable basic tone, of other tones related to it acoustically— because the vibrating medium vibrates in sections as well as a whole.

---

1. The solid circles tell the guitarist exactly where the fingers of the left hand are to be placed in relationship to the strings and frets. The open circles indicate strings that are to be played *open,* that is, without stopping them. Strings without a circle—either solid or open—are not to be played.

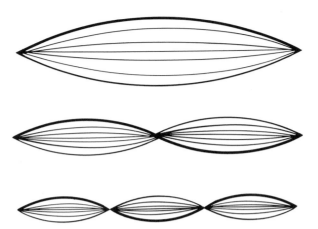

We call the original pitch the *fundamental* and the related ones the *overtones*. Overtones may be demonstrated on the piano as follows. Silently depress the keys of the entire octave from middle C upward to the next C (leaving all of those strings free to vibrate sympathetically) and strike the C an octave below middle C. The middle C string, the G above it, and the upper C will vibrate sympathetically and be heard. These three tones are overtones produced by the fundamental tone, the C that was struck. A similar procedure, accomplished by depressing all the keys an octave higher, will demonstrate that the E and G are also overtones and that they therefore have a close physical relationship to the fundamental tone that was struck. This demonstration can be repeated at any pitch level, but becomes easiest to perceive when the fundamental is a fairly low pitch. In staff notation, the overtones of low C, through the fifteenth overtone, would appear as follows in staff notation:

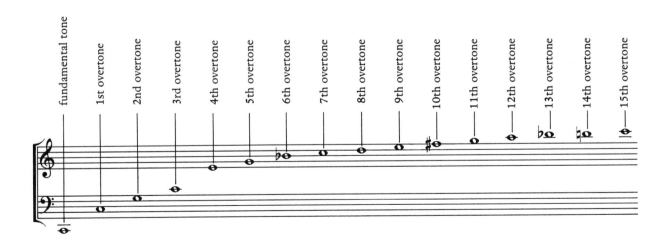

A major chord consists of the fundamental tone and the two overtones that have the closest physical relationship to it. From the preceding example, you can see that G and E are the first two tones in the harmonic series (other than C itself). Therefore, they bear the closest physical relationship to the fundamental tone C.

Because of the close physical relationship between a given tone and the fifth tone above it, the chord based on the fifth tone (known as the *dominant* harmony) bears the closest relationship to the chord based on the key tone (the *tonic* harmony). Thus the natural resolution of the dominant is to the tonic, which is its harmonic generator. The dominant chord may frequently lead elsewhere, to harmonies away from its home base, but its natural resolution is still always to the tonic.

HARMONIC PROGRESSIONS

While chords may be built on any degree of the scale, three chords in each key or to-nality are much more important than the others. If we number the tones of a scale—a C-major scale, for example—the important chords would be the ones based on the first, fourth, and fifth tones of the scale: C, F, and G.

I   IV   V

Musicians frequently indicate these chords by the use of Roman numerals I, IV, and V. They also have names: *tonic* (meaning the chord built on the tone or key center), *subdominant,* and *dominant.*

Often a fourth tone is added to the V or dominant chord. For example, if we take the chord built on G in the key of C major and count every ascending line and space beginning with G as one, we find the newly added note at the top is number seven (which in this case is F). We therefore call this chord a *G-seventh* or *dominant seventh* chord. It can also be indicated as V⁷.

The dominant chord is a very active one; it pulls toward the tonic chord. This at-traction has great importance in music. The use of the dominant chord sets up a ten-sion, a forward motion that does not stop until the tonic chord is heard. This progression from dominant to tonic gives a very strong sense of conclusion. That is why the progression V–I is often used at the end of a phrase, melody, or composition. Such an ending is called a *cadence* (see pp. 44–45). In the song *America,* for example, the penultimate syllable is harmonized with a dominant chord. It resolves to a tonic chord for the last syllable.

Frequently in music we use the term *consonance* to suggest any chord that is stable, static, and suggests repose; we use the word *dissonance* to identify a chord that requires resolution.[2]

CHANGING TONALITIES

The sound of the three basic chords—I, IV, and V⁷—changes when we change key. In the key of F major, for example, the I becomes an F chord, the IV a B-flat chord, and the V⁷ a C⁷ chord:

By listening to these chord progressions in F major and in C major, we discover that the relationship of the three chords *to each other* is the same in both keys.

When we change to the minor tonality, the nature of the tonic and subdominant chords changes: They become minor chords. This is symbolized by the use of lower-case Roman numerals i and iv.

2. The word *dissonance* has two meanings. Most people are aware of only the first: "an inharmonious or harsh sound; discord." In music, when we use the word *dissonance* we refer to the second meaning of the word: "a simultaneous combination of tones [chord] conventionally accepted as being in a state of unrest and needing completion."

If you can find the I, IV, and V⁷ chords on the guitar, the autoharp, the piano, or some other musical instrument, you can accompany or "harmonize" most folk songs. *Home on the Range,* for example, would be harmonized:

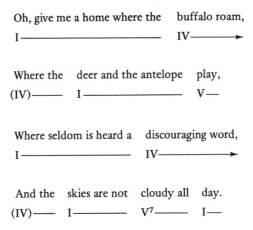

Obviously, more sophisticated music makes use of more sophisticated chords than the basic tonic, subdominant, and dominant. A good example of this more sophisticated type of harmony may be found in the next composition we consider.

Messiah

by GEORG FRIEDRICH HANDEL

Messiah is unquestionably Georg Friedrich Handel's best-known oratorio. The word *oratorio* literally means a "place of prayer," and in sixteenth-century Rome, it was applied to a chapel where religious services were often held. A common feature of these services was the singing of *laude,* songs of popular devotion. These were, in effect, musical "conversations" between God and the soul, heaven and hell, or similar participants. Eventually they evolved into sacred plays with music.

As the form became more elaborate and each section grew longer, the name of the place of performance—the *oratorio*—was adopted as the generic title of the form. In the English edition of Grassineau's music dictionary of 1740, the word *oratorio* was described as "a sort of spiritual opera," and the terms *oratorio* and *sacred drama* at that time

Section of *Messiah* ("I know that my Redeemer liveth") in Handel's own handwriting

were used almost interchangeably. A Handel oratorio was sometimes divided into "acts," or parts.

In his book *Choral Music,* Arthur Jacobs tells us that the published texts of Handel's oratorios "with a large or small helping of imaginary stage directions were sold to audiences. But the stage *was* imaginary, and so Handel could naturally—and quite properly—employ effects of purely musical construction which go against the pace and directness that would be desirable in theatrical presentation."[3]

Since about the year 1600, *oratorio* has come to mean a setting of a text on a sacred or epic theme, scored for chorus, soloists, and orchestra. Performed either in a church or a concert hall, oratorios presented today do not ordinarily involve scenery, props, and costumes as do operas based on religious subjects.

Handel's *Messiah* takes its text from the Bible. It is divided into three parts, focusing successively on the birth of Jesus, his death and resurrection, and man's redemption.

At the invitation of the Viceroy of Ireland, Handel journeyed to Dublin and supervised the first performance of *Messiah* on April 13, 1742. There were 700 people in

3. Arthur Jacobs, ed., *Choral Music* (Baltimore, 1963).

a room designed for 600; to accommodate this crowd, ladies were asked to come without their usual hoops and men were asked to leave their swords at home. The success of the performance and of the work itself was reported in the *Dublin Journal:*

> On Tuesday last Mr. Handel's Sacred Grand Oratorio, the MESSIAH, was performed at the New Musick-Hall in Fishamble-street; the best Judges allowed it to be the most finished piece of Musick. Words are wanting to express the exquisite Delight it afforded to the admiring crouded Audience. The Sublime, the Grand, the Tender, adapted to the most elevated, majestick and moving Words, conspired to transport and charm the ravished Heart and Ear. It is but Justice to Mr. Handel that the World should know, he generously gave the Money arising from this Grand Performance, to be equally shared by the Society for relieving Prisoners, the Charitable Infirmary, and Mercer's Hospital, for which they will ever gratefully remember his Name.

Messiah is divided into fifty-three separate movements, and is scored for four solo voices, a four-voice choir, and an orchestra that includes oboes and bassoons supporting the strings, with trumpets and drums for the great climaxes.[4] In the large choruses, the woodwinds generally play in unison with the strings. The *continuo,* the essential harmonic "filling in," is shared by a cello and a keyboard instrument.[5] These instruments were the nucleus of the typical orchestra of Handel's time, which we know as the Baroque era.

Three of the movements from *Messiah* are described in the following paragraphs; their location in the complete oratorio is indicated by the number preceding the title. Studying these sections of *Messiah* will provide us with an opportunity to compare textures, to *hear* the difference between passages that are developed polyphonically and those that are set in homophonic style, based on chords and the newly emerging concept of harmony.

12. Chorus: For unto us a Child is born

The text of this chorus, cast in fugal form, is from Isaiah 9:6. By *fugal form,* we mean a polyphonic setting in two or more voices built on a *subject*—a theme (long or short) introduced at the beginning by each voice performing or singing it in turn. This subject recurs frequently throughout the composition in either its original form or in a variation. The second entry of the subject is generally on the dominant (the fifth tone of the scale), and is called the *answer.*

---

4. In referring to choral music, musicians speak of a *four-voice chorus* or a *five-voice chorus.* The number does not refer to the number of people who might be singing in the chorus (which would probably run between 15 and 200), but to the number of separate, independent melodic lines in the score. Thus a four-voice chorus would be scored for (1) soprano, (2) alto, (3) tenor, and (4) bass.

5. *Continuo* refers to a bass line in the music of the seventeenth and early eighteenth centuries; it is played as written by a single cello, and is also played as the bass line of a keyboard instrument upon which the performer adds chords that agree with the harmonic structure of the music, thus "filling in" the harmony.

LISTENING OUTLINE

The orchestra is first heard in a brief introduction based on the subject (Example 1) of the fugal section that follows.

In the fugal section, the subject (Example 1) is sung by each of the four voices in turn. The sopranos are heard first. When they finish, the tenors answer with the same melody; the sopranos sing against it a second melody (called the *countersubject*). Altos enter; before they have finished two measures of the subject, the basses answer.

Example 1 (Subject)

Sopranos

For un-to us a Child is born,__ un-to us a Son is

giv-en, un-to us a Son is giv-en;

For unto us a Child is born,
Unto us a Son is given;

A new melodic phrase (Example 2) is introduced by the tenors, who are imitated by the sopranos. Next both altos and basses take up the melody of Example 2 at the same time.

Example 2

Tenors

And the gov-ern-ment shall be up-on His shoul - - - - der;

And the government shall be
Upon His shoulder;
And His name shall be called:

The homophonic passage that follows relies on bold chords to suggest the might and majesty of the text:

Example 3

> *Wonderful, Counsellor,*
> *The Mighty God,*
> *The Everlasting Father,*
> *The Prince of Peace.*

A polyphonic passage follows, with the following text introduced by the altos:

> *Unto us a Child is born*

Tenors respond with

> *For unto us a Child is born*

The altos complete their statement of the tonally adjusted subject (Example 1) and end at the same time as the tenors.[6] Then the sopranos enter, followed by the basses in imitation.

The altos state Example 2; basses answer in imitation.

> *And the government shall be*
> *Upon His shoulder;*

A homophonic passage set in bold chords for the entire chorus follows:

> *And His name shall be called:*
> *Wonderful, Counsellor,*
> *The Mighty God,*
> *The Everlasting Father,*
> *The Prince of Peace.*

Polyphonic imitation on the text *unto us a Child is born* follows, the voices entering in the following sequence:

tenors
sopranos
basses
altos

---

6. So that contrapuntal passages may sound agreeable rather than dissonant, minor changes may be made in a melody when it is repeated on a different pitch level. This is referred to as "tonally adjusting" the melody.

The text *And the government shall be upon His shoulder* (Example 2) returns in the following sequence: the tenors, then the sopranos in imitation, followed by the altos and basses in two-part polyphony on the words *upon His shoulder.*

The concluding section, while containing some polyphonic imitation, is essentially in homophonic style with bold, forthright chords once again used for proclaiming the majesty of the text:

And His name shall be called:
Wonderful, Counsellor,
The Mighty God,
The Everlasting Father,
Prince of Peace.

For unto us a Child is born,
Unto us a Son is given,
And the government shall be
Upon His shoulder,
And His name shall be called:

Wonderful, Counsellor,
The Mighty God,
The Everlasting Father,
The Prince of Peace.

The fugal subject (Example 1) is heard in the violins as this rousing chorus comes to its conclusion with an orchestral ending.

44. Chorus: Hallelujah!

The famous *Hallelujah!* chorus concludes Part II of *Messiah.* Following a tradition established in Handel's time—at a performance when the king stood up for the singing of the *Hallelujah!* chorus, his subjects necessarily following suit—audiences today usually stand for the performances of this chorus.

The text of this chorus is from Revelation 19:6, 11:15, and 19:16. The movement is cast in the mixture of polyphonic and homophonic writing that characterizes *For unto us a Child is born.*

LISTENING OUTLINE

After a brief three-measure introduction, the full chorus proclaims *Hallelujah!* several times in a homophonic passage built of huge, emphatic chords. This passage begins:

Example 4

Hal - le - lu -jah! Hal - le - lu -jah! Hal -le - lu -jah! Hal -le - lu -jah! Hal - le - lu -jah!

In what is actually a *monophonic* passage, the full chorus proclaims in unison:

Example 5

For the Lord God Om - ni - po - tent reign - eth,

For the Lord God Omnipotent reigneth.

Four bold chordal outbursts of *Hallelujah!* for full chorus follow as they respond with additional *Hallelujah!*s.

Alto, tenor, and bass in unison restate the melody of Example 5:

For the Lord God Omnipotent reigneth.

Four more bold chords proclaiming *Hallelujah!* follow.

In a polyphonic passage, the text and melody of Example 5 pass from one voice to another as the other voices state and restate *Hallelujah!* The melody and text of Example 5 successively appear in the following voices:

soprano

tenor and bass

alto and tenor

The dynamic level drops abruptly; with rich-sounding chords, the full chorus proclaims in a homophonic passage:

> *The Kingdom of this world,*
> *Is become the Kingdom of our Lord*
> *And of His Christ, and of His Christ.*

A new polyphonic melody is introduced by the basses:

Example 6

Basses

And He shall reign for - ev - er and ev - er.

In a contrapuntal passage, successive entrances of this melody are made by:

tenors
altos
sopranos

The women's voices declaim the words *King of Kings, and Lord of Lords* in unison on sustained tones, rising in pitch each time they repeat it. The men repeat the words *for ever and ever, Hallelujah! Hallelujah!*

The fugal subject (Example 6) returns in the basses, who are imitated by the sopranos. Altos and tenors have a countermelody.

The tenors now intone the words *King of Kings* on sustained pitches as the other three voices respond with *for ever and ever.*

All voices join in a homophonic setting of the text:

> *And He shall reign for ever and ever.*
> *King of Kings, and Lord of Lords,*
> *King of Kings, and Lord of Lords;*
> *And He shall reign for ever and ever,*
> *For ever and ever, Hallelujah!*

53. Chorus: Worthy is the Lamb

Worthy is the Lamb is part of the majestic closing chorus of *Messiah,* the text taken from the fifth chapter of Revelation. This chorus provides an excellent example of contrasting textures: sections of homophonic texture alternate with sections of polyphonic or contrapuntal texture. It should be noted, however, that changes in tempo—the speed of the basic pulse—do not always or necessarily correspond with changes in texture.

LISTENING OUTLINE

The concluding chorus starts slowly, majestically, with a homophonic passage that begins:

Example 7

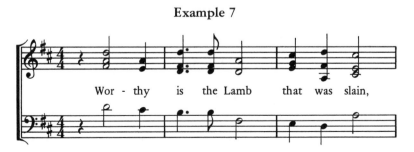

Wor-thy   is   the Lamb   that   was   slain,

Worthy is the Lamb that was slain,
And hath redeemed us to God by His blood,
To receive power, and riches,
And wisdom, and strength,
And honor, and glory, and blessing.

In a variant of the melody of Example 7, the text is repeated in another homophonic passage; starting with *To receive power,* the tempo changes and becomes faster.

Worthy is the Lamb that was slain,
And hath redeemed us to God by His blood,
To receive power, and riches,
And wisdom, and strength,
And honor, and glory, and blessing.

In the following polyphonic passage, the tenors and basses announce the subject in unison:

Example 8

The subject (Example 8) is successively heard in the following voices; a countersubject is heard in counterpoint to it:

soprano
alto
bass

A section of *stretto* (in which each voice enters with the subject before the preceding voice has had a chance to finish its statement) is heard. The first half of Example 8 (the two halves are separable) is sung in turn by:

basses
altos
sopranos
tenors

The tenors (singing the first bar of Example 8) are soon joined by the basses, who restate the subject of Example 8. This leads to a homophonic section which, in turn, is followed by a middle section of three lines that is monophonic and set in unison for altos, tenors, and basses. The concluding section (another five lines) is a homophonic passage:

For ever,
Blessing and honour,
Glory and power
Be unto Him, be unto Him.

Blessing and honour,
Glory and power
Be unto Him, be unto Him.

Blessing,
Honour,
Glory,
And power
Be unto Him.

The final section starts out polyphonically with the text *that sitteth upon the throne*; it concludes in a homophonic fashion, the chorus harmonically proclaiming repeatedly *for ever and ever.*

About the Composer

GEORG FRIEDRICH HANDEL[7]

Born: February 23, 1685
Halle, Germany

Died: April 14, 1759
London, England

Handel was truly a cosmopolitan musician, for he was born a German, became a British subject, composed music in the Italian tradition, and premiered his most famous work, *Messiah,* in Ireland.

Handel's father was a barber-surgeon who had been appointed surgeon and valet to the Duke of Saxe-Weissenfels in Germany. Georg was born of his father's second marriage; his mother was a pastor's daughter. The elder Handel had little training in music and was against his son's following it as a profession. When Georg was seven, the duke noticed his ability at the organ and suggested that Georg be given musical training. The father made no objection to this, and arranged for the boy to have some music lessons for his own amusement. Through his stepbrother, Georg was able to take lessons and practice on the organ in the duke's chapel. As his talent became evident, the boy was also given lessons on the oboe, the violin, and the harpsichord, and studied

7. The original German spelling of the composer's name was Georg Friedrich Händel. Although in later life he adopted the English spelling George Frideric Handel, it was not widely used by others.

counterpoint and fugue. In 1697, when he was twelve, Georg was appointed assistant organist at the cathedral in Halle.

Georg's father had died shortly before that. In fulfillment of the parent's wishes, the boy entered the University of Halle in 1702 as a law student. He remained at the university one year, but at the same time became organist at the cathedral. Then, in desperation, he gave up the study of law. He moved to Hamburg, where he secured a position as a violinist at the opera house. He composed two operas while he was employed at Hamburg.

By the time Handel was twenty-one, he somehow financed a trip to Italy, the opera center of Europe. During his visit to Florence, he composed an opera that was presented there. Another opera, written and produced during his visit to Venice, was a big success with the public. In Rome he completed two large choral works that were given their first performances in that city.

After having spent four years in Italy, Handel returned to Germany in 1710, and was appointed court musician to the Elector of Hanover. During the latter part of that year, Handel made his first visit to London, where one of his operas was presented with success at the Queen's Theater in the Haymarket. Handel returned for a second visit to England two years later, presenting works that were so well received by the public that he was awarded a royal annuity. The enthusiasm of the British public for his works caused him to overstay his leave from his post in Germany. During this time, however, Queen Anne died. Leaving no direct heir to the British throne, she was succeeded by the Elector of Hanover (Handel's patron), who was crowned King George I of England. With his old patron now on the British throne, Handel decided to remain in England, and in 1726 he became a British subject.

Handel enjoyed the royal favor, teaching both the Prince of Wales and Princess Anne. He was appointed a director of the new Royal Academy of Music, his chief function being the production of Italian operas. In a period of a little over ten years, the composer produced eighteen of his own operas. Oxford University conferred upon him the honorary degree Doctor of Music. Next, he was appointed sole director of the Covent Garden Opera House, producing nine of his own works in a three-year period.

After a decline in the popularity of his Italian-style operas, Handel turned to the composition of oratorios, an activity that was to occupy the balance of his life.

Bibliography

Lang, Paul Henry. *George Frederic Handel.* New York: W. W. Norton & Co., 1977.
Schoelcher, Victor. *The Life of Handel.* New York: Da Capo Press, 1979.

A great body of sound is loud, and the opposite is low.

Plato

FIVE/
DYNAMICS

W HEN you listen to one of your favorite songs on a record album or hear a piece you really like performed in a concert, you are very much aware of certain elements in the music. You might say you liked the work because you have been attracted to its tune or melody. Or you could talk about the catchy, infectious rhythm of the piece. Perhaps you might even remark about the lush, romantic chords heard in the background. In essence, what you are getting at are three important elements to be found in most musical compositions: melody, rhythm, and harmony. These are often called the *principal* elements of music—the ones we have been studying so far.

In addition to these three principal elements, there are three *affective* elements that enhance or change the essential nature of a rhythm, melody, or harmonic progression within a composition. These affective elements are so named because they affect or "act on [or] produce an effect or change."[1] These affective elements are timbre, dynamics, and tempo. (For a discussion of timbre, see Chapter 1; for tempo, see Chapter 6.) The affective elements never exist by themselves, but operate in conjunction with the principal elements of rhythm, melody, and harmony.

THE MEANING OF DYNAMICS

When used in reference to music, *dynamics* refers to the softness and loudness of the tones or passage being performed; in other words, the degree of sound-volume. Scientists can, of course, measure the dynamic level very accurately with an audiometer, but musicians (and the listening public), using only the human ear, make a more subjective determination of the dynamic level. Scientists speak of a sound being of an intensity of so many *decibels;* the musician speaks of a musical passage as being *forte* (loud) or *piano* (soft) or some degree thereof.[2]

We may ask why the musician doesn't use an audiometer, marking the pages of music with desired decibel levels instead of *fortes* and *pianos.* There are two good reasons for this. The objective reason is concerned with the ambience or environment in which the sound is produced. Imagine a young student who plays the trumpet. That person might go into the bathroom at home and play a C-major scale using just a fair amount of wind pressure. Because of the acoustical environment of the room—hard-surfaced walls that bounce the sound back and forth many times—the tones of the scale might seem unbearably loud. When that student appears with the school band on the football field, he or she may play the C-major scale again, using the same amount of wind pressure. From just a few feet away it will sound muffled and soft; from a distance it will be almost inaudible unless one is directly in line with the bell of the instrument.

1. *The Random House Dictionary of the English Language* (New York, 1966).
2. The unit for measuring loudness is called a *bel* (after Alexander Graham Bell). The *decibel* (one-tenth of a bel) is the smallest degree of difference in loudness the normal human ear can distinguish. Musical sounds range from about 25 decibels (the softest violin tone) to about 100 decibels (a full orchestra playing *fortissimo).*

It therefore becomes obvious that we must leave it to the individual musician to determine what level of intensity is "loud" for the space or area in which he or she is going to play a passage.

The subjective reason is a little more difficult to describe. It has to do with individual differences, the variety of ways in which people perceive the same object. Perhaps we can best illustrate this by using an extreme example.

For many young people who carry a portable radio-cassette player with them as they walk down the street or turn on the car radio or cassette player as they are driving around, the volume control must be turned up full to achieve what these young people believe to be an enjoyable level of sound. If the grandparents of these young people were asked to listen to the same radio or cassette player, they would probably ask why the volume was turned up so loud, remarking that the music was so very loud "you can't hear what they're playing." This difference of opinion about the dynamic level is a subjective reaction.

We can therefore understand how, on a more subtle level, the performing musician must determine for each passage—yes, even every tone or note in the composition—exactly how loud or soft those tones should be. This act of determination and execution is called *interpreting* the music. Because tastes differ among listeners as well as performers, some people prefer the *interpretation* of one performer over that of another: the "softs" softer, the "louds" louder.

We must bear in mind, however, that dynamics is only one of the three affective elements. The timbre the singer or instrumentalist produces and the tempo (the speed of the basic beat) selected are also part of the interpretation. (The rhythms, melodies, and harmonies of traditional music are all determined by the composer.)

DYNAMIC MARKINGS

The *expression markings* or symbols the composer uses to suggest the relative degree of loudness or softness have changed somewhat over the centuries. Three hundred years ago—during the time of Bach and Handel—only two symbols were used: *f* (*forte*) for loud, and *p* (*piano*) for soft. By the late nineteenth century, with refinements in many wind instruments so that they could play softer and louder than previously, and with composers realizing the desirability of indicating their precise intentions (particularly if they were not going to be in charge of the performance, as Bach, Handel, and others had been in earlier generations when their music was performed)—some composers were using *fffff* and *ppppp* as expression markings.

It should be obvious that soft and loud exist in a continuum—a continuous series of levels, with an infinite number of points between the two extremes.

Before the invention of the piano around 1710, keyboard instruments—spinets, harpsichords, and pipe organs—could only produce a level of sound predetermined by the number of sets of strings or pipes involved.[3] In other words, the keyboard artist might engage only one set of strings or pipes to play a passage softly. Several sets of strings or pipes might be used simultaneously if the artist wanted the passage to sound quite loud. There was no way at that time, however, for a keyboard artist to play a passage so that it would become softer or louder gradually.

For this reason, many artists today think that Bach and Handel's music should be performed using only *plateaus* of dynamic variance. In other words, they believe that all of one phrase or passage should be played at the same dynamic level, with no gradual increases or decreases in the softness or loudness. Other performers believe that, had it been possible to make gradual swells in the sound, composers such as Bach and Handel would have done so. These interpreters, therefore, make free use of gradual swells in the dynamic level when they play the music of Bach and Handel's time.

With the invention of the piano around 1710 and *swell shutters* for the pipe organ around 1712, it became possible to make a smooth, slow, subtle change from soft to loud or loud to soft.[4] We call these gradual increases or decreases in the dynamic level *crescendos* and *decrescendos.* The symbols for them, along with other commonly used accent marks, are as follows:

cresc.	*crescendo*	(growing louder)
decresc. or	*decrescendo* or	(growing softer)
dim.	*diminuendo*	
fp	*fortepiano*	(loud, then immediately soft)
sf or	*sforzato* or	(heavily accented)
sfz	*sforzando*	
		(strong accent)
marcato	—	(stress or pressure)
Λ or V		(heavy pressure)

The general abbreviations for dynamic levels that may be found in music include:

ppp	*pianississimo*	(extremely soft)
pp	*pianissimo*	(very soft)
p	*piano*	(soft)
mp	*mezzopiano*	(medium soft)
mf	*mezzoforte*	(medium loud)
f	*forte*	(loud)
ff	*fortissimo*	(very loud)
fff	*fortississimo*	(extremely loud)

Differences in dynamic levels can be either subtle or bold, or any degree in between. In Ravel's exciting orchestral piece *Bolero,* the subtle changes in dynamic level

3. The piano was originally called *pianoforte* or *piano e forte* ("soft-loud" or "soft and loud") by its Italian inventor, Bartolommeo Cristofori, because it was the first keyboard instrument upon which the performer could subtly control the dynamics from soft to loud by means of the force used to strike the key.
4. *Swell shutters,* sometimes called *Venetian shutters,* are operated by the *swell pedal* on the pipe organ console and are concerned with that section and keyboard of the organ known as the *swell.* Pipes for this section of the organ are placed in an enclosed space for which the only opening is the one behind the swell shutters. When the swell pedal is depressed, the shutters open, thus allowing more sound to issue from the chamber containing the pipes. As the pedal is raised, the shutters close, producing a *diminuendo* or *decrescendo.*

become one of the most important design elements in the composition. Referring to his *Bolero,* Ravel said that what he had composed was "a piece lasting 17 minutes and consisting wholly of . . . one very long, very gradual crescendo. There are no contrasts, there is practically no invention except the plan and the manner of execution."

Not all changes in dynamic level are so subtle. The "surprise" in Haydn's *"Surprise" Symphony* occurs because he places an extremely loud chord at the end of a very soft passage.

DYNAMIC EXPRESSION

Certain types of compositions seem to suggest the appropriate overall dynamic level by their very nature. For example, we expect a lullaby to be soft. A victory march for a football team we expect to be loud.

The overall level, however, is only one aspect of the dynamics of a composition. It is obvious that every musical sound possesses some degree of loudness or softness. By carefully relating the dynamic level of one tone in a composition to all the other tones, a composer is able to achieve subtle dynamic contrasts that provide variety and give expressive meaning to the composition.

A lullaby would be boring if every tone were sung at exactly the same dynamic level, without accent within a measure or phrase, and without contrast between sections of the lullaby. The same boring prospect would exist if a victory march were played throughout at the same dynamic level. In fact, we might not even recognize it as a march, for it is the subtle accent or louder tone produced on the first note of every four-beat measure that gives the flavor of a march to the rhythmic element.

Let us now investigate the ways in which the Russian composer Modest Mussorgsky uses dynamic contrasts for expressive purposes in his *Pictures at an Exhibition.*

Pictures at an Exhibition
by MODEST MUSSORGSKY

In the autumn of 1874, an exhibition of some 400 paintings, watercolors, and architectural designs by the Russian painter and architect Victor Alexandrovich Hartmann was held at the academy of arts in St. Petersburg. The artist, who had died the previous year at the early age of thirty-nine, had been a prominent member of a group of young artists who were striving for the creation of a purely Russian art by the elimination of all foreign influences.

One of the visitors to the exhibit was the composer Modest Mussorgsky, an intimate friend of Hartmann's and himself a member of The Mighty Five, a group of young musicians dedicated to the establishment of a Russian nationalistic school of musical

Victor Hartmann's painting *The Great Gate of Kiev,* which inspired Mussorgsky's composition.

composition, one free of European (particularly German) influences. Inspired by the exhibit and wishing to pay a musical tribute to his friend, Mussorgsky set about translating certain of the pictures and designs into musical terms. He composed a suite of ten piano pieces that he entitled *Pictures at an Exhibition;* these pieces were a musical description of Mussorgsky's interpretation of ten of the pictures in the show.

Once Mussorgsky started to work, ideas came quickly and freely. The composer wrote to his friend, critic Vladimir Stasov, who had arranged the exhibit, saying that his *Pictures* were "bubbling over. . . . Ideas and melodies come to me of their own accord, like the roast pigeons in the story [a reference to the folk tale represented by one of the paintings]—I gorge and gorge and overeat myself. I can hardly manage to put it down on paper fast enough." Mussorgsky completed his piano suite within five months, the quickest work he had ever done on a composition.

Because *Pictures at an Exhibition* was conceived for piano on such a grand scale, and because the writing taxes the tonal resources of that instrument and the technique of the pianist, the suite is usually performed in an orchestral version. In 1922 the distinguished French composer and skilled orchestrator Maurice Ravel made the most famous and most frequently performed transcription for orchestra of these pieces.

The original piano edition contains the following descriptions of the three movements we will study:

I. "Gnomus." A drawing representing a gnome, dragging himself along with clumsy steps by his little twisted legs.

IV. "Bydlo." A Polish wagon with enormous wheels drawn by oxen.

X. "The Great Gate of Kiev." Hartmann's design for the construction of an entrance gate for the city of Kiev, conceived in the massive old Russian style, with a cupola shaped like a Slav helmet.

I. Gnomus

The first of the *Pictures at an Exhibition* that Mussorgsky attempts to portray in music is concerned with a diminutive, misshapen, comical figure—a gnome carved in the form of a nutcracker as an ornament for the Christmas tree at the Artists' Club.

According to the design, a nut could be cracked between the gnome's heavy jaws; the two handles form his legs; there is no body.

LISTENING OUTLINE

The music begins with all the lower woodwinds and strings playing an awkward musical figure:

Example 1

A variation of Example 1 is repeated, minus the bassoons, and the dynamic level drops to *mezzopiano* and finally all the way down to *piano*.

A new theme is introduced by the woodwinds *mezzoforte;* it is repeated several times. (Note that before the woodwinds introduce the new theme, the previous phrase is repeated three more times, with changes.)

Example 2

The celesta repeats all of Example 2 *piano,* accompanied by violins *pizzicato* and harp harmonics on accented chords *piano.*[5] Example 1 returns *fortissimo.* A rising figure begins in the woodwinds and horns *mezzoforte:*

5. The *celesta* is a keyboard instrument in which hammers activated by the keyboard hit small metal bars, producing a bell-like sound.

Example 3

Woodwinds, Horns

Example 1 is heard *fortissimo.*

Example 3 is played again by the woodwinds and horns *mezzoforte.*

This sequence—Example 1 *fortissimo* followed immediately by the opening of Example 3 *mezzoforte*—is heard again.

A repetition of Example 1 *fortissimo* leads to a bold new theme developed out of Example 3:

Example 4

Flutes, Oboes, Clarinets,
Trumpets (muted)

The dynamic level drops to *pianissimo.* Trills and runs are played by the low strings and bass clarinet. Soon the chords from Example 2 *mezzoforte* are heard over the trills and runs.

Pairs of loud chords played by the combined brass follow. A run in contrasting motion (opposite directions), with the upper woodwinds and strings moving upward and the lower woodwinds and strings moving downward, brings *Gnomus* to a conclusion.

IV. Bydlo

In Polish, *bydlo* means "cattle," but in common usage it refers to a crude farm wagon common in Polish agricultural districts. It has enormous wheels made of solid wooden discs. Drawn usually by a pair of stolid oxen, the cumbersome cart—which has no springs—moves along with a halting, irregular rhythm.

LISTENING OUTLINE

In the Mussorgsky-Ravel musical setting, a folklike peasant melody in a minor key is heard over a steady rhythm pattern established by the lower strings and woodwinds. All of this suggests the lumbering Polish oxcart and the sad song of its tired old drayman.

Example 5

Tuba

pp *poco a poco crescendo*

As the dynamic level begins to build, the Mussorgsky-Ravel score introduces a contrasting melodic figure:

Example 6

Violins

mf *sempre cresc.*

After several repetitions of Example 6, each one a little louder than the previous one, the melody of Example 5 returns *fortissimo (fff)* played by the upper woodwinds, strings, and horns.

Soon the dynamic level starts to drop as fragments of Example 5 are heard, the music becoming softer and softer. The lower strings are muted; the music is marked *dimin. e ritard.,* and, in the final three measures, *perdendosi* ("becoming lost").[6] The final two notes, played *pizzicato* by the bass viols alone, are marked *pianississimo (ppp)*.

6. "Muting" or deadening the tone of an instrument can be done with the use of devices called *mutes*. Mutes for stringed instruments are comblike pieces of wood or metal that fit over the bridge of the instrument. Mutes for brass instruments are metal or plastic cones of various sizes and shapes that are placed in the bell of the instrument. There is no effective way of muting a woodwind instrument.

X. The Great Gate of Kiev

The concluding movement of the suite is both the longest and the most dramatic of the ten pieces. Evoking a solemn procession with clanging bells and crashing cymbals, the Mussorgsky-Ravel score musically portrays the massive memorial gate Hartmann sketched out for the old capital of the Ukraine, the city of Kiev. The composer uses two Russian melodies, one proud and forceful, the other hymnlike and serene.

LISTENING OUTLINE

The combined brass—three trumpets, four horns, three trombones, and a tuba—together with the two bassoons and contrabassoon, announce the majestic Russian theme of this final movement. The first half of this theme is quoted in Example 7.

Example 7

The entire theme is repeated by the full orchestra *fortissimo* (*ff*).

In Example 8, the dynamic level drops suddenly and dramatically to *piano* (*p*). Clarinets and bassoons introduce a hymnlike Russian theme that starts out *senza espressione* ("without expression").[7]

Example 8

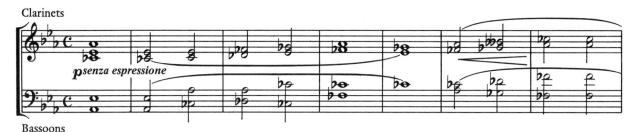

All of a sudden, the majestic opening theme (Example 7) returns, played *forte* by the horns, trombones, and tuba, doubled by cellos, basses, and bassoons in the first half of the first theme and by flutes, oboes, and violins in the second half. This is all accompanied by descending and ascending scale patterns.

The hymnlike theme (Example 8) returns in the clarinets and bassoons, again starting out *piano, senza espressione.*

Resonant chords and clanging bells are heard; this leads to a repetition in varied form of the opening melody, beginning with Example 7.

A tremendous descending scale for woodwinds and strings leads to a forceful repetition of the first theme (beginning with Example 7) against triplet figures. This passage involves the entire orchestra. At its climax, there is a final statement of the melody of Example 7 by full orchestra *fortissimo.*

7. In Example 8, the symbol (♭♭) for double flat is used. It lowers the pitch two half steps.

About the Composer

MODEST MUSSORGSKY   Born: March 21, 1839
                                         Karevo, Russia

                               Died: March 28, 1881
                                         St. Petersburg, Russia

Modest Mussorgsky was born in the village of Karevo where his father was a well-to-do landowner with an estate of over forty square miles, to which he had retired from government service. It was here, according to Mussorgsky's not-too-reliable autobiographical sketch, that he first learned the folk legends of Russia from his nurse and received his first piano lessons from his mother. By the time the boy was seven, he was able to play some short pieces; two years later he gave a recital in his home for friends.

At thirteen, Mussorgsky entered the Cadet School of Guards in St. Petersburg, his chief interests at that time being German philosophy and history. Unfortunately, the Cadet School was a bad influence on Mussorgsky. The morals of the cadets were extremely low, and the cadets considered it beneath their dignity to study. They made fun of Mussorgsky when they discovered him studying, and frequently encouraged him to join in wild drinking sprees.

Mussorgsky left the Cadet School at seventeen and was assigned to the Preobrajensky Guards. A year later, he became acquainted with music critic Vladimir Stasov, who was devoting his time and energies to the promotion of a nationalistic spirit among young Russian composers. Through Stasov, Mussorgsky met several of these younger musicians and, because of the inspiration derived from such associations, decided to become a professional composer.

About this time Mussorgsky had to take a paying job. In 1861 the czar had freed the Russian serfs, which meant that all but a few of the wealthiest landowners had suffered great financial losses. Little was left of the estate Modest and his brother had inherited from their father. Because of this loss, in 1863 Mussorgsky entered government service in the engineering department of the Ministry of Communication. His mother's death two years later greatly affected Mussorgsky's mental outlook. He began to rely on liquor more and more; eventually, after many attacks of delirium tremens, he was forced to move in with his brother and his wife. It took three years for Mussorgsky to recuperate.

When he lost his government job (during a reduction of the staff), he found more time for composition and completed an orchestral tone poem that he called *Night on Bald Mountain;* it was a musical picture of the witches' sabbath on St. John's Eve (July 5). This was his first notable composition, and one that was daring in concept.

In 1867 Stasov published an article in his paper that referred to Mussorgsky and his composer-friends as "the mighty handful of Russian musicians" who were dedicated to the pursuit of a Russian nationalism in music. Other papers followed up on this story and soon were calling Mussorgsky and his fellow composers, César Cui, Mily Balakirev, Alexander Borodin, and Nikolay Rimsky-Korsakov, The Mighty Five, the name by which we still refer to them.

Mussorgsky became enthusiastic about composing an opera, and, after several experiments with other subjects, he became interested in the story of Czar Boris Godunov and the legend of his rise to the throne of Russia through political intrigue and murder. After long struggles with the composition of this great work and two refusals of the score by the opera house, it was finally performed in 1874, the year of the Victor Hartmann exhibit, when Mussorgsky was thirty-five.

The composer then started work on two operas based on Russian historical legends, but he never completed them. Work was slow and his problem with alcohol was increasing to alarming proportions. In 1880 he was forced to leave his government work, which he had resumed in 1869 to help support himself. When he became destitute, his friends came to his aid by providing food and shelter. The following year, after several attacks of alcoholic epilepsy, he had to be moved to the military hospital. His death followed within a few months.

While Mussorgsky's output was small in comparison with that of many other composers—three operas (two never completed), fewer than eight orchestral works (all relatively short), eighteen piano works, and a little over four dozen songs—his impact on music in general and on Russian music in particular has been tremendous. He rejected the old concepts of beauty in music—pleasing sounds and formal structures that involved symmetry, proportion, and balance. In their place Mussorgsky tried to substitute what he believed to be musical *truth;* an expression of everyday people. "I forsee a new kind of melody," he once wrote, "which will be the melody of life. . . . Someday, all of a sudden, the ineffable song will arise, intelligible to one and all. If I succeed, I shall be a conqueror in art—and succeed I must!"

Not even Mussorgsky's friends among The Mighty Five understood him. They decried his use of unusual chord sequences and primitive rhythms, and his return to modal scales. After Mussorgsky's death, Rimsky-Korsakov tried to "correct" many of Mussorgsky's scores, eliminating "ugly" sounds and what he believed to be awkward writing, inept instrumentation, and unschooled harmonizations. Today, however, we realize the fallacy of this misguided effort. Works such as *Boris Godunov* are now frequently produced in the *original* Mussorgsky version with its "crude" instrumentation and "unconventional" harmonies. Mussorgsky and his efforts to "render the straightforward expression of thoughts and feelings as it takes place in ordinary speech, a rendering which is artistic and musicianly" have succeeded.

Bibliography

Calvocoressi, Michel. *Mussorgsky.* New York: Collier Books, 1962.
Riesemann, Oskar von. *Moussorgsky.* Translated by Paul England. Westport, Ct.: Greenwood Press, 1971.

The speed of a work, which is usually suggested by various Italian terms, depends upon its general character and also the speed of the fastest notes and passage work which it contains. Proper attention to these considerations will prevent an *Allegro* from being hurried and an *Adagio* dragged.

Karl Philipp Emanuel Bach

SIX /
TEMPO

THE speed or pace at which we perform certain tasks is an important element in our lives. When we are happy and excited about something, our hearts beat faster, we walk more quickly, our body movements are lively and animated. When we are sad or unhappy, our pace is generally slow, our movements sluggish. Music can and does reflect these moods. We expect lively dance music to be performed at a brisk speed; we anticipate that a blues tune will be slow in pace.

This speed or pace in music is called *tempo,* an Italian word that literally means "time." The fastness or slowness of the underlying pulse is what we mean by the word *tempo.*

Tempo and rhythm are two separate but very closely related elements. The *rhythm* we recognize in our national anthem, for example, does not depend on the tempo at which it is performed, be it fast or slow.

The choice of tempo is one of the most important acts of any performing musician. This interpretation of the proper speed or tempo can lead to an animated, exciting performance or, if an improper choice is made, can lull the audience to sleep with boredom. If a work is played too fast or too slow, it may be robbed of its essential nature or character. A minuet, for example, ceases to be a minuet if it is performed at too fast a tempo.

While composers of all persuasions—classical, pop-rock, jazz, salsa, and so on—attempt to suggest an appropriate tempo for the performance of their music, it is really the solo performer, leader, or conductor who makes the critical choice.

TEMPO MARKINGS

Just as the expressive marks that refer to dynamics have changed from time to time, as we saw in the chapter on dynamics, so the expression marks that refer to tempo have changed over the centuries, as we will discover.

For music composed during the fifteenth and sixteenth centuries, it is rather easy to establish the correct tempo. During those centuries there was essentially only one standard, known as *tactus* or "beat," fixed at about one beat per second. If the composer wanted his piece played at a lively pace, he wrote it out in notes of short time-value, probably eighth and sixteenth notes. If it was to be a slow, funereal bit of music, he probably wrote it out in notes of long time-value: half notes, whole notes, and the now obsolete *breves* and *longas* (double and quadruple whole notes).[1]

As early as 1535, composers started to indicate by expressive words the tempo at which they wanted their music performed. The Spanish composer and lutenist Luis Milán indicated that he wanted sections of his *El Maestro* performed *a priesa* (fast) and

1. While today there is a tendency among composers to write fast music in notes of shorter time-value and slow music in notes of longer value, there is no uniformity; thus the time-value of the notes in recent music often provides little indication of the overall tempo.

others *a espazio* (slow). English composers of the seventeenth century marked their scores with such expressive markings as *fast, drag, away,* and *slow.*

Today we have a rather standard list of tempo markings. The practice of indicating the tempo with Italian expressions stems from the birth of opera around 1600 in Florence, Italy, and its quick adoption by all the musical capitals of Europe. During the late nineteenth century there was a nationalistic revolt against this custom of using Italian words, and the scores of French composers blossomed with expression markings in French, German scores with expression markings in German.

The use of Italian expressions is the common standard in America today. They often indicate, however, more than just the tempo of a work; most indicate the mood or spirit of the piece also. Thus *vivace,* for example, means "vivacious" as well as music to be performed at a brisk tempo; *allegro* originally indicated a "happy" or "cheerful" mood as well as a moderate tempo. *Grave* (pronounced *GHRAHV-eh*) is our English word *grave* and indicates a solemn mood as well as a slow tempo; and *largo* means "wide" or "broad" in spirit as well as slow in tempo. In the following list, we use the expression *andante* as a median, *andante* coming from the Italian verb *andare,* meaning "to go" or "to walk." From this we assume that *andante* means a "walking pace" or moderate tempo of about eighty to one hundred steps per minute, although in the late nineteenth century, composers started to use this expression for a relatively slow tempo.

Grave	Solemn (very, very slow)
Largo	Broad (very slow)
Adagio	Slow (quite slow)
Lento	Slow (moderately slow)
Andante	A walking pace
Andantino	Slightly faster than *andante*
Moderato	Moderate
Allegretto	Moderately fast
Allegro	Brisk (cheerful)
Vivace	Lively (quite fast)
Presto	Very fast
Prestissimo	Very, very fast

There is a series of words that is used to modify the basic tempo markings given in the preceding list. These include:

assai	much
molto	very
meno	less
poco	little
poco a poco	little by little
non troppo	not too much

THE METRONOME

Around the year 1816 Johann Maelzel, a German inventor and close friend of the composer Ludwig van Beethoven, created a device that he called the *metronome*. Its purpose was to establish the exact pace or tempo at which a musical work should be performed.

Metronome

A metronome consists of a pendulum about seven inches long with a pivot about one and one-half inches from its lower end; a permanent weight is fixed to the bottom of the pendulum. There is an adjustable weight on the upper end that can be moved up and down the pendulum and locked at numerous predetermined positions. A clock mechanism propels the rod back and forth; the *escape mechanism* of the clock motor makes a ticking sound each time the rod changes direction. By sliding the upper weight up or down the rod, the metronome can be made to tick anywhere from about 40 to 200 times per minute.

If the sliding weight is locked into the position marked 60, it means the metronome will tick 60 times a minute, or once each second. To indicate this tempo on a musical score, the composer writes M.M. 60, the two *M*s standing for "Maelzel's metronome." Should there be a question as to the musical unit that the composer wants to receive the pulse or beat, the composer may indicate the unit; for example, $\quad$ = M.M. 60.

Beethoven was the first composer to use metronome markings. These more precise markings, however, are not always followed by performers and conductors. The *Harvard Dictionary of Music* states that the tempos indicated on Beethoven's *Sonata No. 29* for piano "and Ninth Symphony are almost impossibly fast, as are those indicated in the works of Schumann."[2]

Although the majority of works written in the last 200 years have metronome indications, not all do. And, whether or not there is a metronome marking, there is nearly always at least one word—usually in Italian—at the beginning of each piece or movement to suggest the correct tempo. Usually the movements of many multimovement works (such as symphonies, sonatas, and concertos) are referred to by their Italian tempo markings.

FLUCTUATIONS IN TEMPO

Although the performer or conductor may decide on a specific pace or tempo for a section of music—or even the entire composition—minor fluctuations generally occur within it. Sometimes these minor fluctuations are indicated by the composer through the use of expression marks such as the following:

2. Willi Apel, *Harvard Dictionary of Music* (Cambridge, 1975).

accel.	*accelerando*	(gradually getting faster)
rit. or	*ritardando* or	(gradually getting slower)
rall.	*rallentando*	
	a tempo	(return to original tempo)
	Tempo I	(original tempo or speed)
	rubato[3]	(a freedom of tempo or speed)
⌢		(*fermata.* This sign indicates that the note or rest over which it appears is to be held longer than its usual period of time.)

There are other instances in which custom and tradition suggest a fluctuation in tempo. For example, a performer or conductor often slows the tempo when approaching a cadence. As early as 1614, Girolamo Frescobaldi, an Italian composer and teacher, wrote that "the nearer you approach a cadence, the more you hold back the tempo."

Some variations in tempo occur within the metrical unit of a measure and thus do not disturb the basic rhythm established by the bass. The rhythmic freedom of jazz in general is a good example of this. Another would be the ever-so-slight hesitation just before the downbeat in a Viennese waltz.

TEMPO CHANGES

While music of earlier eras—the Baroque and Classical eras, roughly 1600 to 1800—was usually without a tempo change within a movement or piece, music of later times frequently makes use of several changes in tempo, sometimes subtle, sometimes bold. The chief design element, for example, in the third movement of Johannes Brahms's *Symphony No. 2* is concerned with tempo changes between its five sections: *slow—fast—slow—fast—slow.*

In almost any musical composition of more than one movement, there is a contrast in tempo between movements. This lends variety and interest to any extended work. Baroque dance suites, for example, alternate between fast and slow dances. Symphonies, sonatas, and concertos are made up of movements in contrasting tempos, usually beginning at a moderate tempo, having a slow movement in the middle, and concluding with a very fast movement.

Let's listen to three contrasting movements from a concerto, noticing the many changes of tempo within each movement and the contrasting tempos of the three movements themselves.

3. *Rubato* refers to a controlled flexibility of tempo, an expressive variation in tempo achieved by depriving some notes of their normal length, and extending others beyond their correct value.

The ūd, the classical Arabian lute (left), and the Spanish vihuela of the sixteenth century (right), both forerunners of the Spanish guitar and the classical guitar (below).

Concerto No. 1 in D for Guitar and Orchestra

by MARIO CASTELNUOVO-TEDESCO

The classic or classical guitar is the ancestor of all other types of guitars, including the Spanish, the flamenco, the folk or western, and the electric guitar. The classical guitar we know today developed in Italy around 1600 and, throughout the seventeenth century, was one of the most important instruments in European music. All the great composers of that era wrote solo pieces for the guitar.

In Spain the guitar developed differently. When the Moors invaded Spain in the fifteenth century, they brought with them an instrument called the *ūd*. This ancient instrument—still in widespread use in Arab countries—together with the lute and Italian guitar, led to the development of an instrument in Spain known as the *vihuela*. This new instrument combined the features of both the lute and the *ūd* and served as the ancestor of the Spanish guitar.

While the guitar dropped out of use in the rest of Europe during the nineteenth century, the Spaniards continued to make guitars and play them. The present worldwide interest in the classical guitar is almost completely the work of one man, Andrés Segovia.

As early as 1932, Segovia approached Mario Castelnuovo-Tedesco about writing for the guitar. After he had completed several highly successful solo works, Castelnuovo-Tedesco was asked to write a guitar concerto—an unusual request, since no one had written a concerto for guitar in over 150 years. Castelnuovo-Tedesco hesitated.

Finally, in 1938, a series of circumstances led him to start work on the guitar concerto. Once Mussolini aligned Italy with Hitler's Third Reich, the political climate in Italy started to become unbearable because of the anti-Semitic campaign (the Castelnuovo-Tedescos were Sephardic Jews). Castelnuovo-Tedesco prepared to leave his native Italy and settle in America. "No one can imagine how this was tearing my heart out," the composer later wrote in his autobiography. He went on to say:

> Full of anguish and worries, I had not composed for the last six months (quite unusual for me who am generally so active). It was then that Segovia did an exquisite thing I shall never forget. At that period when so many of my colleagues turned their backs on me—or, at least, carefully avoided me—Segovia came to [my home in] Florence to spend Christmas holidays with me and encourage me to hope for a better future. He told me not to despair, that I was talented and that in America I would be able to rebuild my life. In a word, he heartened me deeply. And I was so moved by his friendly action that I promised him that my next work would be the *Concerto for Guitar and Orchestra* which I had promised him so many times.
>
> Much more. During his stay in Florence—without further delay—I wrote, all in "one breath,"—the first movement, and we tested it together.
>
> Then Segovia left for South America, and some nine months later, I left for North America. And, in January of 1939, I composed the two other movements and, before leaving Italy, I sent them to him.[4]

The first performance of the *Concerto for Guitar and Orchestra* took place in Montevideo, Uruguay, in October of 1939, and since then it has become the most widely performed and recorded guitar concerto of the contemporary period.

The composer has carefully explained his plan for the *Concerto,* saying:

> It consists of three movements. The first one, *Allegro giusto* [changed by the publisher to *Allegretto*], in a classical style, is simple and graceful; . . . the second one, *Andantino alla Romanza,* is sweet and songlike, a sort of tender farewell to the Tuscan countryside which I was going to leave; the third one, *Ritmico e Cavalleresco,* is typically Iberian and may recall *Romancero,* the *Cantar del Cid,* in short, the Spanish chivalrous ballades.
>
> The guitar, of course, takes a prominent part throughout the movements, with a long *cadenza* in each movement. In the orchestral sections I have tried to suggest the "sound" and not the "size" of an orchestra. Therefore I used a very restricted orchestra: one flute, one oboe, two clarinets, one bassoon, one horn, timpani (always playing very softly) and a small group of strings.[5]

The movements of this concerto are in contrasting tempos:

Allegretto
Andantino
Ritmico e cavalleresco

---

4. Mario Castelnuovo-Tedesco, *Una vita di musica (A Life of Music),* trans. Nick Rossi (unpublished).
5. Castelnuovo-Tedesco, *Una vita di musica.*

And, within each movement, there are subtle changes of tempo. This is especially noticeable in the guitar cadenzas of each movement. In this work, we can also observe the natural ritards as cadences are approached. There also are passages in the concerto marked by the composer *quasi recitativo* (like a recitative), suggesting that the passage —usually for solo guitar—is to be played at a tempo and in a rhythm suggestive of speech.

Allegretto

LISTENING OUTLINE

The *Allegretto* opens at a fairly brisk pace, about 152 beats per minute. Only the orchestra is heard, the soloist not entering until later. Violins immediately announce a lively, dancelike theme that is soon repeated. It begins:

Example 1

Violins

The guitar plays a variant of Example 1 *con bravura* (with flair, bravado). After a brief interlude (based on repeated notes) that includes a ritard and then a pause, the guitar repeats Example 1 as it was first heard. Repetitions and variants of it follow in an extended section.

The orchestra drops out and only the solo guitar is heard. It plays a series of descending broken chords. There is much rubato (slowing down and speeding up) that is part of the guitarist's interpretation of what appears to be, in the printed music, ninety-six equal 32nd notes.

The guitar alone plays the more lyrical second melody; the violins immediately repeat this theme. It begins:

Example 2

Guitar

In the passage that follows, first the orchestra and then the unaccompanied guitar take liberties with the tempo; the brief guitar solo is marked *liberamente* (freely).

A two-note flute figure is heard over rolling chords played by the strings; there is a suggestion of the first theme (Example 1). There are several ritards in this section.

After a pause, the guitar once more takes up the first theme (Example 1). Again there is a slowing up on the repeated notes that follow.

First the guitar is heard in a descending figure; it is repeated by a solo cello. As it is marked *quasi recitativo,* the tempo is broadly interpreted by both solo instruments.

The melody of Example 1 is repeated by the orchestra; it is played in much the same way as it was heard at the beginning. It is then repeated by the soloist.

Castelnuovo-Tedesco marks the next brief passage *Un poco trattenuto* (a little delayed, slowed down). Figures from the last half of Example 1 are heard. After a ritard, the cadenza begins.

In the cadenza, the major solo for the guitarist, the composer indicates several changes in tempo. They are, in succession:

un poco languido	(a little languidly)
un poco trattenuto	(a little slowed down)
a tempo	(in time)
trattenuto	(slowed down, delayed)
𝄐	(a *fermata,* which means to hold the note or rest)
deciso	(decisively)
più mosso	(more agitated)
quasi fanfara	(like a fanfare)
vivo	(very lively)

The orchestra reenters to state the first theme as it was heard at the beginning, the composer marking the music *Tempo I.* The guitar enters with a short variant that slows down; this is not indicated by the composer but is traditional, since the music is approaching the final cadence of the movement.

Andantino —alla Romanza

LISTENING OUTLINE

The slow movement opens with a guitar solo in which there are many subtle changes of tempo. Those indicated by the composer are, in succession:

trattenuto un poco	(slowed down a little)
a tempo	(in time)
movendo un poco	(moving along a little)
cedendo	(yielding)

The guitar solo begins:

Example 3

The orchestra enters with a variant of Example 3. In an extended section, the guitar punctuates with short, upward-moving broken chords this folklike melody played by the flute. Then the violins take over this theme.

The tempo changes to *Appena più mosso e scorrevole* (barely more agitated and flowing). An oboe announces the second folklike tune, which is repeated in a variant by the flute.

Example 4

Two measures later the clarinet is heard with the third folklike theme of the movement:

Example 5

Following an extended section based on the melody of Example 5, the cadenza is heard.

In this cadenza, the composer explicitly indicates certain changes of tempo, while the performer intuitively adds others. Those indicated by the composer include:

appassionato	(passionately)
movendo	(moving along)
trattenuto	(slowing down)
più mosso	(more agitated)
più sostenuto	(more sustained)
rallentando	(gradually losing speed)

As the orchestra reenters, the tempo is marked *Calmo, ma scorrevole* (calm, but flowing). The flute is heard with the melody of Example 4; it is repeated by the oboe, then by the clarinet, and finally by the bassoon.

The music is marked *Calmo—dolcissimo* (calm—sweetly). The violins play the first theme of the movement (Example 3) while the guitar accompanies them with chords.

Eventually the melody of Example 4 returns in the guitar *dolce e triste* (sweet and sad).

The orchestra is heard with Example 5, repeated by the guitar. This leads to the final cadence. In addition to the traditional ritard appropriate for the final cadence of a movement, Castelnuovo-Tedesco indicates the following in these brief three measures:

trattenuto	(slowing down)
Largo	(very slow)
come un ricordo	(like a memory)
perdendosi	(losing itself)

Ritmico e Cavalleresco

LISTENING OUTLINE

The tempo indication Castelnuovo-Tedesco assigned to the finale—*Ritmico e Cavalleresco*—is not a tempo indication in the traditional sense but rather a suggestion of the spirit of the third movement, implying that it must be rhythmical in a cavalier or knightly manner. In this case, the conductor interprets it as a considerably faster tempo than that of the first movement; about 192 beats per minute.

The orchestra immediately announces the principal theme; then it is repeated. It begins:

Example 6

Horn, Violins

f stacc.

The guitar enters over the orchestra with a few measures of introductory material and then plays the principal theme (Example 6).

In a quite extended section, fragments and variants of this theme are played both by the soloist and individual instruments of the orchestra; the oboe and clarinet, playing in turn, are quite prominent.

In the middle of the movement, the tempo changes to *Quasi andante* (like an *andante*). The composer mathematically indicates the exact tempo relationship when he writes "♩ = ♩. of the preceding." In case there is any doubt left, he adds the statement *sempre lo stesso tempo, ma con larghezza di espressione,* meaning "always in the same tempo, but with a largeness of expression."

The guitar plays the melody of this section over an undulating figure in the violins. The guitar theme begins:

Example 7

Flute and bassoon repeat Example 7 to the accompaniment of chords by the solo guitar. Oboe and clarinet soon take over the melody of Example 7. A cadenza follows.

Once again great liberties in tempo occur in the cadenza, some indicated by the composer, others the result of the soloist's interpretation. Those marked in the score are, in order:

più mosso	(more agitated)
precipitando	(rushed)
Tempo I (mosso)	(original tempo; rushed)
più sostenuto	(more sustained)
deciso	(decisively)
mosso	(agitated)
vivo	(lively)

The music is marked *Tempo I* as the orchestra reenters with the first theme of this movement (Example 6), played against a countermelody in the solo guitar.

In an extended section that leads to the conclusion of the *Concerto,* the music is marked *giocoso* — "playful."

The *Concerto* ends *un poco sostenuto (quasi fanfara)* — "quite sustained, similar to a fanfare."

About the Composer

MARIO CASTELNUOVO-TEDESCO

Born: April 3, 1895
Florence, Italy

Died: March 16, 1968
Beverly Hills, California

Mario Castelnuovo-Tedesco has the distinction of possessing the longest family name of any composer in the history of music. How this eighteen-letter name evolved reveals the roots of the family itself.

Mario Castelnuovo-Tedesco, who called himself "musicista fiorentino" (a musician of Florence), was a Sephardic Jew whose ancestors had come from Spain to Italy about 1492, the time of the great "expulsion." They had landed at Livorno (then called Porto Franco), and soon established a home in the Tuscan region of Italy. At that time the family was known as *Castilla Nueva* (New Castile), the name for the Spanish province from which they had emigrated. At what point in time this name was translated into the Italian *Castelnuovo* no one is certain.

"I only know," the Maestro explains in his autobiography, "that my paternal grandfather, Angelo Castelnuovo, was a banker, a common profession of many Jewish people. One of his sisters, Enrichetta, had married Samuel Tedesco, also a banker. [The name *Tedesco*—the Italian word for "German"—is an extremely common name throughout Italy.] The Tedescos did not have any children, therefore they left their property and money to my grandfather with the agreement that the family would assume the Tedesco name so that it would not die. So my father Amadeo became 'Castelnuovo-Tedesco.'"[6]

As a young boy of nine, Castelnuovo-Tedesco learned piano from his mother, who gave him lessons in secret since his rather stern and severe father did not want a musician in the family. About a year later, the boy played two Chopin pieces and one piece of his own creation in a little recital for his father. The elder Castelnuovo-Tedesco was so impressed that he soon made arrangements for his son to study music professionally at the conservatory of music in Florence.

Although several of the composer's songs and piano pieces became quite well known, it was his first opera that won him international fame. That opera, *La Mandragola (The Mandrake)* after Machiavelli's comedy of the same name, won the National Prize when the composer was thirty; it was produced with great success not only in Italy but in Germany as well.

Castelnuovo-Tedesco's music was first introduced in the United States in 1930 by the Italian conductor Arturo Toscanini. A number of major works followed, including concertos for solo instruments as well as orchestral works premiered by the New York Philharmonic and the NBC Symphony.

6. Castelnuovo-Tedesco, *Una vita di musica.*

After Mussolini signed a military pact with Hitler in 1939, the fate of the Italian Jews was sealed. It became necessary for the Castelnuovo-Tedescos to escape from Italy. Leaving behind their family home and all their possessions, the Castelnuovo-Tedescos emigrated to the United States through the assistance of Arturo Toscanini and violinist Jascha Heifetz. The family lived for a year in Larchmont, New York, and then moved permanently to Beverly Hills, California, where the composer was employed for several years writing scores for Hollywood movies. Perhaps the best known of the more than two dozen scores is the music for the 1948 Columbia film *The Loves of Carmen,* which featured Rita Hayworth.

Although Castelnuovo-Tedesco read and spoke more than half a dozen languages, he set more of his songs and choral works to English texts than to those of his native Italian. The sources of much of this inspiration were the Bible and the works of Shakespeare. (He once claimed that he learned English as a boy by reading through those two hefty volumes.)

The composer's catalogue reflects this preference, for he set to music the lyrics of all thirty-three songs from the Shakespeare plays; he made vocal settings of thirty-two of the Sonnets; and his opera *The Merchant of Venice* won the International Scala Prize in 1958. With reference to the Bible, Castelnuovo-Tedesco has made major choral settings—mostly scenic oratorios and cantatas—for the texts of such diverse stories as *The Queen of Sheba, The Song of Songs, Naomi and Ruth, Jonah and the Whale,* and, from the Apocrypha, the story of *Tobias and the Angel.*

Bibliography

Castelnuovo-Tedesco, Mario. *A Life of Music.* Translated by Nick Rossi (Unpublished).

Ewen, David. *The Book of Modern Composers.* New York: Alfred A. Knopf, 1950.

Only when the form is quite clear to you will the spirit become clear . . . .
Robert Schumann

SEVEN/
DESIGN IN MUSIC

AS we look at the world around us, we become aware that the manmade structures we see—be they homes, offices, or supermarkets—have been put together, brick on brick, board on board, according to an organized plan or design. We know that for each building we see, an architect at some time in the past carefully plotted ideas so that all the elements of the building would fit together logically and harmoniously when it was built. And, depending on the skill and talent of the architect, the resulting structure varied in its beauty and usefulness.

When we talk about the masterpieces of architecture—the cathedral of Notre Dame, the palace of Versailles, or the Empire State Building, for example—we realize that the result is more than the sum of its constituent elements—blocks of stone, marble, and masonry. That special relationship of architectural elements, the overall design of the spires, buttresses, windows, pillars, and general shaping of space, makes the cathedral, palace, or building what it is. The aesthetic element, the sheer beauty of each architectural masterpiece, transcends our awareness of the logic behind the structural elements themselves.

In a manner of speaking, a composer is an architect—a designer or builder who works with sounds, putting tone with tone and forming these combinations into some kind of logical design. And, just as a good architect must be concerned with the aesthetic elements of balance and symmetry, of unity and contrast, so the musical architect, our composer, must also be concerned with these elements.

When we talk about the organization of musical elements in composition, we are really referring to musical *design* or *form,* the use and arrangement of the elements of music—melodies, rhythms, harmonies, and so forth—and the manner in which the composer has treated or handled them. In such design, the composer is concerned with building idea on idea until a complex structure exists whose meaning lies in the relationship of one element to another and of each element to the whole.

As we investigate the design elements in music, we must keep in mind the unique quality of music—it exists only in time. This means that we must perceive the design in music, be aware of the relationships between its parts as they are heard successively in time. This perception requires an exercise of memory, an ability to recall later what was heard earlier and to compare this for similarities and contrasts with what is being heard at the moment. This is a skill that develops with time and practice.

PRINCIPLES OF DESIGN

Regardless of the techniques involved, or the specific mold of the music—be it sonata, symphony, or concerto—there are certain principles of design that pervade all musical composition: *symmetry, unity,* and *contrast.*

Whether we are talking about small units such as phrases or melodies, or larger units such as sections or movements, *symmetry* is concerned with the proportion of the parts of the whole to one another with regard to size and form. On an aesthetic level, symmetry refers to the excellence of proportion.

In the world around us we can discover everyday examples of symmetry: a pair of matching windows on either side of a door; a repeated series of pillars across the portico of a building; an old photograph of a man standing and a woman seated.

We can also discover examples of symmetry in music. If we study a short work such as the old French round *Frère Jacques,* we notice that each one-measure phrase is repeated exactly—in words *and* music—before we hear the next, each phrase being balanced by its repetition.[1] These pairs of phrases are symmetrical.

Repetition, especially immediate repetition, is the easiest design element to recognize aurally. Think, for example, of the opening of the Christmas carol *Silent Night.* The melody of the first measure—to the words *Silent night*—is repeated exactly in the second measure for the words *holy night.*

Repetitions of longer passages are also recognizable. Recall the melody of the opening phrase of our national anthem:

> Oh, say can you see, by the dawn's early light,
> What so proudly we hailed at the twilight's last gleaming?

This eight-measure melody is repeated immediately and exactly for the next two lines of the poem:

> Whose broad stripes and bright stars, thru' the perilous fight,
> O'er the ramparts we watched, were so gallantly streaming?

Frequently in Broadway show tunes and popular songs, entire sections are repeated, sometimes with the same lyrics, sometimes with a change. Some sections of larger works are constructed so that they will be repeated as a feature of their form, thus achieving a special purpose such as emphasis on the melody, the words, or the rhythm.

We have several musical symbols that we can use to indicate exact repetitions so that the music does not need to be written out twice. A short section to be repeated may be set off by repeat signs:

$$\|: \quad :\|$$

If the section to be repeated is at the beginning of a work, the initial symbol ‖: is omitted.

---

1. A *phrase* is usually considered to be any short figure or passage complete in itself and unbroken in continuity, somewhat similar to a clause in sentence structure.

When a section of a work is to be repeated after a contrasting section, we some-times see the words *D.C. al Fine* (*da capo al fine,* or "go back to the beginning and play to the end"). This structure, which could be outlined as A-B-A, is called three-part form or *ternary form.* In music of the Baroque era (roughly 1600 to 1750), songs cast in this form are frequently referred to as being "arias in da capo form."

Thus we discover that *balance* is closely related to our concept of symmetry, for balance refers to the placement of the elements of music—rhythm, melody, harmony, and so forth—to produce an aesthetically pleasing or harmoniously integrated whole.

Besides repetition, other types of balance are possible. A melody may be balanced by its harmonic accompaniment, or—as in the case of a fugue—by another melody. In an orchestral work, the sound of the solo instrument may be balanced against the sound of the full orchestra. And, in larger works, one section is frequently balanced against the next. These elements of a composition's design lend it symmetry, the proper and due proportion of the parts to the whole.

Unity and *contrast* are closely related principles of design. *Unity* is "the state of being one; oneness . . . an absence of diversity." As we listen to music, we discover that unity sometimes results from the repetition without change of one or more of the musical elements. The almost endless repetition of the same melody and rhythm in succeeding verses of a folk song such as *Clementine* or in an orchestral work such as Maurice Ravel's *Bolero* gives a work unity.

Contrast provides variety and interest in a composition. In the third movement of Johannes Brahms's *Symphony No. 2,* for example, the composer uses contrasting tempos in its five sections: fast-slow-fast-slow-fast. In the *Hallelujah!* chorus from *Messiah* which we have studied (pp. 63–72), Handel alternates between homophonic and polyphonic textures. Still another type of contrast is employed in a concerto. Mario Castelnuovo-Tedesco contrasts the sound, or timbre, of a solo guitar with that of an orchestra in the *Concerto No. 1 in D Major for Guitar and Orchestra* which we have stud-ied (pp. 91–97). Other types of contrast may also be employed: contrasting high and low pitches in a melody, contrasting meters in the rhythm of a composition, or con-trasting dynamic levels within a work.

DESIGN TECHNIQUES

In considering design elements, we have already encountered some of the techniques or devices that the composer uses to accomplish his or her purpose. We discovered, for example, that unity could be achieved through repetition. Unity, as well as contrast, may also be accomplished by techniques that we call *variation* and *development.*

Not all repetitions are exact. If you look at Paul Klee's painting *Camel in Rhythmi-cal Tree Landscape* on the next page, you will see a visual example of variation. Several patterns, including the orange tree, are repeated over and over in varied form. *Varia-tion* thus refers "to a different form of something; [a] variant."

Paul Klee, *Camel in Rhyth-mical Tree Landscape* (Kunstsammlung Nord-rhein-Westfalen, Düssel-dorf). A visual example of variation within a unified design.

Sometimes in music a motive or melody is repeated, but in varied form. One example of this is called *melodic sequence,* an instance in which a melody or motive is repeated immediately, but on a different pitch level. In the repeated refrain of the old Christmas carol *Angels We Have Heard on High,* shown in the following example, you will notice that the melody within the second bracket is a repetition of that of the first bracket, but on a lower pitch level. This is true also of the repetition of the same melodic figure in the third bracket.

In other instances, variation occurs because some elements remain the same while others change. In Ravel's *Bolero* the melody, rhythm, and harmony remain unchanged throughout; the timbre and dynamics change. Starting very softly, the melody, played by a solo flute, ends many repetitions later with the full orchestra playing *fortissimo.*

The form of music known as *theme with variations* is another example of variation, but on a grander scale. The underlying principle of this form concerns a melody, usually about sixteen or thirty-two measures in length, which, after its initial statement, is varied in many different ways. The first part of Benjamin Britten's *Young Person's Guide to the Orchestra* (p. 14) is a good example of the *theme with variations* form. The full orchestra states the theme (the tune by Henry Purcell), which is followed by a series of variations, first for the woodwind, brass, string, and percussion families, then for each type of instrument in the orchestra.

Compositions of larger stature and greater length usually involve a design element known as *development*. This process is concerned with a motive or perhaps a short theme that lends itself to and serves as a seed out of which larger and more complicated passages can blossom and grow.

There is probably no better example of this than the first movement of Beethoven's *Symphony No. 5.* Beethoven takes a four-note motive,

and immediately repeats it on a lower pitch level (a *melodic sequence*). These four measures, shown in the following example, serve as the dramatic seed out of which the rest of the movement grows.

The principal theme is "developed" out of this motive.

The remainder of the movement, occupying some five minutes in performance time, is further "developed" out of this principal theme and the opening motive. Even when a second, lyrical theme is introduced for contrast, the four-note introductory motive serves as an accompaniment:

Violins

Cellos, Bass Viols

MUSICAL FORMS

While there are an infinite number of ways that design elements can be put together to form musical compositions, certain patterns, or musical *forms,* are employed frequently enough that we should study and understand them. These include single-movement as well as compound forms for both instruments and voices. The following examples of different forms are discussed in this book:

Single-movement instrumental forms

minuet	*Symphony No. 40* (Mozart)	Chapter 16
scherzo	*Symphony No. 5* (Beethoven)	Chapter 8
waltz	*Liebeslieder Walzer* (Brahms)	Chapter 8
	Swan Lake (Tchaikovsky)	Chapter 8
polka	*The Bartered Bride* (Smetana)	Chapter 9
rondo	*Symphony No. 88* (Haydn)	Chapter 16
	Symphony No. 40 (Mozart)	Chapter 16
toccata	*Toccata and Fugue in D Minor* (Bach)	Chapter 15
fugue	*Toccata and Fugue in D Minor* (Bach)	Chapter 15
sonata-allegro	*Symphony No. 5* (Beethoven)	Chapter 8
	Symphony No. 88 (Haydn)	Chapter 16
	Symphony No. 40 (Mozart)	Chapter 16
rhapsody	*Rhapsody in Blue* (Gershwin)	Chapter 11

Single-movement vocal forms

frottola	*El Grillo* (Josquin)	Chapter 14
motet	*O magnum mysterium* (Victoria)	Chapter 14
madrigal	*Now Is the Month of Maying* (Morley)	Chapter 14
	The Silver Swan (Gibbons)	Chapter 14
aria	*La Bohème* (Puccini)	Chapter 8
lied	*Erlkönig* (Schubert)	Chapter 8
	Traum durch die Dämmerung (Strauss)	Chapter 8

Compound (multimovement) instrumental forms

symphony	*Symphony No. 5* (Beethoven)	Chapter 8
	Symphony No. 88 (Haydn)	Chapter 16
	Symphony No. 40 (Mozart)	Chapter 16
ballet	*Daphnis et Chloe* (Ravel)	Chapter 10
	Le Sacre du printemps (Stravinsky)	Chapter 11
suite	*Il primo Libro di Balli* (Mainerio)	Chapter 14
	Water Music (Handel)	Chapter 15
solo concerto	*Concerto No. 1 in D for Guitar and Orchestra* (Castelnuovo-Tedesco)	Chapter 6
concerto grosso	*Brandenburg Concerto No. 2* (Bach)	Chapter 15

Compound (multimovement) vocal forms

opera	*La Bohème* (Puccini)	Chapter 8
oratorio	*Messiah* (Handel)	Chapter 4
passion	*Passio et Mors Domini Nostri Iesu Christi secundum Lucam* (Penderecki)	Chapter 11

Now let's examine some dances by Antonin Dvořák that involve binary and ternary forms, the most elemental and basic forms to be found in music.

Slavonic Dances, Opus 46
by ANTONIN DVOŘÁK

Dvořák originally composed a set of eight *Slavonic Dances* as piano duets; these were published in 1878 with such success that the publishers urged the composer to arrange them for orchestra. In 1886, Dvořák, pleased with the success of the first set, wrote a second series of eight.

Czech dancers perform the furiant, which inspired the first of Dvořák's *Slavonic Dances.*

Slavonic Dance, Opus 46, No. 1

The first *Slavonic Dance* is a *furiant,* a fast and fiery Bohemian dance in ¾ time with shifting accents. Dvořák was one of the first composers to bring this peasant dance to the attention of the concert-going public.

LISTENING OUTLINE

After a crashing chord, the full orchestra launches into a vigorous *Presto* theme, which is repeated. Notice that the first eight measures involve a melodic sequence: measures 5 through 8 are similar to 1 through 4 but are played on a lower pitch level. Notice also that the second half of the theme balances the first half with an almost exact repetition.

Example 1

Flutes, Oboes
Violins, Violas

As indicated by the repeat marks, all of Example 1 is heard again.

A quieter theme, stated by woodwinds, follows; it is stated twice, as the repeat marks indicate. The derivation of this theme from Example 1 is easily recognizable. Also notice the melodic sequence involved in measures 1 and 2, a sequence that is repeated several times.

Example 2

Piccolo, Oboes, Flute

Several repetitions of the first half of Example 1 are heard, the repetitions growing from a dynamic level of *pianissimo* to *forte,* dropping back to *piano,* and then building to a *fortissimo,* then dying away to *pianissimo.*

A sudden repetition of a variant of the first two measures of Example 1 *fortissimo,* followed by a sustained tone played by several woodwinds, leads to the next section.

The middle section is in a much lighter vein and a different key. The *pizzicato* strings and *staccato* woodwinds state a theme that moves mostly by conjunct motion. The bracketed opening figure is heard three times. The second statement of it varies slightly in pitch at the cadence. All of Example 3 is repeated, as indicated.

Example 3

Oboe, Flute

A more lyric theme, presented by the oboe, flute, and piccolo, accompanied by the other woodwinds and the strings, is heard. The second half of this theme is a melodic sequence built on the first half of the theme. Example 4 is accompanied by the clarinets and bassoons, which play a variant of Example 3.

Example 4

Flute, Oboe

Examples 3 and 4 are heard again. This leads to a repetition of the two themes of the first section.

A *coda* based on a combination of Examples 2 and 3 leads to a final statement, marked *più animato,* of Example 1.

By outlining the themes found in this *Slavonic Dance* as illustrated, we can see that there are three principal sections, the third based on the same thematic material as the first. We call this *ternary,* or three-part, form; it is frequently outlined: A-B-A.

A
- Example 1
- Example 2
- Example 1

B
- Example 3
- Example 4
- Example 3
- Example 4

A
- Example 1
- Example 2
- Example 1

Coda
- Example 3/Example 2
- Example 1

Slavonic Dance, Opus 46, No. 3

This *Slavonic Dance* is a *polka,* a dance in moderate duple meter that originated in Bohemia (now Czechoslovakia) around 1830. Dvořák was one of the first composers to introduce the polka in symphonic music.

LISTENING OUTLINE

The first section of the polka opens with a theme presented by the woodwinds against a countermelody played by the second oboe and violas. Note the repetition of the bracketed figure. (All of Example 5 is repeated as indicated.)

Example 5

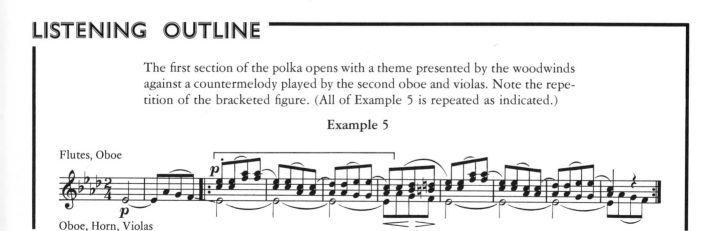

In a bridge passage, variants of fragments from Example 5 are heard.[2]

The second theme is a lively, vigorous melody stated by the full orchestra. Notice the melodic sequence in measures 3 and 4.

Example 6

Violins, Flute (octave higher)

The melody of Example 5 returns in the woodwinds.

For contrast, the tonality changes in the middle section. The first half of a new theme is played by trumpets; the second half, a melodic sequence, is played by a pair of flutes. The entire theme is repeated as indicated.

Example 7

Trumpets   Flutes

Woodwinds and strings announce a new theme characterized by the melodic sequence shown in brackets. The entire theme is repeated.

Example 8

Violins, Flutes, Oboes, Clarinets

The melody of Example 7 returns in the bassoons, violas, and cellos.

Suddenly the tempo becomes faster (*più mosso*) as the full orchestra plays a variant of Example 6. The force of this theme subsides and leads to an interlude that is built out of the melodic sequence of Figure A.

After a ritard, the original tempo returns (*poco allegro*); the flutes, oboe, and a French horn are joined by the cellos (which replace the violas this time) in a restatement of Example 5.

The tempo picks up as the full orchestra is heard with Example 6, which is extended by repetitions of Figure A and variants of it.

2. A brief passage that links two sections is frequently called a *bridge passage*.

Although the internal design or pattern of each of the three sections of this polka differs from that of the furiant, this polka is also in ternary form, the A section encompassing Examples 5 and 6 and the B section comprising Examples 7 and 8.

Slavonic Dance, Opus 46, No. 8

The last dance of this set is, like the first, a furiant in ternary form.

LISTENING OUTLINE

Marked *Presto,* the opening theme is bold and forthright. It is played by the full orchestra and repeated as indicated. Notice the repeated melodic figure in measures 3 and 4.

Example 9

Violins, Flute (octave higher)

A melodic variant of Example 9 is played by the woodwinds and strings *piano;* this variant is repeated.

Example 9 is then played and repeated in its original, full-orchestra version *fortissimo.*

Piccolo, flute, and violins introduce the second theme, which is characterized by a melodic sequence in measures 3, 4, and 5. All of Example 10 is repeated.

Example 10

First Violins, Flute (octave higher)

Second Violins, Oboe

The first theme (Example 9) is heard two more times.

A rhythmic variant of the opening figure from Example 9 is played by the woodwinds.

A crescendo leads to another statement, again repeated, of Example 9 by full orchestra *fortissimo.*

A bridge section based on the melodic figure of measure 1 from Example 10 leads to the middle section, which, for contrast, is in a different key.

The first theme of the middle section is a slow, lyrical melody played by the flute and oboe.[3]

Example 11

Oboe, Flute

The second melody of the middle section follows immediately. Notice that the second phrase is rhythmically identical to the first, but is different melodically.

Example 12

Flute, Piccolo, Oboe

After a ritard, the original tempo returns, and Example 9 is twice repeated by full orchestra.

Two repetitions *piano* are made of the melodic variant of Example 9.

Full orchestra then restates Example 9 two more times.

Example 10 is heard twice.

A short variant of Example 9 with dynamic contrasts between *fortissimo* and *piano* is heard twice. Other variants of Example 9 follow in an extended section.

The melody of Example 10 returns in the full orchestra *fortissimo.*

An extended *coda* is based on fragments of both Example 9 and Example 10, with prominent use of Example 11 in passages.

---

3. The dynamic markings indicated by the composer are ignored by Antal Dorati, who conducts the performance on the records accompanying this book.

About the Composer

ANTONIN DVOŘÁK   Born: September 8, 1841
Nelahozeves, Bohemia

Died: May 1, 1904
Prague, Bohemia

Early in his career, Antonin Dvořák decided that he wanted to join a group of his countrymen who were dedicated to composing music with a flavor of their native land, Bohemia. To do this they had to avoid the prevailing Germanic influences: Bohemia (today part of Czechoslovakia) had long been ruled by Austrians, whose official language was German; and Austro-German composers Haydn, Mozart, Beethoven, Schumann, Schubert, and Brahms had dominated European symphonic music for over two centuries.

Through the use of folk songs, folk-dance rhythms, and Bohemian legends and stories, Dvořák, Bedřich Smetana, and Zděnek Fibich created musical works that were obviously Bohemian in spirit.

Dvořák was the son of an innkeeper and butcher who played the violin and the zither. As a boy of eight, Antonin played in his father's band and sang in the church choir. When he was twelve, his father sent him to the nearby town of Zlonice to learn German from the local schoolmaster, who was both village organist and conductor of his own band.

When the family financial situation took a turn for the worse, Dvořák had to work (like his father) for a short time as a butcher. Fortunately, when he was sixteen, he was able to go to Prague, where he attended the organ school, studying theory and singing and becoming acquainted with the works of the classic masters. He also played in the orchestra of the Society of Saint Cecilia and fell under the influence of the music of Schumann and Wagner.

When Dvořák left school at eighteen, he became a viola player with a local concert band, then joined the orchestra of the Czech National Theatre, in which he served for fourteen years.

His first great success was the performance in 1873 of his cantata *Hymnus* for mixed chorus and orchestra, with strongly nationalistic text, themes, and rhythms. He resigned from the opera orchestra to devote his time to composition; soon he had produced a substantial body of work, but had difficulty securing its publication.

In 1877 he submitted the *Moravian Duets* in a scholarship contest sponsored by the Austrian government and won the award for the third year in a row. Enthused by the beauty of the duets, Brahms encouraged his publisher, Fritz August Simrock of Berlin, to print them. Sales were so successful that Dvořák was able to persuade three separate firms to purchase and publish, between them, eleven of his song settings.

The composer Franz Liszt and the pianist and conductor Hans von Bülow joined Brahms in helping Dvořák secure publication of his compositions and engagements as a conductor in Germany, Russia, and England, where he received an honorary Doctor of Music degree from Cambridge University in 1891.

In 1892 Dvořák was invited by Mrs. Jeannette Thurber, founder of the National Conservatory of Music in New York, to become the school's director. During the next three years in the United States he tried to develop a national school of music but did not succeed, in spite of the success of his symphony *From the New World,* composed and first performed here in 1893.

In addition to its effectiveness as music, this work is interesting. Several sections were thought to be based on spirituals; they were not. These sections were created by Dvořák to suggest spirituals because of his affection for blacks in America. Other sections assumed to have American sources were based on Bohemian airs. This symphony, usually referred to as his fifth, was really his ninth, the confusion resulting from the fact that at one point Dvořák became dissatisfied with some of his work, which he destroyed.

Dvořák excelled in the smaller forms for piano, solo voice, and violin that reveal his most prominent characteristics—his seemingly inexhaustible and spontaneous melodic invention, his rhythmic variety, the intensity of his harmonic effects.

While his longer works do not sustain the dramatic intensity and evolving continuity of the shorter works, they are nevertheless excellent and are frequently heard in the concert hall, including several of the seven published symphonies, the *Piano Quintet in A,* the *Piano Concerto in G Minor,* the *Cello Concerto in B Minor,* and, in Europe, his opera *Rusalka.*

Dvořák was the first musician to be made a life member of the Austrian House of Lords. His funeral took the form of a national ceremony of mourning in Prague.

Bibliography

Clapham, John. *Dvořák*. New York: W. W. Norton & Co., 1979.
Šourek, Otakar. *The Orchestral Works of Antonin Dvořák.* Translated by R. F. Samsour. Prague: Artia, 1954.

PART II

CONCEPTS OF STYLE

The style is the man.
Comte de Buffon

IN Part I of this book we learned about the constituent elements of music, the basic building blocks of the art: tone, rhythm, melody, texture, dynamics, and tempo. Next we considered musical form—both form *in* music and forms *of* music—the ways in which elements combine in a musical work. We are now ready to consider one of the most complex aspects of music, that which we call *style*.

What do we mean by style? Just as we talk about the *style* of a tennis player— meaning the particular way he or she reaches up for the serve, swings, follows through on the forehand, hits the ball deep or short, and so on—so in music *style* means that which makes one type of music or group of compositions different from all others.

When you turn on the radio and hear a piece of music that has already begun, you can classify it within moments as rock or jazz, salsa or disco. Actually, what you are doing is making a reflex judgment based on your existing knowledge of *musical styles*. Without going through a conscious process of analysis, you are perceiving certain features of meter, tempo, rhythm, timbre, and harmony, and relating them to musical labels—rock, jazz, salsa, and disco—that imply the regular use of these elements in the manner in which you have just heard them played.

In music, the word *style* is used in several ways. We talk about the style of eighteenth- or nineteenth-century music. This is a use of the word in its broadest sense. We may also talk about the style of individual composers, referring to *Beethoven's style* or *Schubert's style*. This is a rather specific use of the word. In its most definitive form, style may refer to periods in the creative output of a single composer in which certain characteristics are everpresent. Thus we talk about the style of Beethoven's *early period*, or his *middle* or *late period.*

Your ability to recognize stylistic differences will develop as you learn more and more about music and how composers in different eras of music history used the constituent elements of music in differing and unique ways. Since you are beginning your study of music with this book, you can content yourself for the present with a discovery of the broad stylistic characteristics of the major historical periods of recent times. Later, if you are interested, you can add to this discovery a knowledge of the styles of individual composers, possibly even developing an ability to recognize stylistic periods within the works of a single composer.

In this book, we will not study the style and music of the historical periods in chronological order, as we would do in a music history course. Indeed, we will begin with the Romantic era—roughly the nineteenth century—a period that produced the largest percentage of the music we hear in concert halls and opera houses today. We will also study Nationalism, a unique subdivision of the Romantic era. Next we will consider Impressionism, the style that bridged the turn of the century; we will follow that with music of the twentieth century. Two special types of twentieth-century music will next be studied: jazz and electronic music.

We then turn the musical clock back to the Renaissance, the period that many historians feel to be the foundation of modern culture. From there we will proceed chronologically through the Baroque and Classic eras, which will bring us back to our starting point, the Romantic era.

Music alone expresses the dark and mysterious world of our feelings and the ideal we can never realize.

J. Gaudefroy-Demombynes

EIGHT/
THE ROMANTIC ERA

ON July 14, 1789, ragged crowds of citizens stormed the Bastille, an ancient prison in Paris, where for centuries political prisoners had been held without trial. The protest was against the tyranny of nobles and the king, the crowds demanding "liberty, equality, and fraternity" for *all* French citizens. The revolution that followed shook Europe to its very core.

From that day in mid-July until late in the nineteenth century, the very word *revolution* was a battle cry throughout Europe, carrying a message of hope to all people. The desire for personal liberty and a form of government that represented the people was growing.

Poets, musicians, and painters at that time felt the need for both social and political reform; some even fought in revolutions to achieve these goals. Lord Byron, the poet, died in the Greek revolution against the Turks. Richard Wagner, the German composer, had to flee his native land after taking part in the unsuccessful German revolution of 1849.

This period of great change was known as the Romantic era, an era international in scope. During this period, the man in the street had, for the first time, a chance to express himself and to improve his lot in life. The great French philosopher of the era, Jean-Jacques Rousseau, captured the essence of this when he wrote:

> It is a noble and beautiful spectacle to see a man raising himself, so to speak, from nothing by his own exertions; . . . mounting above himself, soaring in thought even to the celestial regions, encompassing with great strides, like the sun, the vast extent of the universe; and what is still grander and more wonderful, going back into himself, there to study man and get to know his own nature, his duties, and his end.[1]

A true revolution was taking place in the arts as well as on the battlefields of Europe. The courts and nobility were no longer the principal patrons of the artist; they no longer controlled the artist's work, either artistically or financially. At last the artist was free to express himself as he pleased. As T. S. Eliot has said, the poems of the great Romantic visionary William Blake have "a peculiar honesty which, in a world too frightened to be honest, is peculiarly terrifying."

In its early stages, the Romantic movement was led by young men, many of whom did not live to the age of forty. This group included such great English poets as Byron, Shelley, and Keats, and the young giants of music Schubert, Mendelssohn, and Chopin.

Romanticism was a spirit that did not appear in all the arts or in all countries at the same time. It emerged first in England, Germany, and France. Poetry was the first art to feel the influence of Romanticism, painting followed next, and finally music. However, it was in music that the Romantic spirit found one of its strongest expressions.

For inspiration, the artists of the Romantic era began to look to the past. They were attracted to the myths of the Middle Ages, to folk song and folk poetry, to the art

---

1 Jean-Jacques Rousseau, "Discourse on Arts and Sciences" in *Social Contract and Discourses,* p. 30.

of the Orient, and to anything that seemed exotic and picturesque. Perhaps one of the keys to understanding the spirit of Romanticism is its root word, *romant*. In Old French, *romant* means an imaginative story, as opposed to a plain retelling of the facts. The *romant* was a kind of medieval poem that often had as its subject tales of chivalry and love. This led to such important Romantic works as Alfred, Lord Tennyson's twelve long poems on the King Arthur legend, *Idylls of the King* (published between 1859 and 1888), and *The Hunchback of Notre Dame* (1831) by the French writer Victor Hugo. Italian composer Giuseppe Verdi suggests the life of medieval troubadours in his opera *Il Trovatore* (1853); Wagner based operas on the medieval legends of *Lohengrin* (1848) and *Parsifal* (1882).

Painters, too, caught the spirit of this new era. Eugène Delacroix, a gifted Frenchman, pictured bodies rotting in Hades; he painted the savage, barbaric *Massacre at Chios*. No less grim are the vivid portrayals by the Spanish artist Francisco Goya of the horrors of warfare in his native land.

Speaking of Romantic style, the German writer E. T. A. Hoffmann said "Beethoven's music sets in motion the lever of fear, of awe, of horror, of suffering, and awakens just that infinite longing which is the essence of romanticism. He is, accordingly, a completely Romantic composer."

In all the arts, Romanticism brought out imagination and emotion. It was a way of expressing the personal feelings of men and women alike. The point of view was changed: artists and musicians became interested in less exalted subjects than those of the Classic era. In opera, subjects drawn from Greek and Roman mythology gave way to stories of the middle and lower classes of people, the national, and the fantastic. The

Eugène Delacroix, *The Death of Sardanapalus,* 1826 (Louvre, Paris). Inspired by Lord Byron's play, this painting illustrates the Romantics' fascination with savage and barbaric scenes.

Francisco Goya, *The Third of May, 1808,* 1814 (Museo del Prado, Madrid). Goya portrays the horrors of warfare in his native Spain with a scene of a mass execution by Napoleon's riflemen.

John Constable, *The Cornfield,* early 1800s (The National Gallery, London). Constable shows the Romantic painters' love of scenes of everyday life.

tone poem, which became a substitute for the grander symphonic form, was used to suggest a philosophy of life (Liszt's *Les Préludes,* 1856), a fantastic dance of death (Saint-Saëns's *Danse macabre,* 1874), and the romantic hero Don Juan himself (Richard Strauss's *Don Juan,* 1888). Just as the symphonic form grew in length, so its opposite — the miniature form — also excelled. The depth and range of expression in the smaller forms were evidenced in the piano music of Chopin and the art songs of Schubert.

The beauties and mysteries of nature were something the Romantic writers, painters, and composers explored at length. Byron, in his powerful poem *The Ocean,* wrote: "I love not man the less, but nature more." And William Blake, in his *Auguries of Innocence,* commented that one could

> . . . see a World in a Grain of Sand
> And a Heaven in a Wild Flower, . . .

Painters were enraptured with the changing scenes of nature. J. M. W. Turner, an Englishman, showed these changes in his paintings of sun and sea. John Constable, another Englishman, pictured rain-drenched fields and wind-ruffled elms. His works suggest a mood as much as they describe a view.

Nature inspired the German composer Beethoven to call his sixth symphony *The Pastoral* and to describe it as "cheerful feelings awakened by arrival in the country." Felix Mendelssohn, another German composer, tried musically to depict *Fingal's Cave,* a famous basaltic cavern in Scotland, in his orchestral work of the same name.

THE INDUSTRIAL REVOLUTION

While the Romantic artists found comfort in nature, thousands of men and women left the countryside to live and work in smoke-filled factory towns. The inventions that brought about the Industrial Revolution greatly changed the life of the average working person.

In *David Copperfield,* Charles Dickens painfully described his own wretched boyhood as an industrial laborer. In France, Victor Hugo and Honoré de Balzac wrote novels of the life and problems of the working class; they even wrote about prostitutes. And in opera, the French composer Georges Bizet set to music the story of a working girl, *Carmen* — a gypsy of loose moral standards; Giacomo Puccini, an Italian operatic composer, based his *La Bohème* on the tragic story of four unemployed bohemian artists living in Paris.

As the final years of the nineteenth century approached, Romanticism had run its course. A new group of young rebels painted in the garrets and lofts of Montmartre in Paris. They were revolting against the lush harmonies and excesses of the Romantic era. They were seeking to express their thoughts and feelings in new vague forms and new combinations of colors. Composers began to experiment with whole-tone scales and exotic qualities of tone.

The world was witnessing a new kind of revolution.

Symphony No. 5

by LUDWIG VAN BEETHOVEN

As the evening rain beat against the windowpane outside, a lonely figure with rumpled hair bent over a writing table. By the light of a flickering candle he penned a letter to a friend, a prince who had angered him: "Prince, what you are, you are by accident of birth; what I am, I am through my own efforts. There have been thousands of princes and there will be thousands more; there is only one Beethoven."

The prince to whom he was writing had been planning a party and had angered Beethoven by *commanding,* instead of *asking,* him to play the piano for the event.

Beethoven, although of humble birth, believed that his musical talent made him the equal of the rich and noble. This was a bold way to think in the early 1800s.

Young Beethoven admired the ideals of the French Revolution. For him Napoleon, when he was First Consul, was a symbol of human emancipation, "a flaming torch thrust in the face of tyranny, an incorruptible enemy of kings."[2] Beethoven, who had dedicated his *Symphony No. 3* to Napoleon, tore from the score the title page bearing

2. Lawrence Gilman, *Orchestral Music* (New York, 1951).

Title page of Beethoven's *Symphony No. 3,* showing Napoleon's name angrily scratched out.

the name Bonaparte in a furious burst of disillusioned rage when he heard that Napoleon had proclaimed himself Emperor, exclaiming in a bitter fury, "Then is he, too, only an ordinary human being?" The first page was rewritten and only then did the symphony receive the title *Sinfonia Eroica,* "Heroic Symphony."

The *Eroica* is a landmark because it forms the bridge between the earlier Classical style of Beethoven's first two symphonies and the dawning of a new age, the age that expressed an energetic and revolutionary style.

The overall plan for a symphony usually involved four contrasting movements. The first movement was generally an *allegro;* it was a spirited movement based on two contrasting themes. The second movement was a slow, songlike movement. It was followed, in the Classical tradition, by a stately dance movement, the *minuet.* A lively *finale* followed, generally another *allegro,* lighter in tone than the preceding three movements, bringing the work to a close.

With his third symphony, the *Eroica,* Beethoven made major changes in the symphonic form, changes that most later composers adopted. He enlarged the size of the orchestra, writing for a bigger string section and many more wind instruments. He also increased the proportions of the first movement, not only making it longer but using more than the traditional two themes of the Classicists who preceded him. Beethoven substituted a lively, light-hearted *scherzo* for the stately minuet, and made the fourth movement, the finale, more dramatic, a forceful and rousing conclusion to the symphony.[3]

Most of these new traits can be observed in Beethoven's *Symphony No. 5,* the most popular symphony ever written, a work that occupied Beethoven for many years. His sketchbooks show preliminary ideas that are dated before he started work on the *Eroica Symphony.* In those sketchbooks (totaling more than 5,000 pages), we can trace how

3. The *scherzo* retained the minuet's form and meter but was faster in tempo and more lighthearted in spirit.

some rather ordinary melodic ideas were reworked over a period of years until they became the powerful motives we hear today in the *Symphony No. 5.*

The entire first movement, for instance, of Beethoven's fifth symphony grew out of a four-note motive he had jotted down many years earlier:

I. Allegro con brio

It is customary in describing symphonies to call each movement by the tempo marking assigned to it by the composer. Thus we call the first movement of Beethoven's *Symphony No. 5* the *Allegro con brio* or *Opening allegro*. The expression *Allegro con brio* means "with spirit."

Like most first movements, this one is cast in a form we call the *sonata form* or the *sonata-allegro form.* The sonata form is divided into three sections and is based on two themes, a principal theme and a second theme; these themes are in different but related keys.

The first section of the sonata-allegro form is the *exposition,* in which the two themes are "exposed"—and the listener is exposed to them. The next section is the *development,* in which the composer shows off his skill by manipulating bits and pieces of the two themes, constantly shifting keys. The final section is called the *recapitulation;* in it the composer recapitulates, or repeats, the two basic themes essentially as they were first heard in the exposition section. Sometimes the composer adds a closing section to bring the work to a final, rousing climax. We call such a closing section the *coda.*

The *sonata* or *sonata-allegro* form could be outlined as follows:

Exposition (traditionally this entire section is repeated exactly)
    Principal Theme (in key of symphony)
    bridge
    Second Theme (in related key)
    Closing Section (returning to original key)
Development
    Themes and fragments in changing keys and formats
Recapitulation
    Principal Theme (essentially as first heard in Exposition)
    bridge (not modulating this time)
    Second Theme (in key of symphony this time)
    Closing Section
Coda (optional)

LISTENING OUTLINE

The *Allegro con brio* begins with two statements in sequence of the four-note motive of the symphony, played by the entire string section and two clarinets.

Motive

The principal theme, created out of this four-note motive, follows immediately:

Example 1 (Principal Theme)

After the bridge section has modulated from the c-minor tonality of the principal theme to E-flat major (known as the *relative major* of c minor), we hear the second theme, at once less rhythmical than the principal theme and much more songlike and lyrical in nature.

Example 2 (Second Theme)

The exposition ends with its own closing theme—another Beethoven addition to the traditional form.

Example 3 (Closing Theme)

The development section follows; it freely brings in the themes used in the exposition. We should notice how the French horn brings out the four-note motive in this section. A haunting oboe solo leads to the close of the development section.

The third section is the recapitulation, a restatement of the two main themes of the movement. First we hear the principal subject again, but slightly ornamented this time. After the bridge, we hear the second theme—in C major this time instead of E-flat major. The closing theme returns, but this time it is played more loudly, with the addition of trumpets and timpani.

The coda opens with the original four-note motive; this is repeated over and over very loudly. With a bold stroke this late in the movement, Beethoven introduces a new theme:

Example 4

The coda ends with an overpowering, thundering repetition of the four-note motive.

III. Allegro

LISTENING OUTLINE

The third movement, a scherzo, is in ternary form: A-B-A. It opens with a melody that rises from the lowest tones of the string section:

Example 5

After Example 5 is repeated, the second theme, a solemn march based on the rhythm pattern with which the symphony began, is heard.

Example 6

The middle section is based on a theme which, if it were not played by cellos and lumbering bass viols, would sound quite ordinary. Beethoven, however, assigns the melody to the lower strings. This means that the melody becomes quite humorous as the cellos and bass viols try to make it sound light and fast-moving:

Example 7

A return is made to the first section of the scherzo, but the forceful march is now subdued to a whisper. Instead of coming to a full cadence, the strings play a deceptive cadence. The timpani plays a solo. A tremendous crescendo, a passage that only a musical genius could have created, leads directly to the fourth movement, the finale.

IV. Allegro

Beethoven returns to the sonata-allegro form for the finale. (It should be noted that Beethoven was the first composer to make the finale as weighty and important as the other movements; he was also the first to make all the movements relate closely to each other.)

LISTENING OUTLINE

The principal theme is based on the C-major chord and scale:

Example 8 (Principal Theme)

Violins, Woodwinds

The theme has a second half:

Example 9

French Horns, Woodwinds

The violins announce the second theme:

Example 10

Violins

The exposition concludes with an important theme of its own:

Example 11

Violas, Clarinet

The entire exposition section is repeated.

The development section is characterized by rhythm figures and frequent changes of key. Beethoven does something in this section that is most unusual: he brings back the second theme from the scherzo, the powerful horn theme (Example 6) that is derived from the opening four-note motive of the symphony. He also changes the tempo and meter here, from duple ($\frac{4}{4}$) to triple ($\frac{3}{4}$); the tempo speeds up (although there are fewer notes). This too is quite original.

The *recapitulation* is followed by an extensive *coda*. And, typical of Beethoven, it reaches an apparent ending several times only to go on to the true ending, at once powerful and monumental.

About the Composer

LUDWIG VAN BEETHOVEN   Born: December 16(?), 1770
Bonn, Germany

Died: March 26, 1827
Vienna, Austria

At No. 20 Bonngasse in Bonn, Federal Republic of Germany, stands a little house, now the Beethoven Museum, in whose garret apartment Ludwig van Beethoven was born in December of 1770. It was in this same house that Beethoven, as a child, received his first music instruction at the keyboard from his father, a professional singer at the court in Bonn.

When he was sixteen, Beethoven traveled for the first time to Vienna, a city that was soon to become his permanent home. Before long, his name and musical talents—as a pianist, not as a composer—were well known throughout the city. He played at all the important palaces; the aristocrats became not only the friends of the "commoner" Beethoven but his patrons as well. Works were requested by and written for Prince Lichnowsky, Prince Lobkowitz, and Count Razumovsky. Archduke Rudolph, brother of the emperor, became one of Beethoven's pupils and a loyal friend. These commissioned pieces were often performed by the noblemen's private orchestras at musical evenings in their palaces; Beethoven derived much profit from his aristocratic connections.

Eventually Beethoven started to make his mark as a composer. Increasing numbers of public concerts for the emerging middle class provided a wider opportunity for the performance of many of Beethoven's orchestral works and this, in turn, generated an interest in published editions of Beethoven's piano sonatas and chamber music. "I have six or seven publishers for each of my works and could have more if I chose," Beethoven wrote at thirty-one. "No more bargaining! I name my terms and they pay!" For all this, however, money remained a constant problem for Beethoven throughout his life.

In addition to nine monumental symphonies, Beethoven composed thirty-two piano sonatas, works that today still occupy a central position in any pianist's repertory. Likewise, the sixteen string quartets are the heart of string quartet literature. There are five concertos for piano and orchestra that, as well as the *Concerto in D Major for Violin and Orchestra,* are still among the best-known and most frequently performed of all concertos. The *Missa Solemnis,* a sacred choral work, is one of Beethoven's crowning masterpieces.

From about his twenty-eighth year, the malady that later resulted in total deafness made Beethoven's life miserable. He became morose and suspicious of friends. He removed himself entirely from society, taking long walks in the parks and countryside, filling notebooks with musical sketches. He stated, "How could I . . . bring myself to admit the weakness of a *sense* which ought to be more perfect in me than in others?" In 1802 he visited a little house in Heiligenstadt on the outskirts of Vienna and contemplated suicide.

The death of his brother Karl in 1815 left a nephew named Karl in Beethoven's charge. The composer undertook this task with zeal, but the nephew was a scamp and made his uncle's life even more miserable. Beethoven lamented his poverty and believed that all his associates were taking advantage of him in financial matters. Probably because of a suspicious nature resulting from his deafness, he unjustly accused many people of cheating him. Had he been a better manager of funds, he could have lived a life free from financial worries.

Increasing deafness plagued the composer as he worked on the scores of his symphonies. In numerous conversation books preserved from this period of his life, there is a fairly accurate record of his career. His keyboard appearances became less frequent, and he recorded that at times when he was conducting an orchestra, the only way he could tell the musicians were playing was to watch the violinists' bows. On several occasions, according to contemporary accounts, the orchestra was several measures ahead of Beethoven's beat. After 1819, Beethoven was totally deaf. Following a performance he conducted of his mammoth *Symphony No. 9,* the concertmaster had to tug on the composer's sleeve to get him to turn around and acknowledge the applause.

Today, 150 years later, most of Beethoven's compositions are still in the active concert repertory. He was a composer not only for his day but for all time.

Bibliography

Solomon, Maynard. *Beethoven.* New York: Schirmer Books, 1979.

Thayer, Alexander Wheelock. *The Life of Ludwig van Beethoven.* 2 vols. Original in German, 1879; translated by Henry Edward Krehbiel, 1921. Revised and edited by Elliot Forbes. Princeton: Princeton University Press, 1967.

Piano music

by FRÉDÉRIC CHOPIN

If the Classical symphonic form expanded its dimensions during the Romantic era, the form of solo music for the piano tended to do the opposite. The *sonata,* a three-move-ment work comparable to the symphonic form for orchestra, gave way to very short, single-movement works sometimes referred to as *character pieces.* Such works fre-quently had titles that suggested briefness or casualness. The large repertory of charac-ter pieces includes the *impromptus* and *moments musicaux* of Schubert, the *songs without words* of Mendelssohn, and, of course, the *études, preludes, waltzes, nocturnes, polonaises, ballades,* and *impromptus* of Chopin.

The piano became *the* solo instrument of the Romantic era, the supreme Romantic instrument. The nineteenth-century piano, however, was quite a different one from the instrument known in the eighteenth century, the era of Mozart and his contem-poraries. The nineteenth-century piano had been enlarged, reshaped, and improved mechanically; it became even more responsive to the expressive intent of the soloist and enabled even greater flights of virtuosity. The nineteenth-century piano, closely akin to the piano we know today, was capable of producing a full, resonant tone at any dynamic level.

The rise in popularity of the piano during the Romantic era was not caused by mechanical improvements alone. Its accessibility in the homes of the musically literate families suggested that the children in such households, particularly the girls, learned to play it. And, for those whose musical and aesthetic interests lay beneath the surface, the piano proved to be a richly rewarding solo instrument that needed no accompani-ment, and one that could respond to their emotional interpretations.

As a composer of music for the piano, Frédéric Chopin is unique. Born in Poland of a French father and a Polish mother, he learned to play the piano at an early age and was soon writing compositions for it. Although as a youth he tried his hand at writing works for various instrumental and vocal ensembles, after the age of twenty-two he made no excursions into any medium but the piano and no attempts at a large-scale work. Instead, he achieved near-perfection in character pieces of simple, general de-sign but subtle and complex internal structure.

Nocturne in F-Sharp Major, Opus 15, No. 2

The first nocturnes were written by the Irishman John Field, from whom Chopin adopted the name and idea. Field's nocturnes were full of arpeggiated chords, orna-mentations, great climaxes, and sweet melodies that swept ladies of the salons of Paris into an "enthusiasm impossible to describe" (according to one contemporary writer).

Nocturne, of course, refers to a "night piece" or "night music." That night and night music had an appeal for the nineteenth-century Romanticists is undeniable. A fellow composer, Hector Berlioz, wrote of the evening rites at one of Chopin's homes when all the lamps were put out and everyone fell silent, "when the big salon butterflies had gone, when the scandal-mongers had come to an end of their stories, when all the traps were laid, all the treacheries committed, when everyone was all too weary of prose, then, in answer to the prayer of some beautiful, intelligent pair of eyes, Chopin became the poet."

While Berlioz's account might seem wordy and highly romantic, that was the very essence of the period into which the nocturne entered. Chopin, however, was able to avoid in his nineteen nocturnes the hollow indulgences of those of the earlier Field and instill into his compositions an emotional and musical content never quite equaled.

LISTENING OUTLINE

The F-sharp major *Nocturne* opens with a melancholy melody:

Example 1

Example 1 soon becomes heavily embellished with a variety of ornamentations, arabesques, and figurations.

The tempo doubles as a more lively theme is heard:

Example 2

Example 2 is repeated and developed.

The music begins to fade and slow down, but after a slight pause, the first theme (Example 1) returns. It starts as it did the first time but soon becomes very florid in a brief, smooth, cadenza-like passage. (A *cadenza* is a brilliant passage in which the music sounds as though it were being improvised or created at the moment.) The balance of the theme is highly decorated.

The music quickly fades away at the end.

Polonaise in A-Flat Major, Opus 53

Frédéric Chopin's first composition at the age of eight was a polonaise. At twelve and again at sixteen, he composed more polonaises. Yet this form took time for the composer to master; polonaises did not leap from his pen in inspiration and complete mastery of the genre (as did the études, for example).

The polonaise is a slow dance, almost a processional, in triple meter with the following basic rhythm patterns:

The polonaise became the dance of the nobility, a procession in somber and majestic rhythm of princes before their king. In its popular form, the polonaise retains the character of a dance in which one walks, or better, glides.

LISTENING OUTLINE

The A-flat major *Polonaise* opens with an introduction based on a series of chords which move quickly up the scale:

Example 3

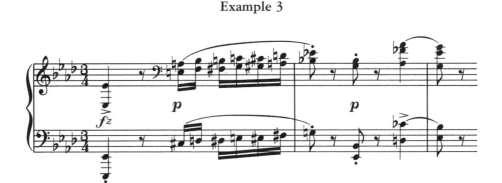

The principal theme is heard immediately after the introduction, accompanied by octaves in the left hand based on the tonic chord:

Example 4

After an extension of Example 4, this melody is repeated more forcefully in octaves.

A new section is built on a figure that keeps moving within the initial octave span:

Example 5

A more lyrical melody is introduced.

Example 6

Example 6 is played in octaves and decorated with trills and runs; it leads immediately to a return to Example 4 in octaves *fortissimo*.

A new section is introduced. The accompaniment pattern is heard first: after a series of rolled E-major chords, the left hand takes up a pattern of four descending notes in octaves, over which the melody appears:

Example 7

The music briefly modulates enharmonically to E-flat major, then returns to E major as Example 7 is heard again.

Once more the modulation to E-flat major occurs, this time more boldly. As the force of the passage subsides, a new and lighter theme is introduced in D major:[4]

Example 8

After Example 8 has been expanded and developed, a crescendo leads to the return of the melody of Example 4 in octaves, *fortissimo*.

A powerful five-octave scale moves up the keyboard, leading to a final statement of Example 4 in the upper octaves of the piano. There is a short closing section consisting of material already heard. A series of chords concludes the polonaise.

4. On the third beat of the second measure, the symbol for an *inverted mordent* (𝄽) above the staff indicates that the performer should quickly alternate the written tone (G) with the next higher tone (A-natural, because of the symbol ♮) as if beginning a trill.

About the Composer

FRÉDÉRIC FRANÇOIS CHOPIN

Born: February 22, 1810
Zelazowa Wola, Poland

Died: October 17, 1849
Paris, France

In the days just before the Second Empire in France, Frédéric Chopin could frequently be found playing the piano in the grandest salons of the French aristocracy. He was the toast of the city of Paris and was in demand at the social gatherings of the cultured, moneyed families. He lived in style, with his own carriage and servants, gave receptions, and was able to dine with his friends at the Café de Paris or at the Maison Dorée. He was witty, elegant, and just a bit of a snob.

The famous portrait of Chopin by Eugène Delacroix, 1857 (Louvre, Paris).

Chopin was not born into an aristocratic family. His father, a Frenchman, was a teacher of French at the Lyceum in Warsaw; the composer's mother had been a tutor in one of the wealthier homes in Poland. Young Frédéric started piano lessons at age six, completed them at age twelve, and never took another piano lesson. At twenty-one Chopin moved to Paris, and for the next ten years was extremely happy. The piano lessons he gave to the children of the aristocracy provided an excellent income, and he greatly enjoyed being a guest in their homes and playing for their social gatherings—although he never enjoyed giving public concerts. These were also some of the most fertile years as far as his compositions were concerned, for he completed a number of preludes, mazurkas, and waltzes.

In 1839, Robert Schumann, who had been one of the first to acknowledge Chopin's ability as a composer, wrote in *Neue Zeitschrift,* the magazine he edited and published: "He is indeed the boldest and proudest poetic spirit of the time." As Chopin's fame as a composer grew, his desire to appear as a pianist declined. He much preferred composition to playing the piano. He disliked technical exercises and hours of practice at the keyboard. When he was twenty-five, he renounced his career as pianist. After that he only appeared infrequently in public recital.

His health, never good, started to decline. During the fall of 1836, he met the famous writer George Sand (the pen name of Madame Aurore Dudevant) through their mutual friend Franz Liszt. "What a repellent woman she is," Chopin wrote. "Is she really a woman? I'm ready to doubt it." Chopin, who had been accustomed to the genteel salons of Paris, was not at first ready to accept this woman with her masculine habits and attitudes. Not only did she assume a man's name, she wore men's clothing and smoked cigars!

In spite of his initial reaction, Chopin was drawn to Sand. Not only was Sand the most famous and brilliant woman of her epoch—and Chopin adored both fame and brilliance—but her masculine traits seemed to complement Chopin's own rather effeminate personality. Sand's older age may have made her more a mother figure for the younger Chopin.

In the summer of 1838 Sand invited Chopin to her château at Nohant. Ill at the time, Chopin welcomed the tenderness and maternal care. That winter Sand's son Maurice—the same age as Chopin—also became quite ill. She suggested that Chopin join Maurice and her on a trip to Majorca, off the Spanish coast, for recuperation. Chopin borrowed some money on the strength of the *Preludes* he was preparing so that he could make the trip.

Majorca did nothing to improve his health. There were no adequate hotels, the rented rooms were poorly furnished, the food inedible, and the rains incessant. Chopin's cough turned into bronchitis, and the people of Majorca treated him as an infected person, forcing him to leave the village of Palma. The customs officials refused to release his piano and he could not complete the *Preludes.* Knowing, however, that he had to finish them in order to pay for the trip, he found an old piano in the basement of the house they were renting. Sand, her son, and Chopin finally left Majorca for Barcelona and then moved on to Marseilles, where Chopin underwent a medical examination. The doctor claimed that Chopin did not have tuberculosis even though he complained of coughing "bowls full of blood."

The trio returned to Paris. Madame Sand became tired of nursing Chopin and arranged for him to live in an adjoining apartment. It was not long before Chopin had many of his old piano students back again and started publishing new works. His financial situation improved tremendously. Unfortunately his health did not improve, and in 1842 he wrote to a friend, "I have to stay in bed all day because I have so much pain in my beastly face and glands." He was already too ill to walk up the stairs to his own room, and his cough grew even worse.

In the spring of 1847 his friendship with George Sand was ruptured. Her son Maurice had never liked Chopin, in spite of their common bond of poor health, and had always resented the composer's presence in his mother's home. With the marriage of George Sand's daughter Solange in May of 1847 and the subsequent quarrels in the house, the situation strained Chopin's friendship with George Sand to the breaking point. Chopin obstinately refused Sand's offers of reconciliation. After the friendship ended, Chopin composed no more.

Bibliography

Gavoty, Bernard. *Frederic Chopin.* Translated by Martin Sokolinsky. New York: Charles Scribner's Sons, 1977.
Orga, Ates. *Chopin: His Life and Times.* Tunbridge Wells, England: Midas Press, 1976.

Erlkönig
by FRANZ SCHUBERT

Songs have been around ever since primitive man discovered that he could modulate his voice and change its pitch to form a melodic line. Over the ensuing millennia two principal forms of songs developed: the everyday folk songs of the common people, which included religious tunes, ballads, songs for entertainment, and, most importantly, work songs; and art songs created by professional composers for the educated nobility.

By the beginning of the nineteenth century, the art song was often a short, strophic song, *strophic* meaning that the same music was repeated for each stanza of the text, much as we today repeat the same music for each verse of a folk song.

In the classic Italian art song and in later derivations, the melody of the vocal line was of supreme importance; the accompaniment was incidental. The rise of a school of great poets in Germany at the beginning of the Romantic era naturally attracted composers who wished to set such poems to music. Many of these were ballads, fairly long poems that related an epic story, alternating narrative and dialogue in a tale full of romantic adventure and supernatural elements.

Because of the length of these poems and the dramatic quality of their stories, it became necessary for composers to devise a new method or style to set them to music. While traces of this new style can be found as early as the eighteenth century, it was not until an eighteen-year-old genius named Franz Schubert developed a style so new and so appropriate that the generic name took on new significance. Up to this point, *lied* (the plural is *lieder*) was simply the common everyday German word for song. Following Schubert's early song of 1814, *Gretchen am Spinnrade (Marguerite at the Spinning Wheel)*, based on a text from Goethe's *Faust, lied* and *lieder* came to refer to this new type of setting, in which the piano part was no longer simply an accompaniment but a partner with the voice in telling the story. The music supported, illustrated, and intensified the meaning of the poetry. The special nature of the new Romantic poetry caused Schubert and his followers to develop a great variety of accompaniment figurations and textures, and they suggested in the music the contrast of moods and movement in the story.

Paul Henry Lang, in his book *Music in Western Civilization,* describes this development:

> Schubert who recognized the new order of things, the new relationship of poet and musician, was far more creative in the purely musical sense than any other song writer, with the occasional exception of Schumann and Brahms. Had he accepted the romantic dictum of the poet's absolute supremacy, merely providing music to the text, he would not have created the modern song; but by consciously elevating such purely musical elements as harmony and instrumental accompaniment to equal importance with poem and melody, he brought to bear upon the atmosphere of the song the force of an overwhelming musical organism, a force sufficient to establish a balance between poetry and music.[5]

Erlkönig (The Erl King) was one of Schubert's early lieder. Although written when he was eighteen, it was by no means his first song. It was published six years after its completion (no one at first wanted to publish such an involved song with a difficult piano accompaniment) and listed by the publisher as Opus 1. It was composed, as were many of Schubert's songs, in a sudden burst of inspiration. One of Schubert's friends, Josef von Spaun, relates in his *Memoirs* how one afternoon he went to see Schubert and found him "all aglow, reading *Erlkönig* aloud from a book. He walked up and down the room several times, book in hand, then suddenly sat down, and, as fast as his pen could travel, put the splendid ballad on paper. As he had no piano, we hurried over to the . . . school, and there the *Erlkönig* was sung the same evening and received with enthusiasm."

The text is by one of the greatest German Romantic literary figures, Johann Wolfgang von Goethe. It describes the night journey of a father who is returning home with

Steel engraving from the title page of the first published edition of *Erlkönig.*

5. Paul Henry Lang, *Music in Western Civilization* (New York, 1941), p. 780.

his child, who is ill with fever. As the child rests in his father's arms, he becomes delirious and thinks he sees the Erlking, a mythological goblin that exercises a fatal influence upon children with alluring promises or visions. The story, except for the first and last stanzas, is told by the characters themselves.

In Schubert's setting, the pitch of the father's speech is low, that of the boy, high. The unearthly Erlking exceeds both in range of his melodic line.

Throughout the song, a repeated octave figure in the piano accompaniment represents the galloping of the horse, which stops just before the end when the father and child reach home. An ominous figure in the left hand of the accompaniment adds tension and mystery to the atmosphere. The distress of the child's cry to the father is sharpened by biting dissonance, and his increasing fear by a rise in pitch, each appeal a tone higher. The Erlking's entreaties are accompanied almost as though they were dance tunes, for indeed the Erlking invites the child to come dance. At the end of the song, when the fatal ride is finished, the music breaks off. The words *war todt* ("was dead") are then sung without accompaniment, followed by two final chords (dominant, tonic) that musically write *finis* to the ballad as no other chords could.

LISTENING OUTLINE

The introduction begins with the repeated figure in octaves in the right hand of the piano, suggesting the rhythm of the galloping horse. In the second measure, a mysterious, ominous motive appears in the left hand.[6]

In the fifteenth measure, a voice inquires:

Wer rei - tet so spät durch Nacht und Wind?

6. The symbol ▲ or ▼ in measures 2 and 3 indicates that the note or chord over or under which it appears is to be played *staccatissimo,* that is, a sharper *staccato.*

Wer reitet so spät durch Nacht und Wind?	Who rides so late through night and wind?
Es ist der Vater mit seinem Kind;	It is the father with his child;
er hat den Knaben wohl in dem Arm,	He has the boy safe in his arms,
er fasst ihn sicher, er hält ihn warm.	He holds him tightly and keeps him warm.

The father speaks:

„Mein Sohn, was birgst du so bang dein Ge - sicht?"

„Mein Sohn, was birgst du so bang dein Gesicht?"	"My son, why do you hide your face?"

The child replies:

„Siehst, Va - ter, du den Erl - kö - nig nicht?"

„Siehst, Vater, du den Erlkönig nicht?	"O father, don't you see the Erlking?
den Erlenkönig mit Kron' und Schweif?"	The Erlking with his crown and robe?"
„Mein Sohn, es ist ein Nebelstreif."	"My son, it is but a fantasy of mist."

The Erlking then speaks to the feverish child:

„Du lie - bes Kind, komm, geh' mit mir!"

„Du liebes Kind, komm', geh' mit mir!	"My dearest child, come with me!
Gar schöne Spiele spiel' ich mit dir;	I'll play games with you
manch' bunte Blumen sind an dem Strand,	Where the flowers bloom along the shore.
meine Mutter hat manch' gülden Gewand."	My mother has many golden robes."
„Mein Vater, mein Vater, und hörest du nicht,	"My father, my father! Don't you hear,
was Erlenkönig mir leise verspricht?"	What the Erlking whispers in my ear?"
„Sei ruhig, bleibe ruhig, mein Kind;	"Be quiet, be quiet, my child.
in dürren Blättern säuselt der Wind."	It is only the dead leaves stirred by the wind."

„Willst, feiner Knabe, du mit mir geh'n?	"Come, my child, will you come with me?
meine Töchter sollen dich warten schön;	My daughters will wait on you,
meine Töchter führen den nächtlichen Reih'n	My daughters will lead you in a merry dance every night.
und wiegen und tanzen und singen dich ein."	And sing and dance and rock you to sleep."
„Mein Vater, mein Vater, und siehst du nicht dort	"My father, my father, don't you see there
Erlkönig's Töchter am düstern Ort?"	The Erlking's daughters in that gloomy spot?"
„Mein Sohn, mein Sohn, ich seh' es genau:	"My son, my son, I see and I know
es scheinen die alten Weiden so grau."	It is only the reflection of the light on the old willow trees."
„Ich liebe dich, mich reizt deine schöne Gestalt;	"I love you; I'm entranced with your handsome looks;
und bist du nicht willig, so brauch' ich Gewalt."	And willing or not, I'll carry you off with me."
„Mein Vater, mein Vater, jetzt fasst er mich an!	"My father, my father, He's grabbing me!
Erlkönig hat mir ein Leid's getan!"	The Erlking has seized me, he's hurting me!"
Dem Vater grauset's, er reitet geschwind,	The father shudders, he rides like the wind,
er hält in Armen das ächzende Kind,	He clasps the pale, sobbing child, tighter.
erreicht den Hof mit Müh' und Not;	He reaches home with fear and dread;
in seinen Armen das Kind war tot.	In his arms the child was dead.

About the Composer

FRANZ SCHUBERT   Born: January 31, 1797
                            Vienna, Austria

                     Died: November 19, 1828
                            Vienna, Austria

Vienna has long been famous for the many coffee houses that line its broad streets.
Had one looked in on the Bognerschen Coffee House on Singerstrasse on a day early

in the nineteenth century, one might have found Schubert having coffee, reading the afternoon newspapers, and discussing the art and politics of the day with his friends. At the end of the coffee hour, the friends would probably have adjourned to one of their homes, where they would have held a *Schubertiad,* an evening during which the famous baritone Johann Michael Vogl would perform some of Schubert's latest lieder accompanied by the composer at the keyboard. Some of the guests would also "perform," reading their latest poems or scenes from plays, or perhaps sketching the gathering itself. The climax of the evening would be dancing and perhaps a game of charades. Each of the members of this close circle of friends had a nickname. Schubert's was "Tubby" (*Schwämmerl,* "little mushroom") because of his short stature (4 feet 11 inches) and his stocky build.

Of the many famous composers known as "Viennese," Schubert was the only one born in Vienna itself. His father was an ill-paid schoolteacher who envisioned the same occupation for his son. As a boy of eight, Franz learned the violin from his father, the piano from his brother Ignaz, and organ and music theory from the organist of the local parish church. In 1808, when Schubert was eleven, he passed the difficult examinations and was admitted as a chorister to the Imperial court chapel, a singing group known today in democratic Austria as the Vienna Boys' Choir.

While a student at the choir school of the court chapel, Schubert wrote his first symphonies and songs, youthful works full of the lyrical melodies that later became his trademark. Although Schubert made many lifelong friends at the school and learned the rudiments of grammar, religion, and ethics in addition to music, he found the living conditions less than ideal, the food usually in short supply. The year before leaving the school (he was then sixteen), he wrote to his brother a humorous letter that read in part:

> I've come to the conclusion that life is pretty good though in some ways it could be better. . . . One could certainly do with a roll and a few apples, particularly when one has to wait eight and a half hours between a moderate sized midday meal and a wretched sort of supper. . . . The few groschen that Father gave me vanished into thin air in the first few days, so what am I going to do for the rest of the time? They who hope upon Thee shall not be put to shame. St. Matthew 3:4. Too true! How would it be if you let me have a few kreuzer each month? You wouldn't notice them and they would make me happy and contented in my tiny room.

The quotation is *not* from St. Matthew; it was fabricated by young Schubert himself.

Soon after leaving the choir school, Schubert, then seventeen, took up duties as an assistant schoolmaster in his father's school. There is no record of how successful he was in the classroom—a position he occupied for a little over a year—but we do know that during this brief period he composed four symphonies, three masses, three operettas, two string quartets, and some 250 songs including the famous *Erlkönig.*

Ill fitted for the role of a schoolteacher, Schubert quit that position when he was nineteen, and was never again gainfully employed in the remaining twelve years of his short life. Like a true bohemian, he lived first with one friend and then another. Many were acquaintances he had first met during his student days at the choir school, and most were active in one of the creative arts, including singing (Vogl), painting (Leopold Kupelwieser), and poetry (Franz von Schober). Schubert was indeed fortunate to be supported by his friends, who—although faithful and generous—were certainly not rich. They had faith in Schubert, they inspired him, and they cheered him up when he was depressed. Thanks to them we have a wonderful legacy of songs and symphonies by Schubert—more than six hundred songs, nine symphonies (of which one is lost, and No. 8, which is called *The Unfinished* because it has only two movements), and a large quantity of chamber and piano music. Although Schubert was intensely interested in writing for the theater, he was less than successful because of his poor choice of dramatic texts to set. Of sixteen operas, none entered the repertory in his lifetime. An attempt was made to revive a few of them during the Schubert sesquicentennial in 1978, but they met with little more success then than had been in evidence at their first performances.

Bibliography

Deutsch, Otto Erich. *Schubert: Memoirs by His Friends.* Translated by Rosamund Ley and John Nowell. New York: Macmillan, 1958.
Wechsberg, Joseph. *Schubert: His Life, His Work, His Time.* New York: Rizzoli International Publications, Inc., 1977.

Die beiden Grenadiere

by ROBERT SCHUMANN

Robert Schumann, who was thirteen years Schubert's junior, came to composition rather late in life, for he had originally intended to become a concert pianist. After a tragic accident to the fourth finger of his right hand when he was twenty-two, he decided to concentrate on composition. Most of his early works were piano solos, but in 1840, when Schumann was thirty, he turned to lieder at the suggestion of his fiancée Clara Wieck. In that momentous year—the year of his marriage to Clara Wieck—and also known as his "year of song"—he composed more than 125 lieder, a varied list that includes many of his finest and best-known songs. They show great inventiveness and a sensitivity to the words—which is not surprising in view of the literary environment in which Schumann was reared; his father was an author, publisher, and bookseller. The songs actually show a greater warmth and vigor, and an even greater wealth of melody and variety of mood, than can be found in his earlier piano works.

Probably because of his background as a pianist, the piano part sometimes tends to overshadow the vocal line in Schumann's lieder, but basically the composer achieves an extraordinarily good balance between voice and instrument. In Schumann's lieder, the piano parts are often very independent, commenting in different ways upon the text. Schumann also attained remarkable success and set a new standard in his sensitive settings of the words of the texts, repeating words and phrases only when he felt that sense demanded it. (Schubert was criticized by the poet Goethe for "repeating" lines of text "that should only have been said once!")

Die beiden Grenadiere is the first of two songs set by Schumann in 1840 to texts by Heinrich Heine and published as part of Opus 49. In his youth, the poet Heine had been a profound admirer of Napoleon, and in *Die beiden Grenadiere* he tells of two French soldiers on their way back from defeat in Moscow who learn of Napoleon's capture.

In the music, Schumann suggests a dead march, solemn and respectful, the rhythm vividly suggestive of disciplined grief. And, with the song's musical quotation of the famous melody from the *Marseillaise,* there can be no mistaking the land of the soldiers' allegiance.

LISTENING OUTLINE

(In the performance by baritone Erich Kunz on this recording, Schumann's original piano accompaniment has been tastefully orchestrated to enhance the stirring nature of the music.)

A very brief, martial introduction by the orchestra leads immediately to the first line of the ballad, a melody characterized by a continuation of this martial rhythm:

Example 1

Nach Frank - reich_ zo - gen zwei Gre - na - dier', die war - ren in Russ - land ge - fan - gen,

Nach Frankreich zogen zwei Grena-   Two grenadiers were returning to
*   dier',   France*
die waren in Russland gefangen,   From prison in Russia,

The melody of Example 1 is repeated for the next two lines of the text:

Und als sie kamen in's deutsche Quar-   And when they arrived at Germany's
*   tier,   borders,*
sie liessen die Köpfe hangen.   They hung their heads in mourning.

A melodic line filled with solemn, repeated tones follows:

Example 2

da hör-ten sie bei-de die trau-ri-ge Mähr', dass Frank-reich ver-lo-ren ge-gan-gen,

Da hörten sie beide die traurige Mähr',
daß Frankreich verloren gegangen,

It was there they heard the sad story,
That France had been crushed and
forsaken,

Besiegt und geschlagen das tapfere Heer

Her glorious armies defeated and
slain,

und der Kaiser, der Kaiser genfangen!

And the Emperor, the Emperor
taken prisoner!

An orchestral interlude leads to a repetition of the melody of Example 1 (there are slight rhythmic alterations in it) with the following text:

Da weinten zusammen die Grenadier',
wohl ob der kläglichen Kunde.

Those two soldiers then wept
After learning of this sad tale.

In an extended passage that gradually builds to a climax, the story continues to unfold:

Der Eine sprach: „Wie weh wird mir,
wie brennt meine alte Wunde!"
Der And're sprach: „Das Lied ist aus,
auch ich möcht' mit dir sterben,
doch hab' ich Weib und Kind zu Haus,
Die ohne mich verderben."

Then one said, "My tears are hot,
But my old wound burns hotter!"
The other said: "The end has come,
My life I'd gladly lay down,
But I've a wife and child at home,
Who would perish without me to
provide for them."

„Was schert mich Weib? was schert
mich Kind?
ich trage weit beß'res Verlangen;
laß sie betteln geh'n, wenn sie hungrig
sind,
mein Kaiser, mein Kaiser gefangen!

"Who cares for wife or child?

A pity they do not awaken,
Let them go and beg if they're hun-
gry!
My Emperor, my Emperor is taken
prisoner!

Gewähr' mir, Bruder, eine Bitt':

One promise you must make my
friend,

wenn ich jetzt sterben werde,
so nimm meine Leiche nach Frankreich
mit,

If this wound should kill me,
You'll carry my body back to France,

begrab' mich in Frankreich's Erde.

And bury me under her soil.

das Ehrenkreuz am rothen Band

And when my cross on its band of
scarlet

sollst du auf's Herz mir legen,	You've placed over my heart,
die Flinte gieb mir in die Hand,	Then put my musket in my hand,
und gürt mir um den Degen.	And belt my sword around me.

Schumann turns to the melody of the *Marseillaise,* the French national anthem, for the next section. It begins:

Example 3

So will ich liegen und horchen still,	So shall I lie there, listening,
wie eine Schildwach' im Grabe,	A sentinel amidst the corpses,
bis einst ich höre Kanonengebrüll	Until I hear the rumble of cannon
und wiehernder Rosse Getrabe;	and the neighing of trampling horses.
dann reitet mein Kaiser wohl über mein Grab,	This will mean that the Emperor rides over my grave,
viel Schwerter klirren und blitzen;	With swords flashing in splendor;
dann steig' ich gewaffnet hervor aus dem Grab,	Then armed for the battle I'll burst from the grave,
den Kaiser, den Kaiser zu schützen!"	And rise as my Emperor's defender!"

A brief, slow passage for the orchestra brings the song to a close.

About the Composer

ROBERT SCHUMANN   Born: June 8, 1810
                              Zwickau, Germany

Died: July 29, 1856
       Endenich, Germany

The marriage of Clara and Robert Schumann is one of the most ideal recorded in the annals of music history. She was the daughter of Robert's piano teacher, Friedrich

Wieck, and at first Robert and Clara regarded each other affectionately as brother and sister. As a youthful composer, Schumann confined himself mostly to the writing of piano music. But as he became aware of his love for Clara, he turned to expressing himself in lyrical songs. A sensitive musician herself, Clara encouraged her husband and soon suggested he try the field of orchestral composition. The composer's *Symphony No. 1* was completed during the first year of their marriage. Clara outlived her husband by many years, and after his death, she traveled throughout Europe giving piano recitals of his music. One of her final concerts was in 1896, forty years after his death.

Schumann's first music lessons with the town organist started when he was eight; a year before, he had first tried his hand at composition. By eleven, he was writing both instrumental and choral compositions without instruction. He graduated from the Zwickau Lyceum (high school), where his principal interest had been in the Romantic writers Byron and Jean Paul Richter. In 1828 Schumann enrolled in Leipzig University to pursue a course in law.

Schumann soon transferred to the University of Heidelberg, where he studied both law and music. While there he heard a concert by the famous violinist Niccolò Paganini, and decided to make music his career. He wrote to his mother requesting permission to move back to Leipzig so that he could devote his full time to the study of music. In 1830, after receiving her permission, he moved into the home of Friedrich Wieck, who was to be his piano teacher.

Eager to perfect his technique—but not being acquainted with the physiology of the hand—Schumann developed a device that made use of a sling and some weights, with which he hoped to strengthen his fourth finger, always a pianist's weakest. The finger, unfortunately, could not take the grueling exercise and torture, and in 1830 it became paralyzed. Schumann then turned his attention to composition rather than performance.

When he was twenty-four, Schumann founded a journal, the *Neue Zeitschrift für Musik.* The paper was dedicated to the promotion of new music and opposed the "decadent Italian music" then frequently heard. Schumann was the sole editor for nine years and contributed many valuable and important articles. It was through this publication that the music world first became acquainted with a new Polish–French pianist by the name of Frédéric Chopin. Much later, the *Neue Zeitschrift* was the first to hail Johannes Brahms as a composer of talent.

Schumann is best remembered today for his lieder and piano music. His character pieces for the piano are the very essence of nineteenth-century German Romantic piano music. His *Carnaval,* for example, is made up of many little pieces that are variations on short melodic fragments with a central carnival theme. There are also two albums concerned with children: *Kinderscenen (Scenes from Childhood)* and *Album für die Jugend (Album for the Young).* His major work for piano is the *Concerto in A Minor for Piano and Orchestra.* He also composed four symphonies, several concert overtures, and choral and chamber music.

Bibliography

Bedford, Herbert. *Robert Schumann, His Life and Work.* Reprint of 1933 edition. Westport, Ct.: Greenwood Press, 1970.

Boucourechliev, André. *Schumann.* Translated by Arthur Boyars. Reprint of 1959 edition. Westport, Ct.: Greenwood Press, 1976.

Traum durch die Dämmerung

by RICHARD STRAUSS

Richard Strauss was among the last of the major German composers of lyric art songs; he was also one of the last of the Romantic composers. Although he lived until 1949, most of his songs were composed before the turn of the century. *Traum durch die Dämmerung (Dream in the Twilight)*, the first of three songs with texts by Otto Julius Bierbaum published as Opus 29, dates from 1894, the year Strauss became thirty.

Melodically, Strauss followed in the tradition of Schumann, writing lyrical melodies that display the beauty and emotional range of the human voice. In the Strauss art songs, however, the piano becomes involved in more modern harmonies, including some dissonance and many complex chords and modulations.

The text of *Traum durch die Dämmerung* is a simple but evocative lyrical rendering of the feeling of longing to be with one's sweetheart at the hour of twilight.

LISTENING OUTLINE

A repeated figure in the lower range of the piano serves both as a brief introduction and as an accompaniment for the opening line of the poem.

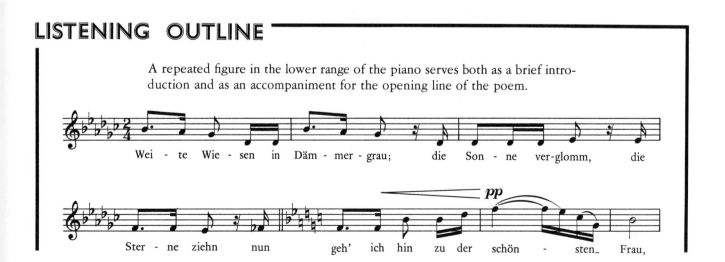

Weite Wiesen im Dämmergrau;	The distant meadow at twilight,
die Sonne verglomm, die Sterne ziehn	When stars appear after the sun has gone down
nun geh' ich hin zu der schönsten Frau,	Leads me to a beautiful young girl,
weit über Wiesen im Dämmergrau,	Leads me across the meadow at dusk,
tief in den Busch von Jasmin.	Deep into the bower of jasmine.

The melody of the example is repeated for the following text:

Durch Dämmergrau in der Liebe Land;	Through evening shadows to the land of love
ich gehe nicht schnell, ich eile nicht;	I go, not too quickly; and then am loath to leave;
mich zieht ein weiches sammtenes Band	I'm led to a soft and velvet bower
durch Dämmergrau in der Liebe Land	In the land of love at the close of day,
in ein blaues, mildes Licht.	In the twilight blue of evening.

The music is marked "slowly and quietly"; the melody is reminiscent of the opening phrase:

Ich gehe nicht schnell, ich eile nicht;	I go, not too quickly; and am loath to leave
durch Dämmergrau in der Liebe Land,	Through evening shadows to the land of love,
in ein mildes, blaues Licht.	In the twilight blue of evening.

About the Composer

RICHARD STRAUSS   Born: June 11, 1864
                             Munich, Germany

                     Died: September 8, 1949
                             Garmisch-Partenkirchen, Germany

Richard Strauss was a genial man who loved his wife, his money, and his art. His home in Garmisch was filled with paintings by such famous artists as El Greco, Tintoretto, and Rubens. He particularly liked to play cards and drink beer, but he usually had to sneak away from his strong-willed wife Pauline to enjoy these diversions (he humorously said that, of his operas, his favorite was *Intermezzo*—the story of a musician and his termagant wife). Strauss loved to make money and hang on to it. According to

one story, he once invited many Parisian celebrities to a postpremiere feast at a leading restaurant, and after he had been praised and cheered for his work and all present had thanked him for being a genial host, he had each guest handed a separate check!

Strauss was the son of the first horn player of the Munich Opera orchestra; the Strauss home was always filled with music. Richard was given his first music lesson when he was four, and at six had composed a little *Polka in C* for piano. His first published work, *Festival March,* was written when he was ten. Most of the other compositions of this period are either in manuscript form or have been destroyed. Strauss was sixteen when the first public performance was given of one of his works, his *Symphony in D Minor.*

Although Strauss did not create the generic form known as the *symphonic poem* or *tone poem* (Strauss himself preferred the latter expression), his works in this idiom are perhaps better known today than those of any other composer. As Strauss envisioned it, a tone poem was an orchestral work in one movement based on an extramusical idea, either poetic or realistic. His first such work—and probably his most successful—was *Don Juan,* completed when the composer was twenty-four. This was followed by *Don Quixote, A Hero's Life, Death and Transfiguration,* the humorous *Till Eulenspiegel's Merry Pranks,* and *Thus Spake Zarathustra* (which became the basis for the title music of the 1968 film *2001: A Space Odyssey*).

Although known more for his operas than for his art songs, Strauss did compose 125 lieder, of which the finest—such as *Traum durch die Dämmerung* and *Morgen (To-morrow)*—are among the masterpieces of the turn-of-the-century repertory. In a letter of 1903, Strauss wrote an extremely interesting confession as to his methods of composing songs:

> For some time I will have no impulse to compose at all. Then one evening I will be turning the leaves of a volume of poetry; a poem will strike my eye. I read it through; it agrees with the mood I am in; and at once the appropriate music is instinctively fitted to it. I am in a musical frame of mind, and all I want is the right poetic vessel into which to pour my ideas. If good luck throws this my way, a satisfactory song results.

Among Strauss's most successful operas are *Salome* (based on Oscar Wilde's play about that biblical character), *Der Rosenkavalier (The Cavalier of the Rose),* and *Die Frau ohne Schatten (The Woman Without a Shadow).* Most of Strauss's operas show the influence of another great German composer, Richard Wagner (see pp. 153–59). This is not unusual, since Strauss's father was a horn player in the Munich opera house where, as a youth, Strauss heard many of the new Wagnerian operas in rehearsal and performance.

Strauss was a gifted and well-known conductor of other composers' works as well as his own. During the early years of the Second World War, he accepted the post of president of Adolf Hitler's Reichsmusikkammer (Government Music Board); but the quickly disillusioned Strauss finally resigned and fled with his family to Switzerland until the war was over. Although at first condemned by the Allied tribunal after the war for having accepted the post, he was later cleared and went on to conduct in London.

Bibliography

Del Mar, Norman. *Richard Strauss: A Critical Commentary on His Life and Works.* 3 vols. London: Free Press, 1962–72.

Marek, George. *Richard Strauss: The Life of a Non-Hero.* New York: Simon & Schuster, 1967.

Die Meistersinger von Nürnberg

by RICHARD WAGNER

During the Middle Ages, the nobility of central Europe established a leisurely manner of life relatively free from the wars and battles that had plagued their ancestors, a life given over to the enjoyment of lavish clothing, ornate furniture, enormous castles, rich food, and much drink. Poet-musicians, writing poems of love, composed their own melodies and sang these songs for the lords and ladies of the manors. In southern France in the twelfth century, these artists were known as *troubadours;* in northern France they were called *trouvères.*

When, a century later, these musicians traveled as far as Germany (largely as a result of the Crusades), they made a great impression on the local people. Soon the German *minnesinger* (love-song singers) were attempting to do for the German nobility what the troubadours and trouvères had done for the French. By the fifteenth century, German commoners—the peasants and craftsmen—began to want to participate in this art of combining original poetry with music, so they formed guilds, much as the cabinetmakers and tanners had earlier formed their craft and trade guilds. The poet-musicians called their guild the *Meistersinger,* meaning "mastersingers."

In the nineteenth century, 400 years later, the German operatic composer Richard Wagner became fascinated by the history of the mastersinger movement and decided to compose an opera whose setting would be medieval Germany during one of the song contests of this musical guild. For a central figure he chose an actual historical personage, one of the greatest of the early German poets—Hans Sachs. The composer chose to call this a "comic opera," attempting to show what fools would-be artists are, who—lacking the least trace of artistic inspiration—attempt to create a work of art by rules and laws alone.

In Wagner's opera, which he called *Die Meistersinger von Nürnberg (The Master-singers of Nuremberg),* a young knight named Walter has fallen in love with Eva, the daughter of a rich goldsmith. The old goldsmith, however, has already promised his daughter's hand in marriage to the winner of the forthcoming song contest.

A stuffy and pompous fellow by the name of Beckmesser is also in love with Eva. Not only that, he is also to serve as a judge of the song contest. His job will be to

The procession of the guilds before the song contest, Act III of Wagner's *Die Meistersinger.* Metropolitan Opera production.

tabulate any errors the contestants make in trying to follow the elaborate set of rules that the guild has established for the creation of a song.

At the contest, Walter's *Trial Song* seems most unusual. Because of this, he makes a poor impression on the masters. Only the middle-aged cobbler Hans Sachs—himself a poet-musician of great ability—recognizes the originality and true beauty of Walter's song. Because Sachs also loves Eva, who is almost like a daughter to him, and because he desires her happiness, he helps Walter to win the contest and, thereby, Eva's hand.

In writing this opera, Wagner said he attempted to "contrast the spirit of folk-art with the narrow-minded, common mastersingers whose quite ridiculous laws and rules for writing poetry I suggested in the person of Beckmesser." The composer went on to say that this story suggests the problem of "an artist like Walter who is faced by the stupid and angry criticism of the crowd." There can be no doubt that Wagner attempted a reference to his own most severe critic, Austrian music critic Eduard Hanslick, for in the third sketch of the opera Wagner called the character Beckmesser—the pompous, stuffy judge of the contest—*Hanslick.*

Overture

LISTENING OUTLINE

The *Overture* opens with the bold Meistersinger theme, the musical emblem of the guild of songwriters. Played by the full orchestra, this twenty-seven-measure theme begins:

Example 1

Violins, Woodwinds

The second theme is introduced by a trill played by the woodwinds and strings. This melody, which in the opera suggests Walter's love for Eva, is played first by the flute:

Example 2

Flute (octave higher)

A rapid and brilliant scale passage introduces the next theme, a Meistersinger fanfare. This melody was adapted by Wagner from an actual tune of the original fifteenth-century mastersingers. It is played by the winds; the strings accompany with ascending runs. The strings then join the winds to complete the statement.

Example 3

Trumpets

A superb expansion of a theme which is heard in the final chorus of the opera, as Hans Sachs delivers his speech in praise of German art, follows:

Example 4

The melody of Walter's *Prize Song* is now heard:

Example 5

Six measures later, this theme (Example 5) is interrupted by a short, impatient melody in the violins, a tune that comes from a song Walter sings in the first act of the opera. This section is marked by several changes of tonality.

Example 6

With a stroke of genius, Wagner now depicts the tottering apprentices of the guild, those doddering men who know the rules so well but who lack the least spark of talent. Wagner uses the majestic Meistersinger theme (Example 1) to suggest the busybody apprentices by cutting the time value of the tones of the theme by one-third (known to the musician as *diminution*). The resulting melody sounds anything but noble and majestic.

Example 7

After several measures of woodwind trills and a rapid succession of 16th notes played by the violins, Wagner, in a magnificent piece of writing, combines three of the major themes. The trumpets and horns start off with the fanfare theme (Example 3); the violins play Walter's *Prize Song* melody (Example 5); and the basses and lower winds take up the majestic Meistersinger theme (Example 1).

Example 8

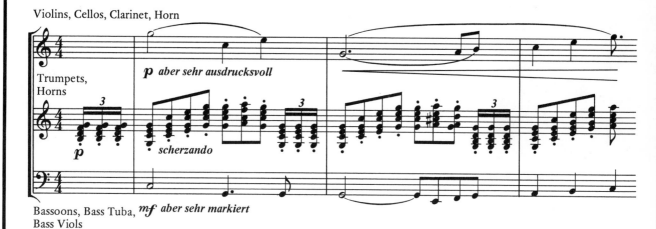

Violins, Cellos, Clarinet, Horn

Trumpets, Horns

p aber sehr ausdrucksvoll

scherzando

Bassoons, Bass Tuba, *mf aber sehr markiert*
Bass Viols

After a dynamic climax, the fanfare theme (Example 3), is boldly restated. The overture concludes with a repetition of the opening Meistersinger theme (Example 1) in a final, dramatic presentation.

About the Composer

RICHARD WAGNER   Born: May 22, 1813
                                         Leipzig, Germany

                             Died: February 13, 1883
                                         Venice, Italy

When Richard Wagner was twenty-two, he purchased a notebook and started writing the details of the life of what he declared to be "one of the world's greatest geniuses." The book became his autobiography, *Mein Leben* (*My Life*). At the time he bought the sketchbook, he was the conductor of a very poor, small opera-house orchestra and the composer of two unproduced operas. The next forty-eight years evidenced a fantastic life. Wagner's biographer, Ernest Newman, sums up the composer's character well when he says:

Wagner is one who stands . . . equally capable of great virtues and great vices, of heroic self-sacrifice and the meanest egoism, packed with a vitality

too superabundant for the moral sense to control it; now concentrating magnificently, now wasting himself tragically, but always believing in himself with the faith that moves mountains, and finally achieving a roundness and completeness of life and a mastery of mankind that makes his record read more like a romance than reality.[7]

Wagner's father, who died six months after the boy was born, was a clerk in the Leipzig police court. Soon after her first husband's death, Wagner's mother married Ludwig Geyer, an actor and playwright who also did some painting. Although Geyer died when Richard Wagner was eight, the effect of a cultured home in which there were good books and plays had an immense influence on the boy. After the death of his stepfather, Wagner transferred from the school in Leipzig to one in Dresden, where he studied, among other subjects, Greek tragedies in their original language. During these student days, his interest was in literature and writing; music had not yet attracted him. His favorite authors included Shakespeare, Goethe, and Schiller.

When he was fifteen, Wagner attended a performance of Beethoven's *Fidelio*. This convinced him that he should pursue a career in music.

After a year at the University of Leipzig, the twenty-year-old Wagner took his first post as a conductor. In addition to those duties in Riga and later in Dresden, and time spent composing such early operas as *The Flying Dutchman, Tannhäuser,* and *Lohengrin,* Wagner found time to write political pamphlets and to champion the cause of the insurrectionists in Germany. For this activity he was exiled, and he moved first to Paris and then to Switzerland in 1849. While in Paris, he ran up huge debts until the French threatened to throw him in prison.

Wagner spent thirteen years in exile in Zurich. During this period, he visited London on a conducting tour in 1855 and in 1858 visited Paris and Venice. In Zurich he started to work on what later came to be known as *Der Ring des Nibelungen (The Ring of the Nibelungs),* a cycle of four operas based on Norse legends. His first original opera in the cycle was called *Siegfried's Death.* He then wrote a second opera describing Siegfried's youth, titled *Siegfried,* in an attempt to prepare the audience for the events in *Siegfried's Death,* which Wagner now called *Götterdämmerung (The Twilight of the Gods).* Yet a third opera seemed necessary to explain events leading up to *Siegfried* and *Götterdämmerung,* so *Die Walküre (The Valkyrie)* was composed. It in turn, however, did not seem to reveal all the details necessary for the development of future events, so a prelude was written: the opera *Das Rheingold (The Rhine Gold).* This cycle of four operas occupied the composer for over twenty-five years, and is the single greatest creative endeavor in the history of opera. It is unique: a single story told via four operas meant to be performed on four successive nights. Wagner gave each opera unity and focus through the use of *leitmotives.*[8]

7. Ernest Newman, *The Life of Richard Wagner* (New York, 1933).
8. A *leitmotive* (in German, *Leitmotiv*) is a short musical idea that is used recurrently to suggest the same person, place, emotion, or object each time it is used.

One of Wagner's most frequently performed operas is *Tristan und Isolde* (1859), a love story based on a Celtic legend from the thirteenth century or earlier. *Tristan,* as well as *Die Meistersinger,* was composed during Wagner's work on the massive *Ring* cycle. This opera makes exacting demands on singers, requiring voices that can produce and sustain an enormous volume of sound. The opera itself—judged by many to be Wagner's greatest achievement—also makes use of leitmotives, and is a work of dramatic unity and clarity of design.

Just when all seemed darkest for Wagner, what with unpaid debts mounting and little prospect in sight for the production of his *Ring* cycle, a miracle happened. At 10 o'clock on the morning of May 3, 1864, the private secretary to King Ludwig II of Bavaria handed Wagner the monarch's signet ring and portrait, bidding the composer come to the palace at Munich and meet the king.

Ludwig II, who was only a boy of 18, had just ascended the throne and admired both Wagner and his music. At the palace meeting, Ludwig explained that when he read the words Wagner had written as an introduction to the poem of the *Ring,* he felt it was a personal message for him. This introduction described a great music festival that could only be given if it were sponsored by a rich prince. The introduction ended with the question, "Will such a prince appear?" Ludwig said that when he read this, he knew that he was that prince.

Wagner wrote in his autobiography, "He wants me to stay with him to work, to rest, to produce. He will give me all the money I need. . . . I am my own absolute master!"

True to his word, Ludwig paid all of the composer's private debts, furnished Wagner with a lavish home in Bayreuth, and helped build that special opera house, the *Festspielhaus,* in which to this day only Wagner's works are produced.

Bibliography

Culshaw, John. *Wagner: The Man and His Music.* New York: Dutton, 1978.
Von Westernhagen, Curt. *Wagner: A Biography.* Cambridge, England: Cambridge University Press, 1979.

La Bohème

by **GIACOMO PUCCINI**

If the symphony was the major orchestral form of the Romantic era, then opera was its principal vocal form. And if Germany and Austria were the centers for symphonic development, then Italy, particularly in the late nineteenth century, was the center for operatic achievements.

Mimi sings *Mi chiamano Mimì* to the impetuous Rodolfo, Act I of Puccini's *La Bohème*. American Opera Center production.

Operas are written for soloists and orchestra, and most make use of choruses and dances. Usually sung throughout, operas are acted on stage with elaborate costumes and fanciful scenery.[9] The solo songs in operas are called *arias,* and take their individual names from the first line of text. There are also ensemble numbers in opera: duets for two performers, trios for three, quartets for four, quintets for five, and sextets for six. In earlier operas, most arias are preceded by a recitative, a type of song-speech employed because it makes the text very easy to understand. Most operas are preceded by an orchestral overture.

Two great musicians dominated the opera field in Italy: Giuseppe Verdi, who was the older, Giacomo Puccini, the younger. Of all the Puccini operas, *La Bohème* is undoubtedly the most popular.

La Bohème is sometimes called a *verismo* opera, *verismo* meaning "realistic." Verismo works deal with scenes of everyday life, in contrast to mythological or historical stories of earlier operas. Many verismo operas are without overture, the composers having felt that such an instrumental piece before the curtain rises destroys the illusion of realism. Most of Puccini's operas are without overtures; in *La Bohème* the curtain goes up quickly on the first note of music.

In *La Bohème,* the time of the action is given as "about 1830." Although this date is

9. Some spoken dialogue may be found in those works known as *opéra comique* (French), *opera buffa* (Italian), and *singspiel* (German).

sixty years before Puccini started to work on the opera, that does not make it a "historical" story, for bohemian artists occupied the Latin Quarter of Paris through the First World War in much the same manner as that depicted in Henri Murger's *Scènes de la vie de bohème* (*Scenes of Bohemian Life*) of 1847, on which Puccini's opera is based. It might be noted that although Puccini dropped the words *Scenes of* from his opera's title, the opera is essentially four separate scenes of bohemian life; there is no real dramatic action, nor is there any real character development.

In the original score, Puccini quoted Murger's novel in his description of the bohemians.

> Mimi was a charming girl specially apt to appeal to Rodolfo, the poet and dreamer. Aged 22, she was slight and graceful. Her face reminded one of some sketch of highborn beauty; its features had marvelous refinement. . . . Gustave Colline, the great philosopher; Marcello, the great painter; Rodolfo, the great poet; and Schaunard, the great musician—as they were wont to style themselves—regularly frequented the Café Momus, where, being inseparable, they were nicknamed the four musketeers. Indeed, they always went about together, played together, dined together, often without paying the bill. . . .

Cast of Characters

The Bohemians	Rodolfo, *a poet*	tenor
	Marcello, *a painter*	baritone
	Schaunard, *a musician*	baritone
	Colline, *a philosopher*	bass
Mimi, *a seamstress and flowermaker*		soprano
Musetta, *a singer and sometime sweetheart of Marcello*		soprano
Benoit, *the Bohemians' landlord*		bass
Alcindoro, *a state councilor*		bass

Time: *About 1830*

ACT I

Scene: *The garret apartment of the Bohemians in the Latin Quarter of Paris*

It is a cold and snowy Christmas Eve. Rodolfo, a struggling poet, and Marcello, an equally struggling painter, are trying to work in their icy garret. Just as Marcello is about to break up a chair to keep their flickering stove burning, Rodolfo remembers the rejected manuscript lying on the table, and decides it would make better fuel than literature. The two friends applaud the "performance" of the play while they warm themselves around the short-lived fire. Colline enters, having unsuccessfully tried to pawn his precious books. Suddenly Schaunard, having earned some money playing music, bursts in with porters bearing food and fuel, and the gloom is lifted. An English lord has paid him handsomely for his music, so he is going to treat them all to a joyous Christmas Eve.

The hilarity is interrupted as Benoit, the landlord, tries to collect their long-over-due rent. The young men invite him in for wine, which loosens his tongue. They induce him to boast about his love life and then, pretending to be horrified by such immorality, they hustle him out of the room. Then the four friends decide to go to the Café Momus to start the evening's celebration. Rodolfo tells them to go ahead while he finishes an article that is due for a newspaper. They leave, urging him to finish quickly.

Alone in the room, Rodolfo waits for inspiration to move his pen. He is surprised by a knock on the door. Opening it, he discovers a young girl standing there with an unlighted candle in her hand. The draft in the stairwell has blown her candle out and she has come seeking a light. As he bids her come in, she is seized with a coughing spasm and falls fainting in a chair. When she has recovered, she asks Rodolfo to light her candle, and then shyly hastens to leave. At the threshold she realizes that she has dropped her key. As she comes back to search for it, her candle goes out again. In hurrying to help her, Rodolfo purposely blows out his own candle, and together in the darkness they grope for the lost key. Rodolfo finds it and quickly puts it in his pocket. Suddenly their hands meet.

Aria: *Che gelida manina*

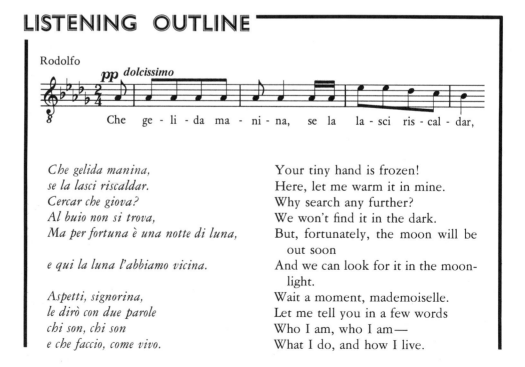

LISTENING OUTLINE

Che gelida manina,	Your tiny hand is frozen!
se la lasci riscaldar.	Here, let me warm it in mine.
Cercar che giova?	Why search any further?
Al buio non si trova,	We won't find it in the dark.
Ma per fortuna è una notte di luna,	But, fortunately, the moon will be out soon
e qui la luna l'abbiamo vicina.	And we can look for it in the moonlight.
Aspetti, signorina,	Wait a moment, mademoiselle.
le dirò con due parole	Let me tell you in a few words
chi son, chi son	Who I am, who I am—
e che faccio, come vivo.	What I do, and how I live.

Vuole? Chi son? Chi son?	Who am I? What do I do?
Sono un poeta.	I am a poet.
Che cosa faccio?	What do I do?
Scrivo. E come vivo? Vivo.	I'm a poet. And how do I live? I live.
In povertà mia lieta scialo	In my poverty I feast as sumptuously
da gran signore rime ed inni d'amore.	As a grand lord on rhymes and hymns of love.
Per sogni e per chimere	For dreams and visions
E per castelli in aria l'anima ho milion-aria.	And for castles in the air, I have the soul of a millionaire.
Talor dal mio forziere ruban	Now and then two thieves rob
tutti i gioielli due ladri:	All the jewels from my jewelbox:
gli occhi belli.	Two beautiful eyes.
V'entrar con voi pur ora,	They came in with you,
ed i miei sogni usati,	And my old dreams,
ed i bei sogni miei tosto si dileguar!	My wonderful dreams have quickly disappeared!
Ma il furto non m'accora poichè,	But the robbery doesn't harm me
poichè v'ha preso stanza la dolce speranza!	Since such wonderful expectation has taken its place.
Or che mi conoscete,	Now that you know me,
parlate voi, deh!	Please, talk to me.
Parlate!	Speak.
Che siete?	Who are you?
Vi piaccia dir!	Please tell me!

Rodolfo releases Mimi's hand, and she drops into a chair.

Aria: Mi chiamano Mimì

LISTENING OUTLINE

Sì.	Yes.
Mi chiamano Mimì,	I am called Mimi,

Ma il mio nome è Lucia.	But my name is Lucia.
La storia mia è breve.	My story is brief.
A tela o a seta ricamo in casa e fuori.	I embroider silk and satin at home or away.
Son tranquilla e lieta,	I am peaceful and happy,
ed è mio svago far gigli e rose.	I pass the time by making lilies and roses.
Mi piaccion quelle cose	I like those things
che han sì dolce malia,	That have a sweetness about them,
che parlano d'amor, di primavere,	That speak of love, of springtime,
che parlano di sogni e di chimere—	That speak of dreams and fancies—
quelle cose che han nome poesia.	Those things that are called poetry.
Lei m'intende?	Do you understand me?

Rodolfo

Sì.	Yes.

Mimi

(The music here repeats that of the opening phrase of her aria.)

Mi chiamano Mimì,	I am called Mimi,
il perchè non so.	But I don't know why.
Sola, mi fo il pranzo da me stessa.	All alone, I cook dinner for myself.
Non vado sempre a messa	I don't always go to Mass,
ma prego assai il Signor.	But I often pray to the Lord.
Vivo sola, soletta,	I live alone, all alone,
là in una bianca cameretta:	In a little white room over there.
guardo sui tetti e in cielo,	I look over the roofs into the sky,
ma quando vien lo sgelo	But when the snow melts,
il primo sole è mio—	The first sunshine is mine—
il primo bacio dell'aprile è mio!	The first kiss of April is mine!
Il primo sole è mio!	The first sunshine is mine!
Germoglia in un vaso una rosa.	A rose bud opens in a vase,
Foglia a foglia la spiro!	Leaf by leaf I inhale its fragrance.
Così gentil è il profumo d'un fior!	How wonderful the perfume of the flowers!
Ma i fior ch'io faccio, ahimè,	But the flowers that I make, alas,
i fior ch'io faccio, ahimè,	The flowers that I make, alas,
non hanno odore!	Have no fragrance.
Altro di me non le saprei narrare:	I don't know anything else to tell you about myself—
Sono la sua vicina	I am your neighbor
Che la vien fuori d'ora a importunare.	Who comes at this odd hour to trouble you.

As Mimi finishes, the other bohemians are heard outside the window beckoning Rodolfo to join them. Rodolfo replies that he is not alone, but tells them to "get a table at the Café Momus, we'll follow soon."

Rodolfo turns and sees Mimi bathed in the soft glow of moonlight. A tender duet, *O soave fanciulla (O Beautiful Girl in the Moonlight)*, closes the scene. The two new lovers pass out the door at the final notes of the duet, and on to the Café Momus.

Duet: *O soave fanciulla*

LISTENING OUTLINE

Rodolfo

O so - a - ve fan - ciul - la,___ O dol - ce vi - so di mi - te cir - con - fu - so al - ba lu - nar,___

	Rodolfo
O soave fanciulla,	O lovely maiden,
O dolce viso	O sweet face
di mite circonfuso alba lunar,	Surrounded by soft moonlight,
in te, ravviso il sogno	As I now see you,
ch'io vorrei sempre sognar!	This is what I have dreamed of!

(The following lines are sung together, and parts of them are repeated.)

	Rodolfo
Fremon già nell'anima	Already passion
Le dolcezze estreme,	Sets my soul on fire.
nel bacio freme!	Love quivers in a kiss!

	Mimi
Ah, tu sol commandi, amore!	Love alone commands me,
Oh! Come dolci scendono	Oh how sweet his flattery sounds
le sue lusinghe al core	To my heart,
Tu sol commandi, amor!	Love alone commands me!

	Mimi
	(as he tries to kiss her)
No, per pietà!	No, please.

	Rodolfo
Sei mia!	Be mine!
	Mimi
V'aspettan gli amici.	Your friends are waiting for you.
	Rodolfo
Già mi mandi via?	You send me away so soon?
	Mimi
Vorrei dir . . . ma non oso . . .	I want to say . . . but I dare not . . .
	Rodolfo
Dì!	Go on.
	Mimi
Se venissi con voi?	Might I come with you?
	Rodolfo
Che? Mimì!	But . . . Mimi!
Sarebbe così dolce restar qui.	It would be lovely to stay here.
C'è freddo fuori.	It's cold outside.
	Mimi
Vi starò vicina!	I shall be near you!
	Rodolfo
E al ritorno?	And when we return?
	Mimi
Curioso!	Wait and see!

Rodolfo
(as he prepares to lead her out the door)

Dammi il braccio, mia piccina.	Give me your arm, my sweet.
	Mimi
Obbedisco, signor!	I obey, Monsieur!
	Rodolfo
Che m'ami dì!	Say that you love me.
	Mimi
Io t'amo!	I love you!

Rodolfo and Mimi
(from the hallway)

Amor! Amor! Amor!	Ah, love, sweet love!

At the Café Momus, Musetta (left) sings her famous waltz in order to attract the attention of Marcello, at the other table. Act II of Puccini's *La Bohème*. American Opera Center production.

ACT II
Scene: *The Café Momus*

The Café Momus, in the heart of the Latin Quarter, is gaily lighted for the evening's festivities. Tables are set outside, and the street is crowded with milling people and hawkers. Schaunard buys an ill-tuned horn and Colline a huge overcoat which is a little the worse for wear. They find a table with Marcello and order supper.

Rodolfo and Mimi enter; Mimi admires a pink bonnet, and Rodolfo buys it for her. Then they see the others and join them. Rodolfo introduces Mimi to his friends with a flowery speech, and they propose a toast to the lovers. Suddenly Musetta bursts upon the scene, attracting as much attention as possible. She has recently quarreled with Marcello, with whom she has been in love. Marcello ignores her. She is with a rich old man, Alcindoro, who is some sort of public official. He nervously tries to keep Musetta quiet, but she is determined to make Marcello take notice of her. She begins what is known as *Musetta's Waltz*.

Aria: Quando me'n vo'

LISTENING OUTLINE

Quan - do me'n vo'___ Quan - do me'n vo' so - let - ta per la via la gen - te sos - ta e mi - ra

Musetta

Quando me'n vo'	As through the streets
quando me'n vo' soletta per la via,	I wander onward merrily,
la gente sosta e mira . . .	I wander onward,
e la bellezza mia	See how the people look around
Tutta ricerca in me,	Because they know
ricerca in me, da capo a piè.	I am a very charming little girl.

Marcello

Legatemi alla seggiola!	Tie me to the chair!

Alcindoro

Quella gente, che dirà?	What will people say?

Musetta
(ignoring the remarks and continuing)

ed assaporo allor la bramosia sottil—	And then I feel the subtle desire
che da gl'occhi traspira	That escapes from their eyes,
e dai palesi vezzi intender sa—	That shows they understand
alle occulte beltà.	My hidden beauties.
Così l'effluvio del desio tutta	Such outpourings of desire whirl
m'aggira, felice mi fa,	about me and make me happy,
felice mi fa.	Make me very happy.

Musetta decides to get rid of Alcindoro. She purposely breaks the heel of her shoe and screams in supposed pain. Alcindoro hastily removes the damaged shoe and hurries off to find a suitable replacement.

Before Musetta is finished with her song, Marcello has weakened and goes over to her table. As the bohemians are about to leave, the waiter brings their bill. They all protest poverty. Schaunard wonders where his fortune has gone. As they talk, the bugle call of an approaching guard of soldiers is heard. The people in the street and the children line up to watch the parade. Musetta calls for her bill, then grandly tells the waiter that Alcindoro will pay both bills. Since she has only one shoe, the bohemians lift her on their shoulders and leave. Alcindoro comes back with a new pair of shoes only to be confronted by an empty table and not one but two bills. He falls back in his chair in bewilderment as the curtain falls.

About the Composer

GIACOMO PUCCINI   Born: December 22, 1858
                                  Lucca, Italy

                         Died: November 29, 1924
                                  Brussels, Belgium

Although Giacomo Puccini came from a family of musicians, everyone gave up hope for the young boy's success in music save his widowed mother. Finally, after having been branded a slow learner by one of his teachers, Giacomo enrolled at the conservatory of music in his native city of Lucca at his mother's request. There he met a teacher who inspired and encouraged him. Progress was quick, and success just over the horizon.

Following his studies in Lucca, Puccini moved to Milan for advanced work at the conservatory there. Although his first opera, *Le Villi* (*The Witch Dancers*), was entered in a contest and lost, it was produced in 1884 at a small opera house where it was well received by the public. Italy's most famous music publisher, Guilio Ricordi, was so impressed that he commissioned another opera from Puccini.

Puccini was now launched on a career devoted exclusively to the creation of operas, works whose leading ladies represented a variety of nationalities: *La Bohème* (French), *Tosca* (Italian), *Madama Butterfly* (Japanese), *The Girl of the Golden West* (American), and *Turandot* (Chinese).

Giacomo Puccini, while a shy man in public, thoroughly enjoyed life. He celebrated the success of *La Bohème* by buying an expensive racing bicycle; his opera *Tosca* by the largest and noisiest automobile he could find; and his American triumph, *The Girl of the Golden West,* with an imported speedboat. He was a man who fell head over heels in love with each heroine he created. Yet above all, he loved the Tuscan soil, the home he built on Lake Massaciucoli called *Torre del Lago*—"Tower of the Lake," his hunting trips into the mountains around the lake, and the little café on the waterfront, Club Bohème.

Bibliography

Carner, Mosco. *Puccini: A Critical Biography.* London: Duckworth, 1958.

Weaver, William, and Hume, Paul. *Puccini: The Man and His Music.* New York: E. P. Dutton, 1977.

Liebeslieder Walzer

by JOHANNES BRAHMS

Although Johannes Brahms is known to the concert-going public primarily as an orchestral composer, much of his early training, experience, and compositional efforts centered around vocal music. At twenty-four, Brahms served the small German town of Lippe-Detmold as a conductor of its choral society, and in 1859, conducted the Women's Choir of Hamburg, for which he composed many of his shorter choral works. In 1863, Brahms moved to Vienna, where he accepted a position as conductor of the Singakademie. Several of his major choral works were completed after this appointment, including the *German Requiem,* a setting of passages from the German Bible concerned with death and resurrection.

In the spring of 1869, Brahms went to Karlsruhe to conduct a performance of this *German Requiem.* He rented an apartment there, and during the first six weeks of his stay, he was truly inspired. He was happy, carefree, and felt encouraged by the public's enthusiastic acceptance of his works. By early July he had completed twenty of the waltzes of the *Liebeslieder Walzer (Love-Song Waltzes).*

Brahms selected eighteen of these waltzes to be published in his first set, Opus 52. The poems he set were from the folk poetry of Russia and Poland. They had been translated into German by Georg Friedrich Daumer and published as a collection under the title *Polydora.* Brahms's original setting of these poems was for four solo voices (soprano, alto, tenor, and bass) and two pianos.

Strangely, the original subtitle states that the music is "for piano duet and vocal parts *ad libitum.*" Although two pianists can make musical sense by playing their part alone, we would then be hearing only half the music and, in some cases, the less interesting half. One writer has suggested that the phrase "vocal parts *ad libitum*" was probably an attempt to woo pianists who could not muster a contingent of singers to join them.

The first performance of the *Liebeslieder Walzer* took place in Karlsruhe in October 1869.

1. Rede, Mädchen

LISTENING OUTLINE

The first waltz is "in slow waltz tempo" and starts with the men's voices; the women's voices eventually reply. The men and women's voices combine in the closing measures.

Tenors

Re - de, Mäd - chen, all - zu lie - bes, das mir in die Brust, die küh - le,

Rede, Mädchen, allzu liebes,	Speak, O maiden all too dear,
das mir in die Brust, die kühle,	Whose glance has aroused
hat geschleudert mit dem Blicke	In my calm heart
diese wilden Glut gefühle!	These wild and passionate feelings.
Willst du nicht dein Herz erweichen,	Will your heart awaken with love,
willst du, eine Über fromme,	Or would you rather keep me wait-ing,
rasten ohne traute Wonne,	Never turning toward me,
oder willst du, willst du, dass ich komme?	Instead of joining me?
Rasten ohne traute Wonne	"Would you rather keep me wait-ing?"
nicht so bitter will ich büssen.	I won't weaken for a moment!
Komme nur, du schwarzes Auge,	Come to me, you dark-eyed maiden,
komme, wenn die Sterne grüssen,	Come when the stars greet us,
komme, wenn die Sterne grüssen.	When the stars greet us.

2. Am Gesteine rauscht die Flut

LISTENING OUTLINE

While the second love-song waltz begins with a brief passage for the tenors, it is essentially in four-part harmony. Both the first and second sections of this swinging gypsy song are repeated. It begins:

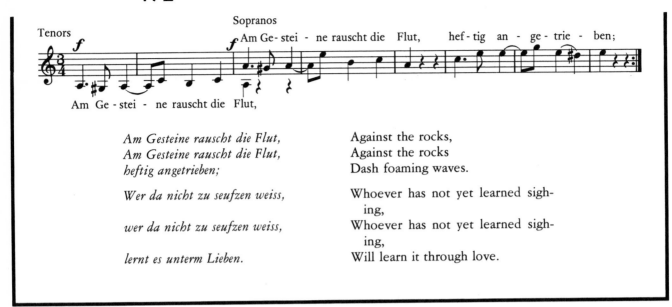

Am Gesteine rauscht die Flut,
Am Gesteine rauscht die Flut,
heftig angetrieben;

Wer da nicht zu seufzen weiss,

wer da nicht zu seufzen weiss,

lernt es unterm Lieben.

Against the rocks,
Against the rocks
Dash foaming waves.

Whoever has not yet learned sighing,

Whoever has not yet learned sighing,

Will learn it through love.

3. O die Frauen

LISTENING OUTLINE

The third waltz is set for men's voices; it is in binary form with both parts repeated. It begins:

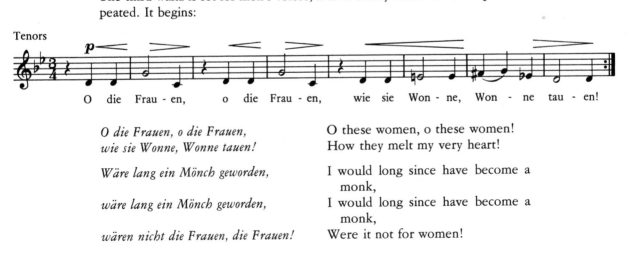

O die Frauen, o die Frauen,
wie sie Wonne, Wonne tauen!

Wäre lang ein Mönch geworden,

wäre lang ein Mönch geworden,

wären nicht die Frauen, die Frauen!

O these women, o these women!
How they melt my very heart!

I would long since have become a monk,

I would long since have become a monk,

Were it not for women!

4. *Wie des Abends schöne Röte*

LISTENING OUTLINE

This waltz is a complement to No. 3, being set for women's voices. Also in binary form with repeats, it begins:

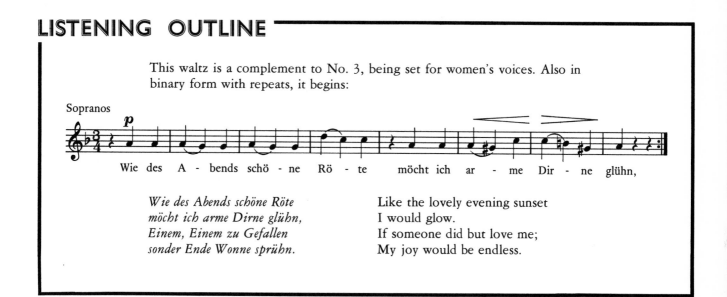

Sopranos

Wie des A - bends schö - ne Rö - te möcht ich ar - me Dir - ne glühn,

Wie des Abends schöne Röte
möcht ich arme Dirne glühn,
Einem, Einem zu Gefallen
sonder Ende Wonne sprühn.

Like the lovely evening sunset
I would glow.
If someone did but love me;
My joy would be endless.

6. *Ein kleiner, hübscher Vogel*

This is the longest and perhaps the most popular waltz in the set. It is a light and gracious waltz that speaks of love which flits about as if it were a bird—sometimes hard to catch, always flighty.

LISTENING OUTLINE

Three pairs of repeated notes serve as an introduction; then the tenors introduce the first melody:

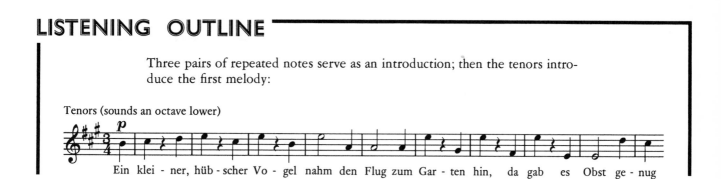

Tenors (sounds an octave lower)

Ein klei - ner, hüb - scher Vo - gel nahm den Flug zum Gar - ten hin, da gab es Obst ge - nug

Ein kleiner, hübscher Vogel nahm	There was a tiny, pretty bird
den Flug zum Garten hin,	Who saw the fruit in the garden,
da gab es Obst genug.	Then took his fill of it.

The other three voices respond (the soprano melody is a melodic and rhythmic variant of the tenor melody above):

Wenn ich ein hübscher, kleiner Vogel wär,	If I were a pretty, tiny bird,
Ich säumte nicht, ich täte so wie der.	I'd fly away and seek a garden lair.

A tenor-bass duet follows; on the second line they are joined by the altos.

Leimruten Arglist lauert an dem Ort,	There are lime twigs hidden to trap him;
der arme Vogel konnte nicht mehr fort,	That unlucky bird didn't know his fate!

These last two lines are repeated.

Next, women's voices, then men's, respond with *nicht fort* ("sad fate") several times.

The tenors introduce the next section; sopranos, altos, and basses respond with a repetition of the text.

Wenn ich ein hübscher, kleiner Vogel wär,	If I were a pretty, tiny bird,
ich säumte doch, ich täte nicht wie der,	I'd rather stay than take a risk as he.

Two repeated sections follow, both very brief and with tenors leading off.

Der Vogel kam, der Vogel kam	That bird found
in eine schöne Hand,	A gentle, loving hand.
da tat es ihm, da tat es ihm,	And there, as a willing captive,
dem Glücklichen, nicht and.	He stands.

The music and text of the opening section are repeated to bring this light-hearted and capricious waltz to a conclusion.

About the Composer

JOHANNES BRAHMS   Born: May 7, 1833
                              Hamburg, Germany

                    Died: April 3, 1897
                            Vienna, Austria

Johannes Brahms was born of an extremely poor family who lived in the slum around the docks of Hamburg. The composer's father was a double bassist in the local theater orchestra; his mother earned additional money for the family by taking in sewing.

At thirteen Brahms accepted his first position as a professional musician: he played in the local taverns for dances. Soon he was earning extra money by playing the offstage piano for the local theater.

Through a friend of his father, Brahms was able to spend the summers away from Hamburg in the little town of Winsen, where he conducted the male chorus of the village, and also tried his hand at composition. He arranged a number of folk songs for men's voices; he also created some original compositions.

When he was seventeen, Brahms had the good fortune to meet the famous Hungarian violinist Eduard Reményi, who requested that young Brahms join him on his concert tour as piano accompanist. During these travels, Brahms met many of the most famous artists of the day: Franz Liszt in Weimar; Robert Schumann at Düsseldorf; and Hector Berlioz at Leipzig. In his journal *Neue Zeitschrift für Musik,* Robert Schumann hailed Brahms as an emerging composer of exceptional talent.

Late in establishing his career as a composer, Brahms did not write his first symphony until he was past forty. This first effort was followed by three additional equally artistic symphonies. Cast in more traditional, Classical form than were the works of his contemporaries, Brahms's symphonies were criticized by many as not living up to Schumann's prophecy of a "new" voice, a modern spirit. Musicians of perception, however, labeled Brahms a "classic Romanticist," an expression that more nearly assesses Brahms's approach—classic in form, Romantic in spirit.

In addition to the *German Requiem* and the *Liebeslieder Walzer,* Brahms produced a large quantity of choral music, a fair amount of which was based on folk material. Along with Schubert and Schumann, Brahms is also one of the major figures in the field of nineteenth-century Romantic German lieder. Besides his four symphonies, Brahms is also known instrumentally for two concert overtures (the *Academic Festival Overture* and the *Tragic Overture*), two concertos for piano, one for violin, and a double concerto for violin and cello. He also wrote some excellent chamber music, and his works for piano frequently appear in piano recitals.

Bibliography

Gál, Hans. *Johannes Brahms: His Work and Personality.* Translated by Joseph Stein. Reprint of 1963 edition. Westport, Ct.: Greenwood Press, 1977.

Niemann, Walter. *Brahms.* Translated by Catherine A. Phillips. Reprint of 1937 edition. New York: Cooper Square, 1979.

A scene from Tchaikovsky's *Swan Lake*. American Ballet Theatre production.

Swan Lake

by **PETER ILYICH TCHAIKOVSKY**

Just as the symphonic form had been the chief concern of the Austro-German composers of the Romantic era and opera the principal idiom of the Italian composers, so ballet attracted the interest of the French during the nineteenth century.

Ballet originated during the fifteenth century at the courts of France and Burgundy. It is a form of dance in which, if it is programmatic and has a story, the entire plot is carried out by action mimed on stage. There is usually neither singing nor speaking.

It was on a visit to France that Peter Ilyich Tchaikovsky, the great Russian composer, first encountered French ballet. Fascinated by it, he made no secret of the fact that he was interested in composing in the idiom.

During the fall of 1875 the stage manager of the Bolshoi Theater offered Tchaikovsky 800 rubles (slightly less than $500) to write such a ballet. In a letter to a friend, Tchaikovsky clearly explained his reasons for agreeing to the commission: "I accepted the offer partly because I need the money, and partly because I had long cherished a desire to try my hand at [the French] type of [ballet] music."

Tchaikovsky made the dramatic sketch for *Swan Lake* himself, basing the story on a tale from the age of chivalry; the legend, possibly of Rhenish origin, tells of Prince Siegfried and his love for Odette, the swan in human form.

Tchaikovsky sketched the music for the first two acts within a couple of weeks, but the balance of the music was not completed until the following March. For some unknown reason, the performance was held up until February of 1877.

Apparently Tchaikovsky did not think too much of his first efforts in the field of ballet music, for he wrote in his diary shortly after *Swan Lake* was first produced: "*Swan Lake* is poor stuff."

There were good reasons for the composer to doubt the quality of his efforts. Performances of *Swan Lake* at the Bolshoi Theater had been flat, shabby, and badly costumed. The conductor had never directed a large-scale, elaborate ballet score before. Some numbers were dropped from *Swan Lake* as "undanceable," and pieces from ballets by other composers used in their place. In performance, perhaps only a third of Tchaikovsky's original score was used, and that not the best.

After the bad reception *Swan Lake* received in Moscow, it was dropped from the performance repertory. Some seventeen years later, during the season of 1894–95 (after Tchaikovsky's death), it was restaged by Marius Petipa, who, after great effort, located the entire score. As presented in the new version at the Maryinsky Theater in St. Petersburg, it was a tremendous success. *Swan Lake* has been almost constantly in the repertory of most major ballet companies since that date. And it is usually performed with choreography derived from Petipa's restaging. In the story, Prince Siegfried, having come of age, is told he must choose a bride at his birthday ball the following night. On the day before the ball, however, he is being feted by courtiers and villagers. He sees a flock of swans pass overhead and decides on a hunt. The prince pursues the flock to the edge of a lake. Arriving just at sunset, he raises his rifle to shoot. Before he can fire, he is astonished to see the birds suddenly change into human form—led by the lovely Odette, the Swan Queen.

She entreats Siegfried not to shoot, and tells him of the spell that has been placed upon her and her companions by the evil magician von Rothbart. By day they must be swans, and only a promise of marriage can free them.

Siegfried immediately falls in love with Odette and secures a promise from her that she will attend the great ball at which their betrothal will be announced, thus ending the spell forever.

But von Rothbart has overheard, and so it is not Odette but Odile—the black swan (his wicked daughter)—made by magic to look exactly like Odette, who is brought to the ball and presented to Siegfried.

The ball is a gala one. Courtiers and dancers have arrived from all over Europe. Siegfried is completely deceived by Odile. At the moment his betrothal is pledged, von Rothbart appears. Suddenly the young Prince sees the white swan outside the window; the sorcerer and his daughter vanish, and Siegfried realizes he has been fooled. He rushes out after Odette.

Siegfried finds Odette at the lake; a storm is coming up. Siegfried asks Odette to forgive him, but she knows that such is not possible. Now only death can free her from the spell. Siegfried decides to die with her, and in this famous final scene they are carried off with a promise of life together at last in another world.

As a composer, one of Tchaikovsky's greatest talents lay in his ability to create beautiful, romantic melodies. In his score for *Swan Lake,* Tchaikovsky not only created some of his greatest melodies but also did something very new and unusual with two of them. For the first time in ballet music, he used melodies as leitmotives or leading motives (see p. 158). That is, he took the tremulous theme of the swans in flight and the hauntingly wistful theme of Odette herself—played by the oboe against soft string and harp arpeggios—and returned to them again and again whenever the story concerned the swans or Odette. It was Tchaikovsky's intention that on hearing such leitmotives, listeners would instantly associate the motives—without benefit of word or dramatic gesture on stage—with the swans in flight or the beautiful Odette.

The full ballet score is seldom performed at orchestral concerts. Rather, various dances are excerpted and played as a suite. We shall examine the music of the *Scène* (in which Odette first appears), the *Waltz* (from the opening ballroom scene), and the *Danse des cynges (Dance of the Swans).*

Scène

LISTENING OUTLINE

The opening movement of the suite consists of music from Odette's dance. Over a soft rippling accompaniment provided by the harp and strings, an oboe sounds the haunting melody that serves as the *leitmotive* for Odette. Marked *piano espressivo* (softly with feeling), it begins:

Example 1

Oboe

p espress.

After the oboe has stated this rather extended melody, the French horns take it up in a much louder, bolder passage; strings and woodwinds provide the accompanying harmonic background. Soon the strings themselves take up this melody. The dynamic level quickly subsides. Flutes, oboes, and clarinet play

The music begins to build toward a tremendous climax; there is a feeling of agitation and foreboding in this tremulous passage. At the climax, flutes, clarinet, and upper strings take up the Odette theme (Example 1) in a passage marked *fff;* the entire brass section provides the harmonic background for the melody. The dynamic level quickly subsides. Flutes, oboes, and clarinet play the first four measures of Example 1; they are answered by bassoons, cellos, and basses playing the same passage four octaves lower. Soft chords bring the dance to a close.

Waltz

Although extremely captivating in its melodic flow and rhythmic drive, the waltz Tchaikovsky wrote for *Swan Lake* is quite conventional in form: a dance made up of many short, repeated sections, all in moderate triple meter.

LISTENING OUTLINE

The brief introduction—some eighteen measures long—begins with a *pizzicato* melody that curves downward in conjunct motion, then turns around and moves upward by disjunct motion. The strings play this melody in unison:

Example 2

Strings

pizz.

f

The violins—using their bows this time—announce the first waltz tune. Notice how it is built out of two eight-measure phrases that begin alike but conclude differently: the first is an imperfect cadence, because it is a momentary conclusion, the second a perfect cadence, because it is a permanent ending.

Also notice the repetition of the four-note melodic pattern (Figure A). It is heard twice at the same pitch level at the beginning of each phrase. It is then repeated one tone lower in the first phrase, this constituting a *melodic sequence.*

Example 3

After its first presentation, Example 3 is repeated by the violins in its entirety an octave higher in pitch. "Noodling," or "busywork" by the flute and clarinet, accompanies it this time.

The second section of the waltz also begins with a melody made up of two eight-measure phrases. This melody also includes a melodic sequence (Figure A) that is heard twice at its original pitch level, then repeated one tone higher. Then it is repeated on the higher pitch level with one chromatic alteration.

Example 4

There follows a short melody characterized by four sustained, repeated tones at its beginning. This serves as a bridge to the next section.

An upward-flowing melody follows; it moves principally by conjunct motion.

An exact repetition is made, starting with the statement of Example 1.

After this lengthy repetition and some new material is introduced and a brief reference to the bridge theme is made, we are introduced to a catchy melody played by the cornet:

Example 5

Soon another new melody is heard; it is first played by the violins.

Example 6

An eighteen-measure passage follows, one characterized by running figures for flutes and violins.

The bold conclusion of the waltz follows. A passage for full orchestra is heard, one that keeps growing in intensity and rising in pitch. The trombones and tuba then boldly proclaim a melodic sequence based on Figure A from Example 3. The violins take over melodically and lead to the stirring final measures of the waltz.

Danse des cygnes

In the ballet, *Danse des cygnes* follows immediately after Odette's dance (another *Scène*). Four dancers, linked closely together and dressed like cygnets (little swans), dance a light, fast, precisely choreographed step to this music.

LISTENING OUTLINE

Danse des cygnes consists of two related melodies, one heard at the beginning and again in the closing section; the other, contrasting but closely related, heard in the middle. Thus the dance is in ternary form.

The light, crisp opening melody is marked *staccato* (the dots under or above each note indicate this). In a *staccato* passage, each tone is separated from the next by a very brief silence.

Example 7

Oboe

The melody of Example 7 is repeated immediately by flutes and clarinets.

The violins introduce the closely related theme of the middle section, a theme heard four consecutive times.

Example 8

Violins

A return is made to the melody of Example 7, which is heard twice. A brief, four-measure coda brings the dance to its conclusion.

About the Composer

PETER ILYICH TCHAIKOVSKY Born: May 7, 1840
Votkinsk, Russia

Died: November 6, 1893
St. Petersburg, Russia

Certainly nothing in Tchaikovsky's early life indicated that he would ever be a creditable or famous composer. He was born in the little mining town of Votkinsk, which is about 1,000 miles east of Moscow. His father was a lieutenant colonel in the Depart-

ment of Mines, and served as chief inspector of the mines and metallurgical works at Votkinsk, a town known chiefly for its manufacture of heavy machinery and engines.

As a child, Tchaikovsky knew a home that contained not only a piano but also an orchestrion, a kind of mechanical organ that was popular at the time. His early efforts in music began with attempts to improvise at the piano.

Tchaikovsky's formal schooling prepared him for civil service, and it was not until after he had graduated from law school and taken a job as a clerk in the Ministry of Justice in St. Petersburg that he decided upon a career as a composer. He enrolled at first for night classes in harmony and composition at the St. Petersburg Conservatory of Music.

After two years of classes, Tchaikovsky resigned from the Ministry and concentrated full time on music. It was a risky step, since his father's financial condition was so poor that he could only provide a very meager board and room allowance for his son. Peter found it necessary to give music lessons to help augment his income. He studied harmony, counterpoint, and composition, the last with Anton Rubinstein. He graduated from the conservatory in 1865, winning a silver medal for his cantata *Hymn to Joy* based on Schiller's text.

The following year Nicholas Rubinstein, Anton's brother, invited Tchaikovsky to join the staff at the Moscow Conservatory of Music. The composer moved to Moscow and started to work on his first symphony, later subtitled *Winter Dreams*. The music did not come easily to him; he stayed awake nights worrying about it; he bordered on a nervous breakdown over its completion; and almost gave up composition as too strenuous for his nerves. When completed, the *Symphony No. 1* was to have been performed at the St. Petersburg Conservatory of Music by Anton Rubinstein, but the latter refused the work, so it was not performed until the following year in Moscow.

Now launched successfully on his career as a creative artist, Tchaikovsky in 1877 became involved with Antonina Milyukova, a young student at the conservatory who was madly in love with him. As Tchaikovsky later wrote in a letter,

> I married not through the urgings of the heart but through a set of circumstances I could not understand, and which forced on me an embarrassing set of alternatives. I had either to desert an honest girl whose love I had thoughtlessly encouraged, or marry her. I chose the latter. In the first place, it honestly seemed to me that I would fall in love with a girl who was so sincerely devoted to me; in the second place, I knew that my marriage was realizing the dreams of my old father and of friends close and dear to me.
>
> The moment the ceremony was over, and I found myself alone with my wife, and realized that our fate was to live inseparably with each other, I suddenly discovered that I did not even have ordinary feelings of friendship for her, but that she was *abhorrent* to me in the fullest sense of that word.[10]

A quick separation followed. In the same year Tchaikovsky became acquainted with Nadezhda von Meck, a rich widow who lived in Moscow. Mme. von Meck greatly admired the music of Tchaikovsky, and made some inquiries concerning his financial situ-

10. John Warrack, *Tchaikovsky* (New York, 1973), p. 115.

ation. When she learned that he was deeply in debt, she sent him a check for $3,000. She attached a strange condition to their relationship: she insisted that they must never meet nor know one another personally. "The more you fascinate me," she wrote, "the more I shrink from knowing you." Tchaikovsky accepted the money, and respected Nadezhda's wish. "I can only serve you," he wrote, "by means of music. Every note which comes from my pen in the future is dedicated to you!"

Although Mme von Meck promised Tchaikovsky a yearly allowance of about $6,000 "for life," the two met briefly only once or twice. But they wrote to each other frequently, and with the deepest intellectual and spiritual intimacy. Mme von Meck became for Tchaikovsky not only his financial backer but also a strong spiritual bene-factor until shortly before the composer's death, when she informed him that she could no longer support him. Tchaikovsky was convinced that her action was the result of learning of the nature of his sexual persuasion. Recent biographers have established however, that Mme von Meck had learned much earlier of the composer's homosexu-ality, and that she was actually in grave financial trouble at that time, being blackmailed by a son-in-law. Her granddaughter Galina asserts that von Meck and Tchaikovsky were reconciled before his death, a claim that has not yet been proved.

Bibliography

Abraham, Gerald, ed. *The Music of Tchaikovsky*. New York: W. W. Norton, 1974.
Warrack, John. *Tchaikovsky*. New York: Charles Scribner's Sons, 1973.

Symphony No. 5
by GUSTAV MAHLER

Gustav Mahler was one of the last great Romantic composers to become intimately involved in the symphonic idiom. He had inherited a form that had grown to immense proportions, a growth that had been started by Beethoven almost a century earlier. With his talent and ability, Mahler expanded the genre even further, enlarging the size of the orchestra to its very limits and increasing the length of the symphonic form.

Six out of the nine Mahler symphonies call for solo voices or chorus, *Symphony No. 8* alone calling for two large mixed choruses, a boys' chorus, eight solo voices, and a mammoth orchestra. (This symphony was called *The Symphony of a Thousand* at its pre-miere, since its first performance involved that many musicians.)

The structure of most Mahler symphonies is equally as gargantuan, some running to as many as six movements, and most of the symphonies lasting over an hour, the longest lasting an hour and forty minutes. Haydn's Classical symphonies, by contrast, last an average of eighteen minutes.

Mahler's nine symphonies (there is a tenth, which is incomplete) have been di-vided into three groups by his biographer Paul Stefan. The first four symphonies are subjective, representing a personal struggle against cosmic forces. The next four are the probings of a musician-philosopher seeking the answer to the riddle of the universe; the personal element is now gone. In *Symphony No. 9* the struggle with himself and the eternal verities is over. Mahler now divorces himself from the problems of the world. Resigned to them, he now seeks inner peace.

Although Mahler usually had a programmatic idea in mind when writing his symphonic works, he was always loath to reveal it to the public. He wanted his listeners to discover the program for themselves from the music. Either through the texts of the symphonies with voices or from Mahler's own prose writings, however, we do know most of the programs Mahler had in mind. Not so with the *Fifth Symphony*. Mahler's good friend and fellow conductor, Bruno Walter, has written:

> Nothing in any of my conversations with Mahler and not a single note point to the influence of extra-musical thoughts or emotions upon the composition of the *Fifth*. It is music, passionate, wild, pathetic, buoyant, solemn, tender, full of all the sentiments of which the human heart is capable, but still *only* music, and no metaphysical questioning, not even from very far off, interferes with its purely musical course.[11]

Mahler himself conducted the first performance of the *Fifth Symphony* at a concert in Cologne, Germany, in 1904. It was immediately called *The Giant Symphony* because of its proportions. It is written in three parts, with the first and last parts divided into two sections each. Thus we may think of the work as having five movements.

Adagietto

The fourth movement, *Adagietto,* is a tiny gem among huge giants. Only 103 measures long, it is scored for strings and harp alone.

LISTENING OUTLINE

Against sustained harmonies and quiet harp arpeggios, the violins play a long, lyrical melody that is the main theme of the movement. It begins:

Example 1

Reprinted by permission of C. F. Peters Corporation.

11. Bruno Walter, *Gustav Mahler,* trans. James Galston (New York, 1973).

Before the rather indefinite ending of the main theme, the cellos play it in augmentation. They do not complete a full statement of it.

After an episode (a brief section in which none of the melodic material appears), the violins take up the melody of Example 1 again, continuing it for ten measures more. The ending is played by the second violins.

The key changes, the pace becomes more animated. The harp is silent through the ensuing passage. The violins eventually introduce a contrasting theme:

Example 2

After a modulation returns the music to the original key, the second violins take up Example 1.

There is a pause on a long-sustained pitch; the cellos respond.

The violins take up the second strain of the main theme (Example 1), leaping to a theme that returns from the first movement (reminiscent of the rhythm of Beethoven's *Fifth Symphony*). After the dramatic *fortissimo* climax, the last chord slowly dies away into nothingness.

About the Composer

GUSTAV MAHLER   Born: July 7, 1860
                            Kalischt, Bohemia

                    Died: May 18, 1911
                            Vienna, Austria

The story has been told that when Mahler was about five years old, his father took him on one of their frequent walks in the forests surrounding their home. Before they had gone far, the elder Mahler remembered a chore to be done at the house. He seated the boy on a tree stump and told him to wait for his return. Unexpected visitors detained the father much longer than he had expected. On his return to the woods, he found Gustav still on the stump, but in a trance—silent and self-absorbed, staring into the deep of the forest as if fixed on some marvelous vision.

In a way, Mahler remained in this trance the rest of his life. His songs and symphonies are filled with a sense of nature. There are even passages in his scores marked

Wie ein Naturlaut ("like a sound of nature"). Certainly the sense of nature pervades *Symphony No. 3,* with its movement suggesting "what the forest tells me" and "what the twilight tells me."

Mahler had been born in Kalischt, a small provincial town in Bohemia, under circumstances that would seem unlikely to produce a world-famous composer. The second of twelve children in a poverty-stricken Jewish home—his father was an ill-paid coachman—Mahler grew up mostly in the small town of Iglau in what was then the Austrian province of Moravia. It was in that small town that he heard the marching bands and bugle calls of the local military garrison, sounds that later echoed in the scores of his symphonies. It was also in Iglau that he heard the special type of cowbell that he insisted be used in one of his later symphonies.

When his father became a tavernkeeper and had enough money to pay for piano lessons, Gustav was taken to a music teacher who was so impressed with the boy's talent that he later helped arrange for Gustav's entrance into the Vienna Conservatory of Music.

After graduation, Mahler took up duties as a conductor at small provincial theaters, most of them with woefully inadequate musical facilities. In spite of an arduous schedule of rehearsals and performances, Mahler spent every spare moment composing.

Finally, when he was twenty-eight, Mahler got his opportunity to be a real conductor. He was appointed artistic director of the Royal Opera in Budapest, Hungary. An assignment in Hamburg, Germany, followed, and then, at thirty-seven, Mahler became director of the Imperial Opera in Vienna, probably the most prestigious position in Europe at that time; he held it for the next ten years. Because no Jew could hold a high public office in the Austrian monarchy, Mahler had to submit to the formality of a religious conversion; he became a Roman Catholic in 1897.

After a visit to the United States in 1906, Mahler returned to New York as conductor of the New York Philharmonic Society in 1907; he also conducted at the Metropolitan Opera House that year. In 1908, he again came to New York to conduct the Philharmonic. Mahler returned to Vienna a very sick man at the end of the 1910–11 season. A rugged conducting schedule had taken its toll, and Mahler's efforts to find time to compose had used up whatever leisure moments he should have had. The composer died in Vienna on May 18, 1911, shortly after arriving there at the end of the season.

Bibliography

Gartenberg, Egon. *Mahler: The Man and His Music.* New York: Schirmer Books, 1978.

Walter, Bruno. *Gustav Mahler.* Revised, edited, and translated by Lotte Walter Lindt. New York: Alfred A. Knopf, 1958.

A great nationalist is one rooted in his own nation, but who grows beyond the limits of his own nation to give something to the whole of humanity.
Gustav Stresemann

NINE/
NATIONALISM

NATIONALISM was a movement that grew out of the mainstream of Romanticism in the last half of the nineteenth century. It was an attempt by a number of composers of various nationalities to affirm their national heritage in a conscious manner.

An awareness of nationalism in its broadest sense was awakened by the French Revolution and the Napoleonic wars (1789–1814). In many countries, resistance to the French armies helped local citizens develop a new patriotic fervor; they became aware of their own language and culture. Eventually this fervor led to the political unification of both Italy and Germany, which had previously been a group of principalities and city-states. There were also revolts against foreign rule in Poland and Bohemia (now part of Czechoslovakia).

In Russia, the freeing of the serfs (serfdom was a form of indentured slavery) in 1861 gave impetus to a national pride that had started to develop at least thirty years earlier. There was renewed interest in the folk legends and national heroes that had appeared in the writings of Alexander Pushkin. Nineteenth-century Russian novelists produced such masterpieces as *War and Peace* (Tolstoy) and *Crime and Punishment* (Dostoevsky), while the artist Ilya Efimovich Repin painted huge canvases depicting scenes of Russian peasant life. In Bohemia, a fight for independence from the Austro-Hungarian Empire inspired a strong movement to eradicate German as the language of newspapers, official documents, and school texts.

In music, Nationalism was a self-conscious and often aggressive movement. Although there had been composers who, out of their own heritage and national pride, had written works of a strong national flavor—Chopin's *Mazurkas* and *Polonaises* and Tchaikovsky's *1812 Overture*, for example—the composers we usually label *Nationalists* made a conscious effort to imbue their works with the flavor of their native land. There is, of course, a great deal of overlapping between these two groups, those with a national flavor in their music and those whom we call *Nationalists*.

Nationalism was accomplished in a number of different ways. Some composers used songs and dances of the people—folk dances and folk songs—as the basis for various compositions. Dvořák's *Slavonic Dances,* Edvard Grieg's *Norwegian Dances,* and Zoltan Kodály's *Variations on a Hungarian Folksong* are good examples.

Some composers based their works on folklore or the life of the peasantry. Good examples would include Rimsky-Korsakov's fairy-tale opera *The Golden Cockerel;* Carl Maria von Weber's *Der Freischütz (The Freeshooter),* an opera that deals with the devil and magical potions and bullets; and Bedřich Smetana's opera of peasant life, *The Bartered Bride.*

Many Nationalists were inspired by and based their compositions on the celebration of a national hero, an event, or the scenic beauty of their native land. Borodin wrote about the twelfth-century ruler Prince Igor and Mussorgsky of the czar Boris Godunov in the operas of those titles; Verdi wrote of the battle of Legnano in the opera of that name; and Smetana praised the beauty of his native Czechoslovakia in *The Moldau,* a tone poem that musically suggests that broad, beautiful river, which flows through Prague.

Because of political upheavals, the performance of some works was inhibited by the rulers and their censors. Names of noblemen and even the country of the setting had to be changed to effect a performance of some Verdi operas. Verdi's own name became an acronym in the Risorgimento, the fight to unite Italy and free it from Austrian, French, and Roman Catholic Church rule. "Viva V.E.R.D.I." stood for *Viva Vittorio Emmanuele, Re d'Italia* (Long Live Victor Emmanuel, King of Italy).

Jean Sibelius's symphonic poem *Finlandia* was not allowed to be played in Finland at the turn of the century when Finland was trying to gain its independence from czarist Russia. The Nazis forbade the performance of Chopin's polonaises in Poland and Smetana's *Moldau* in Czechoslovakia during the Second World War.

As a musical movement, Nationalism started in Russia with the works of Mikhail Glinka (1804–1857), who is known as the father of Russian national music. The first mention in his writing of this new trend occurs in a letter he wrote from Berlin in 1833

Ilya Repin, *Religious Procession in Kursk,* 1880, detail (Tretyakov State Gallery, Moscow). In this scene of an icon shrine carried through a wretched village, Repin seems to combine social comment about the degradation and misery of the Russian peasants with a tribute to official religion during a period of censorship and orthodoxy.

The National Theater, Prague, built to accommodate only Czech operas.

about his opera *A Life for the Czar,* on which he was then working. He said that "in every way it will be absolutely national—and not only the subject but the music."

In 1855 Glinka was visited by a boy of eighteen named Mili Balakirev, who was fascinated by the Russian influences in Glinka's compositions. A mathematician and physicist by training, Balakirev talked of developing a circle of composers dedicated to the creation of a truly Russian music. Although he composed very few works, this guiding spirit was able to attract into his circle four other composers of similar intentions. The first to join was César Cui, an army engineer, who in 1857 introduced into the circle an eighteen-year-old lieutenant from his regiment named Modest Mussorgsky. In 1861 Nikolay Rimsky-Korsakov, who was at that time a seventeen-year-old cadet at the naval academy, became a member of the group. The last to be admitted to this incredible group of composers was Alexander Borodin, a chemist and doctor of medicine. When he first appeared at a meeting at Balakirev's house, Balakirev said by way of introduction, "This is Chemistry! This is Medicine!"

The members of this circle were all amateurs. Not one had attended a conservatory of music; in fact, there was no conservatory in Russia before 1862. But in spite of their diverse backgrounds and lack of formal musical training, they had a native talent. After a concert of their music a few years later, the critic Vladimir Stasov called them "The Mighty Five" (see p. 78).

Bedřich Smetana was one of the early leaders of Nationalism in Czechoslovakia, where the movement culminated in the building of an opera house dedicated exclu-

King Dodon stands at the throne with his Princess; the Astrologer at left; the Golden Cockerel in the cage above. Scene from Rimsky-Korsakov's *Le Coq d'or,* New York City Opera production.

sively to the production of native Czech operas sung in the Czech language. In the northern countries of Europe there were trends toward Nationalism, too, but the split with the mainstream of Romanticism was not nearly as great. Nationalism influenced the music of Edvard Grieg in Norway, especially in his vocal compositions although to a certain degree in his piano and orchestral works as well. Jean Sibelius of Finland was quite Nationalistic in his early works; he returned to the absolute musical style of post-Romanticism in his later works but never quite obliterated the traces of his great patriotic spirit.

Le Coq d'or Suite
by NIKOLAY RIMSKY-KORSAKOV

Nikolay Rimsky-Korsakov, the youngest of The Mighty Five, was greatly attracted to the folk tales and legends of his native Russia. Mythological tales of Slavonic origin, combining poetical allegory with fantastic humor, fascinated him most. With only two exceptions, all of his operas (of which there are sixteen) are based upon national subjects, historical or legendary. Three of these operas as well as many of the composer's solo songs take their texts from Alexander Pushkin's dramatic settings.

Le Coq d'or is a case in point. It is an opera based on a satirical fairy tale by Pushkin. The story was adapted into an opera libretto by Vladimir Bielsky, who observed in the preface that "the purely human nature of Pushkin's *Golden Cockerel* (*Le Coq d'or*)—that instructive tragicomedy of the unhappy consequences following upon mortal passions and weaknesses—permits us to place the plot in any region and in any period." Some have thought that statement a rather feeble attempt to fool the censor.

Fool the censor it did not. Although a performance had been scheduled for the season of 1907, the year the opera was completed, the government censor was unfavorably impressed by the audacity Rimsky-Korsakov had shown in "satirizing the monarchy," and he forbade the production. Rimsky-Korsakov's death in 1908 was thought by some to have been hastened by the censor's prohibition of this, his final opera. The ban was lifted in 1909, and in September of that year the opera was presented for the first time in Moscow; the following year there were performances in St. Petersburg.

Four excerpts from the opera were arranged as a concert suite in accordance with the composer's intentions by Alexander Glazunov, a fellow composer and student of Rimsky-Korsakov.

The opera retells the story of *Le Coq d'or* with a good deal of charm and humor. In the stage presentation, an Astrologer steps before the curtain to introduce the audience to the tale that will follow, one that, he explains to the audience, he has created by magic.

The curtains part to reveal the palace of King Dodon, a senile old monarch who much prefers sleeping to governing. Unfortunately, war is imminent. The Astrologer appears and offers the King a very rare creature, a Golden Cockerel. Place it on the highest watchtower of the palace, the Astrologer says, and it will announce the approach of enemy troops long before that occurrence can be discovered in any other way. If no danger threatens, the Cockerel will so report and allow the King to go back to sleep. The King buys the Golden Cockerel from the Astrologer, offering to pay him later when the price is agreed upon.

The King places the Cockerel on the highest perch in the castle and goes to his chambers to sleep and dream of beautiful ladies. Soon the watchbird gives the alarm. Dodon rises and sends his army to protect the palace. He slumbers again and is once more roused. This time he rises, puts on his armor—which is rusty—and goes forth to meet the foe.

On reaching the battlefield, the King discovers the corpses of his own sons—the royal Princes—as well as those of most of his army strewn about. When the mist clears, he also discovers a tent from which steps a beautiful woman dressed in queenly robes. Dodon is captivated by her charm; he forgets all about the war and invites the queen to marry him. She accepts and the two, with their entourage, set off for the capital.

Now the Astrologer reappears and demands payment for the Cockerel: the Queen. The King refuses and is attacked and killed by the magic bird, who pecks a hole in the royal skull. Amid thunder and lightning, the Astrologer and the Queen vanish.

The Astrologer once again steps before the curtain and tells the audience not to mind all this because all the characters involved are just figments of the imagination. All, that is, except himself and the Queen!

Much of the music of *Le Coq d'or* is highly Russian in spirit. Many of its melodies, if not actual Russian folk songs, are folklike in nature. Made up of highly chromatic melodies and harmonies, some of the themes are based on the old Russian church modes —patterns somewhat similar to major and minor scales but with quite a different musical sound—of which the violin melody in Example 1 of the following listening outline is an example.

Marriage Feast and Lamentable Death of King Dodon

The music of the final movement of the orchestral suite from *Le Coq d'or* is made up of music from the third act of the opera and includes the wedding march and death of King Dodon (as the Cockerel pierces Dodon's brain with his beak).

LISTENING OUTLINE

A march rhythm is established immediately. A fanfare is played softly in turn by the trumpets and flutes, and the violins respond with a martial tune:

Example 1

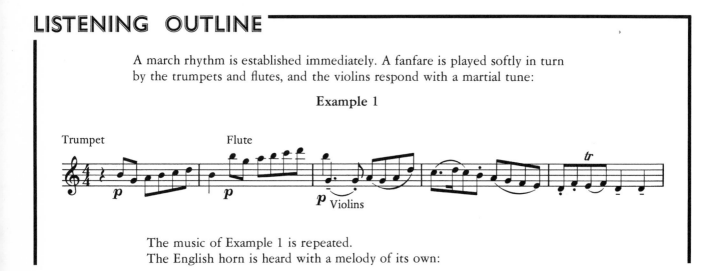

The music of Example 1 is repeated.
The English horn is heard with a melody of its own:

Example 2

English Horn

In an extended passage, the music becomes more intense; fragments of Example 1 are heard throughout it.

Violins, woodwinds, and French horns sound a motive suggestive of the principal melody (Example 4) soon to be heard:

Example 3

Violins, Upper Winds   French Horns

French horns are prominent in the ensuing passage.

A melodic fragment is repeated numerous times by lower strings and woodwinds. Although scalelike in nature, it is strictly Russian in flavor because it is based on a modal progression. Eventually the flute and piccolo play a variant of this melodic fragment above its repetition in the bass.

Trombones—in bold half notes—sound a solemn theme with bassoons, French horn, and lower strings. This too is modal in structure; it is made of rising and falling sevenths.

A moving figure that undulates up and down, played by horns and strings, is heard.

The principal theme of the movement is boldly stated by upper strings, woodwinds, and brass:

Example 4

Violins (octave higher), Upper Winds

The repeated melodic fragment heard earlier returns. Lower woodwinds, strings, and brass take up the rhythm figure ♩♫♩ over which flutes, piccolo, oboe, triangle, and violins play a repeated figure of their own (this figure was the one played at the very beginning by the cellos, which established the march rhythm). This leads to the final chords of the scene.

About the Composer

NIKOLAY RIMSKY-KORSAKOV Born: March 18, 1844
Tikhvin, Russia

Died: June 21, 1908
Liubensk, Russia

Nikolay Rimsky-Korsakov has been called the dean of that Nationalistic group of composers known as The Russian Five or The Mighty Five. He became in many ways the most important figure of that group. His interest in Russian music and Russian composers prompted him, as a conductor, to introduce many new works and new composers to the public both at home and abroad. In addition to this service to Russian music, Rimsky-Korsakov sought to complete and "correct" scores by some of his colleagues whom he thought had insufficient knowledge of the art of music. He revised scores by Borodin, Mussorgsky, and Glinka, among others. His revision of Mussorgsky's opera *Boris Godunov* proved very popular, although today we criticize him for reducing Mussorgsky's original harmonies and melodic lines to the academic standards of that time.

Rimsky-Korsakov's *Symphony No. 1,* completed after a naval cruise, was the earliest work of any importance in this form by a Russian composer. His *Collection of One Hundred Russian Folksongs* was one of the first efforts to preserve in systematic and written form the musical heritage of the Russian people. In addition to his own creations, Rimsky-Korsakov became the composition teacher of a number of young musicians who turned out to be excellent composers in their own right: Alexander Glazunov, Anatol Liadov, Anton Arensky, Mikhail Ippolitov-Ivanov, Alexander Gretchaninov, Alexander Tcherepnin, and Igor Stravinsky. Because of his mastery of orchestration, Rimsky-Korsakov's book on this subject is still one of the primary texts of the craft.

Rimsky-Korsakov had his troubles with the censors of his day. In 1895, troubles came about because his opera *Christmas Eve* had a scene in which the Russian empress Catherine the Great appeared; in 1905, performances of his works were forbidden for two months because he openly supported the student revolutionists; and with *Coq d'or,* the troubles came about because he tried to prevent the censor from altering some of Pushkin's lines that had political overtones. In 1905, he was dismissed from his professorship at the St. Petersburg Conservatory for publishing an article against police surveillance of students; he was not reinstated until the following autumn.

In his music, Rimsky-Korsakov was almost completely committed to program music—music based on, inspired by, and representative of Russian legends, fairy tales, and historical persons. "From earliest childhood I manifested musical abilities," Rimsky-Korsakov has told us in his autobiography.

We had an old piano; my father played by ear rather decently, though with no particular fluency. His repertory included a number of melodies from the operas of his time . . . Rossini and Mozart. . . . My father sang frequently, playing his own accompaniments.

The first indications of musical talent appeared in me at a very early age. I was not fully two years old when I distinguished all the tunes my mother sang to me. Later, when three or four years of age, I beat a toy drum in perfect time while my father played the piano. Often my father would suddenly change tempo and rhythm on purpose, and I at once followed suit. Soon afterward I began to sing correctly whatever my father played. . . . I could, from an adjoining room, recognize and name any note of the piano. When I was six, or thereabouts, they began to give me piano lessons. . . .

It cannot be said that I was fond of music at the time: I endured it and took barely sufficient pains with my studies. . . . I was eleven years old when I conceived the idea of composing a duet for voices with piano accompaniment. . . . I succeeded [and] I recall that it was sufficiently coherent. . . .

I was not studying music with any particular diligence, and was fascinated by the thought of becoming a seaman.[1]

At twelve years of age, Rimsky-Korsakov was enrolled by his parents in the naval college at St. Petersburg. He remained there six years. On Sundays and holidays he found time to take both cello and piano lessons, and it was during his early days at the college that he heard his first opera and attended his first symphony concert. As he had become acquainted with the music of Glinka through his piano studies at home, the appearance of some of Glinka's orchestral music on the programs in St. Petersburg renewed Rimsky-Korsakov's interest in the works of that Russian composer. He was soon spending all his pocket money purchasing scores of Glinka's works.

The year before Rimsky-Korsakov graduated from the naval college, he met Balakirev, who was then twenty-four and already important in the group of nationally inspired composers who were to become The Mighty Five. Rimsky-Korsakov was just beginning to get seriously interested in music through conversations and meetings with this young group when it came time for graduation. The navy assigned him to the ship *Almaz,* which was scheduled for a three-year voyage around the world. He took leave of his friends and sailed from Russia. Aboard the ship he worked on his first symphony, a work that proved difficult for him as he had not had any theoretical training. When the voyage was over he returned to St. Petersburg, where he remained, as his duties for the navy became largely clerical. He renewed his musical acquaintances. His symphonic poem *Sadko* and opera *The Maid of Pskov* date from these years.

Later works by which Rimsky-Korsakov is well known today include the opera *The Snow Maiden,* the symphonic suite *Scheherezade* (probably his best-known work), and the *Russian Easter Overture.* He also wrote songs, piano works, and chamber music.

---

1. Nikolay Rimsky-Korsakov, *My Musical Life,* trans. J. A. Joffe (New York, 1942).

Bibliography

Calvocoressi, Michael D., and Abraham, Gerald. *Masters of Russian Music.* New York: Alfred A. Knopf, 1936. Reprint edition, New York: Johnson Reprints, 1971.

Rimsky-Korsakov, Nikolai A. *My Musical Life.* Translated by Judah A. Joffe. Edited by Carl van Vechten. New York: Alfred A. Knopf, 1942. Reprint edition, New York: Vienna House, 1972.

Prince Igor

by ALEXANDER BORODIN

Dr. Alexander Borodin was by profession a research chemist, by hobby a composer. Like the other members of The Mighty Five, Borodin never received any formal training in composition even though he had a natural aptitude for it. Because Borodin was an expert in his professional field (he was noted for his investigation of the products of condensation of the aldehydes of valerian, enantol, and vinegar) and because he was such a dedicated and active teacher at the academy of medicine and surgery in St. Petersburg, he had little time left for musical composition. His list of works in music is pitifully small, but each is of highest quality: one "opera-farce," three incomplete operas (of which *Prince Igor* is one), two symphonies plus a sketch for a third, a few songs, some piano music, and fewer than a dozen pieces of chamber music.

Borodin described *Prince Igor* as "essentially a national opera, interesting only to us Russians, who love to steep our patriotism in the sources of our history, and to see the origins of our nationality on the stage." He began work on the opera in 1869, using a sketch furnished him by his friend the music critic and writer Vladimir Stasov, who in turn had taken the story from an old national poem, *The Epic of Igor's Army.* The story deals with a twelfth-century expedition of the Russian Prince Igor against the Polovetsi, a nomadic people somewhat akin to the ancient Turks, who have invaded the Russian territory to the east. Igor has been taken captive, but Khan Kontchak, the magnanimous ruler of the Polovetsi, treats him with the utmost cordiality and hospitality, even giving a banquet in the prince's honor. The feast is followed by entertainment that features dances by both the Polovetsian warriors and their womenfolk.

Although Borodin started work on *Prince Igor* as early as 1869, when he was thirty-six, it remained unfinished at his death eighteen years later. This long period of work is best explained in a letter Borodin wrote.

> When you ask about [Prince Igor] I have to laugh at myself. It always reminds me of the magician Finn in [the opera] *Ruslan,* who, though consumed with passionate love for Naina, forgets that time is passing, and cannot bring himself to decide his fate until both he and his betrothed have grown grey with age. I am like him in attempting to write a heroic Russian opera while time

The Prince is captivated by one of the Polovetsian maidens during the *Polovetsian Dances.* Borodin's *Prince Igor,* New York City Opera production.

flies by with the speed of an express train. Days, weeks, months, whole winters pass without my being able to get to work seriously. It isn't that I could not find a couple of hours a day, but because I do not have the leisure of mind to withdraw from occupations and preoccupations that have nothing to do with music.

One must have time to concentrate, to get into the right mood, or else the creation of a sustained work is impossible. For this I have only part of the summer at my disposal. In the winter I can compose only when I am ill and have to give up my lectures and laboratory work. So, reversing the usual custom, my friends never say to me, "I hope you are well," but "I hope you are ill." During Christmas I had influenza and could not go to the laboratory. I stayed home and wrote the Thanksgiving Chorus for the last act of *Igor.* I also wrote Yaroslavna's lament when I was slightly ill.

In all, I have written one act and a half out of four. I am satisfied with what I have done, and my friends are too. The Thanksgiving Chorus, performed by the orchestra of the Free School, was a great success and it is a significant omen for the rest of the work.

As a composer who seeks to remain anonymous, I am shy about confessing my musical activity. This is understandable enough. For others it is their chief business, their occupation and aim in life. For me it is relaxation, a pastime that distracts me from my principal business, my professorship. . . . I love my profession and my science, the Academy and my students. My teaching is of a practical nature and therefore takes up much of my time. I have to be constantly in touch with my pupils, male and female, because in order to direct the work of young people one must always be close to them. I have the interests of the Academy at heart. If, on the one hand I want to complete my opera, on the other hand I am afraid of devoting myself to it too assiduously and thus throwing my scientific work into the shadow.[2]

Polovetsian Dances

In the second act of *Prince Igor* there are several wild, barbaric dances, performed by the Polovetsian tribesmen at the festival Khan Konchak creates for the entertainment of Prince Igor. As an orchestral suite, these *Polovetsian Dances* appear frequently on concert programs. To make the music for these dances as well as for other sections of the opera accurate in every detail, Borodin undertook extensive research. History, archaeology, folk music—all were checked carefully and every discovery carefully studied so that not merely the superficial atmosphere of the time should be reproduced, but its essential spirit made, as far as possible, to live again. And in Borodin's music, that ancient spirit of barbarism, that haunting loneliness of the vast steppes and their nomadic warriors, comes to life again.

Borodin had a natural affinity for pursuing this course, for he was himself the descendant of princes—Caucasian princes. Both in his personal appearance and in his music, there was always a blend of the heroic and Oriental elements.

The *Polovetsian Dances* vary in tempo, rhythm, and symbolism. There are dances of wild men, of young girls and boys, of slave girls and prisoners, dances in praise of the khan, and a wild general dance involving the most vigorous, repetitive rhythms.

Presto

LISTENING OUTLINE

Upper strings and bass drum take up a repeated rhythm pattern.

A descending four-note figure played twice by bassoon and *pizzicato* strings leads to a spirited melody, a rhythmical duet between oboe and clarinet:

2. Letter to Lyubov Ivanovna Karmalina (a singer), dated Moscow, June 1, 1876, quoted in *A. P. Borodin* by S. Dianin (Moscow: State Musical Publication, 1955).

Example 1

In an extended passage, many repetitions of the melodic figures in Example 1 are heard. Sometimes the statements are answered by a descending, highly chromatic figure. Trills in the upper strings are heard toward the end of this passage.

The rhythmic pattern of the introduction returns. Repetitions of Example 1 are heard again. Gradually the music becomes softer and softer.

The tempo changes to *Moderato*. The oboe introduces one of Borodin's most famous melodies:

Example 2

The oboe repeats the melody of Example 2; the English horn responds with a variant of it at a lower pitch level.

The violins, in a passage marked *Cantabile assai* (very "singingly"), repeat the melody of Example 2.

After a brief transitional passage, the oboe takes up the opening figure of Example 2.

The tempo accelerates; the introductory rhythm pattern is heard again.

The melody of Example 1, the duet for oboe and clarinet, is heard again.

The following section resembles that which preceded Example 2.

Another transition passage occurs.

In a section marked *Allegro con spirito* (fast, with spirit), flutes, oboes, and clarinets take up a fast-moving, highly chromatic melody:

Example 3

Flutes, Oboes, Clarinets

Repetitions of Example 3 follow.

A highly rhythmic passage follows, one characterized by many repetitions of a descending three-note figure.

As the music builds dynamically, sweeping runs in the upper woodwinds and strings are heard and lead to the final cadence of the dance.

About the Composer

ALEXANDER BORODIN
Born: November 12, 1833
St. Petersburg, Russia

Died: February 27, 1887
St. Petersburg, Russia

Alexander Borodin was a man of contrasts. A chemist by profession, he was exacting in his scientific research. A musician by inclination, he was genial, easygoing, and most indifferent to unessentials. A sense of humor pervaded all his work, whether scientific or musical. This trait is characterized by his composition *Paraphrases*. One day his adopted daughter wanted him to sit down and play the piano with her, but, she confessed, her knowledge of piano literature was limited to the ability to play *Chopsticks* with one finger of each hand. The genial father sat at the keyboard with her and improvised a polka accompaniment to the only melody in her repertoire. When Borodin told Rimsky-Korsakov about this with enthusiasm, the latter decided to compose some variations on the tune also. Cui and Liadov were persuaded to join the fun and, when the collection was published, it was brought to the attention of Franz Liszt; he was so fascinated by it that he wrote a prelude to it for its second edition.

Alexander Borodin was the illegitimate son of Prince Luke Ghedeanov, a sixty-one-year-old descendant of former kings of the Caucasus, and Avdotia Kleineke, a middle-class young woman of twenty-four. As was the custom of the time, the child was christened for propriety's sake as the son of one of the prince's serfs, Porphiry Borodin. The prince died when Alexander was seven, and he was raised by his mother, a woman of culture and intelligence. With tutoring, the boy was soon proficient in English, French, and German, and a little later in Italian. The boy had keen interests in both music and the natural sciences.

Borodin's first musical experiences were in listening to band concerts. At nine he thought he had fallen in love with a grown woman and composed a polka dedicated to her. According to musical authorities, this composition is more striking for its originality than for its childishness. Because of the polka and the boy's interest in music, lessons were quickly arranged; his teacher was the flutist in the military band. Soon Borodin was to receive piano lessons as well. By the time he was fourteen, his interests both in music and in science were well in evidence: he had composed a number of chamber works, and his room at home had been converted into a laboratory in which he experimented with chemicals, making his own fireworks. Other hobbies included modeling and painting, for which he made his own pigments.

At seventeen, Borodin entered the academy of medicine and surgery, where he specialized in botany and chemistry, eventually limiting his studies to chemistry alone. While attending the academy, he studied the art of the fugue at home and met with a group of string players periodically. The quartet met some seven miles from his home, and he trudged on foot carrying his cello with him to rehearsals in fair weather and foul because he could not afford cab fare. Borodin was a not-very-skilled cellist, and he usually listened to the others play. He would sometimes join in, however, if a fifth player was needed for the music.

After completing his training at the academy, he was appointed assistant to the professor of pathology and therapeutics, and in 1857 he traveled to Belgium as a companion of a prominent oculist to attend a scientific congress. He received his doctorate of medicine shortly after this, having served as a house physician in a hospital that treated serfs. The dressing of wounds displeased him so much that once he graduated, he restricted himself to laboratory work.

In 1859 his journeys for scientific research took him to Heidelberg, Germany, for a winter, Italy and Switzerland for a summer, then back to Heidelberg via Paris. During his stay in the German city, he heard many concerts and met Catherine Protopopova, who was to become his wife in 1863. She was a fine pianist, and through her Borodin became fascinated with the piano works of Chopin and Schumann. Together Borodin and his wife traveled to Mannheim to hear some of the operas of Richard Wagner.

In 1862 Borodin met Balakirev and became his pupil. Borodin's musical interests continued, even though the major portion of his time was occupied by his position as assistant professor of organic chemistry at the academy.

Although Borodin's musical output was small, he remains an important figure in the musical world. He was the first Russian composer to achieve an international reputation. This was probably due in part to his feeling for rhythm and orchestral color. His chromaticism and his skillful use of discords show not only in the instrumental music but also in his songs. He created, notably in his *Second Symphony,* a new type of first-movement form (monothematic, based on development of a single initial theme). He wrote in a lyric and epic-heroic style. Borodin's writing strongly influenced several major composers of the twentieth century: Debussy, Ravel, Sibelius, and Stravinsky.

Bibliography

Abraham, Gerald. *Borodin: the Composer and His Music.* London: William Reeves, 1927.

Calvocoressi, Michael D., and Abraham, Gerald. *Masters of Russian Music.* Reprint of 1936 edition. New York: Johnson Reprints, 1971.

The Bartered Bride

by BEDŘICH SMETANA

The resurgence of interest in both political and artistic freedom that occurred in Bohemia during the last half of the nineteenth century was a nationalistic fervor similar to that which had evolved earlier in Russia. In Russia, the liberation of the serfs had given impetus to the nationalistic movement; in Bohemia, the Czechs were attempting to liberate themselves from foreign rule. Both Russia and Bohemia had been under domination, too, of foreign cultures for an extended period of time: the Russians because the nobility elected to speak French, the Czechs because they were forced to speak German.

From a very early period, music held a central place in the ancient kingdom of Bohemia. As it came to be surrounded by lands of the German empire, Bohemian culture—including music—was strongly influenced by German traditions. The ground was, therefore, already paved for a nationalistic movement in music by the time a composer of such gifts as Bedřich Smetana appeared on the scene. Antonin Dvořák, whose *Slavonic Dances* we studied in Part I, was seventeen years Smetana's junior and also interested and active in establishing a Czech national school of music.

By 1862, the Czech Provisional Theater had been built for the exclusive purpose of presenting operas by Czech composers to be sung in the native Czech language. (It was followed later by the building of a permanent National Theater.) Smetana devoted himself to composing a repertory of such operas, starting with *The Brandenburgers in*

The villagers dance the polka to celebrate the wedding. Smetana's *Bartered Bride,* American Opera Center production.

Bohemia, to a text by Karel Sabina, who also supplied the libretto for *The Bartered Bride.*

Although Smetana thought *The Bartered Bride* the most trivial of his Czech operas, it is the one by which he is best known throughout the world of music. The Czech National Theater alone has presented it more than 2,500 times.

The Bartered Bride is a comedy, its locale a small village somewhere in Bohemia. The story is quite a complicated one, involving a case of mistaken identity. The opera's hero is a peasant named Jenik whose parents are unknown. He has been living in the village for some time, but will not even tell his sweetheart Mařenka about his past, except that he was driven from his home by an unpleasant stepmother. Mařenka is troubled, for her parents are arranging a marriage for her through the pompous marriage broker Kezal. The broker's choice, it turns out, is Vasek, the dimwitted son of Micha, a well-to-do peasant. Mařenka, of course, protests; she will marry no one but her beloved Jenik. To her consternation and that of the entire village, Jenik seems willing to barter her for 300 gulden promised to him by Kezal.

Jenik signs a contract promising to give up Mařenka but insists that it include a clause stating that Mařenka must marry no one but Micha's eldest son. Naturally Kezal agrees, since that is precisely the arrangement he has in mind. At the last moment, when Mařenka has given up Jenik as a mercenary cad and agreed, in anger, to marry the dimwitted Vasek, Jenik discloses that he is Micha's older son. Kezal admits defeat, Mařenka falls into Jenik's arms, and old Micha, glad to have his son home again, blesses the pair. The village peasants—who throughout the opera have been dancing polkas and furiants, drinking great quantities of pivo (the Czech word for beer), and commenting on the events—join in a chorus wishing long life and happiness to the bartered bride.

Polka

During the introduction to the dance, (from Act I), there is a flurry on stage as the older people find seats under the trees in order to watch the young dancers.

LISTENING OUTLINE

In the introduction, strings, horns, and timpani are prominent.
The first of several tunes is introduced by the clarinets and violins:

Example 1

Clarinets, Violins

Following several repetitions of Example 1, the strings introduce a quieter theme:

Example 2

Violins

The theme of Example 2 then becomes the accompaniment to the melody of Example 3:

Example 3

Flute

The strings play a new melody (Example 4), which is lighter in nature, softer and more *staccato.* It is based on the rhythm pattern of Example 2.

Example 4

Violins

The opening melody (Example 1) returns, now livelier than ever. In the original version for stage performance, the villagers join in singing this rousing climax to the dance:

Join our dancing, swaying, dancing
While the tuneful polka's playing;
Cheek to cheek with hand in hand
Twirling to the village band!

Basses growling, cymbals clinking,
'Round our ears the music's tinkling.
Though for quiet we may strive
'Neath our feet the earth's alive.

About the Composer

BEDŘICH SMETANA

Born: March 2, 1824
Litomyšl, Bohemia

Died: May 12, 1884
Prague, Bohemia

At age sixteen, Bedřich Smetana started to keep a diary. In it he said of his childhood: "I was born in Bohemia, the son of a master brewer. I was not quite four when my father taught me how to keep time to music. At five I started to school and studied the piano and violin. I was seven when I first performed in public."

Although Smetana's parents disliked the idea of their son preparing for a career in music, which they thought fine for a hobby but not for earning money, he pursued music as his major interest throughout his schooldays.

After graduation, Smetana confided to his diary that his ambition in life was to become "a Mozart in composition and a Liszt in technique." With a total sum of twenty gold florins from his father, he set out for Prague to become a professional musician.

In Prague, Smetana continued his studies with a renowned teacher, on credit. Before long, Smetana obtained a good position teaching and directing music in the household of the immensely rich Count Thun. Although it was a secure, well-paying position, Smetana was unhappy serving in the home of a German aristocrat and quit the position in 1848.

With money provided by Hungarian pianist-composer Franz Liszt, Smetana opened his own music school. Smetana's compositions were becoming comparatively well known, and he could now afford to marry his childhood sweetheart Kateřina Kolař.

After a number of years, the music school started bringing in less and less income. When Smetana was offered the position of music director of the Philharmonic Society in Göteburg, Sweden, he accepted it, closed his music school, and moved to Sweden. While there, he composed a number of works, none of which showed any trace of his Bohemian ancestry.

During the early part of his tenure in Sweden, Smetana's wife died suddenly. Within a year, the lonely composer found and married another attractive Czech girl, Barbara Fernandini. She, however, disliked Sweden, her homesickness eventually forcing Smetana to give up his position and return to Prague.

At home once more, Smetana became active in the musical life of Prague. He took part in founding the Society of Artists, became prominent as a conductor, contributed criticism to the paper *Národní Listy,* and took over the concerts of the Hlahol Choral Society, a nationalistic group. He then composed his first unmistakably Czech music, a male chorus entitled *The Three Horsemen.* It graphically pictured the triumphant defiance of the Czech people on receiving the news that their leader Jan Hus was burned at the stake. Another chorus, *The Renegade,* was a fierce condemnation of all those who sell out their country or turn their backs on it. Closer to the mature style and spirit of Smetana's creative efforts is the long, descriptive choral piece called *Česká píseň* (Czech Song), a loving hymn to the countryside of Bohemia and its seasonal changes.

With preliminary sketches like these, Smetana was preparing himself for his true work—opera, a form to which he devoted the major part of his efforts for the balance of his creative career.

Unjustly criticized for his use of leitmotives and for an elaborate treatment of the orchestra, Smetana was accused by many of attempting to "Wagnerize" the Czech national opera with works such as *Dalibor*—an opera based on the tragic, semilegendary Czech liberator-leader Dalibor. Such opposition lasted for ten years, and is believed to have preyed on Smetana's mind to the point that it brought on a nervous disorder and breakdown, followed by deafness and death in an asylum. After 1874, when deafness forced him to resign as a conductor, he nevertheless composed two operas (one incomplete at his death), his *String Quartet No. 2,* and the crowning achievement of his orchestral repertory, six pieces (including *The Moldau*) bearing the collective title *Ma Vlast* (*My Country*).

Bibliography

Bartos, Frantisek. *Bedřich Smetana: Letters and Reminiscences.* Translated by D. Rusbridge. Prague: Artia, 1955.

Nejedly, Zdenek. *Frederick Smetana.* London: Geoffrey Bles, 1924.

Who will discover the secret of musical composition? The sound of the sea, the curve of the horizon, the wind in the leaves . . . register complex impressions within us. Then suddenly, without any deliberate consent on our part, one of these memories issues forth to express itself in the language of music.

Claude Debussy

TEN/ IMPRESSIONISM

ALTHOUGH it is a term used in the field of music, *Impressionism* is an expression borrowed from the world of art. The word was first employed by a newspaper critic to describe the style of painting observed in the canvases of Claude Monet at the Paris Exhibit of 1874. The word was actually taken from the title of one of Monet's paintings: *Impression—Soleil levant* (*Impression: Sunrise*).

The artist Claude Monet (1840–1926) and his colleagues Édouard Manet (1832–1883), Edgar Degas (1834–1917), and Auguste Renoir (1841–1919) revolted against the detailed realism of nineteenth-century Romantic painting and concerned themselves with representing on canvas "fleeting glimpses" or first impressions. Rather than trying to provide a photographic likeness of a subject, these artists attempted to suggest an impression of it, what the viewer might see at a hasty glance.

These Impressionist artists, active in Paris during the last half of the nineteenth century, preferred common subjects—still lifes, dancing girls, nudes, scenes of middle-class life such as picnics, boating and cafés—in opposition to the grandiose, drama-packed scenes and heroic subjects of their Romantic predecessors. The Impressionists were concerned with color, light, and shade.

At first the public was offended by this emerging style. It was upset by "grass that was pink, yellow or blue," and used *Impressionism* as a term of derision, of ridicule.

A similar revolt against realism occurred in the 1880s among certain French poets. Known as *Symbolists,* they attempted to suggest a fantasy of imagination rather than describe in detail; they abandoned rhyme and traditional forms; they used a word for its color or flavor rather than for its specific meaning. They preferred to present the symbol rather than to state the thing; to experiment with new sounds and sonorities. Important poets of the Symbolist school included Charles Baudelaire (1821–1867), Stéphane Mallarmé (1842–1898), Paul Verlaine (1844–1896), Arthur Rimbaud (1854–1891), and the Belgian poet Maurice Maeterlinck (1862–1949).

In music, the revolt was centered in Paris and led by Claude Debussy. He attempted to suggest scenes of nature in music—*Springtime* (1887), *Clouds* (1893), *The Sea* (1903–05), *Moonlight* (the well-known *Clair de lune,* 1890), and *Gardens in the Rain* (1903) among other titles—by replacing dynamic development with a succession of orchestral or pianistic colors; he created music that was at once vague, intangible and misty.

Debussy achieved his musical objectives through a new and different concept of form. Themes or musical subjects were no longer of conventional length and symmetry; rather, thematic fragments or short musical figures were used and became patterns. New chordal combinations became common, including chords with added tones (a ninth, eleventh, and thirteenth above the root of the chord [p. 58]); and parallel chords were frequently employed—chords that glide up and down the keyboard. Chords with unresolved dissonances (see p. 62) were another characteristic.

The use of scales other than the traditional major and minor was common among these composers. Debussy used the whole-tone scale, which was alien to the most im-

Claude Monet, *Impression: Sunrise*, 1872 (Musee Marmottan, Paris).

portant aspects of nineteenth-century harmony.[1] The whole-tone scale, along with the use of medieval modes and Oriental scale patterns, imparted a floating, nondirectional quality to the music.

Although music critics referred to this emerging style of Debussy's compositions as Impressionism, Debussy seriously objected to this label. He thought Symbolism more appropriate, for he felt his music followed the aesthetic concepts of the Symbolist poets: it was a music that hinted rather than stated, a music that was concerned with the effects of orchestral sound more than with the development of a musical subject.

The ethereal quality of Impressionism is best in evidence in the compositions of Debussy and Maurice Ravel. It is achieved through the discreet use of orchestral (or pianistic) timbres; that is, by instrumentation—important use of the harp; careful use of percussion instruments of color: the celesta, the triangle, the tambourine, orchestral bells. The timbre of woodwinds is featured, the flute in particular. Drums, when used, are often muffled, and trumpets and trombones frequently muted. String parts are di-

1. The whole-tone scale is made up of tones each one whole step apart, that is, C–D–E–F$^{\sharp}$–G$^{\sharp}$–A$^{\sharp}$–C.

vided into four, eight, or even ten sections. Human voices are used on occasion, usually singing neutral syllables and employed like another orchestral instrument, another tone color in the orchestral palette.

Maurice Ravel cannot be classified as a true disciple of Debussy-style Impressionism, however. His reliance on clear, metrical rhythms and strong cadences and his easily discerned phrase structure and overall form are more in keeping with the earlier, more traditional style of composition. Others who used certain aspects of Impressionism in their compositions included, in France, Albert Roussel and Jacques Ibert; in England, Frederick Delius and Cyril Scott; in the United States, Charles Tomlinson Griffes and John Alden Carpenter; in Spain, Manuel de Falla; and in Italy, Ottorino Respighi.

When Stravinsky's ballet *The Firebird* was first presented in Paris during the season of 1910, the death knell of Impressionism started to ring. Strangely enough, the revolt against Impressionism was also centered largely in Paris. Like Beethoven in an earlier era, Debussy has become a pivotal figure. Impressionism was rooted in antagonism toward Romanticism, yet viewed now from a distance, it is thought by many critics and historians to be the last phase of Romanticism, a *fin de siècle* movement. With

Édouard Manet, *Monet Working in his Houseboat,* 1874 (Neue Pinakothek, Munich). One Impressionist has portrayed another at work, and in a typical setting.

the new music, the twentieth-century music of Stravinsky, Schoenberg, and Bartók, appearing on the musical horizon between 1910 and 1920, and with Debussy's death in 1918, Impressionism had reached its apex. In the words of French poet and novelist Jean Cocteau: "After the music with the silken brush, the music with the axe."

Fêtes

by CLAUDE DEBUSSY

Fêtes is the second movement of an orchestral triptych entitled *Nocturnes,* and is the work that firmly established Debussy as a composer to be regarded with respect. To be sure, his work had achieved success prior to the *Nocturnes,* which date from 1900, but it was this music that made believers out of many musicians and critics who previously had been unwilling to admit the worth of Debussy's music.

Although the composer disliked program notes that attempted to explain musical compositions, feeling that they tended to "destroy the mystery" of the music, Debussy published the following lines in order to define the meaning of the title he had chosen and to explain his artistic intention.

> The title *Nocturnes* is to be interpreted here in a general and, more particularly, in a decorative sense. Therefore, it is not meant to designate the usual form of the Nocturne, but rather all the various impressions and the special effects of light that the word suggests. . . . *Fêtes* gives us the vibrating, dancing rhythm of the atmosphere with sudden flashes of light. There is also the episode of the procession (a dazzling fantastic vision) which passes through the festive scene and becomes merged in it. But the background remains persistently the same: the festival with its blending of music and luminous dust participating in the cosmic rhythm.[2]

LISTENING OUTLINE

Fêtes opens brilliantly with a rhythmical, two-measure introduction in hollow-sounding chords:

Example 1

---

2. Lawrence Gilman, *Orchestral Music: An Armchair Guide* (New York, 1951), pp. 140–41.

The English horn and clarinets play the first theme over a continuation of the rhythmical pattern of Example 1:

Example 2

English Horn, Clarinets

After two measures in which the rhythm of Example 1 is heard by itself *pianissimo,* the flutes and oboes play a modified version of Example 2. Another modification of Example 2 is then played by the bassoons and cellos.

Trombone, tuba, bassoons, and basses sound a *fortissimo* D-flat; the trumpets and the other two trombones play a bold, rhythmical figure:

Example 3

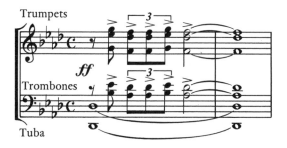

After a harp *glissando* (a rapid scalelike effect produced by sliding the fingers across the strings) the tonality changes. The woodwinds play a figure in ⁱ⁵⁄₈ meter:

Example 4

Woodwinds

The strings take up an abbreviated form of Example 4 in ⁹⁄₈ meter while the oboes and flutes play a melody (Example 5) that is similar to Example 2.

Example 5

Flute, Oboe

Examples 4 and 5 are repeated in turn.
The French horns and bassoons play a bold figure:

Example 6

French Horns

After three measures, the English horn plays an ascending passage that is answered by the oboes with a descending passage. These measures are difficult to hear because of the texture of the music. Each of these two passages is repeated in turn.

Example 7

English Horn

Two measures later, Example 6 appears in the upper strings in a different tonality; it is repeated by the lower strings.

The oboe introduces a melody characterized by the interval between A and C:

Example 8

Oboe

Example 8 is repeated a third higher by the flutes and clarinets.

In the woodwinds, Example 9 (against a rhythmical string accompaniment) is heard three times (the third is an inversion), continually growing louder.

Example 9

Flutes, Oboes, Clarinet

mf sempre cresc.

A sudden *piano* marks the repetition by the clarinets and bassoons of Figure A from Example 8. This is followed by a variant of Example 9 played by the oboes and English horn (a fifth higher this time).

This alternation of Figure A from Example 8 and Example 9 is repeated twice with slight alterations—the first time softly, the second time loudly.

The insistent repetition of a triplet figure grows louder and louder.

Suddenly the orchestra is quiet except for a soft, rhythmical pulsation by the *pizzicato* strings, harp, and timpani. In duple meter, the approach "of the procession . . . which passes through the festival scene" (to quote the score) is heralded.

Example 10

Harp

ppp

Timpani

ppp

The muted trumpets begin the fanfare theme of the procession:

Example 11

Trumpets (muted)

pp

This is immediately repeated by the woodwinds. It gradually grows louder. The French horns and woodwinds alternately play a figure from Example 11.

The military drum is heard with an insistent figure:

The trumpets and trombones play the fanfare theme (Example 11) while the violins and violas repeat a passage derived from Example 2; this mingling of the two themes suggests "the procession which passes through the festive scene and becomes merged in it. But the background remains persistently the same."

Suddenly the volume decreases to a *pianissimo* as flutes play a modified version of Example 2. This is repeated with a gradual crescendo.

The violins play an insistently repeated motive that builds to *fff:*

Example 12

Again the dynamic level drops to *pianissimo;* the figure of Example 4 (in ⅝ meter) is repeated. Example 5 is then heard in the flutes and oboes. Examples 4 and 5 are repeated in succession.

A variant of Example 8 appears in the upper woodwinds over a pulsating figure in the strings and horns.

The fervor decreases, and fragments of Example 8 appear in the bassoons and oboes, answered by fragments of the fanfare theme (Example 11) played by the flutes and brass.

The lower strings continue the pulsating rhythm, but the vitality seems to be waning. The merrymakers are gone, and the festival vision becomes only a memory.

A melancholy theme is played by the oboe and repeated by the flute:

Example 13

Figure B from Example 13 is repeated alternately by oboe, bassoon, oboe, bassoon.

In the twenty-measure coda, the music gradually fades away to a *ppp*. The soft, rhythmical beating of the military drum is heard, leading to the final *pizzicato* chords in the lower strings.

About the Composer

CLAUDE DEBUSSY   Born: August 22, 1862
St. Germain-en-Laye, France

Died: March 25, 1918
Paris, France

During Debussy's happiest days he was frequently seen in the cafés of Montmartre in Paris—the Chat Noir, the Chez Weber, or the Brasserie Pousset. He could always be recognized by the flowing cape he wore, his broad-brimmed hat, and his black beard. Many times the candles on the café tables burned past midnight as he and his artistic friends—writers and painters—discussed both art and current events.

Although Debussy's piano compositions are among his best-known works, his friends claimed that, in the evenings, when Debussy sat for long periods of time at the keyboard of some tired old piano in one of these cafés, his improvisations far exceeded the beauty of his published compositions.

Born of poor parents in a little second-floor apartment above his father's china shop in St. Germain-en-Laye, a suburb about a half-hour's drive from Paris, the boy at first showed no interest in music. His godmother arranged for his first piano lessons; the teacher claimed that the lad had no ear for music, since he banged away at the piano, caring little for tone quality or subtlety in the musical interpretation. By the time he was eleven, Claude was enrolled at the Paris Conservatory of Music, where he studied piano, eighteenth-century harmony, early nineteenth-century form, Classical counterpoint, and other related traditions. He was the problem child of the conservatory and had an erratic record because he objected to the accepted theories of harmony and composition. His fellow students found him both uncouth and sarcastic.

The conservatory's highest award was the *Prix de Rome* (see p. 34), given annually to a student for the best composition of the year. The winner was entitled to three years of study free of charge at the French Academy in Rome. In three years of submitting compositions for consideration, Debussy received a no mention, a fourth place, and a second place. He finally decided to write a work in a more conventional form to

please the judges. Although it is one of his less important and least interesting works, his cantata *L'Enfant prodigue* (*The Prodigal Son*) did win him the first prize.

Debussy was not favorably impressed by the French Academy in Rome. "It would be idle to imagine that new theories of art could evolve here," he wrote home. "This is the home of mediocre art. I have tried to work, but haven't been able to. This just is not the place for me!" Before his three years of study were up, he quit the academy in disgust. "I could no longer drag out a monstrous, easy life. In Rome, I could come to nothing, my musical mind was dead."

Back home in Paris, Debussy listened to the world of music around him, searching for his own idiom of expression. "Music until the present day," he said, "has rested on a false principle. There is too much *writing* of music. Music is made for its effect on paper although it is intended for the ear. Too much importance is attached to the writing of music, the formula, the craft. Composers seek their ideas within themselves when they should look around for them." At another time he said, "I am all for liberty. Music is by its very nature free. Every sound you hear around you can be reproduced. Everything that a keen ear perceives in the rhythm of the surrounding world can be represented musically. To some people rules are of primary importance, but my desire is to reproduce only what I hear."

Debussy learned art and music from every conceivable source around him. In addition to the influences of the art nouveau style, and jazz imported from the United States, he was impressed by the unschooled writing of the Russian composer Modest Mussorgsky—"the art," according to Debussy, "of an inquisitive savage who discovered music at every step made by his emotions." Gregorian chants of the Roman Catholic Church and Renaissance polyphony greatly interested him. And he was also fascinated by the exotic music he heard from Bali and the Orient, which was performed at the Paris Exposition of 1889.

Debussy, in his compositions, gave audible form to his theories and predilections. Of his better-known orchestral works, the *Prélude à l'après-midi d'un faune* (*Prelude to the Afternoon of a Faun*) came first, written in 1894; then the *Nocturnes* for orchestra, 1897–99, followed by his only opera, *Pelléas et Mélisande,* in 1902. His grandest orchestral work came next, in 1905—*La Mer* (*The Sea*). It is an unrivaled tonal picture of winds and waves, sunlight and spray, although Debussy's longest trip by water was crossing the English Channel!

Debussy's works for piano, particularly the *Préludes* and *Études,* added to the resources of piano technique partly because they called for tonal effects created by treating the piano as if its sounds were not produced by hammers hitting strings.

Although Debussy had only visited Spain for one day, his musical evocation of Spanish atmosphere was acclaimed by Manuel de Falla, the great Spanish composer, as better and truer than that of most Spanish composers. Excellent examples of this would include Debussy's *Iberia* (part of his *Images pour orchestre*) and *La puerta del viño* for piano.

Bibliography

Dumesnil, Maurice. *Claude Debussy: Master of Dreams.* Reprint of 1940 edition. West-port, Ct.: Greenwood Press, 1979.

Lockspeiser, Edward. *Debussy: His Life and Mind.* 2 vols. London: Macmillan Ltd., 1962.

Daphnis et Chloé, Suite No. 2
by MAURICE RAVEL

The story of the ballet *Daphnis et Chloé* is based on a legend of the second or third century A.D. attributed to the Greek writer Longus. The excerpts from the story that follow are from the English translation made by George Thornley in 1657.

In the ballet, the opening tableau takes place in a vast meadow before the grotto of the sacred nymphs (three figures carved in stone). The shepherd Daphnis exchanges vows of love with the nymph Chloé. Soon the peaceful fields are invaded by pirates who abduct Chloé.

In the following scene, Chloé is brought before the pirates in their lair. As they command, she dances for them; she then begs them to free her. The pirate chief refuses. Creatures of Pan invade the place; the outlaws fall back in fear, and Chloé is liberated.

The final scene, from which the music for the orchestral *Suite No. 2* is derived, is again set in the meadow. This time it is the hour of sunrise.

> Daphnis . . . started up out of his sleep and, full of pleasure, full of grief, with tears in his eyes, adored the statues of the Nymphs and vowed to sacrifice to them . . . if Chloé should return safe. And running to the pine where the statue of Pan was placed, the legs a goat's, the head horned, one hand holding a pipe, the other a goat dancing to it . . . made a vow for the safety of Chloé. . . .
>
> That night seemed to him the longest of nights, but in it . . . wonders were done. . . .
>
> It was now the time . . . and Daphnis, having spied from a high stand Chloé coming with the flocks, crying out mainly, O ye Nymphs, O blessed Pan! made down to the plains, and rushing into the embraces of Chloé [fell] in a swoon. . . .
>
> Therefore the two . . . fell to dancing . . . Daphnis played Pan; and Chloé, Syrinx. He woos and prays to persuade and win her; she shows her disdain, laughs at love, and flees him. Daphnis follows as to force her, and running on his tiptoes, imitates the hooves of Pan. Chloé, on the other side, acts Syrinx wearied in her flight, and throws herself into the wood. . . . But

A scene from Ravel's *Daphnis et Chloé,* Sadler's-Wells Ballet production.

Daphnis, catching up that great pipe . . . plays at first something that was doleful, and bewailing a lover: then something that made love, and was persuasive.[3]

The composer divided the music of *Suite No. 2* into three sections. The first, *Daybreak,* represents the story from the awakening of Daphnis up to the point at which he is reunited with Chloé. The second, *Pantomime,* accompanies the scene in the ballet in which Daphnis and Chloé mime the story of Pan and Syrinx. The concluding section, the one we shall study, is entitled *Danse générale* and represents the "joyous tumult" of Daphnis and Chloé being brought together again.

3. Maurice Ravel, *Daphnis et Chloé,* score (Paris: Durand, 1913).

Danse générale

LISTENING OUTLINE

After a brief introduction of repeated chords that appear successively in flutes and violins, the theme of the *General Dance* is introduced by the high, piercing sound of the E-flat clarinet:

Example 1

Eb Clarinet (octave higher)

This fast-moving chromatic theme (Example 1) is imitated by other members of the woodwind choir while the strings repeat the moving chromatic passage with chords, recalling the repeated chords of the introduction.

Example 1 returns, building to impressive climaxes.

The trumpets burst in *fortissimo* with repeated chords, followed by a chromatic run as used in the introduction. Dots are used to indicate divisions of a five-beat measure into patterns of 2 plus 3 or 3 plus 2.

Example 2

Trumpets

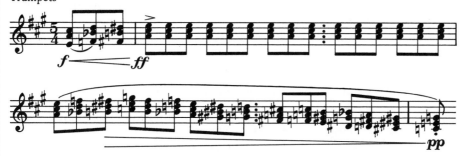

While the woodwinds reecho short segments of Example 2, the strings keep repeating a descending two-note motive.

The trombones enter as a loud dynamic climax is reached.

The orchestral voices start descending in chromatic runs, getting ever softer. Finally only the cellos are heard, sustaining a chord. The bass drum and double basses accentuate a rhythm pattern until the clarinet and cellos enter with Example 1. Chromatic passages keep interrupting this theme until finally the trumpet states it boldly.

As the music again rises to a climax, Example 1 is heard, followed by ascending chromatic scales that dominate the final section. Voices of the chorus are used as another color in the orchestral palette throughout this final section.

After a *fortissimo* climax, the music again rises from a *ppp* to another climax, drops in volume just as suddenly a second time, and builds up into one grand, final surge.

About the Composer

MAURICE RAVEL   Born: March 7, 1875
                              Ciboure, France

                      Died: December 28, 1937
                              Paris, France

Maurice Ravel was a most unusual composer. He was a quiet, dedicated man who wrote music for neither money nor fame; he wrote it because he "had to." He gave piano lessons and usually did not want any payment for them. At concerts that included one of his works, he usually stepped outside during the performance for a "cigarette libératrice." He was neither poor nor wealthy; he made enough money from his musical activities to live the modest life he liked.

Accused first of being an imitator of Debussy and later, with the creation of his *Bolero,* hailed as a composer of originality, Ravel had this to say of his "style":

> I have never been a slave to any one style of composition. Nor have I ever allied myself with any particular school of music. I have always felt that a composer should put on paper what he feels and how he feels it—irrespective of what the current style of composition may be. Great music, I have always felt, must come from the heart. Any music created by technique and brains alone is not worth the paper it is written on.
>
> This has always been my argument against the so-called "modern music" of the younger rebel composers. Their music has been a product of their minds and not of their hearts.

Maurice Ravel was born in the French-Basque seacoast town of Ciboure. Shortly after his birth, his parents moved to Paris. His father, an engineer as well as an amateur musician, saw to it that his son was enrolled in the Paris Conservatory of Music by the time he was fourteen.

At the Conservatory, Ravel was a brilliant student but ran into difficulty with his teachers because he chose not to follow the rules of traditional harmony. In his tries for the coveted *Prix de Rome,* he had even more difficulties than had Debussy before him. In 1901 he submitted a cantata, *Myrrha,* which won second place; the next two years his compositions won nothing, and on the fourth try he was eliminated in the preliminaries that were held to remove those who had no competence.

By the time Ravel was twenty-seven, he had composed *Jeux d'eau* (*Play of the Water*) and *Pavane pour une Infante défunte* (*Pavanne for a Dead Princess*) for piano. His first publicly acknowledged work, his *String Quartet in F Major,* followed in 1903.

In 1909 Ravel was commissioned by the famous ballet impressario Sergei Diaghilev to prepare music for a ballet to be based on the ancient myth of Daphnis and Chloé. After three years of work, it was presented to the Parisian public and earned great popularity.

Ravel was at first criticized for being an imitator of Debussy, who was thirteen years his senior. Today we acknowledge that the lives and works of the two had many similarities, but there were also dissimilarities of enough substance to make Ravel a worthy composer in his own right.

Both Debussy and Ravel rejected the works of Richard Wagner at a time when Wagner was at the height of his popularity in Paris; both Debussy and Ravel admired the works of The Mighty Five, the Russian composers, whose works were just becoming known in the French capital. Both Debussy and Ravel rejected the traditional harmonies being taught at the Paris Conservatory, although Ravel later combined innovation with traditional, classical balance. Both French composers made use of Greek modes, but Ravel alone took care not to destroy the principles of tonality. Although both used the whole-tone scale, Ravel's use of it was minimal. And, while both created great emotional effects, Ravel's were within more conventional limits.

While both Debussy and Ravel wrote works in a variety of forms, Ravel generally opted for the shorter ones. Even his two operas, *L'Heure espagnole* (*The Spanish Hour*) and *L'Enfant et les sortilèges* (*The Child and the Sorceries*), were much shorter than Debussy's lone opera, *Pelléas et Mélisande.*

Ravel wrote several suites for piano, each made up of a number of short movements: *Miroirs* (*Mirrors*), *Gaspard de la nuit* (*Gaspard of the Night*), *Valses nobles et sentimentales* (*Noble and Sentimental Waltzes*), and *Le Tombeau de Couperin* (*Homage to Couperin*), a tribute to friends and acquaintances killed in the First World War, cast in an antique style reminiscent of the French Baroque composer François Couperin.

Both Debussy and Ravel loved children and, just as Debussy wrote his *Children's Corner Suite* for his own little daughter, so Ravel composed for the daughter of a friend a suite called *Ma Mère l'Oye* (*Mother Goose*), a piano duet made up of four movements.

Ravel's *Concerto for the Left Hand,* a unique work that makes some use of the jazz idiom, was written for Paul Wittgenstein, a brilliant young Viennese pianist who lost his right arm during the First World War.

Bibliography

Myers, Rollo Hugh. *Ravel: Life and Works.* Reprint of 1960 edition. Westport, Ct.: Greenwood Press, 1973.

Stuckenschmidt, Hans Heinz. *Maurice Ravel: Variations on His Life and Work.* Translated by Samuel R. Rosenbaum. Philadelphia: Chilton, 1968.

The Pines of Rome

by OTTORINO RESPIGHI

The Italian composer Ottorino Respighi was inspired during his long residence in Rome to compose three major orchestral works commemorating the Eternal City. In 1916 he wrote *The Fountains of Rome;* eight years later he completed *The Pines of Rome.* The final work of this group, *Roman Carnivals,* followed in 1928.

Respighi called these three works *symphonic poems.* Each is in four movements that closely parallel the traditional symphonic form. The style and texture of these works, however, differ from that employed by Debussy in his orchestral works. Respighi is more direct, less vague. The rich harmonies are more traditional and less fleeting. The purpose is more definite and less imaginative. And, of course, the symphonic poems of Respighi are more nationalistic, as evidenced by their titles and subtitles.

"In *The Pines of Rome,*" the composer has said, "I use nature as a point of departure in order to recall memories and visions. The century-old trees which dominate so characteristically the Roman landscape become testimony for the principal events in Roman life."

The four movements of *The Pines of Rome* are *The Pines of the Villa Borghese, The Pines near a Catacomb, The Pines of the Janiculum,* and *The Pines of the Appian Way.*

The Pines of the Appian Way

In the year 312 B.C., the Roman Censor (Supervisor) Appius Claudius Caecus built a road leading out of Rome to Brindisi, a port city on the Adriatic Sea, and a point of departure for ancient vessels sailing for Greece. This time-honored highway is known today as the Appian Way.

The pines of the Roman countryside frequently grow singly by the side of the road rather than in thick groves or clumps. The countryside itself is dreamy and quiet, a rolling plain with hills very far off to the east. Through the plain runs the Via Appia, a reminder of the military empire that built it.

Pines along the Appian Way leading to Rome in the haze of a summer morning.

Today, remnants of the mighty Roman aqueduct along this road suggest its ancient splendor. For half the year the dusty road, the columns of the aqueduct, and the pines are shrouded in mist and haze; for the other half, the hot, boiling sun beats down on them without mercy. This countryside has touched the imagination of countless generations who have seen it, recalling the marching feet of the ancient Roman soldiers, the magnificent chariots of the rulers hastening down the road.

On the title page of the score for *The Pines of Rome,* the composer has written a rather detailed description of what he tries to suggest in *The Pines of the Appian Way:*

> Misty dawn on the Appian Way; solitary pine trees guarding the majestic landscape; the muffled, ceaseless rhythm of unending footsteps. The poet has a fantastic vision of bygone glories. Trumpets sound, in the brilliance of the newly risen sun, a consular army bursts forth toward the Sacred Way, mounting in triumph to the Capital.[4]

4. This and subsequent descriptive quotations from Ottorino Respighi, *Pini di Roma: Poema sinfonico* (Milan, 1925, 1953).

LISTENING OUTLINE

At first only a barely perceptible, insistent rhythm is heard. (The timpani never cease this rhythm until the conclusion of the movement.)

The misty dawn, the solitary loneliness of the undulating countryside is suggested by a melodic fragment played by the bass clarinet:

Example 1

Always underneath this are the timpani, the "muffled, ceaseless rhythm of unending footsteps."

Faintly, as if from a distance, the French horns suggest the military legions of old:

Example 2

A hint of the fanfare to come is softly suggested by the clarinets:

Example 3

"The magic landscape," which is guarded by "solitary pine trees," provides food and shelter for countless flocks of sheep. The tune of an ancient shepherd is suggested by an English horn solo of some fourteen measures. It begins:

Example 4

English Horn

The bassoon and French horn repeat the fanfare theme of Example 3 softly. It is echoed by the clarinet and another French horn.

As if from a distance, two trumpets play a variant of the fanfare:

Example 5

Flugelhorns[5] (isolated and stopped)
as from a distance

After a variant of Example 3 has been heard again in the winds, the distant brass play Example 5.

"The brilliance of a newly-risen sun" breaks forth as two unmuted trumpets loudly proclaim the fanfare theme (a variant of Example 3).

"A consular army bursts forth toward the Sacred Way," advancing brilliantly from this point to the end of the composition. Winds and upper strings play a loud, slowly ascending scale, over which the brass brilliantly play Example 6, which is derived from previous thematic material.

Example 6

Trombones

Trumpet, Oboes

Soon the brass take over the slow, sustained, ascending scale, while from the depths of the orchestra the tubas proclaim Example 5.

The drive of the timpani beat (augmented by low winds, strings, and bass drum) is incessant; the dynamic climaxes come closer together, each more brilliant than its predecessor, the pipe organ adding to the total sonority of sound. Theme overlaps theme as "trumpets sound . . . a fantastic vision of bygone glories. The consular army bursts forth, . . . mounting in triumph to the Capital."

5. Respighi calls for this passage to be played by two *flicorni,* a flicorno being an Italian type of flugelhorn (an instrument similar to a cornet but with a different bore).

About the Composer

OTTORINO RESPIGHI

Born: July 9, 1879
Bologna, Italy

Died: April 18, 1936
Rome, Italy

Although the roster of well-known Italian opera composers of the late nineteenth century is long, there is but one name that appears on the roster of serious symphonic composers—that of Ottorino Respighi. An expert craftsman at orchestration, having studied with Rimsky-Korsakov, he adopted many of the techniques of the Impressionistic composers. *The Pines of Rome,* he said, was an attempt to use "nature as a point of departure in order to recall memories and visions." Of contemporary schools and styles of composition, Respighi said:

> The future course of music? Who can say? I believe that every composer should first of all be an individual. As for dissonance, it has its place as a medium of tone-color. . . . For its own sake it is abhorrent to me, but as a means to expression it has important uses. . . .
>
> So far as modern Italian musicians are concerned . . . they had their beginning in impressionism. We stem from this school, but for some years we have not been of it. The Italian genius is for melody and clarity. Today there is a noticeable return to the less sophisticated music of our past—in harmony to the church modes and in form to the suites of dances and other charming forms. This is no doubt good, providing we all cling to our own individualities and really express them.

Respighi was born of a musical family; his grandfather had been a choir director for all the churches of Bologna, and his father was a pianist and teacher at the Bologna Liceo Musicale. It was only natural that, after piano lessons from his father, young Ottorino should be enrolled in his twelfth year at the Liceo Musicale. At the same time he was also taking violin lessons.

At nineteen Respighi started his work in composition, studying for two years in Bologna. His last year in Bologna also saw him earning his diploma in violin. In order to enlarge his musical knowledge, he traveled in his twenty-first year to St. Petersburg, Russia, where he secured a position as first violist with the orchestra of the opera theater. This same year his first composition, *Symphonic Variations,* was given its first school performance.

After his first year in St. Petersburg, Respighi was able to study both composition and orchestration with Rimsky-Korsakov. After five months of study with the Russian master, he moved to Berlin, where he continued his studies in composition. In 1905 his first work to be played publicly, *Notturno,* was performed at the Metropolitan Opera House in New York. Some of his compositions were published soon after this.

In 1913 Respighi was appointed an instructor of composition at the Academy of Santa Cecilia in Rome, and he became its director some ten years later.

In his musical works, Respighi reflected both the training in classical forms that he received in Bologna under the tutelage of the teachers Torchi and Martucci, and the training in orchestration from the master of that art, Rimsky-Korsakov. Respighi made frequent use of ecclesiastical modalities and Gregorian themes from the liturgical music of the Roman Catholic Church and he arranged works by the early Italian masters Monteverdi, Vitali, Pergolesi, Cimarosa, and Marcello.

His biography was written by his wife, a concert singer and the composer of an opera, a symphonic poem, and numerous songs. She also completed Respighi's last opera, *Lucrezia*.

Bibliography

Respighi, Elsa. *Ottorino Respighi: His Life Story.* London: G. Ricordi, 1962.

We stand in the midst of one of the most revolutionary periods in the history of art music. At no time in the past have so many conceptually opposing musical developments existed side by side: tonal vs. atonal music; highly organized (serial) vs. freely organized (chance) vs. probabilistic (stochastic) music; music for traditional instruments vs. music for electronic instruments; and even music with sounding elements vs. music without sound!

Gary Wittlich

ELEVEN/
THE TWENTIETH
CENTURY

THERE is no universally accepted name for the period under discussion in this chapter. "Twentieth-century music" is being used, but "new music" or "contemporary music" are also encountered from time to time. "Twentieth-century music," however, is not being used in its all-inclusive sense. No mention will be made in this chapter of composers who, although they lived and worked in the twentieth century, were essentially nineteenth-century Romanticists (such as Richard Strauss). Neither is mention made of the Impressionists, whose developmental and creative periods crossed from the very late nineteenth century into the first decades of the twentieth (Debussy, Ravel, and Respighi, discussed in Chapter 10, for example). Because electronic composers of the twentieth century are discussed in Chapter 12 and the great jazz artists of the twentieth century in Chapter 13, no mention is made of them here.

The composers of the twentieth century have been a very busy group, lashing out in many directions, seeking new sounds, employing every means available to create new music. This new music represents a revolt against German Romanticism of the last century and all that it stands for. No single, universally accepted style has become representative of the present era, however. Many composers have started with one technique, then experimented with and successfully used others. The degree to which twentieth-century music has been accepted varies with the composers and the techniques they have used. We are too close in time to this era really to know which composers and which compositions will remain meaningful for future generations.

The objections of most contemporary composers to nineteenth-century Romanticism have centered on the use in that music of the major and minor scale patterns and the feeling of a tonal center, the use of regularly recurring accents within the formal limits of measures of fixed length, and the use of lush, rich harmonies. Even the programmatic implications of much late nineteenth-century music have come under fire. This revolt could first be detected in the titles and expression marks of works by the French composer Eric Satie (1866–1925), pieces with such titles as *Trois Morceaux en forme de poire* (*Three Pieces in the Form of a Pear,* 1903) and *Embryons desséchés* (*Dried Embryos,* 1913), with its indication to the pianist to play a passage "Comme un rossignol qui a mal au dent" ("Like a nightingale that has a toothache").

Among the many influences on the music of the twentieth century, composers have experimented with jazz: Stravinsky wrote his *Ragtime for Eleven Instruments* in 1918; Copland composed his *Two Blues* in 1926; and the Frenchman Darius Milhaud wrote his *Trois rag caprices* in 1922.

Perhaps the most obvious direction music has taken in this century has been the revolt against a "key feeling" or tonality. Several different techniques have been used to avoid the sense of a tonal center. *Polytonality* is one such technique, the use of two or more keys or tonal centers simultaneously. The first well-known work to make use of polytonality was Stravinsky's ballet *Petrouchka* of 1911, although compositions by Charles Ives that were hidden away in cardboard cartons in his barn antedate Stravinsky's work.

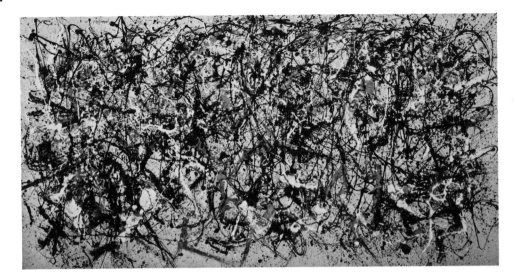

Jackson Pollock, *Autumn Rhythm,* 1950 (Metropolitan Museum of Art, New York). Pollock applied the paint by dripping and with sticks, trowels, and knives. This element of chance parallels the aleatoric movement in music.

Alexander Calder, *Lobster Trap and Fish Tail,* 1939 (Museum of Modern Art, New York). Interest in nontraditional media led Calder to create mobiles. Composers like Pierre Boulez joined acousticians, electronic and computer scientists, and instrument-makers in an attempt to create new musical media.

Arnold Schoenberg proceeded in a different direction. At first he was concerned simply with "the absence of tonality"—*atonal* music. As he continued experimenting and reworking his theories he developed (to quote his own words) "a procedure or method of composing with twelve tones which are related only with one another." Works that were based on this method have been called *twelve-tone* or *dodecaphonic* compositions.

There was a trend toward greater freedom in rhythm, an element that became extremely important. The works of Stravinsky and Béla Bartók show a greater diversity of rhythmic effects than is found in most nineteenth-century music. Asymmetrical melodies became dominant; bar lines disappeared in some of the music; compositions that still made use of meter signatures frequently varied them from measure to measure. Sometimes two or more meters were employed at the same time, hence the adjective, *polyrhythmic.*

There has been a tremendous enlargement of the orchestral palette in the twentieth century. Electronic synthesizers have been used with symphony orchestras, and the use of percussion instruments has increased greatly. *Ionisation* (1931) by Edgard Varèse (1884–1965), is scored for thirty-seven instruments of "percussion, friction and sibilization," the latter consisting of two sirens (one high in pitch, the other low). Harry Partch (1901–1974) created twenty-eight original musical instruments of his own design, including a seventy-two-string kithara, marimba-like reeds he called boos, glass bells called cloud-chamber bowls, and the bloboys, made of bellows, three organ pipes, and an auto exhaust pipe. Partch also devised a forty-three-tone scale in contrast to the conventional twelve-tone scale of most Western music.

Two iconoclastic concepts about musical composition have been proposed by the American composer John Cage (b. 1912) and the French composer Pierre Boulez

(b. 1925). Cage shocked the music world in 1952 with his composition *4'33"*, a piece four minutes and thirty-three seconds long in three movements of specified length, but containing not a single note. Silence. Cage has a logical explanation for this.

> In this new music nothing takes place but sounds: those that are notated and those that are not. Those that are not notated appear in the written music as silences, opening the doors of the music to the sounds that happen to be in the environment. . . . There is no such thing as an empty space or an empty time. There is always something to see, something to hear. In fact, try as we may to make silence, we cannot.

Thus Cage suggests that the audience, for the four-and-a-half minutes, should listen to the sounds of the concert hall and the people around them rather than to tones produced by the musical instruments on stage.

Pierre Boulez coined the word *aleatoric* from the French word for chance, *alea,* to suggest a new concept that employs chance techniques within a controlled framework, a type of music more related to improvisation than to true indeterminacy.

An attempt has been made by certain musical historians to define a twentieth-century Nationalism. This new Nationalism contrasts to nineteenth-century Nationalism in its philosophy. The composers of the last century—Rimsky-Korsakov, Smetana, and Dvořák among others—determined, as their primary objective, to make their music representative of their native lands. Hence those composers relied heavily on folk melodies, peasant dance rhythms, and folk-tale subject matter. The twentieth-century Nationalists philosophically have been concerned only with conveying universal musical ideas. But because these composers represent musical traditions of their own native lands, they frequently find that folk melodies and folk-dance rhythms automatically creep into the works they create. Bartók's use of Hungarian melodies or Ives's quotation of countless American folk songs might be cited as examples.

Top, Pablo Picasso, *Les Demoiselles d''Avignon,* 1907 (Museum of Modern Art, New York). Above, Edvard Munch, *The Scream,* 1893 (Munch Museum, Oslo). Like twentieth-century composers, twentieth-century artists went in many stylistic directions. Picasso's style here is Cubism; Munch's style is Expressionism. Expressionists in music were Schoenberg, Berg, and Webern.

The course of twentieth-century music has been shaped somewhat by the many advances of science. Radio has brought music to thousands who have never attended a concert. Works have been commissioned especially for radio performance; the American composer Randall Thompson's opera *Solomon and Balkis* (1942) is a good example. When sound was added to motion pictures in 1929, another field opened for serious composers. Successful film scores include Serge Prokofiev's *Lt. Kije* (1933) and Virgil Thomson's *Louisiana Story* (1948). Phonograph records have brought music to the most isolated parts of the world, and have provided each listener with an almost unlimited choice of repertory. Works such as Roy Harris's *Four Minutes and Twenty Seconds* (1934) were composed especially for recording purposes. The most recent contributor to music in the electronic field is television, which commissioned Gian-Carlo Menotti's Christmas opera *Amahl and the Night Visitors* in 1951 and Igor Stravinsky's ballet *The Flood* in 1962.

Undoubtedly the best way for us to understand the music of our own time is to become acquainted with a wide variety of twentieth-century musical idioms. Only by listening can we understand.

The Fourth of July

by CHARLES IVES

Charles Ives was both one of the most unusual and one of the greatest of American composers. Leonard Bernstein has referred to him as "our first really great composer . . . our Washington, Lincoln and Jefferson of music." The noted composer and writer on contemporary music Henry Cowell has said that "Ives can, in fact, be shown to be one of the four great creative figures in music of the first half of the twentieth century. The others are Schoenberg, Stravinsky and Bartók."

It was around 1945 that Arnold Schoenberg singled out Ives for special recognition. Up to that time Ives was known only to a small number of music lovers, mostly professional musicians. On the surface this did not seem to concern the composer very much, for he always appeared to be rather apathetic to either praise or criticism. When his *Symphony No. 3* (completed in 1904) won the Pulitzer Prize in 1947, Ives's response was that "prizes are the badges of mediocrity." He immediately proceeded to give the prize money away.

Charles Ives was a rugged individualist, a man of immense physical energy and competence in practical affairs and of vigorous originality and independence. Between 1890 and 1910, he had effected revolutionary ideas in the composition of music that would not occur to the mainstream of European composers until a decade or two later. He was writing atonal music, that is, music without a key center or tonality; he was composing polyrhythmic works, works with one or more meters set against another; he was also concerned with polyharmonies, the juxtaposition of two or more incongruent harmonies or chords simultaneously.

Charles Ives was also one of the most successful insurance executives the United States has ever produced, a man who made millions in the field, a man who wrote one of the most important books on the subject. He helped found the firm of Ives & Myrick in New York City and, at the time of his retirement in 1930, it was the largest insurance agency in the United States.

The work that today is called *The Holidays Symphony* or sometimes *New England Holidays* is, in a certain sense, a synthetic symphony. The last movement, *Thanksgiving,* was composed first, as an independent orchestral piece, in 1904. The idea of a four-movement symphony did not occur to Ives until, in 1909, he wrote *Washington's Birthday,* the opening movement. The second movement, *Decoration Day,* was composed in 1912, and the third movement, *The Fourth of July,* was completed in 1913. Ives placed the four scores in a folder labeled "4 N. E. Holidays" and added the note that they were "Recollections of a boy's holidays in a Connecticut country town. . . . These movements may be played as separate pieces. . . . These pieces may be lumped together as a symphony."

The Fourth of July is dedicated to Julian Myrick, Ives's business partner. The hot New England atmosphere explodes in a finale of fireworks. Writing about this movement in his *Memos,* Ives said:

> *The Fourth of July* was a thing I'd had in mind for a good while. It was finished, and the part that represents the explosions (or other parts where the full orchestra is playing) was completely scored in the summer of 1912. . . . This is pure program music—it is also pure abstract music—"You pays your money and you takes your choice. . . . "
>
> I remember distinctly, when I was scoring this, that there was a feeling of freedom as a boy has, on the Fourth of July, who wants to do anything he wants to do, and that's his one day to do it. And I wrote this, feeling free to remember local things etc., and to put [in] as many feelings and rhythms as I wanted to put together. And I did what I wanted to, quite sure that the thing would never be played, and probably *could* never be played.[1]

Throughout *The Fourth of July* there can be heard the strains of the old patriotic tune of 1843 by David Shaw, *Columbia, the Gem of the Ocean* (later called *The Red, White, and Blue*). Ives uses this tune much as Johann Sebastian Bach had, 200 years earlier, used chorales and hymn tunes as the basis for his multimovement sacred choral works (*cantatas*).

In addition to numerous musical quotations of *Columbia, the Gem of the Ocean,* Ives makes use of melodies from a number of other tunes. Although listeners will probably recognize only a few of them unless they closely study the score, experts have identified the following: *Assembly, The Battle Cry of Freedom, Marching Through Georgia, Sailor's Hornpipe, The Battle Hymn of the Republic, Fisherman's Hornpipe, Reveille, The Girl I Left Behind Me, London Bridge, St. Patrick's Day, Katy Darling, Yankee Doodle, Dixie,* and *Kingdom Coming.*

As you will discover by listening to *The Fourth of July,* Ives reverses the usual custom in symphonic form and presents the development first, the theme last.

In the manuscript of *The Fourth of July,* Ives described the program he had in mind by saying:

> Everybody knows what it's like—if everybody doesn't—Cannon on the Green, Village Band on Main Street, fire crackers, shanks [valves] mixed on cornets, strings around big toes, torpedoes, Church bells, lost finger, fifes, clam-chowder, a prize-fight, drum-corps, burnt shins, parades (in and out of step), saloons all closed (more drunks than usual), baseball game (Danbury All-Stars vs. Beaver Brook Boys), the pistols, mobbed umpire, Red, White and Blue, runaway horse,—and the day ends with the sky-rocket over the Church-steeple, just after the annual explosion sets the Town-Hall on fire.[2]

---

1. Charles Ives, *Charles E. Ives: Memos,* ed. John Kirkpatrick (New York, 1972).
2. Ives, *Memos,* quoted in *The Fourth of July,* score (New York, 1959), p. 1.

LISTENING OUTLINE

The Fourth of July begins with a very slow, quiet introduction. At first only muted strings are heard, the violins playing a variant of the *Columbia* tune:

Example 1

Violins (muted)

The bass viols are heard with a rhythmical variant of Example 1.

Heard, in turn, are short figures played by woodwinds: clarinet, oboe, flute.

Several measures later the flute and piccolo play their variant of the *Columbia* tune:

Example 2

Piccolo, Flutes (one and two octaves higher)
etwas schneller

A loud chord is heard; the dynamic level quickly subsides. Brass and woodwinds play short fragments from the *Sailor's Hornpipe.*

The violins take up a phrase from *The Battle Hymn of the Republic:*

Example 3

Violins

The brass respond with fragments of the *Fisherman's Hornpipe*. Hints of other tunes are heard. *Columbia* is also among these fragments, played by the trombone.

The piccolo takes up *The Girl I Left Behind Me:*

Example 4

Piccolos (octave higher)

Geschwindmarsch

The entire orchestra enters *con furore* (with fury) in an extended, loud, and dissonant passage. The dynamic level subsides to a *ppp*. Violins are heard with sustained tones; woodwinds play short melodic figures.

Drums are heard; a soft, pulsating march rhythm is taken up. Hints of *Columbia* and *Reveille* are heard in the brass.

The *Columbia* tune, at last, is boldly proclaimed by trumpets, as other tunes (including *The Battle Hymn* and *Yankee Doodle*) are played in counterpoint to it by other wind instruments. The *Columbia* tune, however, easily predominates:

Example 5

Trumpets

The tune continues as only an amateur village band might play it, complete with wrong notes, stuck valves, out-of-tune notes, missed beats, and spontaneous variants of the melody.

At the dynamic climax there is a pause, then a bell (*pppp*) is heard. The full orchestra soon enters *ffff*. The dynamic level quickly subsides to *pianissimo*. A few descending string chords lead to the final one marked *pppp*.

About the Composer

CHARLES IVES   Born: October 20, 1874
                            Danbury, Connecticut

              Died: May 19, 1954
                      New York, New York

Charles Ives was born in Danbury, Connecticut, not far from where his forebears had settled shortly after the landing of the Pilgrims. His father had been a band director in the army during the Civil War, his mother a music teacher in Danbury. Once out of the service, the elder Ives continued his interest in music by playing the piano for dances and the organ for Sunday church services, and by leading the town band and occasionally arranging music for them to play.

Charles's father was also an experimenter, always trying to find new sounds and learn how to use them effectively. In effect, he was a student of acoustics as well as a teacher of piano, violin, and theory. For one experiment, he built an instrument with twenty-four violin strings stretched over a clothespress, so that he could play quarter-tone music (that is, dividing the present chromatic scale of half tones into intervals half the size of those we know).

Such continued experimentation on the part of the father was bound to fascinate and interest the son. In addition, young Charles attended many outdoor camp meetings and heard countless revival songs. He heard many of Stephen Foster's tunes: in fact, Foster had been a friend of his father. When Charles was eight, his father discovered him thumping out rhythms on the family piano, trying to make it sound like the percussion section of a marching band. Father Ives promptly took the boy down to the barbershop and turned him over to the German barber, who was also the drummer in the Danbury town band. By the time he was twelve, Charles himself was the drummer in the band. His father also saw to it that Charles had lessons in piano, violin, cornet, sight-reading, harmony, and counterpoint. A year earlier Charles had started organ lessons, and within two years was the organist for the Congregational Church of Danbury, playing two Sunday services and giving frequent recitals.

Several years earlier Ives had begun to compose, his first work being a *Dirge for Chin Chin,* the family cat. His father's band performed one of his pieces, but for the performance Charles begged out of playing. As the band marched down the street loudly blaring forth the melody of his composition, the lad played handball against the side of the house and appeared to completely ignore it all.

At twenty, Ives enrolled at Yale to study composition. As far as can be determined, his teachers seem to have ignored the daring new compositions that Ives was writing and looked only at the standard harmony exercises required of the students. While at Yale, he wrote music for a theater orchestra for amusement, played on the football team, and was a member of the baseball team. Ives's *Symphony No. 1* dates from his college days; it is a work filled with dissonances and written in many tonalities simultaneously.

As Ives approached graduation, he determined that he wanted a full and comfortable life and, although marriage was still eight years away, he decided that a musician simply did not earn enough money to support a family in such style. He, therefore, chose a career in insurance.

While Ives pursued his active career as an insurance executive in New York during the nine-to-five workday, he spent his evenings composing. The patriotic songs of his youth not only inspired Ives but also found their way into his compositions, as did melodies from church anthems, popular dance tunes of the day, and marches. Creative American literary artists also inspired him, leading him to write such works as his *Piano Sonata No. 2* (composed between 1905 and 1915, and first publicly performed in 1939). Subtitled *Concord, Mass., 1840–1860,* the sonata is in four movements: *Emerson, Hawthorne, The Alcotts,* and *Thoreau.* Numerous works of his refer to life in early rural America: *Hallowe'en* (1911) for piano and strings; *The Pond* (1906) for orchestra; *The Gong on the Hook and Ladder* (1911) for chamber orchestra; *Lincoln, The Great Commoner* (1912) for chorus and orchestra; *A Revival Service* (1896) for string quartet; and *Children's Day at Camp Meeting* (1915) for violin and piano.

Ives retired from business in 1930; about the same time, he was compelled to give up composing because a diabetic condition made it impossible for him to hold a pen. In a letter of January 1934 he complained: "my hands and arms have been bothering me again and it's hard to hold a pen, but the meanest part is not to be able to play the piano when I want."[3] He grew the beard that appears in all his later photographs at this time, for the same reason: he could not hold a razor.

Recognition came late for Ives. His works, written in the early years of the century, were not first performed until decades later—and then in one case, as previously mentioned, won the Pulitzer Prize. Ives, however, published at his own expense the *Concord Sonata* in 1919 and, in 1922, a volume of 114 songs (written between 1884 and 1921) which he distributed free to public libraries throughout the United States. *Three Places in New England,* perhaps his best-known orchestral work, although written between 1903 and 1914, was not publicly performed until 1931!

Paradoxically, this business executive came home from the office at the end of the day and spent his evenings writing music at his desk because he enjoyed it. As he filled the sheets of score-paper, he tossed them on the floor. When the piles of music became too high, he packed them in cardboard boxes and hauled them out to the barn on his estate in Connecticut for storage.

Always planning to look over these disordered boxes of manuscripts, he did, during the fall of 1949, do some rummaging around. He found a sheaf of dusty pages that turned out to be his *Symphony No. 2,* begun in 1897. Painstakingly, individual parts for the performers were copied out. A few months later Leonard Bernstein and the New York Philharmonic Orchestra gave the world premiere of the symphony some fifty-

3. David Wooldridge, *From the Steeples and Mountains: A Study of Charles Ives* (New York, 1974), p. 299.

four years after it had been written. Since it was the first time one of Ives's symphonies was to be performed by a major orchestra, Bernstein invited the composer to be his guest at the premiere. When the composer declined, Bernstein offered to conduct a rehearsal of it at any hour and date that would suit Ives. Furthermore, Bernstein would leave the auditorium dark so that no one would know that the composer was present. When Ives refused even this offer, the best the conductor could do was to have Mrs. Ives as his guest of honor for the premiere.

When she returned home after the concert, she told her husband how successful the work had been and how much the public had liked it. Ives sneaked down to the kitchen a week later and listened to a broadcast performance of it on the maid's little radio. This was his only experience hearing one of his major works performed.

Bibliography

Ives, Charles E. *Charles E. Ives: Memos.* Edited by Ralph Kirkpatrick. New York: W. W. Norton, 1972.

Wooldridge, David. *From the Steeples and Mountains: A Study of Charles Ives.* New York: Alfred A. Knopf, 1974.

Concerto for Orchestra

by BÉLA BARTÓK

Béla Bartók, one of the major composers of the twentieth century, will probably be best remembered by posterity for his *Concerto for Orchestra,* the work that not only has found widest favor with concert audiences, but also is his most frequently performed composition. This concerto, in the words of one critic, "calls forth not merely admiration for its musical architecture; many listeners feel toward it the kind of affection reserved for those universal expressions of a basic humanity that transcend all questions of style in any art."

During the Second World War, Bartók with his wife and son escaped from his native Hungary. Plagued by illness, he settled the family in New York. Although both Columbia University and the American Society of Composers, Authors, and Publishers (ASCAP) made grants of money available to the composer, these hardly covered minimum living expenses exclusive of doctors and medicines. Two close friends, the violinist Josef Szigeti and the conductor Fritz Reiner, suggested to the conductor of the Boston Symphony Orchestra, Serge Koussevitzky, that a work be commissioned from Bartók. The circumstances surrounding this commission were concealed from Bartók lest he think that it was meant as charity. Serge Koussevitzky offered Bartók a thousand dollars to write an orchestral work in memory of the conductor's first wife.

After years of consulting specialists and being prescribed endless medication, Bartók wrote to his friend Josef Szigeti in 1944:

> At present I feel in the best of health, no fever, my strength has returned, I take fine walks in the woods and mountains—actually I climb the mountain (of course only with due caution). In March my weight was 87 pounds; now it is 105. I grow fat. I bulge. I explode. You will not recognize me.[4]

The composer did not attribute the improvement in his condition to medicine or doctors. He debated whether he was able to complete the Koussevitzky commission because he felt better, or felt better because he was able to complete the commission.

Bartók said of his *Concerto for Orchestra:* "The title of this symphony-like orchestral work is explained by its tendency to treat the single orchestral instruments in a concertant or soloistic manner."[5]

Second Movement: *Giuoco delle coppie* (Game of the Couples)

This movement is marked *Allegretto scherzando.* Of it Bartók said:

> The main part of the second movement consists of a chain of independent short sections, by wind instruments consecutively introduced in five pairs (bassoons in [intervals of] 6ths; oboes in [intervals of] 3rds, clarinets in [intervals of] 7ths, flutes in [intervals of] 5ths, and muted trumpets in [intervals of] 2nds.) Thematically, the five sections have nothing in common. A kind of "trio"—a short chorale for brass instruments and side-drum [snare drum]—follows, after which the five sections are recapitulated in a more elaborate instrumentation.[6]

LISTENING OUTLINE

An introduction is played by the side drum in a syncopated rhythm:

Example 1

Snare Drum (without snares)

4. Halsey Stevens, *The Life and Music of Béla Bartók* (New York, 1964).
5. Program notes for first performance.
6. Béla Bartók, quoted in *The Concert Companion: A Comprehensive Guide to Symphonic Music* by Robert Bagar and Louis Biancolli (New York, 1947), pp. 24–25.

The first theme is introduced by bassoons in parallel sixths—both bassoons move in the same direction at the same time at the interval of a sixth:

Example 2

A pair of oboes play Example 3, a melody in parallel thirds:

Example 3

Two clarinets in parallel sevenths are heard with Example 4:

Example 4

The flutes are heard next, in a somewhat longer thematic passage built out of parallel fifths:

Example 5

The muted trumpets, in seconds, complete this section of the movement:

Example 6

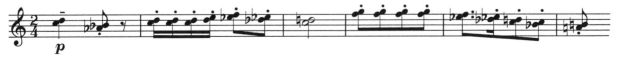

The *trio,* played by brass instruments, is scored for five voices: two trumpets, two trombones, and a tuba. The side drum accompanies the chorale (Example 7).

Example 7

The themes of the first section return in their original order, played by the same pairs of instruments, which are now joined by additional ones. After a brief hint of Example 1 in the side drum, the bassoons return with Example 2; a third bassoon has been added with a running sixteenth-note figure.

The oboes repeat Example 3, joined by a pair of clarinets, which start off playing Example 3 in inversion.

Example 4, played by the clarinets in sevenths, is doubled by a pair of flutes also playing in sevenths. The flutes, however, play their melodic line a fourth lower than the clarinet melody.

The flutes, with a continuation of Example 5, are joined by all the woodwinds.

The muted trumpets, with Example 6, are accompanied by two harps with glissandos.

The movement ends with a side drum solo based on Example 1.

About the Composer

BÉLA BARTÓK   Born: March 25, 1881
Nagyszentmiklós, Hungary

Died: September 26, 1945
New York, New York

Béla Bartók was a quiet, shy, and retiring man, a composer largely unheralded and ignored during his lifetime. No label such as Impressionism or Expressionism has been affixed to his style by the critics; he did not develop a "method" or inspire a group of

ardent student followers. Yet his contribution to twentieth-century music is of epic proportion; few works of other composers are the equal of his best, and none are better.

Although Hungarian by birth, Bartók first became familiar with music in the German tradition, especially that of Brahms. Later he discovered the adventuresome, highly chromatic music of Richard Strauss; this opened new vistas in harmony, style, and structure. Bartók became acquainted with the folk music of Hungary and later that of Romania, Turkey, and the Arabs of North Africa, and his music was affected by these influences.

The musical training of Béla Bartók, the lad with perfect pitch, began on his fifth birthday when his mother gave him his first piano lesson; less than a month later the two of them were able to play a duet for his father. The death of Béla's father two years later caused the family to make a number of moves to widely separated parts of Hungary. His mother gave piano lessons to help support the family; a private teacher was found for Béla, and he acquired a solid foundation in the music of the Classical and Romantic eras.

By the fall of 1899, Bartók was ready to enter the academy of music in Budapest. He took courses in piano, composition, score-reading, and orchestration. Bouts with ill health—a bronchial condition among other problems—seemed for a time to preclude a career in music for him. A professor at the academy advised his mother that the life of a professional musician was much too strenuous for a person of such frail stature and precarious health. Undaunted, Bartók resolutely continued with his studies at the academy.

During Bartók's student days, a new nationalism was starting to sweep across the country. There was an interest by scholars in reviving the old Hungarian culture, in republishing some of the early Hungarian writers, and in resurrecting patriotic songs, all suppressed since the catastrophic uprising of 1848–49. Through this renaissance of authentic Hungarian culture and history, Bartók became interested in national music.

Bartók set out to locate, investigate, notate, and classify the original folk music of Hungary. He discovered that he accomplished his purpose best if he went to the little rural villages and hamlets and lived with the peasants, eating simple foods at their tables, living in their primitive homes. In this manner he gained their respect and friendship, finding them willing to share music-making with him. For such scientific purposes, he took with him a primitive spring-wound Edison cylinder phonograph; sometime later he transcribed these melodies into a system of musical notation of his own, which could record microtones, and vocal effects.

In 1907 Bartók was appointed to the staff of the academy of music in Budapest, a post he was to occupy for thirty years. He did not, however, teach composition; this he always refused to do, probably fearing that it would affect and interfere with his own style and method of composition. He took brief leaves from the academy from time to time, occasionally because of ill health, frequently to go on folk-song collecting trips.

The death of Bartók's mother in 1939 severed Bartók's last strong tie to his beloved Hungary, and he emigrated with his wife to the United States; soon his son followed. A position was found for him at Columbia University at a salary of $3,000 a year doing folk-song research. When that special fund was exhausted, a position was found for him at Harvard, but his health was already seriously undermined. He also was depressed by the war and the fate of his homeland.

After the commission for the *Concerto for Orchestra,* Bartók completed all but seventeen bars of his *Piano Concerto No. 3;* the following work, a *Concerto for Viola,* was left in manuscript at his death in 1945.

The premiere of the *Concerto for Orchestra* by the Boston Symphony Orchestra on December 1, 1944, was followed by a thunderous ovation, probably the only spontaneous demonstration of enthusiasm the composer ever received. Had he lived a few more years, he would have discovered that his other major works gained an acceptance they had not known in his lifetime, works such as his ballets *The Wooden Prince* (1916) and *The Miraculous Mandarin* (1919), his *Music for String Instruments, Percussion and Celesta* (1936), and his *Sonata for Two Pianos and Percussion* (1937).

Within a few months after Bartók's death in the fall of 1945, there were forty-eight important performances of his larger works, including the premieres of his last two concertos. Within two years of his death, several all-inclusive Bartók cycles were performed in several different cities and, within the following three years, all of his important works became available on records, including all six string quartets.

The dual aspects of Bartók's style—his use of elements of Hungarian folk music and his use of the modern devices of polytonality and extended harmonies—inspired many young composers who were reluctant to abandon national melodic expression.

Bibliography

Moreux, Serge. *Béla Bartók.* Translated by G. S. Fraser and Erik de Mauny. New York: Vienna House, 1974.

Ujfalussy, József. *Béla Bartók.* Translated by Ruth Pataki. Boston: Crescendo, 1971.

Le Sacre du printemps
by IGOR STRAVINSKY

Igor Stravinsky's first efforts for the Russian ballet impresario Sergei Diaghilev were concerned with the orchestration of two piano works of Chopin for the ballet *Les Sylphides.* The two artists then collaborated in three of the twentieth century's outstanding ballets: *L'Oiseau de feu (The Firebird), Petrouchka,* and *Le Sacre du printemps (The Rite of Spring).*

In his autobiography, Stravinsky details the origin of the third and finest of the three ballets.

The Sacrifice from Stravinsky's *Sacre du printemps,* production of Maurice Bejart's Ballet of the Twentieth Century.

One day while I was finishing the last pages of *The Firebird* in St. Petersburg, I had a fleeting vision that came to me as a complete surprise. I saw in my imagination a solemn pagan rite: Sage elders, seated in a circle, watching a young girl dance herself to death. They were sacrificing her to propitiate the god of spring. Such was the theme of *The Rite of Spring.* I must confess that this vision made a deep impression on me, and I at once described it to my friend, Nicholas Roerich, he being a painter who specialized in pagan subjects. He welcomed my inspiration with enthusiasm, and he became my collaborator in the creation. In Paris, I told Diaghilev about it, and he was at once carried away with the idea, though its realization was delayed by the production of *Petrouchka.*[7]

7. Igor Stravinsky, *An Autobiography* (New York, 1962).

The Rite of Spring, subtitled *Pictures from Pagan Russia,* recreates a primitive story in highly sophisticated music. Harsh dissonances, polyrhythms that create a barbaric atmosphere, and polytonality characterize the score, but the music never loses its vibrating transparency. The work is scored for a very large orchestra: two piccolos, three flutes, alto flute, four oboes, two English horns, the shrill E-flat clarinet, three regular clarinets, two bass clarinets, four bassoons, two contrabassoons, eight French horns, a high D trumpet, four regular (C) trumpets, a bass trumpet, three trombones, two tenor tubas, two bass tubas, five timpani, bass drum, tam-tam, cymbals, antique cymbals, triangle, guiro, tambourine, and the usual complement of strings.

The ballet is divided into two parts, *The Adoration of the Earth* and *The Sacrifice.* Each of these "acts" is further subdivided. *The Adoration* begins with an *Introduction* played before the curtain rises; it is intended to suggest "the mystery of the physical world in spring." It leads without pause into the *The Augurs of Spring—Dances of the Young Girls,* a ceremonial worship of the earth, danced in forceful steps to a system of curiously placed accents.

The scandal created by the music—sounding harsh and dissonant as it did to the opening-night audience—is one of the well-known legends of twentieth-century music. Stravinsky had not expected anything unusual, as he later said, since "at the dress rehearsal to which we had, as usual, invited a number of actors, painters, musicians, writers and the most cultured representatives of society, everything had gone off peacefully and I was very far from expecting such an outburst."

Then came that fateful night of May 29, 1913, at the Théâtre des Champs-Elysées in Paris. Nijinsky, the leading dancer of the company, had done the choreography, Pierre Monteux was to conduct.

> The first bars of the prelude [Stravinsky later said] evoked derisive laughter. I was disgusted. These demonstrations, at first isolated, soon became general, provoking counter-demonstrations and very quickly developing into a terrific uproar. During the whole performance I was at Nijinsky's side in the wings. He was on a chair screaming: "Sixteen, seventeen, eighteen!"—they had their own methods of counting to keep time. Naturally the poor dancers could hear nothing by reason of the row in the auditorium and the sound of their own dance steps. I had to hold Nijinsky by his clothes—he was furious and ready to dash on stage at any moment and create a scandal.[8]

Fortunately for the composer, who escaped through a dressing room window with the conductor after that first performance, a concert performance of the music a year later was more peaceful. Stravinsky said of it:

> It was a brilliant renascence of *The Rite,* after the Théâtre des Champs-Elysées scandal. The hall was crowded. The audience, with no scenery to distract them, listened with concentrated attention and applauded with an enthusiasm I had been far from expecting and which greatly moved me. Certain critics

8. Igor Stravinsky and Robert Craft, *Dialogues and A Diary* (New York, 1963).

who had censured *The Rite* the year before now openly admitted their mistake. This conquest of the public naturally gave me intense and lasting satisfaction.[9]

Introduction

LISTENING OUTLINE

The *Introduction* is scored almost exclusively for woodwinds (the French horns being equally a part of this family); only in a few places does Stravinsky employ the strings. The high D trumpet is used once, the other brass and percussion not at all. It opens with a bassoon solo, scored very high in its register (Example 1). At first this melody is unaccompanied; two soft French horns enter contrapuntally in the second measure; in the fourth bar, the clarinets join in. The bassoon melody (Example 1) is Stravinsky's adaptation of a Lithuanian folk song that he discovered in an anthology and whose character he changed by adding a shortened chromatic phrase to the end of the originally symmetrical tune.

Example 1

A measure later the solo bassoon repeats a truncated variant of the first three measures of Example 1. An English horn, sounding almost like a shepherd's pipe, responds. The bassoon, in turn, answers with a one-measure excerpt from Example 1.

9. Stravinsky and Craft, *Dialogues and a Diary*.

The tempo becomes a little faster; three bassoons and the English horn are heard in a highly chromatic and contrapuntal passage. Four quick *pizzicato* notes in the violas and cellos introduce the shrill soprano clarinet, which plays a highly chromatic melody whose compass is only a fourth (tones no more than four steps apart).

A melody of widely spaced leaps for the flute follows; an oboe solo is heard in counterpoint to the flute melody. An alto flute responds to this flute-oboe duet. The English horn again becomes prominent and is soon joined contrapuntally by the bass clarinet.

A legato passage for three flutes and English horn is almost organlike in its texture. It is interrupted by a persistent rhythm established by the alto flute alternating with the bass clarinets and a single cello *pizzicato,* which stops only for a one-measure bassoon passage. Its resumption is short lived; the solo bassoon enters again. Soon the shrill voice of the soprano clarinet is heard above it, then the flute.

The oboe introduces a new melody (Example 2), which is folklike in nature:

Example 2

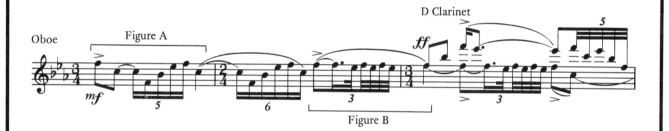

Clarinets become prominent against muted strings in harmonics; a cello (*pizzicato*) and two bassoons supply the rhythmic pulse of this passage. Flute and piccolo arpeggios are answered by "flutter-tongued" (a sound produced by rolling the tongue, as in the pronunciation of the letter *r* in Spanish or Italian), descending, chromatic chords by the oboes, flute, and clarinet. A muted trumpet is heard with Figure A from Example 2; this is followed by Figure B from the same example. The texture then becomes very thick.

Suddenly the original tempo returns with the solo bassoon playing a variant of Example 1. A clarinet trill against violins *pizzicato* interrupts it. A descending figure for clarinets leads to a string chord. The pizzicato figure in the violins concludes the *Introduction,* leading without pause to the following dance.

The Augurs of Spring — Dance of the Young Girls

LISTENING OUTLINE

The tempo doubles—*Tempo giusto* ("a moderate, strict tempo")—at the opening of this dance. A very syncopated rhythm (Example 3) is established immediately by the strings; horns punctuate the accented beats. The harmony in this passage is polytonal, an E-flat chord (with an added seventh) superimposed on an F-flat chord. Stravinsky claimed that this polytonal chord, with its double "axis" (E-flat and F-flat) was the fundamental musical idea of the entire score.

Example 3

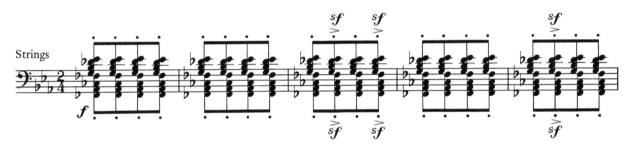

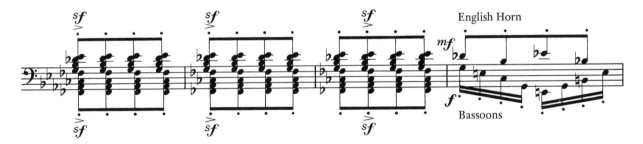

Soon a descending chromatic figure (Example 4) moves back and forth between the muted trumpet, oboe, and violins *pizzicato,* while the rest of the strings continue the rhythmic chords of Example 3.

Example 4

As the texture becomes thicker, brief figures for the piccolos and flutes can be heard.

A return is made to the opening rhythmical passage (Example 3). This *ostinato* (repeated figure) suddenly becomes softer as a theme emerges from it in the bassoons:

Example 5

Bassoons (in octaves)

Over a continuation of the ostinato, pert figures are heard in the oboe, the flute playing in concert with them. The music then halts suddenly; the pounding of the timpani, with the bass drum, and the tubas holding the octave F *fortississimo,* echoes in the listener's ear.

A descending *arpeggio* in the woodwinds and brass leads to a solo violin and bassoon trill. A solo trumpet, *staccato,* takes up an insistent, repetitive four-note figure. A bassoon and violin trill interrupts, leading to a new theme (Example 6), the principal theme of the dance (again in folk-song style), played by the French horns; it is accompanied by strings *col legno,* that is, the strings played by the wood of the bow rather than the horsehair.

Example 6

French Horns (mais en dehors)

A countermelody for solo flute appears over the sustained tones of the French horn melody. Soon a figure in repeated tones is heard in the oboes; twice the trumpet answers this with Figure C from Example 4.

The alto flute plays the principal theme (Example 6). Figures from it are then repeated.

Pairs of trumpets introduce a new polytonal melody, one based on the tonal centers of D-flat and G-flat.

Example 7

Trumpets

Figures from Example 7 are extended over the following ten measures.

The dynamic level suddenly subsides; only the strings are heard. After the woodwinds start to punctuate the string passage, a piccolo enters with a variant of the principal theme (Example 6).

From this point on, the texture thickens, the dynamic level increases, the pulse becomes stronger. Cellos are heard undergirding the rhythm; trumpets enter with insistent figures. The music builds, moving inexorably to its bold conclusion.

About the Composer

IGOR STRAVINSKY   Born: June 17, 1882
Oranienbaum, Russia

Died: April 6, 1971
New York, New York

Igor Stravinsky has said of himself: "I was born out of time in the sense that by temperament and talent I would have been more suited for the life of a small Bach, living in anonymity and composing regularly for an established service and for God."[10]

But such was not to be his fate. His fame and popularity have greatly overshadowed that of the other two major composers of the twentieth century—Schoenberg and Bartók. And so has his longevity—more than four generations: he lived from the days of Wagner, Tchaikovsky, and Brahms, to the time of the most avant-garde composers of the late twentieth century.

Stravinsky was born in Oranienbaum, Russia, a summer resort a short distance from St. Petersburg (now Leningrad). His father was the leading bass at the St. Petersburg Opera and, because of this, Igor grew up surrounded by the world of French, Italian, and Russian opera. By the age of nine, he could play the piano and had begun reading through his father's library of opera scores.

At first no thought was given either by Igor or his family to the possibility of a professional career in music. The boy hated the routine piano exercises he was assigned and was bored by the lessons in traditional harmony. He decided finally on a career in law and entered the University of St. Petersburg to study jurisprudence. At this time Stravinsky became acquainted with Nikolay Rimsky-Korsakov and requested lessons in composition. From 1903 until Rimsky-Korsakov's death in 1908, the two worked closely together.

This entire early phase of Stravinsky's career was shaped by the events that followed the first performance of his youthful *Fantastic Scherzo* at a concert in St. Petersburg in 1909. The Russian ballet impresario Sergei Diaghilev heard the performance

10. Igor Stravinsky, *An Autobiography.*

Igor Stravinsky at age 25 (left) sits beside his teacher Rimsky-Korsakov with relatives in a 1907 photograph.

and was so impressed that he requested Stravinsky to arrange and orchestrate Chopin's *Valse brillante* and one of his *Nocturnes* for the proposed ballet *Les Sylphides,* to be given in Paris the following season. Diaghilev was pleased with the results; he next commissioned Stravinsky to compose a ballet based on the Russian fairy tale *The Firebird.*

From this association of Diaghilev and Stravinsky in Paris came three of the masterpieces of twentieth-century music, the three ballets *The Firebird,* 1910; *Petrouchka* (named after the puppet who is the center of the story), 1911; and *The Rite of Spring,* 1913. All three reflect Stravinsky's Russian background. In spite of their unconscious nationalistic character, these works established a musical idiom for the twenty-eight-year-old composer that was unique and individual. He revolutionized the concept of rhythm, with units of seven, eleven, or thirteen beats in a measure; a continual shifting from one meter to another; and a dislocation of accents by means of intricate patterns of syncopation. This tended to give the music powerful but controlled thrust and tension. He avoided the lush chromaticisms of the late Romantics; instead, he changed tonalities frequently and at times employed polytonality. No matter how complex in structure, however, his melodies and harmonies always seemed to revert back to or center around a basic key and tonality. His orchestrations were superb, for he was a pupil of one of the greatest authorities on orchestration the world of music has ever known—Rimsky-Korsakov.

The First World War disrupted all of Europe and its music-making. Stravinsky spent the years 1914–18 mostly in Switzerland, where he continued to compose; Russian subjects continued to dominate his creative imagination. After the war ended, Stravinsky settled in Paris for fifteen years, becoming a French citizen. The First World War and its economic aftermath—a tremendous depression—caused Stravinsky to make important changes in his next major composition, a ballet and choral work entitled *Les Noces* (*The Wedding*), based on the customs of Russian folk weddings. Originally he had planned to use an orchestra of about 150 to accompany the chorus and soloists. When he finally readied it for the stage after the war (during the height of European postwar inflation), the composer pared the accompaniment down to four pianos and percussion.

American jazz exerted an influence on Stravinsky. As the composer later recalled:

> Ernst Ansermet [a Swiss conductor], returning from an American tour, brought me a bundle of ragtime music in the form of piano reductions and instrumental parts, which I copied out in score. With these pieces before me, I composed the *Ragtime* in [*The Soldier's Tale*] and, after completing [it], the *Ragtime for Eleven Instruments*.[11]

One of the choral masterpieces of the twentieth century, the *Symphony of Psalms,* was written by Stravinsky in 1930 on a commission from the Boston Symphony Orchestra for its fiftieth anniversary. Scored for chorus and orchestra (omitting violins and violas in order to achieve a richer, deeper sound), *Symphony of Psalms* is based on the Latin text of the Vulgate Bible—Psalms 38, 39 and 150 (Psalms 39, 40 and 150 are

11. Igor Stravinsky, *An Autobiography.*

the equivalent in the King James version) and is in three sections played without pause. The first is a call for divine pity (Psalm 38: *Hear my prayer, O Lord*), the second an expression of gratitude (Psalm 39: *I waited patiently for the Lord, and He inclined unto me*), and a hymn of praise and glory (Psalm 150: *Praise ye the Lord*).

In 1939 the composer was invited by Harvard University to deliver a series of lectures; he was there when the Second World War broke out, and decided to remain in the United States, moving to Beverly Hills, California, where he became a United States citizen in 1945.

During the Second World War a strange series of works flowed from his pen. "These were journeyman jobs," the composer stated in defense of them, "commissions I was forced to accept because the war in Europe had so drastically reduced the income from my compositions." These "commissions" included a *Circus Polka* (a ballet for elephants) requested by the Ringling Brothers and Barnum and Bailey Circus in 1942; *Scenes de ballet* for Billy Rose's 1944 review *The Seven Lively Arts; Ebony Concerto* for Woody Herman's Band in 1945; and *Praeludium* (1937, revised 1953), a work of thirty-odd bars meant as a signature for a dance band. He also composed an opera, *The Rake's Progress* (1950), during this period.

The composer's eightieth birthday, in 1962, was celebrated by his first return to Russia in fifty-three years. In addition to conducting concerts of his music in Moscow and Leningrad, he spent an afternoon visiting with then Soviet premier Nikita Khrushchev. "He is like a composer playing you the composition he is working on," said Stravinsky of Khrushchev as he rode away from the Kremlin, "a composition of which he is very proud."

Bibliography

Stravinsky, Igor. *An Autobiography.* New York: M. & J. Steuer, 1958; W. W. Norton, 1962.

Libman, Lillian. *And Music at the Close: Stravinsky's Last Years, a Personal Memoir.* New York: W. W. Norton, 1972.

Rhapsody in Blue
by GEORGE GERSHWIN

George Gershwin was neither the first nor the last composer to adapt the jazz idiom to concert music, but of all of them—including Stravinsky—Gershwin was by far the most successful. His initial effort in this hybrid form was the *Rhapsody in Blue.*

The idea that Gershwin should compose something of larger scope than Broadway musical comedy scores came from the bandleader Paul Whiteman. He was planning an "educational" concert at Aeolian Hall in New York, and he wanted Gershwin to write something for it.

Gershwin did not take Whiteman very seriously. It was, therefore, quite a shock for Gershwin to read in the *New York Tribune* of January 4, 1924, that Whiteman had scheduled his concert for February 12, and that "George Gershwin is at work on a jazz concerto." Here is the composer's own story of what happened after that.

> Suddenly an idea occurred to me. There had been so much talk about the limitations of jazz, not to speak of the manifest misunderstanding of its function. Jazz, they said, had to be in strict time. It had to cling to dance rhythms. I resolved, if possible, to kill that misconception with one sturdy blow. Inspired by this aim, I set to work composing.
>
> I had no set plan, no structure to which my music could conform. The *Rhapsody,* you see, began as a purpose, not a plan. I worked out a few themes, but just at this time I had to appear in Boston for the premiere of [my Broadway show] *Sweet Little Devil.* It was on the train, with its steely rhythms, its rattlety-bang that is so often stimulating to a composer (I frequently hear music in the very heart of a noise), that I suddenly heard—even saw on paper—the complete construction of the *Rhapsody* from beginning to end. No new themes came to me, but I worked on the thematic material already in my mind, and tried to conceive the composition as a whole. I heard it as a sort of musical kaleidoscope of America—of our vast melting-pot, of our incomparable national pep, our blues, our metropolitan madness. By the time I reached Boston, I had the definite plot of the piece, as distinguished from its actual substance.
>
> The middle theme came upon me suddenly as my music often does. It was at the home of a friend, just after I got back to New York. I must do a great deal of what you might call subconscious composing, and this is an example. Playing at parties is one of my notorious weaknesses. As I was playing, without a thought of the *Rhapsody,* all at once I heard myself playing a theme that must have been haunting me inside, seeking outlet. No sooner had it oozed out of my fingers than I realized I had found it. Within a week of my return from Boston I had completed the structure, in the rough, of the *Rhapsody in Blue.*[12]

In the ensuing weeks before the concert, Gershwin worked on revisions of the *Rhapsody.* The composition was written for two pianos, with a few suggestions of instrumentation jotted down in the music. Because of the pressure of time and because Gershwin had little experience in orchestration, Whiteman's arranger Ferde Grofé made the setting for an enlarged dance band and, later, for symphony orchestra. The final version of the solo part was not even ready at concert time, and there were whole blank pages of piano music which Gershwin improvised on the spot. Whiteman must have had his hands full conducting a score that in one long blank space bore the notation, "Wait for nod."

For the Aeolian Hall concert at which the *Rhapsody* was premiered, Whiteman had invited as guests the famous violinists Fritz Kreisler and Jascha Heifetz, the conductors Walter Damrosch and Leopold Stokowski, and the composers Sergei Rachmaninoff

---

12. Isaac Goldberg, *George Gershwin: A Study in American Music,* pp. 138–39. Copyright © 1931 by Isaac Goldberg. Copyright © 1959 by Ruth Solomon and Bernice Stein. Reprinted by permission of Simon & Schuster, a Division of Gulf & Western Corporation.

and Igor Stravinsky. Suddenly, at the last minute, panic overtook Whiteman. What had he done, inviting all the biggest names in music to hear an "educational" experiment in American music like this? "Black fear simply possessed me," he later recalled. "I paced the floor, gnawed my thumbs and vowed I'd give $5,000 if we could stop right then and there."

But the concert went on. The program was a very long one, with more than twenty selections, of which *Rhapsody in Blue* was to be the next to last. The audience received the earlier works on the program with mild applause and no enthusiasm. (A jazz selection written by Victor Herbert was quite bad; he could compose the world's most successful operettas, but not jazz.)

Finally it came time for the *Rhapsody*. Ross Gorman, the band's brilliant clarinetist, lifted his instrument and let out that famous, slowly ascending wail that opens the *Rhapsody* (a glissando that other clarinetists of the time said was impossible to play). The conductor could feel the attention the audience was giving this new work. "Somewhere in the middle of the score I began crying," Whiteman later recalled. "When I came to myself I was eleven pages along and to this day I cannot tell you how I conducted that far." The final bold, brash notes died away, and the audience rose to its feet and gave the *Rhapsody* a wild ovation. Thus its career was successfully launched.

By definition, the *Rhapsody* is in a free, rhapsodic form, ideally suited to Gershwin's purposes. Melodically there are five ideas involved, three of which occur at the very beginning and are variants of the old jazz trick of using the final chord of a piece as the basis for melodic and harmonic variants.

LISTENING OUTLINE

The first melodic idea is heard immediately: the long, slowly ascending, seventeen-note *glissando* (slide) of the clarinet and the theme that follows it.

Example 1

Rhapsody in Blue (George Gershwin). © 1924 New World Music Corporation. Copyright Renewed. All Rights Reserved. Used by permission.

The second musical idea follows almost immediately. It is played by the bass clarinet, tenor saxophone, and one French horn while other woodwinds and strings sustain a long-held pitch.

Example 2

Bass Clarinet, Horn, Tenor Saxophone

Bassoons, Horns, Low Strings

Introduced by a clarinet glissando, a trumpet using a wha-wha mute plays Example 1; after a very brief piano interlude, the full orchestra repeats it.

The piano introduces the third melodic idea (Example 3) in an extended solo passage of some forty-eight measures that also involves the idea of Example 1.

Example 3

Piano

The full orchestra plays the melody of Example 1 *fortissimo,* then elaborates on its melodic idea.

Trumpets in octaves announce the *Rhapsody*'s fourth melodic idea:

Example 4

Trumpets

The clarinet, followed by the full orchestra, returns to the melodic idea of Example 2.

The orchestra, *marcato,* moves on to new melodic material in an extended and lengthy development that begins:

Example 5

Saxophones, Bass Clarinet, Bassoons

A lengthy passage for solo piano, suggestive of a cadenza, is based on the thematic material thus far introduced.

The tempo changes to *Andantino moderato con espressione;* the strings and reeds introduce the *Rhapsody's* most famous theme:

Example 6

After an extended passage, in which the theme of Example 6 builds to one dynamic climax after another, the solo piano is heard again in a cadenza built out of the melodic material of Example 6.

In the closing section of the *Rhapsody,* the order of the thematic ideas is reversed. Example 6 is heard first, played by the brass. Example 3 follows in the piano, *agitato,* building to a climax. Example 2 appears in the solo piano; it is accompanied by woodwinds and strings.

A final, bold, and brief statement of Example 1 brings the *Rhapsody* to a swift conclusion.

About the Composer

GEORGE GERSHWIN   Born: September 26, 1898
Brooklyn, New York

Died: July 11, 1937
Beverly Hills, California

At the age of fifteen, George Gershwin announced to his parents that he was quitting school to go into the music business. Before he could say another word, his parents—immigrants from Russia who had no use for music—exploded. Quit school? Impossible! Nobody got ahead without an education. Musicians were always out of work. But, George protested, he *had* a job. One that would pay fifteen dollars a week! The following day, George Gershwin began his professional career in music as a Tin Pan Alley song-plugger. He worked for Remick's, a music publisher, in a cubicle about the size of a self-service elevator, pounding out songs on the piano for entertainers who came looking for new material.

Gershwin studied piano with Ernest Hutcheson and Charles Hambitzer in New York, and took lessons in harmony from Edward Kilenyi and Rubin Goldmark. Later, when he was a famous composer of popular music, Gershwin continued private studies, including counterpoint with the composers Henry Cowell and Wallingford Riegger. Gershwin applied to Maurice Ravel for lessons in composition, only to be turned down by Ravel, who said that he could only "teach him [Gershwin] to compose bad Ravel, whereas you [Gershwin] now compose superb Gershwin."

While song-plugging during the working day, Gershwin spent his spare time writing original songs, and soon got a chance to play one for Sophie Tucker, a rising young singer who was later to become known as the "Red Hot Mamma." She liked the song, recommended it to a publisher, and, at eighteen, Gershwin was a published composer. The song made him neither rich nor famous (he earned a grand total of five dollars in royalties from it), but the time was not far distant when the boy from the Lower East Side of New York would be represented on Broadway by such hit tunes as *Swanee, Fascinatin' Rhythm, The Man I Love,* and *Embraceable You* —and, in the process, earn enough money to afford a penthouse on the Upper East Side.

As he matured, Gershwin wrote a set of piano *Preludes* that incorporated some of his reflections on jazz in music. A trip to Paris to supervise some concerts of his music at the Opéra led to another fine work for orchestra, the tone poem *An American in Paris.* While in Europe, Gershwin became acquainted with Ravel, Stravinsky, and Prokofiev in Paris, and Alban Berg, a pupil of Schoenberg, in Vienna. Days were now crowded with work for the composer, but he found time to take up painting, demonstrating far more than average talent.

He composed one of his best Broadway shows, *Girl Crazy,* in 1930. (Playing in the pit orchestra for it were the now legendary jazz artists Benny Goodman, Gene Krupa, Glenn Miller, Jack Teagarden, and Red Nichols. On stage, a new singer was making her debut; Ethel Merman, in a secondary role.)

In the meantime, Gershwin had been working on an opera inspired by the novel *Porgy* by DuBose Heyward. The author lived in South Carolina, scene of the story, so Gershwin moved south for the summer both to be near his librettist and, more importantly, to absorb the atmosphere of the setting of this tale about the South's poor blacks. Gershwin moved from his New York penthouse to Folly Island and a primitive shack with an old iron bedstead and a few pieces of crumbling furniture. Drinking water had to be brought in five-gallon jugs to the little island. An old upright piano was moved in for composing. Here, unshaven and usually clad in a bathing suit, Gershwin lived by the sea and sand under the hot summer sun and worked with an excitement bordering on ecstasy that he had never known before.

In September he returned to New York with the music for the opera more or less sketched out. He could write a Broadway show tune in half an hour and make a fortune from it, but to complete complex choral passages, contrapuntal writing, and orchestration for *Porgy and Bess* took another whole year. It was on September 2, 1935, that Gershwin marked the 600-page score finished.

The opera was put into six weeks of rehearsal, and on September 30, 1935, just four days after Gershwin's thirty-seventh birthday, it opened in Boston, and then moved to New York for a highly successful run. The opera has been successfully revived in New York and elsewhere, and received international recognition in 1955, when an American company of black singers took it on tour throughout South America and Europe, reaching a climax of success with several performances in Russia—the first American opera troupe to visit the Soviet Union.

When sound was added to movies, it was only natural that Hollywood would want to make use of Gershwin's talents. After *Girl Crazy* and *Of Thee I Sing* (1931), George and his brother Ira, who wrote the lyrics for many of his tunes, moved to Beverly Hills, California, where together they wrote music for the movies.

While Gershwin was writing music for Samuel Goldwyn's movie-musical extravaganza, *The Goldwyn Follies,* it was discovered that he had a brain tumor. A delicate operation revealed to the doctors that it was in a part of the brain from which it could not be removed. Gershwin never regained consciousness and died on July 11, 1937, at the age of thirty-eight.

Bibliography

Ewen, David. *George Gershwin: His Journey to Greatness.* Reprint of 1970 edition. Westport, Conn.: Greenwood Press, 1977.

Kimball, Robert E., and Simon, Alfred E. *The Gershwins.* New York: Atheneum, 1973.

Estancia

by ALBERTO GINASTERA

The title *Estancia* could probably best be translated as "The Estate," for *estancia* is the term for the large ranches where cattle are raised in Argentina. It is the land of the *gauchos,* the hard-riding herdsmen of the *pampas* who traditionally have played such an important role in Argentine history, folklore, legend, and literature.

Argentinian composer Alberto Ginastera (pronounced heen-ah-STEH-ra) has said of this countryside:

> Whenever I have crossed the pampa or have lived in it for a time, my spirit felt itself inundated by changing impressions, now joyful, now melancholy, some full of euphoria and others replete with a profound tranquility produced by its limitless immensity and by the transformation that the countryside undergoes in the course of the day. . . .

View of an estancia.

From my first contact with the pampa, there awakened within me the desire to write a work that would reflect these states of my spirit. In some moments of my ballet *Estancia* the landscape appears as the veritable protagonist, imposing its influence upon the feelings of the characters.[13]

The story of the ballet *Estancia* is derived from one of Argentina's literary masterpieces, *Martín Fierro,* a bit of that country's *gauchesco* literature written in 1872 by José Hernandez. The scenario of the ballet depicts the activity on an *estancia* from dawn to dawn, thus providing the composer with an opportunity for a succession of typical dances. The actual story itself must also have been close to the composer's heart, for it concerns a girl so enamored of rural life that she turns a cold shoulder to her city-bred suitor, until he proves his mettle by mastering the difficult and dangerous skills of the gaucho.

Danza Final (Malambo)

In the orchestral suite derived from the ballet, the finale, or fourth movement, is a *malambo,* the most vigorous and typical dance of the *gauchos.* The *malambo* is an agile,

13. Alberto Ginastera, program notes for *Pampeana No. 3,* recording (Louisville Symphony Orchestra, 1954).

footstamping dance generally performed by one man alone, or by two men in competition. The basic metrical pattern of six beats to the measure embodies the typical feature of the *malambo*—the *zapateo* (from the Spanish word *zapato,* "shoe"), the term applied to the energetic footwork of this virile and rustic dance.

LISTENING OUTLINE

The introduction is a brisk *Allegro* in $\frac{6}{8}$ meter. Upper woodwinds, muted trumpets, and strings (including the piano) are prominent in a sixteen-measure passage that establishes the rhythmic pulse of the movement.

The violins and upper woodwinds introduce the first melody of the dance:

Example 1

Soon a new, bolder melody is played in octaves by the violins:

Example 2

The following rhythmic passage contains measures sometimes divided into duple and sometimes triple meter, although the signature is always $\frac{6}{8}$. The end of this passage is highly syncopated.

The opening rhythmic passage is repeated, followed by a restatement of Example 1 and its succceeding measures.

At the point of dynamic climax, the music is marked *Tempo di Malambo.* The upper woodwinds—piccolos, oboes, and clarinets—as well as the trumpets and xylophone, introduce the principal theme (Example 3), which is repeated twice.

Example 3

Piccolos, Oboes, Clarinets

sempre f

The French horns boldly proclaim a malambo motive of their own against a string accompaniment.

The upper woodwinds, trumpets, and xylophone return to the principal theme (Example 3), playing it three times.

The brass play a prominent melodic figure.

Again the upper woodwinds, trumpets, and xylophone counter with statements of Example 3—three repetitions this time, and sometimes beginning with the second measure. Some episodic passages are added.

The brass are now joined in their melodic figures by oboes and clarinets.

The principal theme (Example 3) returns triumphant, boldly holding sway until the final climax of the dance.

About the Composer

ALBERTO GINASTERA   Born: April 11, 1916
                                              Buenos Aires, Argentina

Alberto Ginastera is Argentina's most famous composer, a creative artist who has earned an international reputation as a Nationalist composer through such works as his ballets *Panambi* and *Estancia* and orchestral works such as *Concierto Argentino* and *Sinfonia Porteña*—although his latest operas, *Bomarzo* and *Don Rodrigo,* are in a more universal musical idiom.

Ginastera's paternal grandfather immigrated from Catalonia in Spain; his maternal grandfather from Lombardy in Italy. Thus his parents, Luisa Bossi and Alberto Ginastera, were second-generation Argentines who had settled in the *gran aldea* (big village) of Buenos Aires. It was there that the composer was born.

No one else in his family was musically inclined, but from about the age of five, young Alberto showed an unusual interest in toy trumpets and drums. Two years later

he started taking piano lessons, and at twelve he was enrolled in the Conservatorio Williams, where he studied for eight years. In 1936 he entered the National Conservatory of Music in Buenos Aires, first studying composition with a graduate of the Schola Cantorum in Paris, thus absorbing French influences of lasting effect.

During his student days, Ginastera composed a large body of works in many different forms. He later destroyed most of them, claiming they were immature. At that time he was most impressed by two contemporary works—Debussy's *La Mer* (*The Sea*) and Stravinsky's *Le Sacre du printemps* (*The Rite of Spring*).

Ginastera's first published work was *Impressions of the Puna,*[14] printed in 1934. Scored for flute and string quartet, its local color is derived from the northern highland region of Argentina, where the surviving remnants of Indian tradition are found. In 1937 he completed the ballet *Panambi,* a "choreographic legend" based on an indigenous legend of the Guarnaní Indians. It was successfully produced at the Teatro Colón in Buenos Aires three years later. Several piano works of this era likewise reflect a strongly national influence: *Argentine Dances* (1937), *Three Pieces* (1940), and *Danzas Criollas* (*Creole Dances,* 1946).

In 1941 Ginastera completed his second ballet, *Estancia.* It had been commissioned for the American Ballet Caravan which, because of the United States' involvement in the Second World War, dissolved before producing it. A concert performance of the suite from *Estancia* was given at a Colón concert in 1943, and the ballet itself was finally produced on that stage in 1952.

Ginastera was awarded a Guggenheim Fellowship in 1942, but because of the war he postponed his visit to the United States until 1946. He spent most of his time in New York and was commissioned to write several works while in this country. It was in 1947 that he completed the first of three works to which he has given the generic title of *Pampeana,* derived from the word *pampa,* referring to the immense grassy plains of Argentina.

The composer returned to Argentina in 1948 and, in the city of La Plata, organized the Conservatory of Music and Scenic Art of the Province of Buenos Aires, of which he became director. He was removed from that position in 1952 by the regime of president Juan Perón, just as the Peronistas had removed him from his professorship at the National Military Academy in 1945. In 1956, after Perón's overthrow, Ginastera had the satisfaction of being named Interventor (Supervisor) of the Conservatory of La Plata.

Ginastera's music is colorful, often flamboyant, and appealing in a most uncerebral way. Although its vocabulary is modern (derived in his later works by serial procedures, a further achievement of Schoenberg's "twelve-tone" system), the syntax of Ginastera's music is almost invariably familiar. "Music," he says, "must be expressive. All of the great composers have been expressionists in this sense: Mozart, Beethoven, Schubert, Mahler, Schoenberg, Berg." Ginastera asserts that "most modern composers have become frozen and sterile."

14. *Puna* refers to the high, cold, arid plateaus of the Andes.

Bibliography

Chase, Gilbert. "Alberto Ginastera: Argentine Composer." *Musical Quarterly,* 43 (October 1957), 439–60.

—"Alberto Ginastera: Portrait of an Argentine Composer." *Tempo,* 44 (Summer 1957), 11–16.

Passio et Mors Domini Nostri Iesu Christi secundum Lucam

by KRZYSZTOF PENDERECKI

The contemporary Polish composer Krzysztof Penderecki (pronounced "CHRIS-toff Pen-der-ET-ski) has written many large works for chorus, orchestra, and soloists. One of the finest is his oratorio called in English *The Passion and Death of Our Lord Jesus Christ According to St. Luke.*

Begun in 1963 and completed in 1965, Penderecki's *Passion* was commissioned by the West German Radio to mark the seven hundredth anniversary of the Münster Cathedral and was first performed in the cathedral itself in 1966.

Just before that performance, Penderecki told some reporters:

> I am a Roman Catholic. In my opinion, however, one does not have to belong to a church to compose religious music. The only condition is that one is willing to confess one's religious convictions. Therefore, you can without any objection consider my music as "avowal" music: in that respect I am a Romanticist.[15]

The *St. Luke Passion* is scored for a large orchestra; soprano, baritone, and bass soloists; a narrator, whose part is spoken; a children's choir; and three adult, mixed choirs. The work is divided into two halves, each of which is through-composed—that is, with no section being repeated. Being a modern work, it is not really in any of the traditional tonalities or keys, although much of it centers around the pitch D. In style, the work includes many polyphonic passages in traditional canonic style; some chorus parts are declaimed or spoken rather than sung; and there is a bit of aleatoric writing, passages that are performed a different way each time the work is heard, leaving to chance the actual sound.

Following the tradition of Johann Sebastian Bach's *St. Matthew Passion* and *St. John Passion* of over 200 years earlier, Penderecki's work tells the story of Jesus's last seven days, using the words of the Gospel according to St. Luke along with both personal and communal liturgical responses to the story—excerpts from the Psalms, the Gospel according to St. John, and sections of the Roman Catholic prayerbook including special chants called *sequences.* Thus the soloists and chorus all function as characters

15. "Penderecki: A Portrait," notes to accompany recording (Candide/Vox CE 31071).

in the drama. The St. Luke Gospel portion of Penderecki's *Passion,* in Latin, starts with chapter 22, verse 39, and concludes with chapter 23, verse 46. Penderecki omits some thirty verses from these chapters because of the time element.

What makes Penderecki's *Passion* a completely individual work are the powerful and dramatic effects he achieves in his treatment of both instrumental and vocal sounds. The conductor's score is full of most unusual directions for the players, telling them to do such things as to rub the back of the violin bow on a hard surface, and aleatoric or chance passages that allow the players to choose a series of tones between the high and low notes in their instrument's range. Many of the things the composer suggests are the result of his own experiments with the nature of sound. His choirs make hissing and jeering sounds to suggest the rabble of the crowd as Jesus is brought before Pilate. Sometimes Penderecki even divides the syllables of a word between different voices in the choir, thus giving an almost three-dimensional effect of space and distance such as would be occupied by the babbling crowd. Yet, in their seemingly confused fragments, the words are still recognizable and can be understood.

Penderecki's methods, however, are not tricks or gimmickry for its own sake. He follows the tradition of seventeenth- and eighteenth-century German composers such as Heinrich Schütz, who tried in his *St. Matthew Passion* to imitate the sound of a cock crowing during Peter's denial, and Bach, who attempted in his Passions to make realistic suggestions of angel wings fluttering and of angels ascending to heaven.

Stabat Mater

Stabat Mater is scored for three adult, mixed choirs singing *a cappella* (without instrumental accompaniment). The text is a thirteenth-century sequence probably written by the Franciscan monk Jacopone da Todi (*c.* 1228–1306).

LISTENING OUTLINE

The tenors of the first choir introduce the first line of the text to a chantlike motive of three closely related pitches. This figure becomes the melodic and harmonic basis for the *Stabat Mater.*

Example 1

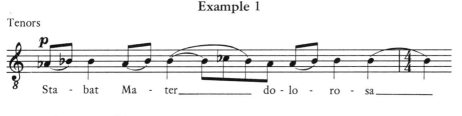

Stabat Mater dolorosa   Stood the Mother

The lower voices of all three choirs—altos, tenors, and basses—enter softly, one by one, with long-sustained pitches. (The most important unifying factor of this passage is the steady pedal-point on A in most of the voices.) The sounds are unusual, for each voice exaggerates the mouth sound of the particular vowel it is enunciating. With the words *Dum pendebat Filius* ("Where the Son hung"), Penderecki introduces an interesting sustained chord of many different pitches.[16]

Stabat Mater dolorosa	Stood the Mother, stood there sighing
Iuxta Crucem lacrimosa,	Tearful, 'neath the cross, where dying
Dum pendebat Filius.	Hung her only Son and Lord.

The next section marks the first entry of the sopranos. The sopranos of all three choirs begin the section with an outcry on E (in unison), *forte* on the word *Quis.*

Soft, sustained pitches predominate, but the section is punctuated by an outburst on the first *Christe* of the text. This passage has a fortissimo climax on the words *si videret.*

Quis est homo, qui non fleret,	Who the man
Matrem Christi si videret	his tears withholdeth

The following section, based on the repeated text, is highly rhythmical, the text being rendered in songlike speech and whispers rather than sung:

In tanto supplicio?	On her martyrdom profound?

The altos of the first choir enter with the melodic figure of Example 1 to the text *Eia Mater, fons amoris.* Tenors and then basses enter with variants of this melodic figure.

Eia, Mater, fons amoris,	Mother, fount of love the purest,

16. Because the staff notation for the pitches of this complex chord involves adjoining spaces and lines, it is necessary to print the chord as shown.

The tenors repeat the last part of the melodic figure of Example 1 to another line of the text. They are imitated, in turn, by all the other voices of the three choirs. This section culminates in a short and loud chordal proclamation of the word *Christe.* (These chords contain all twelve pitches of the chromatic scale.)

Me sentire vim doloris	All the anguish thou endurest,
Fac, ut tecum lugeam.	Make me feel to mourn with thee.
Fac, ut ardeat cor meum	Make my heart with ardour glowing,
In amando Christum Deum,	In the love of Christ still growing,
Ut sibi complaceam.	Unto him well-pleasing be.
Christe,	Christ,

The altos of all three choirs then very softly intone *quasi una litania* ("like a litany") the text:

Christe, cum sit hinc exire,	Christ, where hence my spirit's lifted,
Da per Matrem me venire	Through thy Mother be I gifted
Ad palmam victoriae.	With the palm of victory.

Discordant outbursts of *Christe* occur, one by each choir.
The litany continues, each choir starting at a different point in time:

Christe, cum sit hinc exire,	Christ, where hence my spirit's lifted,
Da per Matrem me venire	Through thy Mother be I gifted
Ad palmam victoriae.	With the palm of victory.

Once again the text is sung; the melodic line is a variant of the melodic motive found in Example 1.

Christe, cum sit hinc exire,	Christ, where hence my spirit's lifted,

The altos of the first choir introduce the closing, contrapuntal section, in which the voices of all three choirs enter one by one with long-sustained pitches. The final *gloria* comes as a surprise ending—in contrast to all the modern sounds and intervals in the rest of the *Stabat Mater*—a centuries-old, traditional tonic chord.

Quando corpus morietur,	When my mortal flesh here dieth,
Fac, ut animae donetur	Grant my soul in glory flieth
Paradisi gloria.	Swift to Paradise with Thee.

About the Composer

KRZYSZTOF PENDERECKI   Born: November 23, 1933
Debica, Poland

The world's great catastrophes seem to fascinate Poland's avant-garde composer Krzysztof Penderecki. In both his *Threnody to the Victims of Hiroshima* and *Dies Irae* (an oratorio in memory of the dead of Auschwitz), Penderecki treated mass annihilation with moving intensity, stretching the limits of orchestral and vocal writing so far that he had to invent new notational symbols to convey the meanings in his scores. In *The Passion and Death of Our Lord Jesus Christ According to St. Luke* and his opera *The Devils of Loudun* (concerned with the torture and execution of a seventeenth-century Jesuit priest), the composer has treated mass hysteria, crucifixion, and murder. For a 1976 Bicentennial commission from the Chicago Lyric Opera, Penderecki chose as the basis of his work Milton's epic, *Paradise Lost,* with its story of Satan's rebellion against God. "My music has been obsessed with death and the tragic," the composer has freely admitted.

Krzysztof Penderecki was born in the small town of Debica, in eastern Poland, in 1933. His father, a lawyer, gave him a violin when he was thirteen, and by fourteen the boy was playing in the local orchestra. As a teenager, Penderecki wanted to be a virtuoso in the manner of the great Paganini and composed fiery and difficult violin pieces. He abandoned this ambition when he was twenty and, deciding to be a more serious composer, entered the Conservatory of Music in Cracow. His teacher was an archconservative who taught in the then popular style of the neoclassical school that emerged briefly between the two world wars. "We heard no early Stravinsky—*Le sacre du printemps* or *Petrouchka,*" the composer later recalled. "And, of course, no Schoenberg or Berg. For me, I feel this was good. Not having to study all the modern styles, I was free to work on creating my own musical language, devising new possibilities of string technique, also new notation."

In Poland, ideological pressures on the arts were relaxed in 1956, which resulted in the opening of the Warsaw Autumn Festival. This has grown, in Penderecki's estimation, to be "the biggest new music festival in the world." The same year, Penderecki began working in the Warsaw Studio of Electronic Music, where he wrote scores for experimental theater and films, and developed notions of sound textures that he would later apply to traditional instruments.

Public attention was first drawn to Penderecki when, in 1959, he anonymously entered three different compositions in a competition sponsored by the Youth Circle of the Association of Polish Composers and won all three first prizes. With the prize money, Penderecki went to Italy for six weeks, his first "contact with the outside world," as he termed it.

International recognition came two years later, when his *Threnody for the Victims of Hiroshima* won the UNESCO prize from the Tribune Internationale des Compositeurs. Although Penderecki is concerned with writing for various-sized instrumental groups, for orchestra, and—rather unusual with a contemporary composer—for chorus, utilizing religious texts, and continually experiments with the production of unusual sounds from traditional instruments or the human voice, he has not been concerned with electronic music. "Electronic music is too primitive," he says in a gentle put-down. "The symphony orchestra and the human voice are still the greatest resource for variety of tone." Even so, he allows that, "I write instrumentally for the voice."[17]

Penderecki has taught at Yale and Florida State Universities. In 1973, when the Chicago Lyric Opera commissioned Penderecki's *Paradise Lost* for the Bicentennial celebration, a great hue and cry went up from native-born American composers because a Bicentennial commission had been given to a foreigner. (Penderecki is still a Polish citizen and usually divides his time between Poland and the United States.) Because the scope of the opera—which the composer later chose to call a "dramatic presentation"—kept growing, the premiere of the work had to wait until the 1978–79 season. In spite of much time, talent, and money expended on both its first United States performance and its subsequent presentation in Europe, both music critics and the general public responded with indifference and apathy.

In recent years, Penderecki has abandoned serial and totally dissonant music in favor of a simpler, more direct form of expression. His *Symphony No. 2* (1980), subtitled "Christmas," is neo-Romantic in style, tonal throughout, and incorporates parts of the traditional Christmas carol *Silent Night.* His *Te Deum,* also of 1980, for chorus and orchestra and written in honor of Pope John Paul II, follows in the Romantic tradition, as does his later *Concerto No. 2 for Cello and Orchestra,* written for cellist Mstislav Rostropovich.

"Music should serve to touch the depth of human emotion, not merely for posters or realistic effects," Penderecki has been quoted as saying. "I believe in man, his goodwill and the triumph of that quality. To me, music is a humanistic art. Anything else is nonsense."[18]

Bibliography

Hiemenz, Jack. "A Composer Praises God as One Who Lives in Darkness." *New York Times,* February 27, 1977, section II, p. 19.

17. Hewell Tircuit, "A Composer Speaks," *San Francisco Chronicle,* January 15, 1969.
18. Tircuit.

Four Movements for a Fashionable Five-Toed Dragon

by CARMAN MOORE

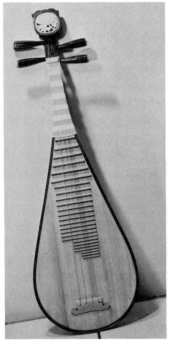

Some of the instruments used in Moore's piece. Above, harpsichord; below, pi'pa; facing page, Chinese opera drum.

Carman Moore is one of the most talented of America's younger composers, a creative artist who is not afraid to speak through the contemporary voice of music, whether it be the sounds of jazz, soul, rock, or the traditional sounds of a symphony orchestra. Moore has written works cast in the traditional European-American symphonic idiom; he has also made use of classical jazz styles and the gospel sounds of black Americans. On occasion, even the rhythm of modern rock can be heard pulsing through his music. This blending (or "fusing," to employ the verb Moore used in the title of one of his most frequently performed works) is not done for the sake of novelty but is a natural outgrowth of both a knowledge of and love for many types of music. "There are several kinds of music screaming in my head," the composer has said, "and there must be a way for all of them to come out at the same time."

Moore has felt that the realities of an age in which cultures and individuals incessantly cross paths mandate this fresh approach to contemporary music-making. In *Gospel Fuse,* for example, Moore fused the sound of the traditional symphony orchestra with the forceful and haunting strains of gospel music in a work the composer describes as "a twenty-two-minute atomic age gospel cantata." And in *Four Movements for a Fashionable Five-Toed Dragon* (1976), the manner in which the composer has blended elements of classical Chinese music, the modern rhythms of rock, the improvisations of jazz, and the traditional symphonic form along with the sounds of the Baroque harpsichord produces a work that is intensely interesting and highly dramatic.

Although some might wonder at the relevance of having a new symphony performed in association with a commercial fashion show, the executive director of the Hong Kong Trade Development Council, Len Dunning, who conceived the idea behind the Carman Moore commission, gave a succinct response.

> Fashion is no longer simply what you wear. Like music, fashion is a life-style in itself, reflecting the moods of an era. It is inspired by, and in turn inspires all aspects of the visual and aural media. And, as new fashion constantly evolves, so does new music.
>
> In [our] presentation, the cross-stimulation and the cross-fertilization of the two separate elements—fashion and music—has resulted in an experimental and totally new artform: fashion inspiring music and music inspiring fashion. The result: *Four Movements for a Fashionable Five-Toed Dragon.*

Since 1976, the year of the commission, was known according to the Chinese lunar calendar as "The Year of the Dragon," it was only natural for Carman Moore's thoughts that year to turn to this ancient Oriental symbol. And, since it was to be music for a fashion celebration, it had to be a "fashionable" five-toed dragon.[20]

20. "Four Movements for a Fashionable Five-Toed Dragon: Tone Roads to Hong Kong '76," notes to accompany recording (Hong Kong Trade Development Council).

Although Moore conceived this work as a symphony in the usual sense of the word, he did not attempt or intend to follow the traditional forms. Thus, while the first movement might be analyzed in relation to sonata-allegro form, this was not the intent of the composer. Moore envisioned the first movement as suggesting a pastoral scene, like a meandering through the countryside. During this wandering, the listener encounters a feeling of the European Middle Ages as the sounds of the harpsichord are heard. There is even a "mind-bending" experience (to use the modern parlance of the composer) as the listener discovers that the Oriental theme is a parody or a movie notion of what an Oriental theme should sound like. And, since Moore enjoys the sounds of nature, there are pseudo-naturalistic sounds, including not only the snort of the five-toed dragon, but the braying of donkeys and the bleating of sheep and goats.

Musically, the listener becomes involved in a bit of chinoiserie as the sounds of the pi'pa—the Oriental "guitar," which has jangling sound values and is an age-old symbol of classical Chinese culture—and opera drums are heard in triple meter over a European medieval "grounding."

As the sound of the harpsichord emerges (with European-Baroque references) from this tapestry, the harpsichord begins to propose the notion of jazz, and before the music is finished, the listener has been transported to the world of bebop.

Overture and Pastorale

The program for the first performance included these words by the composer:

> A rustic mood. The sophisticate's dream of the uncomplicated country life. Petticoats and baskets, aprons and shawls; or tough and sturdy workwear that takes mountains and city canyons in equal stride.

LISTENING OUTLINE

The *Overture* begins with the sound of a Chinese opera gong. Soon harp glissandos up and down the scale are heard, accompanied by high hissing sounds produced by a synthesizer (see Chapter 12) suggesting the snorts of the five-toed dragon. A brass fanfare breaks forth:

Example 1

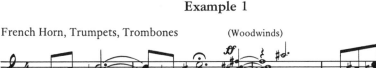

French Horn, Trumpets, Trombones   (Woodwinds)

Four Movements for a Fashionable Five-Toed Dragon (*Tone Roads to HK '76*) by Carman Moore. © Copyright 1978 by Southern Music Publishing Co. Inc. International Copyright Secured. Used by Permission. All Rights Reserved.

The brass are joined by woodwinds and then strings in a passage in which echoes of the fanfare can be detected. The sounds of both Chinese cymbal and opera drums are also heard.

A brief solo for muted trumpet is heard, followed by a solo clarinet with a descending figure that soon turns around and moves upward.

The sound of the full orchestra is heard as the music builds to a dramatic moment, a *Largo,* in which the principal theme is presented:

Example 2

Violins (octave higher)

This theme and variants of it are heard several times in succession.

As the music builds to another dynamic climax, a fanfarelike motive is played by upper woodwinds and brass. This motive is derived from Figure A of Example 2. After several repetitions, an ascending run for flute and upper strings against a descending figure in bassoon and lower strings brings the *Overture* to a conclusion.

The *Pastorale* begins with wind sounds produced by the synthesizer; eerie, reedy sounds are also heard, produced by double-reed players who remove the reeds from their instruments to buzz on them in imitation of the sounds of braying donkeys and bleating sheep and goats.

An electric bass enters with a four-note bass figure that is repeated many times. Woodwinds and brass enter over this with sustained chords. A harp glissando and Chinese drums are heard.

Soon the Oriental theme is introduced by the reeds and pi'pa in unison:

Example 3

Oboe, English Horn, Clarinet, Soprano Saxophone

On a repetition of Example 3 by the woodwinds, the sound of the pi'pa is more prominent than it was the first time.

The brass, with the sound of the French horns predominating, are heard with both rhythmic and melodic variants of Example 3.

After a brief interlude in which the sound of the strings is heard, clarinet and English horn play their soft, lazy, and lyrical variant of Example 3.

Once again the strings are heard; French horns enter, soon joined by the trumpet.

All but low strings drop out as the pi'pa enters with an extended, improvised solo.

The violins eventually take up a countermelody derived from Example 3, while the pi'pa continues with its improvisation.

After a passage for low strings and woodwinds in which both opera gong and tiger gong are heard, the sound of the harpsichord emerges from the orchestral texture. As the harpsichordist improvises a rather extended solo, the sound of the electric bass and low strings accompany. Eventually the double reeds—English horn and bassoon—enter.

An ascending run by the harpsichord leads to a reentrance of the French horns. The bass drum gives a strong accent to the downbeat as the electric guitar enters. Woodwinds and strings, in unison, play a descending figure accompanied by the Chinese opera gong.

The flute and violins then take up the melody of Example 3. A lyrical variant of this melody follows.

As the dynamic level drops, the soprano saxophone enters with an improvised solo. Low strings and the jazz drum set provide a rhythmical accompaniment. There are accents by the brass throughout this passage.

Almost imperceptibly the rhythm turns into a rock beat, as sounds of the Chinese opera drum are heard in contrast to it.

A brief solo cadenza by the soprano saxophone follows in a jazzlike section and leads to a return of the rock beat. A slightly longer solo cadenza for the soprano saxophone follows.

The orchestra reenters and takes up the rock beat as the brass play melodic fragments and variants of Example 3.

As the dynamic level drops once more, the harp is heard with an ascending figure.

After a very short, upward-moving passage for strings, the French horns take up a new melodic figure:

Example 4

French Horn

The horn repeats Example 4.

Following several harp glissandos and a repeated rhythm pattern established by the upper woodwinds, the full orchestra reenters. The soprano saxophone is heard; it is soon joined by the harpsichord and electric bass with jazz improvisations over rhythmic chordal figures in the strings, bassoon, and tuba.

The traditional orchestral instruments drop out as a brief passage for percussion, jazz drum set, electric guitar, and electric bass is heard.

From lowest to highest, the instruments of the string and then woodwind families reenter. The final brief section returns us to the melody of Example 2 from the introduction, which is heard three times in succession: first for full orchestra; then played by woodwinds; and, finally, by the harp as the music dies away into nothingness.

About the Composer

CARMAN MOORE   Born: October 8, 1936
                             Lorain, Ohio

Carman Moore's background is as diverse as his music. His mother played piano— "everything from Liszt to jazz"—and his grandmother sang spirituals to him. His grandmother's father was a Creek Indian. His own double-take first name was not a masculine version of Bizet's heroine, but his parent's phonetic stab at Carmine, the name of an Italian fishing buddy of his father's.

Growing up in Elyria, Ohio, Moore was an outstanding tennis player and a member of the high school team. He chose music over tennis as a profession, though, and graduated from Ohio State University. He then came to New York to study composition with Hall Overton, and he later worked with Luciano Berio as well as several other composers. Moore developed a distinct leaning toward the avant-garde, and most of his early scores—chamber pieces—received, at the time, fleeting exposure in such centers for advanced thought as the New School. In 1966, Lincoln Kirstein commissioned a piece for the New York City Ballet. It was called *Catwalk,* and Jacques d'Amboise was to choreograph it. The City Ballet ended by not playing it at all. "Too difficult, I guess," the composer later commented. In 1968, he and a few colleagues founded the Society of Black Composers, which now has about fifty members across the country.

The composer's "big break" came in 1975 when not one but two major orchestras wanted him to write works. For Seiji Ozawa and the San Francisco Symphony, Moore composed *Gospel Fuse;* for Pierre Boulez and the New York Philharmonic he wrote *Wildfires and Field Songs.* How did these opportunities come about? The composer recalls that "about three years earlier a private student of mine, Peter Yarrow—yes, the Peter, Paul and Mary guy—got me together with Ozawa, who is a friend of his. I told Ozawa my idea for *Gospel Fuse* and he loved the idea, got really excited about it. He seems to be into jazz and a lot of other stuff besides the classical orchestra repertory."

The Boulez connection came a couple of years earlier when Moore was interviewing Boulez, then the Philharmonic's music director, for the *Village Voice,* a New York City weekly newspaper. In 1975, Boulez and a panel from the orchestra selected

Moore to receive a $10,000 commission under a grant from the New York State Council on the Arts; the result was *Wildfires and Field Songs.*

In these two works Moore epitomizes the twentieth-century style of composition that utilizes the entire heritage of music, past and present. In Moore's works can be detected musical ideas derived from slave chants, from Mozart, from Berio, from Aretha Franklin, from bluegrass. After all, Moore has written books on Bessie Smith and Afro-American music. At Ohio State he played French horn in the marching band, the lead horn in the concert band, and cello in the university orchestra. Occasionally he played horn in the Columbus symphony.

He also has done more than dabble in pop music, having written the words for more than a dozen rock songs, including *Rock'n'Roll Outlaw* and *Foghat* (Felix Cavalieri, the lead singer of the group called the Rascals, composed the music). "One of the problems in twentieth-century music has been that until now all music was folk-based. To me music must be a product of a person working with the community on some level." For most modern composers, Moore feels, "that kind of feed-in simply is not available. Part of the composer's mission—part of his art—is writing for a general audience. I suppose my artistic ideal is Shakespeare. His work is commercially viable with all classes of people. There are always enough murders to keep everybody interested, but also this incredible poetry going on over the top."

Apparently Moore has been successful in achieving his ideal. In 1978, the music students at LaGuardia Community College in New York City honored the composer with a month-long festival of his music, a series of concerts that included everything from an atonal sonata for piano to his *Theater Music Suite* for jazz ensemble, based on his incidental music for the Broadway play *JoAnn.* In 1979 he was commissioned by the mayor of New York City to write a work for performance at Gracie Mansion, the home of the city's chief executive. This was one of the first commissions by city officials since those of the Italian Medicis of Florence during the Renaissance.

Bibliography

DeRhen, A. "New York Philharmonic: Moore Premiere." *HiFi/Musical America* 25 (May 1975), MA 29–30.

Michener, C. "Double Header." *Newsweek,* February 3, 1975, p. 71.

> If the experience of electronic music is important, and I believe it is, its significance lies not in the discovery of "new" sounds but in the possibility it gives the composer of integrating a larger domain of sound phenomena into a musical thought.
>
> Luciano Berio

TWELVE/ ELECTRONIC MUSIC

THE world of electronic music is one full of fascinating, captivating sounds. Sometimes this music conjures fantastic scenes that might seem to come out of the latest science-fiction novel. At other times, it may entrance us with the strange timbres it can produce, the unusual scale patterns it can develop, the extremely complicated polyrhythms that it can evolve.

Electronic music is a great deal more than mere technology. Electronic music has been concerned with expanding the horizons of music. It was never intended, of course, to replace the music of Bach, Beethoven, Brahms, and their successors, for, just as those worthy gentlemen expanded the existing literature of their own day, so electronic composers are expanding the repertory of our day.

There are two basic kinds of electronic music: *tape music* and live *electronic music.* Unlike traditional music, in which there are always performers involved, tape music exists—as its name implies—only on tape, and can be realized in sound only by playing it back through an amplifier-loudspeaker system. In tape music, the composer's equipment consists of various sound sources, electronic apparatus to change and enhance the sound, and tape recorders to record the newly emerging sound. In the final stage, an amplification system is necessary for reproducing the sound captured on tape.

We encounter most live electronic music today in the area of rock and disco. The development in the mid-1970s of sophisticated *performance synthesizers* made it possible to use such electronic devices in concert or live performances, along with such other electronic instruments as electric guitars and pianos, as well as traditional musical instruments.

The tape composer—as opposed to the composer writing for traditional instruments—is no longer limited to the seventy or eighty pitch levels of the standard keyboard, the six or seven dynamic levels from *pp* to *ff*, and half, quarter, and eighth notes with their dotted and syncopated values. The tape composer now has the entire range of frequencies, from fifty to fifteen thousand cycles (or vibrations) per second; forty or more precisely calculated dynamic levels calibrated on dials; and an infinite number of durational values, measured on tape in thirty-seconds of an inch or in centimeters. And whereas the traditional composer is limited to the tone qualities associated with a given instrument, the composer using tape, synthesizer, or computer has an infinite number of timbres available. The live-performance musician using traditional instruments is similarly limited in timbre and dynamics, whereas the live electronic performer now has available the dynamic and rhythmic freedom that the tape composer enjoys.

The tape composer has two sources for sounds with which to work: natural sounds from the everyday world captured on tape by means of a microphone, and sounds synthesized or created electronically. Sound-synthesis, as practiced in electronic music, is the creation of a musical tone by purely electronic means. Its opposite function, sound-analysis, has been known to scientists for generations. Sound technicians in a laboratory have been able to take a musical tone (any pitch produced by an instrument) and break it down, analyzing it so that its fundamental and numerous overtones—the individual "pure" components—could be noted.[1] The first electronic composers' idea was to reverse the process: instead of analyzing, or breaking down, a musical tone into its pure components, the pure components would be put together to create, or synthesize, a musical tone. The discovery of the sine-wave generator—the main source of "pure" tone—made all this possible. Thus sound-synthesized music was born.

HISTORY OF ELECTRONIC MUSIC

We sometimes assume that anything even remotely connected with electronic music started only yesterday. The historical record contradicts this belief. For hundreds of years, scientists and musicians have attempted to change the timbre of natural sounds and create new artificial ones.

More than 2,400 years ago in India, a teacher and scholar named Panini experimented with the relationship between the shape of the mouth and the timbre of the sound produced. In 1627, English philosopher Francis Bacon wrote about "sound houses," in which all kinds of musical sounds could be produced and modified. About the same time, a drawing was published in Nuremberg, Germany, showing one of the first mechanical instruments. Operated by means of a turning crank, it attempted to imitate the sound of a string ensemble. Such mechanical instruments—and there was a wide variety of them—became very popular. Haydn, for example, loved the mechanical trumpet and composed music for it. Mozart was attracted to the glass harmonica, an instrument brought to perfection by the American statesman-inventor Benjamin Franklin. It consists of a series of interlocked water glasses of various sizes; rotated in a trough of water by means of a footpedal, they produce a delicate, ringing sound when the fingertips are placed on the rims. Mozart composed quite a few works for this instrument.

Beethoven became fascinated with a mechanical instrument invented by his friend Johann Maelzel, who had already invented the metronome and who also made Beethoven's hearing aids for him. Beethoven composed his *Wellingtons Sieg* (*Wellington's Victory at the Battle of Victoria*) especially for Maelzel's mechanical instrument, the Panharmonion.

The orchestrion, a form of pipe organ–player-piano with percussion effects, became very popular in the late nineteenth century. Tchaikovsky first became familiar with the works of Mozart played on the orchestrion in his childhood home.

In the last quarter of the nineteenth century, discoveries and inventions by such men as Thomas Edison paved the way for the electronic music of the twentieth cen-

---

1. A *natural* musical tone (as opposed to one created electronically) consists of a *fundamental*—the pitch we most easily perceive—and a series of *overtones* (higher and softer pitches indistinguishable by the human ear as separate pitches). It is these overtones, along with attack and release, that give a musical tone its timbre and thereby help us distinguish a middle C played by a trumpet from a middle C played by a clarinet.

tury. In 1877, Edison made his first successful "talking machine"—a phonograph that recorded sound on a cylinder covered with tinfoil. Edison also developed dynamos that could generate electricity. This invention led to one of the very first electrical instruments: the *Dynamophone* (also called *Telharmonium*), invented by Dr. Thaddeus Cahill around the turn of the century. A demonstration of the instrument took place in Holyoke, Massachusetts, on March 10, 1906. The machine produced music by means of a series of dynamos, or motors, run by alternating current. The machine was the largest musical instrument in the world; it weighed over 200 tons.

Although the Dynamophone could be adjusted to produce any number of different pitches within the span of each octave, the instrument was too big to be practical, and the delicate wires of that period could not carry its necessarily complex signals.

In 1920, a Russian, Leon Theremin, invented an electrical instrument that bears his name. An aerial-like rod is attached to the top of the Theremin. The pitch of the electrically produced tone varies as the performer's hand is brought closer to the rod. The dynamics are controlled by bringing the left hand closer to the side of the instrument. The Theremin has been most successively used in the score for the 1945 film *Spellbound,* giving the music an ethereal, out-of-this-world quality.

In 1928, Maurice Martenot, a French musician and engineer, demonstrated an electrical keyboard instrument he had created which he called the Ondes Martenot, or "Martenot's Sound Waves." The Ondes could produce, one at a time, the tones of the traditional scale by means of the keyboard, or it could produce a glissando by means of the finger ring attached directly above the keyboard. For the Ondes, Martenot provided not only the traditional type of speaker but a special "cymbal" speaker for a metallic effect, a speaker in which the voice coil is attached to an orchestral cymbal instead of the regular cardboard loudspeaker cone.

During the early 1930's, Friedrich Trautwein, a professor in Berlin, Germany, developed an electrical instrument that made use for the first time of neon tubes to produce sound. He called his instrument the Trautonium. Many composers were attracted to its unusual timbres. Paul Hindemith, the most famous German composer of that era, wrote a *Concertino for Trautonium and Strings* (1931). Hindemith, for his own part, also tried using phonograph records in unusual ways: he scratched them to produce rhythmic effects; he tried playing them backwards; and he even cut them with a knife to produce unusual sounds.

In 1929, the American electronic engineer Laurens Hammond founded a company for building the Novachord and other electronic organs. His best-known product was the Hammond organ, first produced in 1935. It was the first practical instrument to produce by completely electronic means more than a single tone at a time; the Hammond organ could play chords. (Most modern performance synthesizers are based on the principles of the Hammond organ.)

The first music made completely by electrical-mechanical means was created in Paris shortly after the Second World War. Pierre Schaeffer tried working with recorded sound effects and noises. He created his piece *Steam Train Étude* by recording

A classic electronic music studio.

the sound of a locomotive at the old phonograph speed of 78 rpm (revolutions per minute), and playing it back at the long-playing speed of 33⅓ rpm. It made the steam train noises sound like those of a blast furnace. Schaeffer called this type of composition *musique concrète,* since he worked with actual, concrete sounds in its creation rather than with abstract symbols. The following year, the French radio network organized the Research Group on Concrete Music with a specially equipped studio for technical and artistic research.

The big interest in electronic music did not start, though, until the tape recorder was fully developed and became commercially available, which was around 1950, the year the first bit of tape music was publicly performed in France. A year later, an electronic music laboratory was established in the broadcasting studio of Radio Cologne in Germany.

In 1952 the first tape music was heard in the United States, performed at Columbia University. Vladimir Ussachevsky, a Columbia faculty member, was the composer. He created his compositions on an Ampex tape recorder that had been given to the university for the purpose of recording student concerts. The chairman of Columbia's composition faculty, Otto Leuning, was fascinated by the sounds of this new music, and invited Ussachevsky to present his experiments at the 1952 Bennington Composers Conference in Vermont. At the conference, Ussachevsky took control of the tape recorder and conducted a series of experiments involving violin, clarinet, piano, and vocal sounds. Leuning became involved too, and with earphones and flute, began experimenting himself. Leuning reported that after the demonstration a number of composers solemnly congratulated him, saying: "This is it!"—*it* meaning the music of the future.

A year later, the German composer Karlheinz Stockhausen created a piece of music entirely by electronic means. Instead of starting with the sound of a piano or flute or voice, he used a sound created electrically, produced by an oscillator, or tone generator, borrowed from an electrical engineer. Three years later, the engineers at RCA completed what they called the Olson-Belar sound synthesizer. It was followed by an improved model known as the Mark II synthesizer. The Mark II was twenty feet long, seven feet high, and cost a quarter of a million dollars. This synthesizer contained various sound-wave-creating devices: tuning fork oscillators, frequency amplifiers, and sine-wave generators. It also contained all kinds of electrical gadgets for changing and modifying these sound waves: ring modulators, high and low filters, reverberation units, and so on. In 1957, the electrical engineer Robert A. Moog (pronounced *Mohg*, the *o* as in *no*) had developed a synthesizer using tiny transistors instead of the bulky heat-producing vacuum tubes found in the RCA Mark II. This meant that the synthesizer could occupy much less space and would cost a small fraction of the cost of the big RCA model.

The original 1960s group of synthesizers produced only one tone at a time, and therefore a musician was limited in what could be performed with such instruments at a live concert. On tape, of course, the 1960s musician could, by backing up the tape several times, superimpose tone on tone (called "sound on sound" or "superimposition").

By the mid-1970s, laboratories were producing performance synthesizers, largely for use by rock and disco groups. These could produce, simultaneously, as many tones as there were keys on the keyboard. Today, various keyboard "combos" are sold in most music stores for the home market; these instruments, as their name implies, are combinations of electric piano, electric organ, and synthesizer, and can play simultaneously as many different pitches as there are keys or switches. The performer thus can play easily either polyphonic or homophonic music on them.

SYNTHESIZERS

The synthesizer is an instrument capable of producing almost any sound. It produces sounds with electrical circuits able to control precisely the three properties of sound—pitch, timbre, and loudness. Each property of sound is determined by a specific synthesizer function.

The pitch of a sound is produced by the synthesizer's oscillators (of which there are several different kinds). The timbre of a sound is controlled by the synthesizer's filters. In terms of dynamics, it is necessary for the composer to create a beginning, a middle, and an end to each sound. This is called the *envelope* of the sound. The general loudness of the sound is determined by the *amplitude shaper* (sometimes called a *voltage-controlled amplifier*).

Closeup of the basic Moog synthesizer.

LISTENING TO ELECTRONIC MUSIC

Listening to a piece of electronic music is quite similar to listening to a work composed in the more traditional idioms. First you try to discover from listening to the work its *sound source,* just as you would try to learn what instrument is playing a passage in a traditional composition. Second, you try to discover how this sound is modified: has echo been added, have the high frequencies been filtered out, and so on. You also try to discover if there is melodic movement involved and, if so, which melodic figures return or reappear in varied form. Are rhythm patterns apparent in the work? If so, what function do they serve? Do they unify the work? Add dramatic excitement? And, of course, is there a recognizable overall pattern or design to the work: binary or ternary, theme with variations, or any of the many other forms of music.

Thema (Omaggio a Joyce)

by LUCIANO BERIO

Luciano Berio's *Thema (Omaggio a Joyce),* or *Theme (Homage to Joyce),* which dates from 1958, is an excellent example of tape music. In it no use is made of any electrically produced sounds; the sound source is the speaking voice, recorded on tape, of Cathy Berberian reading the beginning of the eleventh chapter of James Joyce's novel *Ulysses.* Of his work on this composition, Luciano Berio has written:[2]

If the experience of electronic music is important, and I believe it is, its significance lies not in the discovery of "new" sounds but in the possibility it gives the composer of integrating a larger domain of sound phenomena into a musical thought. . . .

The beginning of [the eleventh chapter of *Ulysses*] is a sort of overture, a prelude to the chapter itself. From the mass of sounds through which characters and events are disclosed Joyce selects a series of main themes and isolates them from their contexts to form a sequence of [motives] freed of discourse connections. These are phrases which can be grasped musically; they form a kind of [sound-melody] in which the author has used references to the most common artifices of musical performance:

Imperthnthn thnthnthn..	trill
Chips, picking chips..	staccato
Warbling. Ah, lure!...	appoggiatura[3]
Deaf bold Pat brought pad knife took up..............	martellato[4]
A sail! A veil awave upon the waves.....................	glissando, portamento[5]

2. Luciano Berio, *Poesia e musica—un' esperienca,* translated by the author (Milan: Edizione Suvini Zerboni, 1958). Reprinted by permission of Edizione Suvini Zerboni, and Boosey & Hawkes, Inc., sole agents.
3. An *appoggiatura* is a very short adjoining note preceding a longer-held one.
4. *Martellato* means that notes are to be played with a "hammered" tone.
5. A *glissando* is a slide from one note to another; a *portamento* is a smooth gliding from one note to another.

LISTENING OUTLINE

The original Joyce text heard at the beginning of Berio's composition is as follows:

Bronze by gold heard the hoofirons, steelyrining imperthnthn thnthnthn.
Chips, picking chips off rocky thumbnail, chips. Horrid! And gold flushed more.
A husky fifenote blew.
Blew. Blue bloom is on the
Gold pinnacled hair.
A jumping rose on satiny breasts of satin, rose of Castille.
Trilling, trilling: Idolores.
Peep! Who's in the . . . peepofgold?
Tink cried to bronze in pity.
And a call, pure, long and throbbing. Longindying call.
Decoy. Soft word. But look! The bright stars fade. O rose! Notes chirruping answer. Castille. The morn is breaking
Jingle jingle jaunted jingling.
Coin rang. Clock clacked.
Avowal. *Sonnez.* I could. Rebound of garter. Not leave thee. Smack.
    La cloche! Thigh smack. Avowal. Warm. Sweetheart, goodbye!
Jingle. Bloo.
Boomed crashing chords. When love absorbs. War! War! The tympanum.
A sail! A veil awave upon the waves.
Lost. Throstle fluted. All is lost now.
Horn. Hawhorn.
When first he saw. Alas!
Full tup. Full throb.
Warbling. Ah, lure! Alluring.
Martha! Come!
Clapclop. Clipclap. Clappyclap.
Goodgod henever heard inall.
Deaf bald Pat brought pad knife took up.
A moonlight nightcall: far: far.
I feel so sad. P.S. So lonely blooming.
Listen!
The spiked and winding cold seahorn. Have you the? Each and for other plash and silent roar.
Pearls: when she. Liszt's rhapsodies. Hissss.[6]

The composer has given a rather detailed account of his transformation of this taped reading. Berio has said:

The text is broken down into sound families, groups of words or syllables organized in a scale of vocal colors (from [a] to [u]) and a scale

6. James Joyce, *Ulysses*, Ch. 11, quoted in *Thema*, notes to accompany recording (Vox).

of consonants (from voiced to unvoiced), the ordering of which is determined by noise content. The extreme points of the latter scale, for instance, are constituted by the "b" grouping (from "Blew. Blue bloom . . . ") and by "s" (from the last line of this exposition, a real cadence on noise: "Pearls: when she. Liszt's rhapsodies. Hissss."). The members of these sound families are placed in environments other than their original textual contexts, the varying length of the portions of context establishing a pattern of degree of intelligibility of the text. Twice, a language other than English is used, French, from the translation by Joyce and V. Larbaud, for the phrase "Petites ripes, il picore les petites ripes d'un pouce reche, petites ripes" ("Chips, picking chips off rocky thumbnail, chips"), which serves as a modulating pattern for the transformation of continuous sounds derived from the English text, and Italian, from the translation by E. Montale et al., which allows development of periodic patterns from the rolled "r" of the words "morbida parola" ("soft word"). When highly elaborated, the vocal material is often not recognizable, as such transformations, however, are always related to the following scheme, based on three articulatory categories of the original material:

Discontinuous $\longrightarrow$ Periodic $\longrightarrow$ Continuous
(as in "Goodgod, he never heard inall")
Continuous $\longrightarrow$ Periodic $\longrightarrow$ Discontinuous
(as in sibilants)
Periodic $\longrightarrow$ Continuous $\longrightarrow$ Discontinuous
(as in "thnthnthn")

All transformations are accomplished by tape editing, through superimposition of identical elements with varying time relations (phase shifting, especially where Joyce is concerned with musical onomatopoeia), through wide frequency and time transpositions and through ⅓ octave filtering. Though at certain points it would have been a simple matter to extend the transformations by introducing electrically produced sounds, this was not done because the original intention was to develop a reading of Joyce's text within certain restrictions dictated by the text itself.

Finally, with *Thema* I attempted to establish a new relationship between speech and music, in which a continuous metamorphosis of one into the other can be developed. Thus, through a reorganization and transformation of the phonetic and semantic elements of Joyce's text, Mr. Bloom's day in Dublin (it is 4 P.M., at the Ormond Bar) briefly takes another direction, where it is no longer possible to distinguish between word and sound, between sound and noise, between poetry and music, but where we once more become aware of the relative nature of these distinctions and of the expressive character inherent in their changing functions.[7]

7. Luciano Berio, *Poesia e musica.*

About the Composer

LUCIANO BERIO   Born: October 24, 1925
                              Oneglia, Italy

Luciano Berio has been one of the leading figures in contemporary Italian music since the 1950s. He was born in Oneglia (now Imperia) on the Italian Riviera. He is the third generation of composers in his family; both his father and his grandfather were church organists and composers. Young Luciano began his musical studies with his father and, like his father, he completed his training at the conservatory in Milan.

The composer later said with ire, referring to Mussolini's regime:

> It was not until 1945 that I first had the opportunity to see and hear the works of Schoenberg, Stravinsky, Webern, Hindemith, Bartók and Milhaud. I was already nineteen years old! Of that crucial period let me simply say that among the many thoughts and emotions aroused in me by those encounters, one is still intact and alive within me today: anger—anger at the realization that Fascism had until that moment deprived me of knowledge of the most essential musical achievements of my own culture; . . . [8]

While carrying on his conservatory studies, Berio was employed as coach and accompanist for the classes of two well-known opera stars. Before graduating in 1950, Berio gained wider practical experience as pianist-coach, conductor, and occasional timpanist for a small opera company that toured northern Italian provincial cities and towns. The year after his graduation from the conservatory, a Koussevitzky Foundation Fellowship enabled him to travel to the Berkshire Music Center at Tanglewood, Massachusetts, to study composition further.

On his return to Italy, Berio joined the staff of the Italian State Radio where, in 1954, he established a Studio di Fonologia Musicale for the study of and experimentation in electronic music. The following year he launched a series of concerts of contemporary music that he called *Incontri Musicali (Musical Encounters)* and edited a

8. Luciano Berio, "The Composer on His Work," *Christian Science Monitor,* July 15, 1968., p. 5.

progressive music magazine of the same name. He also became active as a conductor (chiefly of his own music) at La Scala Opera House in Milan, the Teatro Fenice in Venice, and the Rome Opera, and he has conducted the Chicago Symphony and the New York Philharmonic Orchestras as well.

During the 1960s Berio traveled widely, with many trips to the United States. He held composition classes in Darmstadt, Germany, and in the United States at Mills College in California and at Tanglewood. From 1965 to 1972, Berio was on the staff of the Juilliard School of Music in New York City.

In addition to his purely electronic works such as *Omaggio,* Berio is known for such works as his *Concertino* (1951) for solo violin, clarinet, harp, celesta, and strings; his *Concerto for Two Pianos and Orchestra* (1973); and *Chemins IV* (1975) for viola and orchestra.

Bibliography

Beckwith, John, and Kasemets, Udo, eds. *The Modern Composer and His World.* Toronto: University of Toronto Press, 1961.

Berio, Luciano. "The Composer on His Work." *Christian Science Monitor,* July 15, 1968, p. 5.

Bowery Bum (Study After Jean Dubuffet)
by İLHAN MIMAROĞLU

Jean Dubuffet, *Bowery Bum No. 112,* 1951 (Secretariat de Jean Dubuffet, Paris).

İlhan Mimaroğlu (accent the *mar* and omit the *g*) composed *Bowery Bum* in May of 1964. An example of tape music, its sound source and title were inspired by Jean Dubuffet's sketch *Bowery Bum,* which that artist accomplished through a single material: India ink. Mimaroğlu chose to use the sound of a single rubber band as his sound source. The techniques he used in transforming the sound of that rubber band were purposefully limited: amplification, filtering, speed variation, and superimposition.

The composer has said that his *Bowery Bum*

> is the piece that occasioned my association with Dubuffet and opened the way to my discovery of his own extraordinary music. The visual impetus of the Dubuffet drawing, one of the Bowery Bums, suggested the form, the content, and even the sound source—the sound of a sole rubber band used as a counterpart to the India ink of the drawing. The outer formal character of the piece was determined by that of the drawing—a seemingly random maze of lines, through which appears a human figure, pathetic and droll.[9]

9. İlhan Mimaroğlu, letter to the author, June 14, 1977.

Intermezzo

by İLHAN MIMAROĞLU

Mimaroğlu's *Intermezzo* is an example of electronic music, music that makes use of electronically generated sounds rather than natural sounds. Created in December of 1964, *Intermezzo* was composed at the Columbia-Princeton Electronic Music Center in New York City, in whose studios Mimaroğlu has created most of his electronic works.

The Columbia-Princeton Music Studio was made possible by a Rockefeller Foundation Grant given to Columbia and Princeton Universities in 1959. It represents the typical "classical studio" known in both Europe and America, with specialized equipment devoted to the production and modification of sound materials by the traditional electronic methods common to all electronic music studios. Thus materials of either purely electronic or nonelectronic origin, recorded on tape, may be manipulated by tape-speed variation, electronic filtering, several types of frequency modulation, artificial reverberation, and so on. Tape-cutting and splicing by hand occupy much of the composer's time in preparing sound patterns and arranging them in longer sequences. Techniques are available to create certain types of rhythmic patterns and timbre variations by semiautomatic methods, but the materials produced by these methods are of limited use.

At the time Mimaroğlu was working on *Intermezzo,* the studio did not have a synthesizer.[10] He therefore used independent electronic sound sources—sine-wave generators, square-wave generators, and a white-noise generator.[11] Such sound modifiers as an electronic switch, ring modulators, equalizers, echo chamber, and tape-speed controls were used.

About the piece, the composer has said that

> *Intermezzo* was so named because it was composed as a diversion between two projects that proved (and to some extent were designed) to be technically and procedurally laborious. I realized it with an improvisatory ease that I did not think was possible in the medium of the classical studio, and in the process gained an awareness of the inner workings of an experimental style that certainly existed before me, yet seemed to yield its secrets only to me. . . . *Intermezzo* remains as my favorite among my earlier tape-music pieces.[12]

10. "At that time, Columbia-Princeton Electronic Music Center did not have what is defined today as a synthesizer. But it did have the RCA Mark II Electronic Sound Synthesizer, a unique, one-of-a-kind instrument which, nonetheless, *cannot* be regarded as a prototype or an ancestor of today's synthesizers." İlhan Mimaroğlu, letter to the author, May 9, 1980.

11. So called because—like the color white, which in the visual spectrum represents the presence of all colors—"white noise" represents the presence of all frequencies. (It sounds like a radio that has been turned on but not tuned to any station.)

12. Mimaroğlu, letter to the author, June 14, 1977.

About the Composer

İLHAN MIMAROĞLU Born: March 11, 1926
Istanbul, Turkey

Since İlhan Mimaroğlu is well known in musical circles as an author of several books on music as well as a composer, his own words about his youth give a better picture of those years than any other source. He has written:

> I am told that my father (known as the foremost Turkish architect of his generation, and I never knew him as he died when I was only a year old) wanted me to grow up with music; for this purpose, he provided me with a phonograph and a good collection of classical records. Those records were my only toys and I knew them by heart. But as I grew up, I began to wonder whether there ought not to be more to music than that. The school I was attending (a prestigious boys' school in Istanbul, where I spent twelve years of my young life for what corresponds to the primary, secondary and high school education) taught me quite well in the rudiments of music, but not so well in the so-called musical culture. (As I was to find out later, schools doing well in that particular department are hard to come by anywhere, and on any level.) So I

was still on my own in the discovery of other musical "truths." The mid-30s were the years when Turkish music (traditional/classical, folkloric, and popular) was banned as part of the effort of the country's westernization. I had never heard any Turkish music until the ban was lifted in the late 30s, and when I first heard it its effect on me was that of a mere novelty and I soon lost all interest in it. Indeed, I thought that the ban was justifiable. It was also the time when occidental popular music was becoming more and more hard to avoid. It only urged me to keep on in my explorations, but provided an avenue by which I "discovered" jazz. There really *was* more to music than anything I had known before. For several years I studied jazz with an intense and exclusive dedication (my first article, published in 1943 in an Istanbul magazine, was on jazz), and I overlooked an exploration of the *classical* music that I kept on hearing around me. I didn't pay too much attention to it. But the late 40s were the days of experimentation in jazz, and one thing led to another. It did not take long for the newer classical music to come my way. When, among other things, I first heard Debussy's *String Quartet* and Berg's *Lyric Suite* I decided to compose a quartet of my own. I had never studied composition before, so I had to teach myself to do it. I did not look for a composition teacher and I did not want to go to the conservatory, because I feared that they would teach me the wrong things. Years later I had no fears anymore of the teachers and, in general, academia, because I was more secure of myself as to what I wanted to compose, hence I knew what I wanted to learn.

As to electronic music, the first experiments reached me in the early 50s, but somehow I did not want to engage myself in it as immediately as I had with the string quartet. By that time I had established a reputation in Turkey as a writer and broadcaster on music (somebody had to pass the word around about jazz and new music). The Rockefeller Foundation heard about me and had me visit New York for a program of studies at Columbia University where I studied composition . . . and musicology. . . . It was then that I came into closer contact with the work in electronic music conducted at Columbia University.[13]

In 1959, Mimaroğlu returned to New York to establish residence, in order to further his studies at Columbia with a program centered around electronic music. He also received his master of arts degree in music education from Columbia's Teachers College. He served as technical and teaching assistant at the Electronic Music Center, where he realized the majority of his electronic pieces. He has also worked in the studios of the Groupe de Recherches Musicales led by Pierre Schaeffer in Paris. In 1971 he was awarded a Guggenheim Fellowship in musical composition.

Bibliography

Mimaroğlu. Pamphlet. New York: Broadcast Music, Inc., n.d.

13. Mimaroğlu, letter to the author, June 14, 1977.

Drum on your drums, batter on your
  banjos,
sob on the long cool winding
  saxophones.
Go to it, O jazzmen.

Carl Sandburg

THIRTEEN/
JAZZ

WHEREVER music is known in the world today, jazz is heard. It is a unique type of music created in the United States around the turn of the century by numerous, often anonymous, black American musicians.

The details of the exact date and birthplace of jazz are lost in history, because jazz is an aural art and was not written about until decades later. We do know, however, that jazz was born shortly after the turn of the century among the black populations of several Southern urban centers. While more has been written about jazz as it developed in New Orleans, other cities of the Deep South were also active. St. Louis was famous for its ragtime; Memphis became famous because of W. C. Handy (1873–1958), known as the "Father of the Blues." Atlanta and Baltimore were musically alive, too.

Jazz is an art created out of a cultural heritage that reaches all the way back to Africa. Highly complex rhythms and syncopation are important characteristics of African music, traces of which are found in the spirituals that the blacks developed in the South shortly after the turn of the nineteenth century. The use of repeated rhythmic and melodic patterns that were further embellished with each repetition, as well as the use of "call and answer" patterns, were part of the African song tradition. This latter element—the "call and answer" patterns—probably led to the jazz technique of alternating solo *breaks* with choruses played by the entire combo, or group of players.

Other musical traditions inherited from African culture include the rhythmic accompaniment of foot-tapping, hand-clapping, percussion instruments, and a freer, less inhibited style of singing that included glissandos, falsetto, and other sounds not normally found in a trained singer's voice.[1]

The *blues*—which had been a popular form of music among black people since long before the Civil War—was, in essence, a secular form of spiritual that was incorporated into jazz. Basically, a blues tune is an eight- or twelve-bar strain with lyrics in which the first stanza is repeated. It gets its "blue" quality from its "blue notes," the somewhat flatted third and seventh tones of the scale.[2]

If the blues was the sad music of the blacks, *ragtime* was their happy music. Ragtime was essentially piano music and was the immediate precursor of jazz. Like jazz, ragtime itself was a combination of cultural heritages. The steady two-beat rhythm of the left hand was derived from the brass street-band music of the South's urban areas, while the syncopated right-hand rhythm came from the music of the plantation banjos. Combined, they gave a syncopated effect, later to be one of the chief characteristics of jazz.

Other forms of black music from the slave years that led to the birth of jazz were work songs, field hollers, shouts, children's songs, and dances.

A unique series of political circumstances led to the development of jazz in the urban centers of the South, particularly in and around New Orleans. During the last

1. *Falsetto* occurs only in men's voices and is the high, artificial voice equivalent in range to that of the unchanged male or normal female voice.
2. Actually the blue notes are about a quarter tone flat, as opposed to a normally flatted tone, which is a half tone lower in pitch.

quarter of the nineteenth century, New Orleans was essentially two cities—an American city west of Canal Street (known as uptown) and a French city east of Canal Street (downtown). The east side, the area of the upper class, was an active cultural center with French opera, chamber ensembles, and well-rehearsed dance orchestras. It numbered among its citizens whites, black servants, and Creoles of Color—families of mixed blood who, while not accepted socially, were successful in business.

By contrast, the newly freed blacks who lived uptown were poor, uneducated, and lacking in all the cultural and economic advantages available to the Creoles of Color.

In 1894, New Orleans passed a restrictive racial segregation code that threw the Creoles onto the other side of the tracks. This meant that the professional, well-trained Creole musicians were brought together with the unskilled black musicians. They did not get along well at all.

In 1897, the city council passed another ordinance that would have an even greater effect on the musical life of the city. It voted to move all the prostitutes (there were more than 2,000 of them—licensed by the city at that time) to a thirty-eight-block area that became known as Storyville, the city's legendary red-light district. The sporting houses of Storyville, which vied with one another for business, employed everything from string trios to ragtime pianists and brass bands. Storyville brought black and Creole musicians together, not altogether in a willing manner, as described in *Bourbon Street Black:*

> The 1890s had been an especially tough period for middle class and poor people in [New Orleans]. The younger Creoles of Color, whose parents had struggled for two generations, reached out for economic stability wherever they could find it. Storyville was there. For most, the pay was small, but anything was a gain. Young Creoles like Sidney Bechet often worked the District without their proud relatives' knowledge, because, for many Creoles of Color, playing in Storyville meant a loss of status within their own community. Jelly Roll Morton's grandmother kicked him out of the house when he was fifteen for playing in Storyville. She loved music, but said people who played in such places were bums, and she didn't want him to be a bad influence on his sisters. Many of the "dark" Negroes, though, "didn't give a damn" if it was a whore house they were playing in. They had an opportunity to play the music they loved and got paid for doing it.[3]

Although a few photographs of these early combos still exist, we have no idea of the sound such combos produced because the first jazz record was not made until January 1917—and then it was recorded by a white band rather than a black one. We do know, however, the makeup of these early groups. The rhythm section became standardized with three players—piano, bass, and drum set. The bass of these early groups was frequently a tuba, because both player and instrument could be borrowed from the brass street bands that played regularly for weddings, funerals, and other ceremonial occasions.

3. Jack V. Buerkle and Danny Barker, *Bourbon Street Black: The New Orleans Black Jazzman* (New York, 1974).

The other members, known as the *front line,* included the melody instruments—clarinet, cornet, and trombone. The trumpet or cornet was the key melodic instrument of the combo and basically played the melody in ragtime—that is, the player *ragged* or syncopated the tune. When the cornet or trumpet player stopped at the end of a phrase to catch a breath, the trombone or clarinet player would improvise a *fill* to occupy this space in time. The rhythm group, like that in most jazz styles that followed, operated simultaneously on three levels—the quarter-note pulse of four beats to a bar; the half-note harmonic unit; and the eighth-note melodic or ornamental unit.

RHYTHM IN JAZZ

Originally, jazz as it developed in New Orleans around 1910 had two pulses, or beats, to a bar, or measure, but after 1930 it became customary to have four to a bar. (A popular song of the 'thirties was called *Bounce Me, Brother, with a Solid Four.*) In modern jazz, which developed in the late 'forties and early 'fifties, other units were used. Dave Brubeck became famous for his *Take Five,* based on five beats per measure.

Syncopation—the occurrence of accents where the listener does not expect them —is one of the chief characteristics not only of jazz rhythm but of the idiom itself. This ability to stress the "off" beat probably came from the black spirituals. Notice, for example, the syncopation that occurs in the spiritual *Deep River* at the points indicated by the arrows. This syncopation is caused by holding the weak second syllable of the words *river* and *Jordan* through the strong third beat of the measure.

Or in *Nobody Knows:*

A similar type of syncopation can be found in the jazz tune of the twenties, *I Want to Be Happy:*

"I Want To Be Happy" (Vincent Youmans-Irving Caesar). © 1924 Warner Bros. Inc. Copyright Renewed. All Rights Reserved. Used by Permission.

Another important aspect of rhythm in jazz concerns note values. In traditional European music, it is customary for the performer to give each note its full, mathematically correct time value. Jazz musicians, in contrast, never play a rhythm exactly the way it is notated. Some scholars call this *delayed syncopation*. For example, if a jazz musician were asked to play a melody such as the following (which is made up entirely of equal-value eighth notes):

it would sound like *something* between

and

It is absolutely impossible to write out in the European system of notation the rhythms played by most jazz performers. At best, only an approximation can be given.

MELODY IN JAZZ

Just as most melodies in traditional European music are made up of tones selected from a predetermined set—a particular major or minor scale—so in jazz, melodies are frequently made up of tones selected from a special set known as the *blues scale.* The use of this scale, with its *blue notes,* probably developed around the time the early black jazz musicians tried to work with seven-tone European major and minor scale patterns. Much African music (as well as that of much of the world except Europe) is based on a five-tone, or pentatonic, scale:

This is, in reality, the European major scale minus its fourth and seventh tones:

Many of the spirituals known by the early jazz musicians, including *Deep River* and *Nobody Knows,* were based on the pentatonic scale.

Apparently, when the black musicians attempted to improvise jazz tunes based on the seven-tone European scale, they tried to accommodate the two additional tones and slightly flatted (lowered) the third and seventh degrees. Today we call these two different tones blue notes, and a scale that makes use of them the blues scale:

While most instruments used in jazz can play these blue notes, the piano cannot. There is no key on the piano between the E of the major scale and the E-flat of the minor scale. Therefore, in jazz piano works, we sometimes find a melody that makes use of the minor tonality accompanied by harmony in the major tonality. This gives the feeling of hovering between the two.

HARMONY IN JAZZ

As it originated in and around New Orleans at the beginning of the century, jazz made use of only the three basic chords of our harmonic system, the I (tonic), IV (subdominant), and V^7 (dominant seventh). Such a simplified harmonic structure was undoubtedly patterned after the music the jazz creators regularly heard, a repertory that included popular dance music of Spanish or French origin—the quadrille, habanera, and tango; popular American music of the blacks themselves—the cakewalk and minstrel songs; military music; light classical music; and Baptist hymns. All of these were based on a simple harmonic system centered on the three basic chords.

As jazz developed, this harmonic structure became the basis of improvisation, the skeleton around which the players would weave their extemporaneous melodic lines.

And as jazz became more sophisticated, more complex chords and harmonies were used. The progressive style of jazz that developed around 1940 made use of extremely complicated chords and a harmonic structure that easily wandered from one key or tonality to another. By the 1950s, jazz musicians such as Miles Davis abandoned the harmonic structure, with its major and minor tonalities, as a basis for improvisation and used the early modal scale patterns instead.[4] Davis's *So What?* is an excellent example of a tune based on the Dorian mode (on the piano, the scale using all the white keys from D to D):

European music, both classical and folk, is usually made up of phrases and periods eight or sixteen measures in length. Jazz, however, developed a twelve-bar harmonic pattern. This pattern is usually established at the beginning of a performance and repeated numerous times while improvised melodies are played above it, the harmonic structure serving as the unifying element.

Because jazz is a *way of playing,* many jazz musicians are unaware of the *theory* of harmony; they instinctively know which chord is appropriate. For this reason, composers and arrangers of jazz indicate chords by letter names (C, G^7, F) rather than by function in a structured harmonic system (I, V^7, IV). A typical chord progression for piano and guitar might be written:

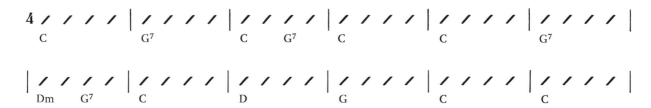

JAZZ TIMBRE

Jazz has a unique sound. This is the result not only of the instruments used in a jazz ensemble but also of the unusual ways in which they are sometimes played.

The original New Orleans-style jazz band was made up of easily available instruments such as clarinet and trumpet (which could be picked up for almost nothing at any hockshop) and homemade instruments such as broomstick bass, washboard scraper,

4. For a description of modes, see Chapter 14, page 338.

and gutbucket percussion.[5] The front line usually consisted of melody instruments—one or two cornets or trumpets, a trombone, and a clarinet.[6] The rhythm section was usually made up of banjo or guitar, string bass, piano, and drum set. As jazz developed in the 1920s and '30s, the drum set came to consist of a bass drum played with a foot pedal, a side drum with snares that was played with either sticks or wire brushes, two tom-toms, a single suspended cymbal known as a *ride cymbal,* and a *high-hat cymbal* worked with a foot pedal. During the 1920s, the saxophone joined the group of melody instruments in most jazz ensembles.

By the Big Band era of the late 1930s and early '40s, as many as thirty musicians could be found in some jazz groups. After the Second World War, most jazz groups became small ensembles again for economic reasons. Today most jazz groups include:

Brass: trumpet and trombone

Woodwinds: clarinet; alto, tenor, and baritone saxophones; flute

Rhythm: piano, guitar, and bass (each of which can be acoustic or electric);

drum set; vibes (vibraphone)

As the search for more exotic sounds continues, other instruments, including strings, are sometimes used. They are frequently amplified to balance the tonal output of the louder brass instruments. In addition to the basic drum set, several Latin percussion instruments are occasionally employed—small bongos; the large conga drum; a cowbell hit with a stick; a tambourine; a chocolo (tube-shaped rattle); a pair of maracas (seed-filled gourds); claves (two thick, hardwood sticks clapped together); and a güiro (grooved gourd scraped with a stick).

In addition to the instruments themselves, there are special ways of playing them that are widely used in jazz:

Vibrato: A slight undulation or variance in pitch, weaving back and forth a little above and a little below the note itself

Glissando: Sliding from one pitch to another

Smear: The approach to a note from slightly below its exact pitch, holding this out-of-tune effect for the desired time, and then sliding up to the correct pitch

Fall: The reverse of a smear; the player sounds the correct pitch and then lets it fall rapidly to an indeterminant tone much lower in pitch

Bend: The pushing of a note above (or below) the exact pitch and then returning to the pitch

Growl: The sound produced by the player growling at the back of the throat while playing a note

5. A broomstick bass consisted of an inverted washtub that served as a resonator and a broomstick resting on the center of the inverted tub bottom. A string was connected to the top of the broomstick and stretched to the side of the inverted tub; the left hand "stopped" the string at different lengths as it moved up and down the broomstick; the right hand plucked the string to produce the tone. A washboard scraper was the simplest of the rhythm instruments: a stick was rubbed up and down the corrugated surface of the washboard to produce a rhythmic effect. A gutbucket was simply an inverted tub (gutbucket) used as a drum.

6. A cornet is similar to a trumpet, but is slightly easier to play and more mellow in sound because the bore is different. (See photo p. 10.)

Left to right: straight mute, derby, wha-wha mute, cup mute.

Flutter: Similar to *flutter-tonguing* in traditional music, achieved by rolling an *r* while playing

Mute: The use of a metal or plastic device to change or deaden the tone of a brass instrument. Such devices include:

1. The *straight mute,* which produces a thin, hard tone
2. The *cup mute,* which produces a more rounded tone than the straight mute
3. The *wha-wha mute,* which produces a sound similar to its name
4. The *derby* or *hat mute,* which allows the player constantly to change the sound by repositioning the hat closer to or farther away from the bell of his horn.

FORM IN JAZZ

Most jazz can be considered as cast in the *theme with variations* form. The theme itself is usually in simple binary or ternary form, possibly a twelve-bar blues melody, the chorus of a popular dance tune, or a specially composed melody.

Sometimes a short introduction precedes the theme. Then the theme is played by the entire group—the band or combo—followed by a series of variations known as *choruses.* The harmonic structure that accompanies the theme is very important as it becomes the basis of all the variations that follow.

As with traditional European music cast in this form, the first chorus, or variation, usually stays quite close to the original theme and is only slightly "decorated." As the music progresses, the melody and rhythms become more complex, sometimes so much so that the theme almost gets lost in the welter of extra notes and complicated rhythms. The final variation seems to recapitulate or recapture the essence of the first presentation of the theme.

The improvisations that occur during a piece may be played either by a soloist or by the entire band or combo. When a soloist improvises, that person is free to do as he or she pleases (always keeping the harmonic structure in mind, of course); the other players combine to accompany the soloist with the established rhythmic-harmonic background of the theme. When everyone in the group improvises simultaneously, it is called a *jam session,* the melodic lines developing polyphonically—but always blending harmoniously together, because they are all based on the established rhythmic-harmonic pattern of the theme.

Sometimes a small cadenza occurs at the end of a phrase with a long note or rest; this is called a *break,* a chance for the soloist to "show off" unaccompanied. A *riff* is a short phrase, usually of two to four bars, repeated many times over the changing harmonies of the theme. This may occur in the accompaniment pattern, or it may be used by an instrumentalist in the course of a solo.

In the original New Orleans bands, written or printed music was never used; in fact, most of the greats among the early players could not even read music. But as bands became larger during the 1930s, it became necessary for someone to write out the music for each instrumentalist. Total improvisation had become impractical because there were so many musicians.

In jazz, the *composer* is the person who writes the original theme on which the variations are created. The musician who develops the variations on the theme and writes them out is known as the *arranger*.

JAZZ STYLES

As jazz evolved from its turn-of-the-century birth in the South, it passed through several stylistic periods, some named after the city of origin, others after key words associated with the transformation in style.

New Orleans or Dixieland (1900–1920) *New Orleans jazz* refers to the early development in the urban centers of the South sometime between 1890 and 1917. The principal musicians of that period wandered from city to city, playing aboard riverboats and being heard in Natchez and Vicksburg, Memphis and St. Louis. Such music was not confined to the dance hall or theater but was social in the widest sense. "There were countless places of enjoyment that employed musicians," recalls the guitarist Danny Barker, "as well as private affairs, balls, soirees, banquets, picnics at the lake front, country hay rides, and advertisements of business concerns."[7]

For the early New Orleans musicians, jazz was "night music"; they had other jobs in the daytime. Zutty Singleton, a great drummer, said, "They were bricklayers and carpenters and cigar makers and plasterers. Some had a little business of their own—coal and wood and vegetable stores. Some worked on the cotton exchange and some were porters." "King" Joe Oliver, the great jazz trumpeter, worked as a butler; his protégé, the later-legendary Louis "Satchmo" Armstrong, carried coal.

New York, Chicago, and Kansas City (1920–1935) Between 1910 and 1920, nearly a million people—white as well as black—migrated to the North. The population of the "black belt," the black community lying on the south side of Chicago, doubled in five years. This meant that by the beginning of the 1920s—the First World War had ended in November of 1919—there was a large audience for music and its entertainers in the northern cities, particularly New York and Chicago.

Ironically, while it was the closing of Storyville in 1917 that sent many jazz musicians northward, it was the beginning of Prohibition in 1920 that provided the new setting for jazz. The Eighteenth Amendment to the Constitution prohibited the sale of any alcoholic drink and led to the establishment of chains of "speakeasies"—illegal drinking clubs. Jazz flourished vigorously in such corrupt surroundings. The free and easy attitude of the city authorities in both Chicago and Kansas City allowed club

7. Nat Shapiro and Nat Hentoff, eds., *Hear Me Talkin' to Ya* (New York, 1966).

owners to do more or less as they liked; this in turn meant plenty of jobs for jazz musicians. At the same time it meant that the function of jazz narrowed considerably. The musicians who had played for all kinds of community activities in New Orleans were now confined to work in nightclubs, the theater, and dance halls.

"In some ways," according to Charles Fox, a leading jazz critic, "'Chicago Style' was not so much a style as a collision of sympathetic musicians, almost a forerunner of the jam session. The music came out sounding tough and brittle and slightly bitter, a perfect reflection of the society in which it was created, the mobster's jungle bossed by Al Capone and Dion O'Bannion."

Boogie-woogie, principally a pianistic style of jazz, originated in Chicago around this time. It made use of a repeated bass pattern, often eight notes in a bar:

This rhythm pattern made use of the harmonies of the twelve-bar blues, while the right hand played variations on the sequence of chords.

Jazz took New York by storm. Recordings made in January and February of 1917 by the Original Dixieland Jazz Band—the first jazz records ever made—sold in the millions.

During the 1920s and early '30s, New York and Chicago were not the only meccas of jazz. The Midwest, centering on Kansas City, Missouri, and including the nearby states of Texas, Arkansas, Kansas, and Oklahoma, witnessed some lively developments. Although the early bands in this part of the country appear to have performed New Orleans-style jazz, nine- and ten-piece orchestras, using sections of brass and reeds like their counterparts in Chicago, were beginning to emerge. One of the chief characteristics of the *Kansas City style* was the development of the riff, used to build up to a dramatic climax.

New York and Swing (1932–1942) In New Orleans, jazz had been a response to a social need; in Chicago, it was an answer to the demand for a widely popular style of music; in New York during the 1930s, it was a response to the needs of the music industry. By this time, New York City had become the theatrical capital of the United States and the center of its record industry. The city abounded in music publishers and variety-act agents. New York was the place to which ambitious young songwriters traveled as soon as they had the fare. It was on Broadway that the now-famous jazz pianist James P. Johnson, who a decade or so earlier had written the song that made the Charleston famous, first staged *Running Wild,* an all-black musical.

Jazz, then still a racially segregated art form, attracted many white players who wanted steady work playing in the pit orchestras of New York or in radio and recording sessions. It also attracted black artists who played for large white audiences in nightclubs and dance halls. Fletcher Henderson, for example, gained success with his

Ella Fitzgerald with Dizzy Gillespie
(right) and Ray Brown (left).

orchestra playing at the Roseland Ballroom on Broadway. Duke Ellington and his orchestra performed at the Cotton Club on Lenox Avenue in Harlem for white audiences, blacks not being allowed to enter as patrons. Prohibition had ended in 1933, and the speakeasies disappeared. In their place, lots of small clubs with dance floors and bars with live entertainment opened. These provided the setting for some of the big bands of the 1930s.

The 1930s were also known as the era of *swing,* a title derived from one of Duke Ellington's songs, *It Don't Mean a Thing if It Ain't Got That Swing.* Swing musicians used a less strident tone than their predecessors, and the harmonic structure of their music became more complex and varied. Nonjazz-related rhythm patterns such as the rhumba became popular.

During this period, the most successful swing bands were all white. Although all-black orchestras like Duke Ellington's and Jimmie Lunceford's were at their peak, they never enjoyed anything like the same popularity as the white bands; neither did Count Basie's Orchestra, which had arrived from Kansas City in the winter of 1936.

Although earlier attempts had been made to desegregate jazz, it remained for Benny Goodman to successfully bridge the gap. He regularly used two black musicians, pianist Teddy Wilson and vibraphonist Lionel Hampton, in his Trio and Quartet. (Hampton, in turn, was one of the first to exploit the amplified electronic instruments that began to appear in the thirties.)

Blues singers who rose to fame during the swing era of the thirties included Ella Fitzgerald, an orphan who had been discovered in a talent contest; Billie Holiday; and Mildred Bailey, the wife of the xylophone-player and bandleader Red Norvo and the first nonblack woman to sing successfully in the jazz idiom.

Swing, as interpreted by Benny Goodman and countless others, differed from the style that had gone before in four principal ways. First, the size of the bands increased from an ensemble of eight to ten musicians to groups as large as twenty-five or more. Second, because these groups became too large to allow for free improvisation, arrangements had to be made and music copied for the performers. (Fletcher Henderson, another great bandleader, made his principal claim to immortality in the world of jazz in his role as the first jazz arranger.) Third, the characteristics of solos changed. The melodic patterns tended to become set on standard arpeggios and scales that were obviously derived from classical exercises. Tone quality and pitch became more refined, especially among the reed instruments, and the bawdy, raw sound of classic jazz began to disappear.

Fourth, swing changed the nature of jazz rhythm. The swing drummers remodeled the Dixieland beat. They still played $\frac{4}{4}$ on the bass drum, and it was a very insistent and pervasive beat; but they also began to ride the high-hat cymbal with a pattern that set up cross-rhythms:

With both feet going—one on bass drum and one on high-hat cymbal, four beats on the right and two on the left—the swing drummer used his hands for decorations and accents: one to ride the high-hat, and the other to lead off on the snare drum, crash cymbal, or whatever else was available.[8]

Bebop (1940–1950) *Modern jazz* was a product of the 1940s and '50s and was characterized by several styles, of which *bebop* or *bop* was the first and possibly the most important.

"No man or group of men started modern jazz," Dizzy Gillespie has said. "Some of us began to jam at Minton's [Playhouse in Harlem] in the early '40s. But there were always some cats showing up there who couldn't blow at all, but would take six or seven choruses to prove it. So on afternoons before a session, Thelonious Monk and I began to work out some complex variations on chords and the like. And we used them at night to scare away the no-talent guys."[9]

These pioneer jazz players of the early forties tried to make a complete break with anything suggestive of swing. The name itself—*bop, rebop,* or *bebop*—originated in the jazz musician's practice of vocalizing or singing instrumental melodic lines with nonsense syllables (*scat singing*). Bebop phrases frequently had abrupt endings with a 3–2 pattern ("beeee-bop!"):

8. *Ride* is a jazz expression meaning, in this instance, "to play." It is also used as an adjective to mean "the one to be played," as in *ride cymbal.*
9. Shapiro and Hentoff, *Hear Me Talkin' to Ya.*

Undoubtedly the most important musician of this period was the saxophonist Charlie "Bird" Parker. Although some critics claim that Coleman Hawkins and Lester Young had anticipated some of Parker's rhythmic devices—notably his habit of breaking up time, basing solos on half-beats rather than those actually played by the rhythm section—it was Parker who synthesized the technique within his style. It was *where* Parker placed a note—its rhythmic more than its pitch value—that remained the secret of his success. Another characteristic was the manner in which his melodic line broke away from the traditional twelve-bar pattern of earlier musicians. Parker introduced an element of apparent discontinuity, long and short phrases fitted together in a way that seems suggestive of the old call-and-answer patterns.

Cool Jazz (1949–1955) In 1948, the trumpeter Miles Davis made recordings with a small band that was to reach another turning point in jazz. It was a nine-piece group, and it used written arrangements that combined bop harmonies and rhythms with a melodic style of improvisation made famous by the saxophonist Lester Young. "The result," one writer has said, "was cool jazz—cool, almost legitimate-toned music as opposed to the hot tone of traditional jazz and bebop, its variation economical, 'understated,' and its relaxed rhythm giving the effect of being almost behind the beat."[10]

New Wave or Free Form (1957–) Free-form jazz was one of the most controversial developments in the history of jazz. It became the ultimate in improvisation, a search for complete harmonic freedom. Saxophonist Ornette Coleman was the leader in this direction, which began around 1957; other important figures in the movement included saxophonist Eric Dolphy and bassist Charles Mingus. John Coltrane came to be one of the central figures in free form, the acknowledged leader of the group. He had begun by improvising from modes and scales instead of from chord progressions, when he was with Miles Davis in the 1950s. He next worked with Thelonious Monk for five or six years, developing new insights into improvisation that led him into experimenting with free-form or free improvisation.

Present and Future (1980–) Jazz in the '80s is moving in many directions and developing new and eclectic styles. There is jazz-rock or "fusion," gospel jazz, third-stream music (the blending of jazz with elements of classical music), electronic jazz, and Latin jazz.

When the first summer Wolf Trap International Jazz Festival was held at Wolf Trap park near Washington, D.C., in 1980, such disparate performers as the National Symphony Orchestra and the violinist Yehudi Menuhin from the classical realm were scheduled along with traditional jazz musicians from all over the United States and visiting artists from Europe and Japan.

10. Avril Dankworth, *Jazz: An Introduction to Its Musical Basis,* (London, 1968).

Ornette Coleman

Back o' Town Blues

by LOUIS ARMSTRONG

In 1943, *Esquire* magazine held the first of a series of jazz polls, and Louis Armstrong won in popùlarity in both the trumpet and vocal classifications. It was only natural, then, that when *Esquire* presented the first jazz concert held at the Metropolitan Opera House the following year, Louis Armstrong should be one of the featured artists. The other musicians included Jack Teagarden on trombone, Coleman Hawkins on tenor saxophone, Art Tatum on piano, Oscar Pettiford on bass, Al Casey on guitar, Lionel Hampton on vibes, and Sidney Catlett on drums. One of the highlights of this concert was a tune by Armstrong called *Back o' Town Blues.*

The style of *Back o' Town Blues* is Dixieland, which implies group improvisation. Throughout the performance there is much reliance on counterpoint, which in this style is known as *call and answer.* There is no exact melody or tune as such in *Back o' Town Blues,* but rather a "decorated improvisation," with a melodic formula in the last two bars of each chorus.

LISTENING OUTLINE

There is a four-bar piano introduction.

The following twelve-bar harmonic chorus, with its closing formula, is heard seven times:

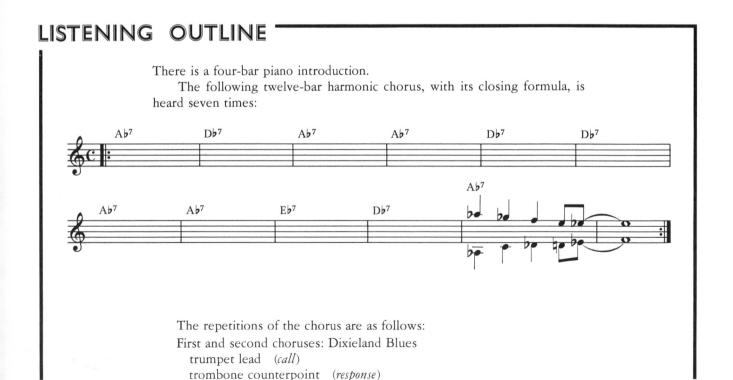

The repetitions of the chorus are as follows:
First and second choruses: Dixieland Blues
trumpet lead   *(call)*
trombone counterpoint   *(response)*

Third, fourth, and fifth choruses: Vocal
vocal lead by Armstrong *(call)*
clarinet
muted trombone } *(response)*
second voice
Sixth chorus: Trombone solo
piano — fill-ins (background)
muted trumpet — countermelody
Seventh chorus: Dixieland — free improvisation
trumpet lead
There is a fermata (⌢) over the final three chords:

$$| \overset{\frown}{\text{Ab}^7} \quad | \overset{\frown}{\text{Eb}^{+9}_{7}} \quad | \overset{\frown}{\text{Ab}^7} \quad \|$$

About the Composer

LOUIS "SATCHMO" ARMSTRONG

Born: July 4, 1900
New Orleans, Louisiana

Died: July 6, 1971
New York, New York

Born in the poorest section of New Orleans in 1900, Daniel Louis Armstrong was interested in everything musical, from his earliest years on. "I was brought up around music," Armstrong later recalled. "I can't see how I could have thought of anything else. My mother took me to church when I was ten, I sang in the choir. Before ever I played trumpet I was singing in a quartet, that was my hustle, we used to sing in the streets and pass the hat around."[11]

When he was only thirteen, he borrowed a .38-caliber revolver, joined the noisy crowd at the corner of Perdido and Rampart streets, and fired the gun into the air to help celebrate New Year's Eve. An elderly detective arrested him immediately.

Armstrong was taken to court and sentenced to a waifs' home. "After a short while," Armstrong later recalled, "I had got so used to the home that I forgot all about the streets. When other kids started calling me nick-names, I knew everything was all right! Then, as now, I had a pretty big mouth, so the kids hit on that and started calling me 'gate mouth' or 'satchelmouth,' and 'satchelmouth' has stuck to me all my life, except that now it's made into *Satchmo* — 'Satchmo' Armstrong."[12]

11. Quoted in *Louis: The Louis Armstrong Story,* by Max Jones and John Chilton (Boston, 1971).
12. Louis Armstrong, *Satchmo: My Life in New Orleans* (New York, 1955).

The director of the band at the waifs' home talked Louis into taking up a musical instrument so he could play in the band. First Louis tried the tambourine, but soon gave that up in favor of the bugle and cornet, which he liked better. "I improved so much with the band," Armstrong later recalled, "that Mr. Davis, our Director, began to be proud of us. He began to take us to outings and street parades. We were glad to get a chance to see the city again."[13]

After eighteen months, Louis was released from the waifs' home and returned to his mother. In the daytime, Louis hauled coal for 75¢ a day; he augmented his income by playing in a jazz band for $1.75 a night. He later wrote of this experience:

> Speaking of Storyville, well, I was born in what they called the poor man's Storyville. Of course, it was later on they changed the name to that, after a man called Story. But it was always the Red Light District, or just District, to me. . . .
>
> By my being raised up in that place at that time, I spent all my young days around whores and pimps and gambling fellers and some of the baddest people that was ever born. And there were some bad cats came from what we called the Swamp, known to carry a big .45 under their jacket and will shoot it at the drop of a hat. . . . [14]

In 1922, when King Joe Oliver sent Armstrong a telegram and asked him to join the Creole Jazz Band in Chicago, it was the finest jazz group of its day. This band repre-

13. Armstrong, *Satchmo.*
14. Letter by Louis Armstrong, quoted in Jones and Chilton, *Louis.*

sented the final great flowering of the classic New Orleans ensemble style. Aside from its two cornetists Oliver and Armstrong, its stars were the Dodds brothers, clarinetist Johnny and drummer Baby. Baby Dodds brought a new level of rhythmic subtlety and drive to jazz drumming. Along with another New Orleans-bred musician, Zutty Singleton, Baby Dodds introduced the concept of swinging to the jazz drums.

Armstrong left Oliver in late 1924, accepting an offer from New York's most prestigious black band leader, Fletcher Henderson. According to jazz critic Dan Morgenstern, "The elements of Louis's style, already then in perfect balance, included a sound that was the most musical and appealing yet heard from a trumpet; a gift for melodic invention that was as logical as it was new and startling; and a rhythmic poise (jazzmen call it 'time') that made other players sound stiff and clumsy in comparison."[15]

About a year later Armstrong left Henderson's band and returned to Chicago, where he joined his wife's band—Lil Armstrong's Dreamland Syncopators. It was around this time that Satchmo made his first recordings with the Hot Five, a group he got together just for recording purposes. By 1927, he had formed his own large band —Louis Armstrong and His Stompers. He also continued to appear with other bands, and in 1930, played an extended engagement at the Cotton Club in Los Angeles. His first tour of Great Britain took place in 1934; this was followed by a short residence in Paris. A year later he returned to Chicago, where he temporarily gave up the trumpet because of a problem with his lip. During this period he sang with Duke Ellington's orchestra.

During the early years of the Second World War, Armstrong made several coast-to-coast tours, and in 1944 took up permanent residence in New York City, where he lived the rest of his life.

Louis Armstrong, whose career paralleled the development of jazz up to the time he died in 1971, had a tremendous influence on the entire field of music, symphonic as well as jazz. Martin T. Williams probably summed it up best in his seventieth-birthday tribute to Armstrong, when he said:

> Armstrong's music has affected all our music, top to bottom, concert hall to barroom. No concert composers here or abroad write for brass instruments the way they used to, simply because Armstrong has shown that brass instruments, and the trumpet in particular, are capable of things that no one thought them capable of before he came along. Our symphonists play trumpet with a slight, usually unconscious vibrato that is inappropriate to Beethoven or Schubert, because Armstrong had one.[16]

Bibliography

Jones, Max, and Chilton, John. *Louis: The Louis Armstrong Story, 1900–1971.* Boston: Little, Brown, 1971.

Panassié, Hughes. *Louis Armstrong.* New York: Scribner, 1971, 1979.

15. Dan Morgenstern, *The Jazz Story* (New York: Jazz Museum, 1973).
16. Martin T. Williams, "For Louis Armstrong at 70," *Down Beat* 37 (July 9, 1970), pp. 22–23.

Magenta Haze

by DUKE ELLINGTON

Duke Ellington's unique gift as composer-arranger-pianist was coupled with his ability to organize and lead a band. From 1927 to 1941, with very few exceptions and occasional additions, the personnel in the band remained unchanged—a record no other band leader has been able to match.

In *Magenta Haze,* which was recorded in 1946, we hear several of these long-time faithfuls—baritone saxophonist Harry Carney, who had joined the band in 1927 when he was seventeen and who remained with it until he died in 1974; Johnny Hodges, whose alto saxophone sound was one of the glories of jazz, who had joined the band in 1928 and, except for a period from 1951 to 1955, stayed with the band until his death in 1971; and drummer Sonny Greer. Other Ellington artists who are heard in this recording include Shelton Hempill, Francis Williams, Taft Jordan, and Harold Baker on trumpet; Ray Nance doubling on trumpet and violin, Claude Jones, Lawrence Brown, and Wilbur de Paris on trombone; Russell Procope doubling on alto saxophone and clarinet; Jimmy Hamilton doubling on tenor saxophone and clarinet; Al Sears on tenor saxophone; Fred Guy on guitar; Oscar Pettiford on bass; and, of course, the Duke himself on piano.

Magenta Haze is one of Ellington's works in mood style, a genre he described as "portraits in sound." Many of those "portraits" have titles that name colors. The Duke once wrote, "I think of music sometimes in terms of color. I like to see flames licking yellow in the dark and then pushing down to a red glow." In addition to *Magenta Haze,* there are *Black and Tan Fantasy, Blue Bubbles, Mood Indigo, Sepia Panorama, Azure, On a Turquoise Cloud, Golden Cress, Silver Cobweb,* and *Red Garter.*

Actually, *Magenta Haze* is as much one of Ellington's works in concerto style as it is a mood piece, for, with the exception of a brief introduction by the Duke on piano and a short interlude by the entire ensemble in the middle, the work is essentially one long, beautiful solo for saxophonist Johnny Hodges. The English jazz critic G. E. L. Lambert calls the tune a "delightful miniature [concerto] in which the almost classic beauty of Hodges's melodic line keeps the music well clear of any undue sentimentality."

Magenta Haze consists essentially of two full choruses of a twenty-bar tune in ternary form, separated by a six-measure brass interlude.

LISTENING OUTLINE

There is a four-bar piano introduction.

The twenty-bar tune follows; the first four bars (at Letter A), an alto saxophone solo with unison accompaniment, are repeated. An eight-bar bridge follows at Letter B with a countermelody in the saxophone section; it has a chordal accompaniment. At Letter C, a four-bar restatement of the theme.

Courtesy Tempo Music, Inc.

There is a six-measure brass interlude; a pedal-point (a sustained low C) occurs in the last four bars.

The chorus (Example 1) is repeated in slightly varied form:

Letter A: four bars of free improvisation
                 four bars of decorated melody

Letter B: four bars of free improvisation
                 four bars of slightly altered melody

Letter C: four bars of slightly decorated melody

(There is a fermata on the final chord, a polytonal chord. Muted trumpets end with a G chord over a harmonic background built on an F chord.)

About the Composer

DUKE ELLINGTON   Born: April 29, 1899
                                 Washington, D. C.

                       Died: May 24, 1974
                                 New York, New York

If Louis Armstrong was responsible for the expansion of the role of the soloist in jazz, then Duke Ellington was equally responsible for the development of the ensemble. Together, these two trends led away from the more folklike qualities of early jazz.

While Armstrong featured high notes, scat singing with nonsense syllables, tricky melodic figures, involved syncopations, and the development of motives, Ellington was known for music characterized by rich chords, chromatic progressions, and varied, lush, and frequently contrasting sounds.

Edward Kennedy Ellington was born in Washington D.C., in 1899. His family was quite well to do for a black family living in the nation's capital at that time (his father was on the White House staff). The family provided their son with every educational advantage, and at six started him on piano.

"The first thing I ever wrote," Ellington later recalled, "was *Soda Fountain Rag.* I was 14. I worked as a soda jerk in Washington. I also had a job as a piano player. I worked for 75¢ a night. I got other jobs—with bands. Then I formed my own. I studied some, but I could hear people whistling and got all the Negro music that way. You can't learn that in any school."[17]

The Duke got his nickname during his high-school days from a buddy who thought Ellington was a sharp dresser with lordly manners. Ellington never changed. Throughout his career he was known as a snappy dresser as well as a gourmet, bon vivant, humorist, sophisticate, and lover of beautiful women.

Referring to his youth, Ellington once recalled, "I was going to be a painter. I won a scholarship at Pratt. I had planned to go there after one more year, but I got mixed up in this music and I was doing all right. At 18 I had bought a house and a car."[18]

From Washington, Ellington moved his band to New York in 1922, where the group took up lodgings with a young married couple the Duke knew. "We like the way you kids play," the wife said. "You can stay here as long as you want. Don't worry about the rent. You can pay when you get it, because we think you kids are really going somewhere."[19]

And go somewhere they did! Beginning with their first European tour in 1933, Ellington and his band went on to play in almost every major city in the world, except those in China and Siberia. He dined with presidents and kings, had the Prince of Wales accompany him on drums, played piano duets with a president of the United States, was presented on television performing his music in Japan, Sweden, England, and the United States, and conducted symphony orchestras in various countries. He wrote more than 5,000 pieces of music, including Broadway musicals, a ballet with the choreographer Alvin Ailey, orchestral music for the conductor Arturo Toscanini and the Paris Symphony Orchestra, film music for the director Otto Preminger, and special shows for television.

In 1943, Ellington gave the first of a series of annual concerts at Carnegie Hall in New York City, in which he introduced some of his longer, more complex works. *Black, Brown, and Beige,* lasting some fifty minutes, was one of the most popular of this genre.

His series of *Sacred Concerts,* among his most important accomplishments, in his own opinion, was presented in cathedrals from Coventry and London to Barcelona, from New York to San Francisco. Few people who knew the Duke were aware of his

17. Duke Ellington, "The Composer on His Work," *Christian Science Monitor,* June 10, 1968.
18. Ellington, "The Composer on His Work."
19. Edward Kennedy Ellington, *Music Is My Mistress* (New York, 1976), p. xi.

Performing Ellington's *Sacred Concert* at the Fifth Avenue Presbyterian Church, New York, 1965.

religious convictions before he became involved with the sacred concerts. While he was a boy, his mother had taken him to two different churches every Sunday. By the time he was fourteen, he was sent to Sunday School as well. Before he was out of his twenties, Ellington claimed that he had read the Bible completely four times. He read it through three more times for consolation after his beloved mother's death in 1935. Once asked in a newspaper interview what his best habit was, he responded, quite simply, "prayer."

In 1965, the Duke was invited to present a concert of sacred music in Grace Cathedral, San Francisco, as part of a year-long series celebrating the completion and consecration of that great Episcopal cathedral atop Nob Hill. "I recognized this as an exceptional opportunity," Ellington later wrote. " 'Now I can say openly,' I said [to Dean C. J. Bartlett and the Rev. John S. Yargan], 'what I have been saying to myself on my knees.' "[20] The concert was such a success that it was repeated at the Fifth Avenue Presbyterian Church in New York. *Duke Ellington Talked to the Lord in Grace Cathedral Last Night* read the headlines above a United Press International report in hundreds of newspapers across the country. "These were musicians offering what they did best— better than any others in the world—to the glory of God," said the *Saturday Review,* in an article entitled "The Ecumenical Ellington." Other sacred concerts followed, culminating in one at Westminster Abbey in London seven months before the Duke died at age seventy-six.

Bibliography

Ellington, Edward Kennedy. *Music Is My Mistress.* New York: Doubleday, 1973.
Jewell, Derek. *Duke: A Portrait of Duke Ellington.* New York: Norton, 1977.

Makin' Whoopee

by **BENNY GOODMAN**

In 1934, Benny Goodman and his band started a series of radio broadcasts that were to become among the most popular on the airwaves at that time. The first broadcasts were sponsored by the National Biscuit Company, three-hour programs entitled "Let's Dance." These were followed by "sustaining broadcasts" (without a commercial sponsor) that originated in whatever city the Goodman band happened to be playing in. During the 1937 season, while it was appearing for an extended engagement at the Madhattan Room of the Hotel Pennsylvania in New York, the band was heard at least once every night—after all, it was the hottest property in show business.

One of the biggest hits of the October 30 broadcast was a Walter Donaldson tune called *Makin' Whoopee.* Part of its success was undoubtedly due to the fact that the audience heard not only the solo clarinet work of Benny Goodman but also the lead trumpet work of Harry James. Others in the group included Ziggy Elman and Chris Griffin on trumpet, Red Ballard and Vernon Brown on trombone, Hymie Schertzer and George Koenig on alto saxophone, Art Rollini and Vido Muso on tenor saxophone, Jess Stacy on piano, Allan Reuss on guitar, Harry Goodman on bass, and the inimitable Gene Krupa on drums.

20. Ellington, *Music Is My Mistress,* p. 261.

Makin' Whoopie consists of four choruses of a thirty-two-bar tune. The ternary form of the chorus could be outlined A-A-B-A.

LISTENING OUTLINE

A four-bar introduction leads to the thirty-two-bar tune.

Example 1

First chorus:

In the A section, with its repeat, the lead shifts between the brass and woodwind sections.

In the B section, the lead is taken by the woodwinds; the brass provide a chordal accompaniment.

Section C is a repeat of the A section.

There is a four-bar woodwind interlude:

Example 2

Second chorus: This is a clarinet solo with a chordal, sectional background.
Third chorus:

    The A section with its repeat is a trumpet solo.

    The B section is a saxophone solo.

    The C section, another trumpet solo, is cut one bar short.

A modulation from G major to F major follows:

Example 3

Fourth chorus:

    The A section with its repeat features the brass and woodwinds in counterpoint.

    The B section is characterized by a clarinet solo.

    The concluding C section features the full band.

About the Composer

BENNY GOODMAN   Born: May 30, 1909
                           Chicago, Illinois

Almost from the inception of the style, Benny Goodman has been known as the King of Swing. It must be said, however, that Goodman did not invent swing, Duke Ellington, Fletcher Henderson, and such other black musicians as Don Redman and Benny Moten did that. But Goodman made swing popular and set the standards for its performance. Jazz writer Frank Tirro summed up Goodman's contribution well when he wrote:

> The decade from 1935 to 1945 has become known as the swing era, and no single musician did more to crystallize the style, establish the technical standards, and popularize the music than Benny Goodman. Practically all by himself, he revolutionized the dance-band business. As a result, he was loved,

Benny Goodman (right) with Illinois Jacquette (center) and Lionel Hampton (left).

admired, and respected by millions, including the jazz musicians themselves. When BG became "King of Swing," he made this music the most vital and exciting kind of social-dance music ever created in America.[21]

Benjamin David Goodman was born in Chicago on May 30, 1909, the eighth of twelve children of an immigrant tailor. At the age of ten, he was already able to play some clarinet, and at twelve he was alternating professional imitations of Ted Lewis — then the current popular success — with scales and arpeggios forced upon him by his teacher Franz Schoepp, clarinetist with the Chicago Symphony. Between the ages of fourteen and eighteen he listened to the jazz performances in Chicago of such masters as King Joe Oliver, Louis Armstrong, Johnny and Warren "Baby" Dodds, cornetist Paul Mares, trombonist George Brunis, and clarinetist Leon Rappolo, and played in bands with the Austin High gang of Jimmy McPartland, Frank Teschemacher, Bud Freeman, Dave Tough, and Muggsy Spanier. In August of 1923, at the age of fifteen, Goodman played with Bix Beiderbecke on a riverboat gig, or job. By the time he was sixteen, word of Goodman's excellent musicianship had spread all the way to Califor-

21. Frank Tirro, *Jazz: A History* (New York, 1977).

nia, and Ben Pollack asked him to join his band. Goodman had built a considerable reputation by the age of twenty, when he left the Pollack band. For the next five years he played on radio and for recording companies in New York.

Benny Goodman's first recording as leader of a group was made for Vocalion Records in 1927, and a year later Benny Goodman's Boys recorded with Jimmy McPartland and Glenn Miller. Jazz impressario John Hammond liked what he heard and secured a place for Goodman and a small band on NBC's three-hour Saturday night radio program "Let's Dance." By 1935, Goodman was leading his own big band, making use of a number of Fletcher Henderson arrangements. This was followed by a cross-country tour for the band. But few people came to hear them, making the tour appear to be a failure. Then Goodman's band hit Los Angeles, and what happened is best described by Goodman himself:

> After traveling 3,000 miles, we finally found people who were up on what we were trying to do, prepared to take our music the way we wanted to play it. The first big roar from the crowd was one of the sweetest sounds I've ever heard in my life—and from that time on, the night kept getting bigger and bigger, as we played about every good number in our book.[22]

That remarkable night is usually designated as the beginning of the *Swing Era,* an era that was to last for at least a decade. As its "King," Goodman knew exactly what he wanted to hear and what he expected from his musicians. Popsie Randolph, once Goodman's bandboy, remarked that "Benny wanted what he wanted, that's all. If a guy worked for him he had to do the job right. Sure, he was changeable, all right, like the weather—a little fickle you might say. But man, he was a perfectionist. A guy would come into the band one day and two days later Benny'd say he was no good—and out he'd go."[23]

Goodman was the first bandleader to force the issue of integration. It had been possible for black and white musicians to jam together in after-hours clubs and to record together, because neither was a visual situation (one in which they would be visible to an audience). But neither the white nor the black public wanted to see a "mixed" band. When Goodman hired Teddy Wilson, in 1935, and Lionel Hampton, in 1936, he had to pretend that they were not regular members of his band. Finally, he simply acknowledged that these musicians were part of his band and that the public would have to see and hear his music on his terms. He stated it in a very simple way: he was not selling prejudice or integration, but music.

Benny Goodman has been active not only in the performance of jazz for well over sixty years but also equally involved in the field of symphonic music. He commissioned and recorded *Contrasts for Clarinet, Violin, and Piano* by Béla Bartók and clarinet concertos by Aaron Copland and Paul Hindemith; he has performed the solo clarinet part in works by Mozart, Debussy, and Brahms with such orchestras as the Boston Sym-

22. Benny Goodman, quoted in notes for *Benny Goodman: The Golden Age of Swing,* recording (Victor LPT 6703).
23. Shapiro and Hentoff, *Hear Me Talkin' to Ya,* p. 322.

phony, the Cleveland Symphony, and the NBC Symphony as well as the Budapest String Quartet.

In 1955, Universal-International made a movie of his life story; Goodman himself recorded the soundtrack and acted as musical director. The following year he played to sell-out audiences in Hong Kong, Singapore, Tokyo, and Bangkok. In 1958 and 1959, his overseas tours took him to Belgium, Germany, Sweden, Denmark, France, Switzerland, Austria, England, Australia, Central America, South America, and Alaska. Since the mid-'60s, Goodman has appeared regularly at jazz festivals. Throughout the 1970s, he continued to make appearances at New York City's prestigious Carnegie Hall; Goodman's band had been the first swing band to play a concert there when they appeared during the 1938 season.

Bibliography

Baron, Stanley. *Benny: King of Swing, A Pictorial Biography Based on Benny Goodman's Personal Archives.* New York: Morrow, 1979.

Goodman, Benny, and Kolodin, Irving. *The Kingdom of Swing.* Harrisburg, Pa.: Stackpole, 1939.

Koko

by **CHARLIE PARKER**

The ensemble form of the bop era was one of small combos with three to six members. The standard procedure was to perform without written music, a visible and practical sign of rebellion by these musicians against the written arrangements of swing. Usually the melody was played in its entirety once (twice if it was a twelve-measure blues), then followed by several choruses consisting of solos improvised to the accompaniment of the rhythm section. A repeat of the melody of the first chorus would bring the piece to an end. Throughout the tune, the rhythm section (usually piano, bass, and drum set) maintained the structure of the piece by repeating the harmonic pattern (the *changes*) of a complete chorus. Parker's performance of *Koko* with his Quintet is a good example.

Parker has told us how *Koko* came into existence:

> "I remember one night I was jamming in a chili house [Dan Wall's] on Seventh Avenue between 139th and 140th [in Harlem]. It was December, 1939. Now I'd been getting bored with the stereotyped changes that were being used all the time, at the time, and I kept thinking there's bound to be something else. I could hear it sometimes, but I couldn't play it. Well, that night, I was working over *Cherokee,* and, as I did, I found that by using the higher intervals of a chord as a melody line and backing them with appropriately related changes, I could play the thing I'd been hearing. I came alive.[24]

24. Quoted in *Hear Me Talkin' to Ya,* ed. Shapiro and Hentoff.

Actually, what Parker accomplished was a remarkable transformation. He totally discarded Ray Noble's old tune *Cherokee,* and composed his new melody *Koko* over the chord progression of *Cherokee.* A comparison of one of the melodic lines of Parker's *Koko* with the opening of Ray Noble's *Cherokee* shows that the bop transformation is complete. Nothing of the original remains.

Parker's *Koko*

Noble's *Cherokee*

The recording of *Koko* used for this book was made at a live performance, probably in 1948. The Quintet at that time consisted of Charlie Parker on alto saxophone, Kenny Dorham on trumpet, Al Haig on piano, Nelson Boyd on bass, and Max Roach on drums.

Charlie Parker's improvisations are well described by the jazz critic Whitney Balliett, who wrote:

> The heart of Parker's style was his unceasing and uncanny projection of surprise. It was composed, principally, of long and short melodic lines, legato and staccato phrases, simple one-two-three rhythms and intense Stravinsky-like rhythms, a sometimes whiney tone and a rich, full-blooded sound, as well as that rare thing among jazz musicians, an acute grasp of dynamics.[25]

LISTENING OUTLINE

Koko consists of an improvised bebop line over the chord changes of the old jazz standard, *Cherokee,* a thirty-two-bar chorus in the traditional ternary form: A-A-B-A. The original tune, which is dropped in *Koko,* is shown in the following example, along with the chord changes that become the basis of *Koko.*[26]

25. Whitney Balliett, "The Measure of 'Bird,'" *Saturday Review* 37 (March 17, 1956), p. 34.
26. Added to the chord designations in the score are certain symbols, used in jazz to indicate alterations or additions to the basic triad indicated by the capital letter, such as Δ major seventh chord;—minor seventh chord; and 7 dominant seventh chord.

Cherokee

As *Koko,* the entire tune is in double time, that is, twice as fast as the original tempo of *Cherokee.*

The introduction is sixteen bars in length:

a four-bar passage for trumpet and sax in unison is heard;

a four-bar passage, in which the muted trumpet improvises, follows;

a four-bar passage follows next, featuring improvisations by the saxophone;

the final four-bar passage returns to the trumpet and saxophone in unison.

First and second choruses: The solo sax improvises on the thirty-two-bar harmonic structure of *Cherokee.*

There is a sixteen-bar drum solo.

Coda: The sixteen-bar coda is similar to the introduction.

About the Composer

CHARLIE PARKER   Born: August 29, 1920
                                Kansas City, Kansas

                        Died: March 12, 1955
                                New York, New York

More than to any other musician, the credit for the birth of modern jazz belongs to Charles "Yardbird" Parker—known to his friends and fans simply as "Bird." His virtuoso technique, melodic genius, and inspired improvisations helped launch a new era in jazz, an era that began with bop and culminated in the cool or modern jazz of the fifties. His brilliant handling of the alto saxophone inspired a generation of jazz musicians; without him there would have been no John Coltrane, no Ornette Coleman, no jazz as we know it today.

The Bird was born Charles Parker, Jr., on August 29, 1920, in Kansas City, Kansas. His father, a native of Memphis, was a singer and dancer who had settled in Kansas City, when a vaudeville show with which he had been touring finished their season there. Shortly after that, Charlie, Sr., married a local girl, seventeen-year-old Addie Boyley. When their son was seven, the Parkers moved to Kansas City, Missouri. Which was at that time a center for much good jazz.

At fifteen, Charlie was learning music the same way most jazz players learned their trade: by listening and attempting to imitate. By the time he was sixteen, Charlie could be found standing around in the alley behind the Reno Club in Kansas City, listening to Count Basie's band. Another of his favorites was saxophonist Lester Young.

After having quit high school and having played in some of the clubs around Kansas City, Parker moved to New York in 1939 and supported himself washing dishes. "I played at Monroe's Uptown House. Nobody paid me much mind at first at Monroe's except Billy Moore, one of Count Basie's trumpet players. He liked me. Everybody else was trying to get me to sound like Benny Carter. There was no [salary schedule] at

Charlie Parker (left) and Miles Davis.

Monroe's. Sometimes I got 40¢ or 50¢ a night. If business was good, I might get up to $6."[27]

After playing for a while at the Uptown House, Parker left town to tour with Jay McShann's band; by the time the band returned to New York in 1942, Parker was a mature musician. Jam sessions at Minton's Playhouse followed, and Parker, together with Dizzy Gillespie, became one of the most talked-about musicians in the new school of jazz called bop.

In 1942, Parker quit the blues-oriented band of Jay McShann, and saxophonist Budd Johnson urged bandleader Earl Hines to hire him. When Hines's band separated, Billy Eckstine hired most of the avant-garde players—including Parker—for his own band. In 1944, as the band started a tour headed for St. Louis, a trumpet player became ill and was replaced by a teenager named Miles Davis. Thus began the legendary association of Charlie Parker and Miles Davis.

Parker's first job as a bandleader in his own right was at the Spotlight Club on Fifty-second Street, New York's jazz street in 1944, after he had left Eckstine. Most jazz experts concede that some of Parker's finest recordings were made with his Quintet in 1945–46. During that period, he was paid $1,200 a week by the same people who had hired him earlier for $2 a night.

To the world at large, Parker was known as *"Yardbird,"* or more commonly, just *"Bird."* (The famous jazz club Birdland was named after him.) Sometimes when he was introduced, he would smile benignly and say, "People call me Bird"; and he would recite from the *Rubaiyat:* "The Bird of Time has but a little way to flutter—and the Bird is on the Wing."

For Parker, the world of music knew no bounds. He wanted to listen to everything by Stravinsky, Bartók, Varèse, and Alban Berg. He planned to compose seriously. This interest in the broader aspects of music was to help him free jazz of many of its traditional limitations. He began stretching his improvisational line beyond the thirty-two-bar, one-chorus limit as far as his sense of design would allow and his inspiration would support. (Today, a lyric statement by a jazz soloist can last any number of bars.)

Outside the world of music, Parker had a number of problems. He was a man of enormous appetites that matched his great gifts, and his offstage antics were marked by chronic overindulgence and defiance—whether he was throwing his saxophone out of a hotel window, walking into the ocean wearing a new suit, standing up to the promoter of a jazz concert in Paris, drinking sixteen double whiskies in two hours, eating twenty hamburgers at a sitting, riding a policeman's horse into a well-known Manhattan tavern, or accommodating the steady stream of women who followed him.

Although Parker could be quite charming off stage, he seldom smiled when on it. There he was a deadly serious musician. Requests were ignored unless people happened to call for a tune he liked or had recorded. "Even then it was scarcely recognizable," one of his record producers commented, "for it was played with new variations. Psychologically Charlie seemed incapable of repeating himself. One improvisation simply led to another. Each set was played as if he were trying to shake down the walls of a

27. Robert G. Reisner, ed., *Bird: The Legend of Charlie Parker* (New York, 1975), p. 238.

modern Jericho. After he had gone for several weeks at this killing pace, he would be exhausted, become difficult, unreliable, or revert to his bad-boy style."[28]

In 1946, Parker spent seven months in Camarillo State Hospital in California. By 1949, because of a combination of ulcers, drugs, and alcohol, his playing started to decline. He was not considered a reliable risk by booking offices, so getting regular gigs started to become a problem. When his daughter Pree died of pneumonia, Parker seemed to decline for the last time, both musically and physically. He died on March 12, 1955, at less than thirty-five years of age. The jazz critic Ralph Gleason wrote: "Parker's was a sentence of death from youth, waiting to be consummated, like the racing driver out to see how many times he can get away with it, knowing that in the end the odds will catch up with him."[29]

Bibliography

Reisner, Robert, G. ed. *Bird: The Legend of Charlie Parker.* New York: Da Capo Press, 1975.

Russell, Ross. *Bird Lives! The High Life and Hard Times of Charlie (Yardbird) Parker.* New York: Charterhouse Books, 1973.

Simple Like

by JOHN COLTRANE

Simple Like is an original Coltrane tune that he recorded in 1960, the year he organized his own quartet, at New York's fabled club Birdland during the quartet's summer appearance there. The group included, in addition to Coltrane on tenor saxophone, McCoy Tyner on piano, Steve Davis on bass, and Billy Higgins on drums.

About the time *Simple Like* was recorded, the New York *Daily News* reported on the Trane's appearance in New York:

> Run, do not walk or otherwise loiter on your way. . . . The reason is John Coltrane, a tenor saxophonist who has the future coming out of his horn.
>
> This musician is phenomenal. Few jazzmen possess such a thorough knowledge of their instrument plus the combined imagination and feeling to translate that knowledge into great music. Coltrane is not just a player. He is a composer, practicing his craft every moment he is on the stand. He creates huge patterns of interwoven themes united in a beautifully-knit whole. The sounds he produces are often weird, like they shouldn't be coming out of that horn at all, but somehow he makes them seem natural. It's as if these notes were hiding inside all along, just waiting for someone to appear and release them.[30]

28. Ross Russell, *Bird Lives! The High Life and Hard Times of Charlie (Yardbird) Parker* (New York, 1973).
29. *San Francisco Chronicle.*
30. "Trane Stops in the Gallery," New York *Daily News,* Sunday, May 15, 1960.

LISTENING OUTLINE

Simple Like consists of six choruses of a thirty-two-bar tune in ternary form: A-B-A. The example is the melody of that tune in a simplified form, without an embellishment.

In both sections A and C, the minor-chord roots outline a diminished D chord (D–F–A-flat).

In the B section, the minor chord roots outline an augmented D-flat chord (D-flat–F–A).

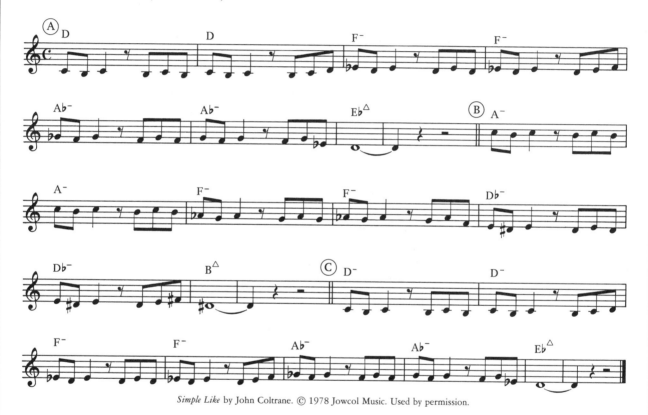

Simple Like by John Coltrane. © 1978 Jowcol Music. Used by permission.

First chorus: melody in the tenor saxophone.

Second chorus: improvisation by the tenor saxophone over a complex rhythmic background that contains elements of music.

Third chorus: tenor saxophone solo continues; the rhythm changes to swing.

Fourth and Fifth choruses: piano solo.

Sixth chorus: melody in the tenor saxophone again.

About the Composer

JOHN COLTRANE Born: September 23, 1926
Hamlet, North Carolina

Died: July 17, 1967
Huntington, New York

John Coltrane was one of the most influential jazz musicians of our time, on a par with Louis Armstrong and Charlie Parker. Coltrane—more frequently known as "The Trane"—was an important innovative force. He revolutionized the timbre and technique of playing the saxophone as well as contributing innovations to the style of jazz composition.

Coltrane's style of playing was once described, in the jacket notes for his recording *Soultrane,* as "ripping, roaring, hotly pulsing, cooking, aircleaning"—which is one view. Another is that of the jazz critic Mimi Clara, who said "Coltrane's playing is like an electric fan turned on and left on." What was Coltrane's style? It was characterized in his improvisations chiefly by two things: an extremely fast pace and the use of the higher harmonics of chords as the source of his melodic line.

Coltrane had great coordination between his fingering of the saxophone and his *tonguing* (the technique of articulating each tone). This ability allowed him a fast-paced technique; he played arpeggios so rapidly that they were referred to as Coltrane's *"sheets of sound."* These sheets of sound were actually constructed vertically, since Coltrane thought of these runs as if they were chords on top of chords.

Playing jazz was always a spiritual experience for Coltrane. A deeply religious man —a Muslim by faith—he felt he should share his feelings with listeners.

> The main thing a musician would like to do is to give a picture to the listener of the many wonderful things he knows of and senses in the universe. That's what music is to me—it's just another way of saying this is a big, beautiful universe we live in, that has been given to us, and here's an example of just how magnificent and encompassing it is. That's what I would like to do. I think that's one of the greatest things you can do in life, and we all try to do it in some way. The musician's is through his music.[31]

John William Coltrane was born in Hamlet, North Carolina, on September 23, 1926. His father, a tailor and the son of a minister of the African Methodist Episcopal Zion Church, played ukulele and violin and sang. His mother, who had wanted to become an opera singer, played the piano in church and sang with the choir.

When he was twelve, young Coltrane got his first instrument, a school clarinet. The following year both his father and grandfather died; it was the same year in which John's band instructor at school talked his mother into buying the boy an alto saxophone. After he and his mother moved to Philadelphia, which was to become his hometown, John studied for a short while at the Ornstein School of Music and then at

31. Gleason, *Jam Session.*

the Granoff Studios, where he won scholarships for both performance and composition.

After joining the Navy, Coltrane played with a band in Hawaii in 1945–46. Following his discharge, he worked with the big bands of King Kolax and Dizzy Gillespie and the blues groups of Eddie Vinson and Earl Boston. He joined Miles Davis in 1955, and first came to the attention of the public with that group. In 1960, Coltrane formed his own quartet. In 1965, Alice McLeod (Mrs. John Coltrane) joined the ensemble. The Trane's short career ended with his death on July 1, 1967, at the age of forty.

The Trane's contributions to music both as a performer and as a composer were tremendous during this brief career. As the principal jazz magazine *Down Beat* reported:

> Coltrane came, and he made music. He built on existing foundations. He and his music lived in inexorable relation to other lives, other ideas, other musics. But how he built! The musical structures are changed forever because of him."[32]

Bibliography

Cole, Bill. *John Coltrane.* New York: Schirmer Books, 1976.

Thomas, J. C. *Chasin' the Trane: The Music and Mystique of John Coltrane.* New York: Doubleday, 1975.

32. Gordon Kopulos, "John Coltrane: Retrospective Prospective," *Down Beat* 38 (July 22, 1971), p. 14.

What frightening vitality there must have been in those Renaissance Italians, living amid violence, seduction, superstition, and war, yet eagerly alive to every form of beauty and artistry, and pouring forth—as if all Italy had been a volcano—the hot lava of their passions and their art, their architecture and assassinations, their sculpture and their liaisons, their painting and their brigandage, their madonnas and grotesques, their hymns and macaronic verse, their obscenities and piety, their profanity and prayers!

Will Durant

FOURTEEN/ THE RENAISSANCE

COLUMBUS and his men sailed in three small ships on an unchartered ocean and discovered a new continent. Gutenberg printed the Bible in movable type, and unlocked the world of the printed word. Artists rediscovered the glories of Greek sculpture; scholars read with renewed interest of the philosophy of Plato and Aristotle. In the words of Erasmus, "the world was coming to its senses, as if awakening from a deep sleep."

During this marvelous time, roughly 1450 to 1650, Michelangelo lay on his back, high on a scaffold, painting the powerful figures of *The Creation of Adam* on the ceiling of the Sistine Chapel in Rome. The restless genius Leonardo da Vinci sketched his plans for a flying machine and a submarine, and painted the famous and mysterious *Mona Lisa.* It was a time of tremendous artistic achievement by Raphael, Botticelli, Titian, and Cellini; by Ghiberti, Donatello, Fra Angelico, and Luca della Robbia; and by Veronese and Correggio.

The Renaissance is set off from the Middle Ages by several important milestones. The fall of Constantinople—the capital of the eastern Roman Empire—to the invading Ottoman Turks in 1453 forced hundreds of Greek scholars to flee to the West (many to the city of Florence in Italy), bringing with them such books and manuscripts as they could save. The introduction of gunpowder brought an end to the age of knighthood and left the protection of the old walled cities and castles ineffectual. The invention of printing with moveable type in about 1450 made it possible to print books in quantity instead of hand-lettering each one, and to disseminate such books throughout Europe. (By 1500, almost 20 million copies of 40,000 different editions had been printed.) And, of course, the development of the compass made it possible to sail on the high seas—as did Columbus (1492), Vasco da Gama (1498), and Ferdinand Magellan (1519–1522)—and discover new lands and new people.

With the growth of trade and industry during the Renaissance, merchant princes became fabulously wealthy. They controlled city-states. Many, like the two dukes of Florence, Cosimo de' Medici and Lorenzo "the Magnificent," patronized artists and sculptors and, in the process, developed one of the finest collections of art in the world.

During the Renaissance, an important change in intellectual outlook called *humanism* took place. Interest focused on human life and its accomplishments rather than on heaven and hell in an afterlife, the prime concern of the intellectuals during the Middle Ages. The people of the Renaissance became interested in the pagan cultures of ancient Greece and Rome, including their art and literature. Sculptors and painters once again presented the nude body as an object of beauty rather than as one of shame and concealment, as had been the style during the Middle Ages.

Just as literature and art turned from an exclusive concern with religious subjects, so music became involved in secular forms as well as liturgical ones. The subject matter rather than the style now determined whether a work was sacred or secular. Just as the painters of the era used the same local models for their madonnas as for their Aphrodites and nymphs, so the composers of the Renaissance used similar melodies for both sacred and secular works. The music for Latin love poetry, for example, could also be

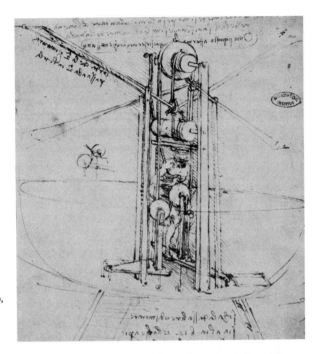

Leonardo da Vinci, *Flying machine with a man operating it, c.* 1488 (Bibliotheque Nationale, Paris). Leonardo, the supreme example of Renaissance genius, was both a great artist and a scientist.

Michelangelo Buonarroti, *The Creation of Adam,* detail of Sistine Chapel ceiling, 1508–12 (Vatican, Rome).

used to accompany a portion of the Mass, and popular songs of the era could be and were used as the themes on which composers based sacred motets and even entire Masses.

A *cappella* singing—vocal music without instrumental accompaniment—became more important during the Renaissance; polyphonic settings for four or more voices became common; and a counterpointing of rhythm between voices became as important as the melodic counterpoint between them. The Renaissance also marked the beginning of the development of instrumental music written for organ, lute, and ensemble.

Although in the field of art and the humanistic movement the Renaissance began and developed in Italy before moving northward, the flow of creative ideas in music moved in a contrary motion. The court and church composers of northern France and the Low Countries were true Renaissance artists. They were "individualistic, materialistic, and experimental. They had mastered the art of music and took great pleasure

Raphael Sanzio, *The School of Athens,* 1509–11 (Vatican, Rome). This fresco epitomizes the Renaissance reawakening to ancient Greek culture. It depicts Plato, Aristotle, Pythagoras, Euclid, and other wise men of antiquity in an idealized temple of philosophy.

demonstrating their compositional skills with a variety of intricate canons and musical puzzles for educated amateurs."[1]

The Franco-Flemish composers traveled to Italy in a search for new materials and ideas. These well-schooled composers were fascinated with the simple folk melodies and dance tunes of Italy, which provided them with new opportunities for polyphonic devices and techniques. In turn, Italian composers added some of the complexities of the northern style to their creations. Increased travel led to interaction between the two musical cultures that, in turn, led to the rise of an international style of music.

El Grillo

by JOSQUIN DES PREZ

El Grillo (*The Cricket*) is a *frottola,* one of the first aesthetic forms of secular music. Frottole were a product of the late Renaissance, and were composed mostly by musicians living in and around northern Italy. Between 1504 and 1514, following the invention of a satisfactory method of printing music, eleven books of frottole were published in Venice.

A frottola could be in duple or triple meter (triple was more common), and was usually composed for four voices, with a prominent melody and a strong harmonic bass. The two middle voices were of less significance and filled in the harmony. The four voices moved in a square-cut manner, the rhythm always being precisely balanced with the meter of the text. The texts were frivolous or humorous poems written by the leading poets of northern Italy. Some musical historians believe that frottole were meant to be sung with instrumental accompaniment, probably with the lute.

As with *El Grillo,* the poems were usually stanzaic. Repetitions of rhymes and stanzas of the poem were usually set similarly by the composers. As the century progressed, the frottola gave way to new forms—the *canzone* (which were also frivolous) and madrigals (which were very noble in character).

El Grillo points up the general characteristics of most frottole: a simple, chordal piece in four parts or voices; its phrase lengths determined by the poetic lines; the text closely related to the top voice, which, though having a narrow range and frequent repeated notes, is quite tuneful. The bass line is angular, since it provides harmonic support to the tune. The inner parts (which were usually filled in last by the composer) were simply devised to round out the harmonic texture.

---

1. Neal M. Cross, Robert C. Lamm, and Rudy H. Turk, *The Search for Personal Freedom.* (Dubuque, Iowa, 1978).

LISTENING OUTLINE

The first section begins:

Example 1

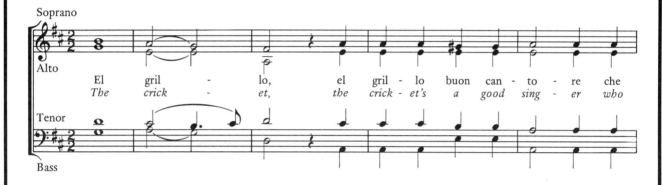

In the next passage (which follows immediately), the treble and bass voices answer each other in a humorous exchange:

Example 2

All four voices sing simultaneously:

Dalle, dalle	Chirping, chirping
beve, beve	drinking, drinking
grillo, grillo	cricket, cricket
canta.	sing!

The meter changes from duple to triple after the word *cantore* in the following passage:

El grillo, el grillo è buon cantore.	The cricket's a good singer.
Ma non fa come gl'altri uccelli,	But unlike birds of all description,
come li han cantato un poco,	Noble crickets for fun keep singing.
van' de fatto in altro loco,	And, unlike many others which fly away when their song is finished,
sempre el grillo sta pur saldo.	Crickets keep on singing!

In a passage in which the melodic setting is derived from the melody of both Examples 1 and 2, the story is brought to its conclusion:

El grillo, e grillo è buon cantore.	The cricket's a good singer.
Quando la maggior el caldo	When the heavy heat is greatest
Alhor canta sol per amore,	He sings alone: for love alone he sings,
canta sol per amore.	He sings for love alone.

The opening section of *El Grillo* (through musical Example 2) is repeated.

About the Composer

JOSQUIN DES PREZ   Born: *c.* 1450
                        Hainault (now in Belgium)

               Died: August 27, 1521
                        Condé-sur-Escaut, France

Josquin des Prez was honored as one of the greatest composers of his own day; and even now, some 450 years later, musicians give him credit for being one of the great composers of all time. Donald J. Grout says in *A History of Western Music:*

> Out of the extraordinarily large number of first-rank composers living around 1500, one, Josquin des Prez, must be counted among the greatest of all time. Few musicians have enjoyed higher renown while they lived, or exercised more profound and lasting influence on those who came after them. Josquin

was hailed by contemporaries as "the best of the composers of our time," the "Father of Musicians." "He is the master of the notes," said Martin Luther.[2]

Little is known of Josquin's life, and even the dates of his service at various chapels and courts are confused, since the dates of his tenure at the Papal Chapel were incorrectly recorded. He was born in Hainault, an area then ruled by Burgundy, and served as a chorister at the Collegiate Church at St. Quentin, which is now in northwestern France. He later became a canon and choirmaster there.

When he was about twenty-five, Josquin served as a chorister at the court of Duke Sforza in Milan, Italy. About eleven years later he served as a singer in the Papal Choir at the Vatican in Rome. By that time he had gained universal admiration. Adrianus Petit Coclico, in his *Compendium musices* of 1552, gives an account of Josquin's method of teaching:

> My teacher Josquin . . . never gave a lecture on music or wrote a theoretical work, and yet he was able in a short time to form complete musicians, because he did not keep back his pupils with long and useless instructions, but taught them the rules in a few words, through practical application in the course of singing. As soon as he saw his pupils were well grounded in singing, that they had good enunciation, that they knew how to embellish melodies and how to fit the text to the music, then he taught them the perfect and imperfect intervals and the different methods of inventing counterpoints against plainsong. If he discovered, however, pupils with an ingenious mind and promising disposition, then he would teach these in a few words the rules of three-part, and later of four-, five-, and six-part writing, always providing them with examples to imitate. Josquin did not, however, consider all fit to learn composition; he judged that only those should be taught who were drawn to this delightful art by a special natural impulse.[3]

From Rome Josquin returned north to France, where for a time he served at the court of Louis XII. Several examples of his music from this period reveal his sense of humor—*El Grillo* is an excellent one. Apparently, Louis XII had offered a position at one of the local churches in return for Josquin's services at his own court. When such a position was not forthcoming, the composer wrote a motet based on Psalm 119 and had it performed in the presence of the king. The first line of the text was repeated in the music so many times that the king could not miss the point: "Deal bountifully with thy servant that I may live."

At another time, the king requested Josquin to compose a little piece in which he might sing a part. The completed work was a canon for the two upper voices; the part for the king (*vox regis,* the tenor line) was a single continuous note held throughout the composition; and the bass line, which the composer sang himself, consisted of an alternation of the root and fifth of the chord—so that on every other note he reinforced the pitch the king was singing to help hold the king true to his part.

2. Donald J. Grout, *A History of Western Music* (New York, 1960), p. 173.
3. Quoted in *Music Through the Centuries* by Nick Rossi (Boston, 1963), p. 32.

Having served at numerous courts, including those of Ferrara and Florence, Josquin returned to northern France toward the end of his life; he served as canon of the collegiate church at Condé-sur-Escaut, and died there.

Bibliography

Lowinsky, Edward E., ed. *Josquin des Prez.* New York: Oxford University Press, 1976.

O magnum mysterium
by TOMÁS LUIS DE VICTORIA

O magnum mysterium (*O Great Mystery*) by Tomás Luis de Victoria is a *motet* intended for the Christmas season. Although generically the motet was the most important form of early polyphonic music (particularly during the Middle Ages and Renaissance), it is almost impossible to give it a general definition because of the great changes it underwent during the more than 500 years of its existence. If, however, we limit ourselves to the period in which Victoria was active—roughly 1560 to 1600—a motet could be described as a short composition intended primarily for unaccompanied singing, written in polyphonic style on a Latin text that is usually liturgical or quasi-liturgical in nature.

As with much of the writing of this period, composers occasionally employed *word painting* in motets; that is, they attempted to represent musically specific poetic images. For example, the words *descending from heaven* might be set to a descending melodic line; the words *the flight of angels* might be accompanied by rapidly repeated arpeggios in imitation of the flapping of angel wings. The relation of words and music was of primary importance and concern. Gioseffe Zarlino, a leading musician and writer of the period, said: "When one of the words expresses weeping, pain, heartbreak, sighs, tears, and other similar things, let the harmony be full of sadness."

LISTENING OUTLINE

O magnum mysterium, which is written in the Dorian mode,[4] opens in imitative counterpoint—that is, each voice or part imitates its predecessors.[5] The sopranos enter first with a haunting melody, one filled with wonderment and awe

4. The twelve *modes*, or *church modes*, used in medieval and Renaissance music are scale patterns, each with a particular set of half steps and whole steps (see p. 41). Each mode is associated with a key; the Dorian mode is equivalent to playing all the white keys on the piano keyboard between any two adjacent D's.
5. In most imitative polyphony, the second and succeeding even-numbered voices usually enter at the interval of a fifth higher or a fourth lower than the pitch of the first voice.

(an excellent example of word painting). The altos enter next, five tones lower in pitch. The tenor entrance is at the original pitch of the sopranos, but one octave lower in range; the basses enter last. The pitch of their entrance coincides with that of the altos but one octave lower in range:

Example 1

O magnum mysterium   O great mystery
et admirabile sacramentum   and wondrous sacrament

Three measures later, in a very brief passage, the texture becomes chordal in nature, all voices moving in the same rhythm at the same time, and all singing the same text at the same time:

Example 2

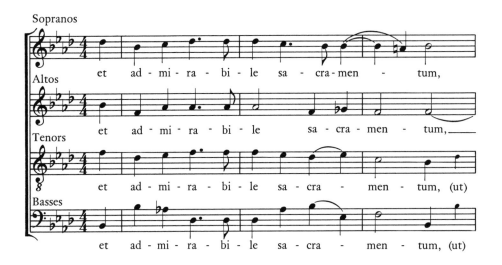

et admirabile sacramentum   and wondrous sacrament

At the conclusion of Example 2, the texture immediately becomes polyphonic again as the men's voices—singing in thirds (three tones apart)—are imitated by the women's voices:

Example 3

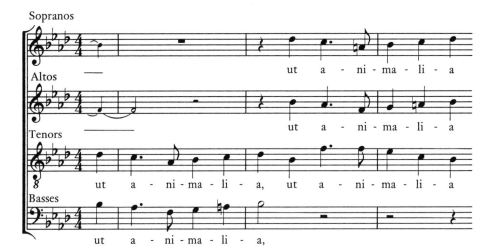

ut	*animalia*	*viderent*	*Dominum*	That animals might see the birth of
natum,				the Lord,

The writing continues in imitative counterpoint in an extended passage, with each line of the text being repeated several times in each voice:

viderent Dominum natum,	see the birth of the Lord
jacentem in praesepio.	Lying in a manger.

After a brief pause, the second part begins. It consists of a prayer followed by an Alleluia. The prayer opens in chordal style, although some imitative counterpoint can be heard in the second line:

O beata Virgo,	O blessed virgin,
cujus viscera meruerunt	Who was worthy
portare Dominum Jesum Christum.	Of bearing our Lord Jesus Christ.

The closing Alleluia is slightly faster in tempo, is in triple meter, and is divided into two very short sections. The first is more chordal and harmonic in nature, although imitative counterpoint is a pervasive part of its structure. It begins:

Example 4

The closing section, again in quadruple meter, is in strict counterpoint; the basses and tenors entering first, followed by the altos and then the sopranos.

Example 5

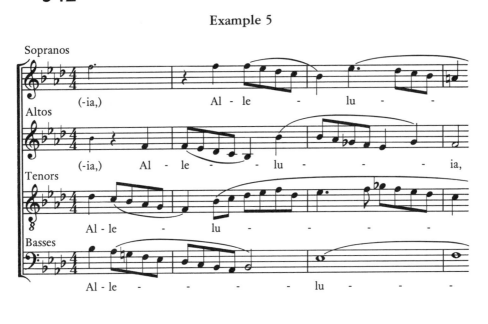

Sopranos

(-ia,) Al - le - lu -

Altos

(-ia,) Al - le - lu - ia,

Tenors

Al - le - lu -

Basses

Al - le - lu -

About the Composer

TOMÁS LUIS DE VICTORIA

Born: *c.* 1548
Avila, Spain

Died: August 27, 1611
Madrid, Spain

Tomás Luis de Victoria (frequently spelled Vittoria in Italian) was born in or near Avila in Old Castile, Spain. He studied at Segovia and, when he was seventeen, obtained a grant from the king to study in Rome. He enrolled at the Jesuit Collegium Germanicum, not as a music student but to study theology. The Collegium Germanicum had been founded by St. Ignatius Loyola to combat the Lutheran movement in Germany. Within a year after entering, Victoria was singing in the choir.

After leaving school he became the choir director and organist at the church of Santa Maria di Monserrato in Rome, the national church of the Spaniards of Aragon. He then succeeded Palestrina as musical director at the Roman seminary. His first published works, mostly motets, were printed in Venice when he was twenty-four. At twenty-seven he was ordained a priest, and shortly after that came into the service of the widowed Empress Maria, daughter of Charles V and sister of Philip II of Spain.

Victoria served as her chaplain, but it was some time before either of them moved from Rome back to Spain. With such royal patronage, many of Victoria's works were published in handsome editions.

Although Victoria acknowledged Spain as his home when he was forty-six, accounts are not clear as to his actual activities after that year. It is known that he made some trips back to Rome, but he spent the latter part of his career as a chaplain in the seminary where the Empress Maria's daughter was a nun.

Victoria composed no secular music. His works were largely unaccompanied polyphonic church music, although one of his last compositions includes an organ part. His music was touched by a sense of mysticism from his Spanish background. His music was well known in his lifetime, and his works were printed in Italy, Germany, and Spain. He left a legacy of about twenty-one masses, eighteen magnificats, thirty-five four-voiced hymns, and two settings of the Passion.

Bibliography

Tend, J. B. "Tomás Luis de Victoria." *Musical Times,* April 1925.

Now Is the Month of Maying

by **THOMAS MORLEY**

Thomas Morley was and is one of the best-known Elizabethan musicians, a composer known throughout Renaissance England for his brilliant and well-liked creations: motets, songs, and madrigals. The *madrigal* was a form he, together with other English composers of that day, had inherited from Italy, where it was one of the most uniquely Italian art forms of the Renaissance.

Since Elizabethan England was interested in things Italian—translations of Italian literary works, employment of Italian musicians at court, and even the Arcadian movement in English poetry, led by Sir Philip Sidney—it was only logical that the English try their hand at creating madrigals. What emerged, and emerged most successfully, was quite a different entity from its Italian progenitor.

English madrigalists tended to select their texts (usually dealing with country life or nature) from the works of minor or popular poets. This tended to give the English madrigals a wider, more popular appeal. The Italians had chosen their texts from the highest quality poetry, and this in turn had attracted an audience made up largely of nobility and educated scholars.

The English madrigalists also emphasized a simplicity of texture—no involved counterpoint for them! Most English madrigals tended to be either light and happy, or filled with remorse and sadness—either "merry" or "melancholy," as one writer put it.

Sebastian Florigerio pictured some madrigal singers in his painting *A Musical Entertainment, c.* 1540.

For those madrigals that fell in the merry category, there was a strong dependence on rhythm, the settings often making use of dance rhythms. The harmonic structure of the English madrigals was quite direct and simple, too, in contrast to the highly chromatic harmony of the earlier Italian madrigals.

A number of characteristically English madrigals, of which *Now Is the Month of Maying* is perhaps the best example, make use of *fa-la* refrains. Morley's models for this form were the Italian *balletti* of Giovanni Gastoldi, published in 1591, which were dancelike vocal compositions written in simplified madrigal style and usually provided with a fa-la refrain that was probably danced.

Now Is the Month of Maying is quite simple in structure. It is made up of two melodies, each of which concludes with a fa-la refrain and each of which is repeated. The first, third, and fifth stanzas of the poem are sung to the first melody; the second, fourth, and six stanzas are sung to the second melody. In effect, *Now Is the Month of Maying* is binary in form, repeated twice to accommodate all the stanzas.

LISTENING OUTLINE

Now Is the Month of Maying is set for five voices.[6] The opening line has a fa-la refrain:

Example 1

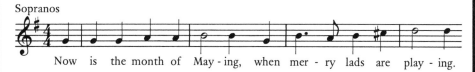

This opening section is repeated, as the sign indicates.

A second melody is introduced; it also has a fa-la refrain.

Example 2

The third stanza is sung to the melody of Example 1, the fourth stanza to the melody of Example 2:

> *The Spring, clad all in gladness,*
> *Doth laugh at Winter's sadness.*
> *Fa la la la la . . .* etc. (repeated)

> *And to the bagpipes' sound*
> *The nymphs tread out their ground.*
> *Fa la la la la . . .* etc. (repeated)

6. In polyphonic music, we use the term *voice* to mean an independent melodic line, whether instrumental or vocal. Thus "set for five voices" means that there are five independent melodic lines; each of the lines may be played or sung (in the case of vocal music) by one or more musicians.

The fifth stanza is sung to the melody of Example 1, the final stanza to the melody of Example 2:

Fie then, why sit we musing,
Youth's sweet delight refusing?
Fa la la la la . . . etc. (repeated)

Say, dainty nymphs, and speak,
Shall we play barley break?
Fa la la la la . . . etc. (repeated)

About the Composer

THOMAS MORLEY   Born: 1557
                            London, England

                     Died: October 1602
                            London, England

Thomas Morley was a pupil of the great English composer William Byrd, and received his bachelor of music degree from Oxford University in 1588. He served as an organist at St. Paul's Cathedral in London, where he was undoubtedly heard by Queen Elizabeth I. Morley also served as a Gentleman of the Chapel Royal.

The works of Morley are unusually melodious. In addition to his church music—motets and anthems (the English derivative of the motet, meant for use in the Anglican Church)—Morley composed songs and madrigals; he also wrote the first theoretical work on music in England. In was published in 1597 as *A Plaine and Easie Introduction to Practicall Musicke.*

Morley was the composer of at least two of the songs in the original productions of Shakespeare's plays and probably was acquainted with the great bard.

Little else is known of his life. Church records reveal that he was married once, possibly twice, and that he probably had three children, two girls and a boy.

As a composer, Morley was highly regarded by his contemporaries, some of whom believed that he was the finest musician of the era. Thomas Ravenscroft, the most important music editor of the Elizabethan age, wrote after Morley's death that it was "he who did shine as the Sun in the Firmament of our Art, and did first give light to our understanding with his Precepts."

Morley's ability to write cheerful, tuneful works led to his popularity. He became known for his light-hearted *balletts* (dancelike vocal works in simplified madrigal style) and for his *canzonets* (sometimes short, dancelike vocal works similar to the balletts, and frequently instrumental works—often *fantasies*—scored for viols).

Although the majority of his works were in the lighter forms, his few works of a more serious nature, such as his *Burial Service,* were highly praised by the music critics of his time.

Bibliography

Kerman, Joseph. "Morley and 'The Triumph of Oriana.'" *Music and Letters* 34, 1953.
Morley, Thomas. A *Plain and Easy Introduction to Practical Music.* Edited by John Harmon. London: Dent, 1952.

The Silver Swan

by ORLANDO GIBBONS

Orlando Gibbons was one of the most original of that group of English composers known as the madrigalists. Less influenced by the Italians than his contemporaries, his works have greater depth and grandeur and are marked by an individuality that sets them apart from the works of other composers of Jacobean England.

Gibbons's compositions include a set of five-part madrigals, keyboard pieces, music for viols, and sacred works for the Anglican service. Several of the five-part madrigals (including *The Silver Swan*) are less contrapuntal creations in the English madrigal tradition than beautifully harmonized *lute ayres* (airs), songs for soprano solo with lute accompaniment. Gibbons achieves the effect of solo song with accompaniment, as opposed to that of a contrapuntal madrigal, by keeping the soprano solo—the melody—separate from the lower voices, and by keeping the counterpoint simple in texture.

LISTENING OUTLINE

An example of the "melancholy" rather than "merry" group of English madrigals, *The Silver Swan* is cast in simple two-part (binary) song form, the second section being repeated. Notice in the opening phrase how the soprano line is frequently an octave above the alto line, while the lower four voices are singing in close harmony, the notes seldom separated by large intervals.

Example 1

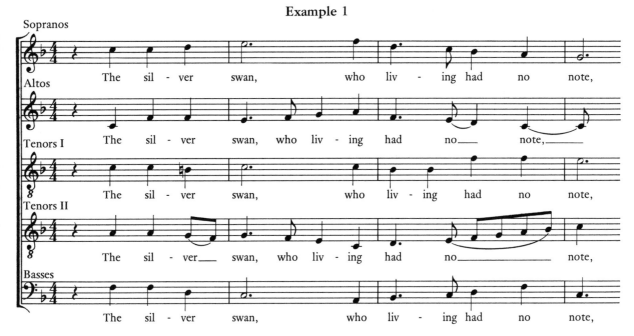

The text of the first section concludes:

When death approached
Unlocked her silent throat.

The second section (the entrances of the voices overlap with the conclusion of the last section) begins:

Example 2

The text of the second section continues:

> *Thus sung her first and last,*
> *And sung no more.*

To a repetition of the music of the second section, which begins with Example 2, the text concludes:

> *Farewell all joys,*
> *O death come close mine eyes,*
> *More Geese than Swans now live,*
> *More fools than wise.*

About the Composer

ORLANDO GIBBONS   Born: December 25, 1583
                                  Oxford, England

                        Died: June 5, 1625
                                  Canterbury, England

Orlando Gibbons, in addition to being one of the best-known composers in Renaissance England, was also an outstanding keyboard player, without a rival in England as a performer on the organ and virginals.[7]

Born in December of 1583, the son of a town councillor, he grew up in Cambridge, where his parents moved when he was five years old. At twelve, he entered the choir of King's College, Cambridge, and sang regularly with them until he was fifteen. A few years later (1602 and 1603), the college was paying him for original compositions written for special occasions.

On March 21, 1605, when he was only twenty-one, Gibbons was appointed organist of the Chapel Royal, a position he held the rest of his life. Best known for his church music, Gibbons wrote only for the Anglican service—there is not a note of his for the better-known Latin rite. In 1612 he published his set of *Madrigals and Mottets of 5 Parts: apt for Viols and Voyces,* which among its thirteen selections included *The Silver Swan.* (In this instance, it is believed Gibbons used the word *mottet* in his title to indicate the serious type of madrigal rather than the more limited religious form also known by the same term.) Gibbons also wrote a number of *fantasies* for three stringed instruments (usually viols—see p. 351) that have been described as the first music ever "cut in copper" (engraved) in England, placing their publication around 1610.

7. The *virginals* (a single instrument in spite of the plurality of the word itself) is a keyboard instrument, an earlier and smaller version of the harpsichord, built in an oblong case with the strings running from left to right. The strings are plucked by leather quills to produce the tone.

In 1623 the organist at Westminster Abbey died, and Gibbons, who at the age of thirty-nine had already been organist of the Chapel Royal for almost nineteen years, was appointed to that position, which he held for the final two years of his life. During that short period he was responsible for conducting the music at one state function of importance: the funeral of James I. In less than two months, Gibbons himself was dead. He had been summoned to the Chapel Royal to attend the new king, Charles I, at Canterbury, where Charles was to await the arrival of his queen, Henrietta Maria, from France. Before the arrival of the queen, Gibbons was seized with an apoplectic fit and died on Wednesday, June 5, 1625. He was buried the next day in Canterbury Cathedral.

Bibliography

Fellowes, Edmund H. *Orlando Gibbons; A Short Account of His Life and Work.* London, 1925.

_____. *Orlando Gibbons and His Family.* London, 1951. Reprint edition, New York: Shoe String Press, 1970.

Il Primo libro di balli

by GIORGIO MAINERIO

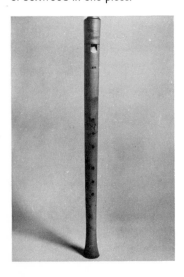

Renaissance tenor recorder, made of boxwood in one piece.

Instrumental music had first achieved independence during the Middle Ages primarily by providing music for dancing. Since social dancing was more widespread and more highly regarded during the Renaissance than at any other time in Western history, it was only natural that both the instruments themselves and the music they played become much more refined than in medieval times. More music was written down than ever before, and books were published that for the first time described the various musical instruments then in widespread use. Such books as Sebastian Virdung's *Musica getutscht und ausgezogen* (*A Summary* [*of the Science*] *of Music in Germany*) of 1510 were published not in the traditional Latin for theorists but in the vernacular German, so that craftsmen could use the descriptions and woodcuts as guides in building musical instruments.

The most interesting and complete book of this type was Michael Praetorius's *Syntagma musicum* (*Treatise of Music*) of 1618. It includes an extraordinary number and variety of wind instruments known and used during the Renaissance. Most of these instruments were available in sets, or families, so that music could be played with the same timbre from the highest to lowest voice in the ensemble. Such *chests* or *consorts* usually consisted, for example, of three to eight recorders, ranging from the high *sopranino* through the *soprano, alto, tenor,* and *bass,* and on to the *big bass* or *great bass* recorder.

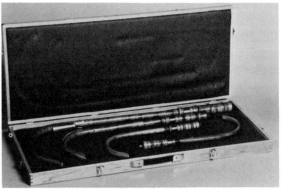

In addition to recorders, the principal wind instruments of the Renaissance, there were *shawms* (double-reeded, oboe-type instruments); *crumhorns* (also double-reeded instruments) and a family of strange-looking instruments known as *racketts,* both described in detail in the list on page 352; *cornetts* (made of wood or ivory with a cup-shaped mouthpiece); trumpets (quite similar to our modern bugles); and trombones. The bowed string family consisted of *viols* of different sizes. These differ from our modern violin family. The necks of the viols were fretted (gut bands were placed across the fingerboard to stop the strings, similar to the frets on our modern guitars). There were six strings, tuned a fourth apart with a major third in the middle (for example, A–D–G–B–E′–A′), and the tone was more delicate and thinner in quality than that of our modern stringed instruments. Since less vibrato (slight fluctuation of pitch) was used, the instruments were less expressive than their modern descendants.

Probably the most common instrument to be found in the Renaissance home was the *lute.* It had been introduced to Europe from Persia around 1000 A.D. and was originally confined to the Arabian and Moorish parts of Spain. From there it spread slowly across continental Europe. During the Middle Ages the lute had been played with a quill plectrum, and therefore only a single melodic line could be performed. During the Renaissance, the quill was abandoned; the fingers were used instead to play the strings. This enabled the performer to play chords, runs, ornaments of all kinds, and even contrapuntal pieces.

Usually made of costly materials and highly decorated, lutes were built in different sizes. All were pear-shaped, with fretted fingerboards and a pegbox bent back at a right angle. Lutes have one single and five double strings tuned G–C–F–A–D′–G′.

The collections of music printed during the Renaissance were usually made up of sets of contrasting dances, commonly grouped in twos or threes, precursors of the *dance suites* of the Baroque era. Since the Renaissance collections were used to accompany dances rather than serve as music for listening (as were the later Baroque dance suites), they had clearly marked, quite regular rhythms, and were divided into distinct sections. Essentially there was no contrapuntal interplay between parts; rather, a melody—frequently highly ornamented—was heard in the highest or soprano voice; the other instruments accompanied it.

Above, left, lute, c. 1600. Right, crumhorns.

Renaissance tenor viol. The body is made of pine, the fingerboard and tailpiece of ebony.

Giorgio Mainerio's *Primo libro di balli* (*First Book of Dances*), published in Venice, Italy, in 1578, is an excellent example of the dance collections printed during the Renaissance. It is a collection of twenty-one separate dances, ten of which are paired with a *saltarello* (a fast, lively Italian country dance). We shall concern ourselves with four examples from Mainerio's collection:

Ballo anglese (*English Dance*)

Ballo francese with its *saltarello* (*French Dance*)

Tedescha with its *saltarello* (*German Dance*)

Ungarescha with its *saltarello* (*Hungarian Dance*)

It was not the custom of Renaissance composers to indicate in the musical score which type of instrument was to play each voice. For practical reasons it was left up to the performers. If, for example, they happened to have a consort of four recorders at the time they wished to perform a four-voice work such as Mainerio's, they used recorders. If, on the other hand, there was a consort of four crumhorns, they used them. But, if they only had two recorders and two crumhorns, then that is what they used to perform the work (this combination of instruments from different families is called a *broken consort*). Fortunately, in our recording, the Boston Camerata makes use of several very interesting musical instruments of the Renaissance in addition to those already mentioned. The wind instruments listed below, which will be heard in the Mainerio piece, are all available in four sizes: soprano, alto, tenor, and bass.

Recorders: A family of end-blown or "whistle" flutes, usually made of wood, although a few were carved from ivory. Their tone is soft and breathy except in the higher register, where it becomes shrill and penetrating.

Crumhorns: A family of double-reeded instruments that was the forerunner of the oboe family. The mainly cylindrical tube of the crumhorn is curved upward like the letter *J*. There is a pierced cap on top that contains a large double reed. The player's lips do not touch the reed, the cap serving as a wind chamber so that the reed is set in vibration by the moving air inside. Crumhorns have an extremely piercing, buzzing sound.

Racketts: A family of double-reeded instruments. Racketts have short, squat bodies of solid wood that are pierced lengthwise by ten cylindrical channels connected so as to form a continuous tube; numerous fingerholes occur on the outside of the body. Racketts have a rich, reedy sound.

In addition to consorts of wind instruments, the Boston Camerata make use of:

Jew's-harp: A simple metal instrument, the frame horseshoe shaped. It has a vibrating metal tongue attached to the bottom of the horseshoe. The jew's-harp is played by holding the frame between the teeth (some think that the name *jew's-harp* might be a corruption of *jaw's-harp*). The metal tongue is plucked with the finger, causing it to vibrate in the player's mouth. It produces only one pitch, although the quality of that tone can be varied by changing the shape of the mouth. The jew's-harp is used to provide a drone, or long, sustained note.

Tabor: A small, bowl-like drum.

Antique cymbals: Small cymbals approximately three inches in diameter.

Copy of a Renaissance rackett. Its pitch is very low—the tubing inside is nine times the instrument's height.

Ballo anglese (English Dance)

Ballo anglese is a moderately slow dance in duple meter. Cast in binary form, A-B, the A section (Example 1) is made up of two identical four-measure phrases; the B section (Example 2) is made up of two six-measure phrases.

LISTENING OUTLINE

A one-measure drum solo establishes the moderately slow tempo of the dance.

A consort of viols (treble, tenor, and bass), assisted by a rackett, plays the first statement of the dance (Example 1 followed immediately by Example 2). The treble viol carries the melody.

Example 1

(Viols, Rackett)

Example 2

(Viols, Rackett)

A consort of recorders joins the consort of viols and rackett for a repetition of the dance. Some slight ornamentation is added to the melodic lines.

Ballo francese (French Dance)

The second dance, *Ballo francese,* is paired with a *saltarello. Ballo francese* is in a moderately fast duple meter; the *saltarello,* a lively Italian dance involving a jump step, is in a fast triple meter—so fast, actually, that the ear perceives the measures in groups of two that make it sound like a dance in $\frac{6}{8}$ meter.

    Ballo francese is cast in binary form. The A section (Example 3) is made up of two identical four-measure phrases. The B section is made up of two identical eight-measure phrases (Example 4 is repeated).

LISTENING OUTLINE

The first time the *Ballo francese* is heard, the melody (Example 3 followed by example 4 played twice) is played by a treble viol; a lute accompanies it.

Example 3

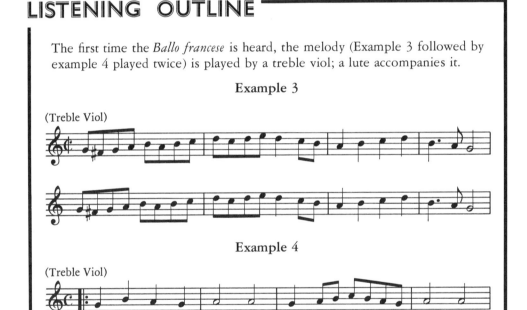

Example 4

(Treble Viol)

The entire dance (Example 3 followed by Example 4 played twice) is repeated. The instrumental roles are reversed: the lute plays the melodic line; treble, tenor, and bass viols accompany *pizzicato.* A pair of antique cymbals reinforces the beat.

    The *saltarello* follows without pause. Its melody is a variant—both melodically and rhythmically—of that of the *Ballo francese.* The *saltarello* is also in binary form: a sixteen-measure A section made up of two identical eight-measure phrases, Example 5, linked by a four-measure bridge (made out of the first four measures of the opening melody of the B section) to a B section made up of two twelve-measure phrases, in which the first six measures are identical. Example 6 is the first phrase.

A soprano recorder, accompanied by a consort of viols and a single tambourine for rhythm, states the opening melody (Example 5).

Example 5

(Soprano Recorder)

A four-measure bridge, also played by soprano recorder accompanied by the consort of viols and the tambourine, follows. Its melody is identical with the first four measures of Example 6.

The B section consists of an eight-measure melody played twice (Example 6). There is a slight variation in the last four measures of its repetition.

Example 6

(Soprano Recorder)

Tedescha (German Dance)

The *Tedescha* is a dance in moderate duple meter, cast in binary form. The A section (Example 7) consists of two identical four-measure phrases; the B section (Example 8) is made up of two identical six-measure phrases. A *saltarello* follows immediately.

LISTENING OUTLINE

The *Tedescha* is first played by a rackett accompanied by a consort of crumhorns and a tabor. The A section (Example 7) is heard first. The B section (Example 8) follows immediately.

Example 7

(Rackett)

Example 8

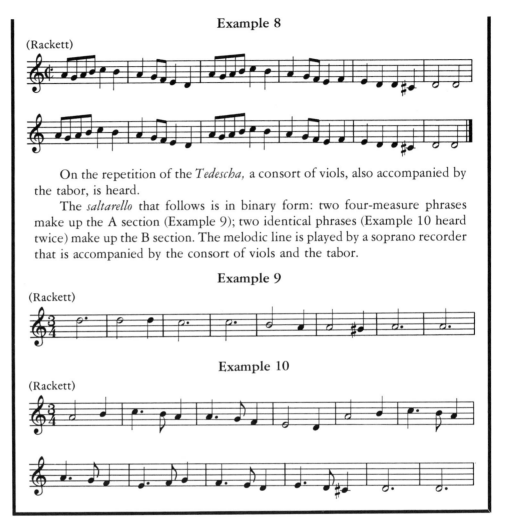

On the repetition of the *Tedescha,* a consort of viols, also accompanied by the tabor, is heard.

The *saltarello* that follows is in binary form: two four-measure phrases make up the A section (Example 9); two identical phrases (Example 10 heard twice) make up the B section. The melodic line is played by a soprano recorder that is accompanied by the consort of viols and the tabor.

Example 9

Example 10

Ungarescha (Hungarian Dance)

The *Ungarescha* is a lively dance in duple meter; it is coupled with a *saltarello* in fast triple meter.

LISTENING OUTLINE

A Jew's-harp establishes the underlying pulse in a four-measure introduction. The Jew's-harp then serves as a drone throughout the *Ungarescha.*

The melody of the *Ungarescha* (Example 11 followed by Example 12 heard twice) is sung by a woman's voice using the syllable *la.* Two women's voices sing the repeat of the dance in unison.

Example 11

(Soprano Voice)

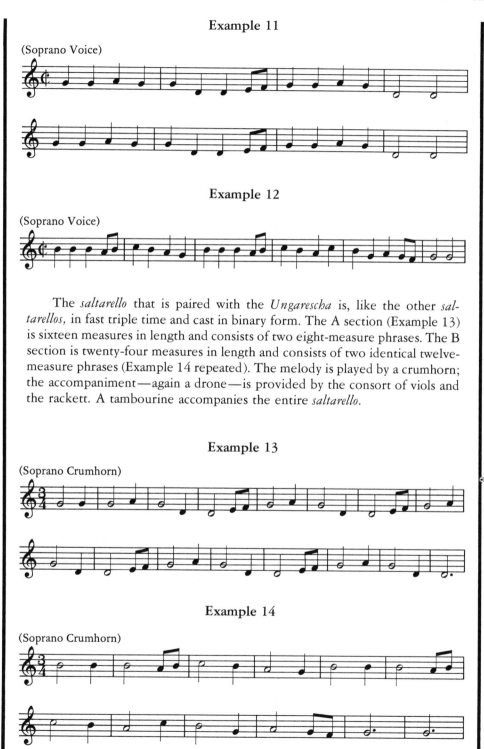

Example 12

(Soprano Voice)

The *saltarello* that is paired with the *Ungarescha* is, like the other *saltarellos,* in fast triple time and cast in binary form. The A section (Example 13) is sixteen measures in length and consists of two eight-measure phrases. The B section is twenty-four measures in length and consists of two identical twelve-measure phrases (Example 14 repeated). The melody is played by a crumhorn; the accompaniment—again a drone—is provided by the consort of viols and the rackett. A tambourine accompanies the entire *saltarello.*

Example 13

(Soprano Crumhorn)

Example 14

(Soprano Crumhorn)

About the Composer

GIORGIO MAINERIO   Born: *c*. 1535
                                       Parma, Italy

                   Died: May 4 (?), 1582
                                 Aquileia, Italy

Little is known about the early life of Giorgio Mainerio, who at one time or another spelled his name Mayner, Meyner, and Maynerius. He was born in Parma, Italy, around 1535, and, according to a later account, he loved music from earliest childhood.

Apparently having decided on the priesthood, Mainerio was appointed chaplain at the Udine Cathedral in 1560, when he was probably in his mid-twenties. Within five years, he was promoted to *mansionarius* (choral curate), in charge of eighteen singers and eight chaplains who not only had to perform their regular church duties but had to sing and play various instruments—both string and wind—for the holiday services. From his years at the cathedral, Mainerio became acquainted with some of the best music and finest musicians to be found in northern Italy.

Mainerio left Udine toward the end of March 1570, and on April 2 was appointed Mansonarius at the cathedral of Aquileia, after having successfully passed a rigorous test that confirmed his qualifications in "speaking and singing." On May 25, he became director of the San Canciano Chapel, and for several years (at least from 1575 to 1578) had the title of *dapifero e sescalo* ("manager") of the Aquileia Chapel. From registers that still exist, we are informed that he took this post with utmost sincerity and paid a great deal of attention to the details of his work.

The first known appearance of Mainerio as a composer occurred in 1574 when a Magnificat of his was performed in Aquileia. He was awarded fifteen gold scudi for the work along with a promise that he would be given a choir of his own at the first available opportunity.

The following year, on October 29, he was rewarded with the choir of San Ellaro; in addition, he was asked to teach voice to the choirboys of the cathedral.

On July 23, 1576, Mainerio suffered pain in one of his legs and had to be replaced temporarily. The following spring, he again fell ill and went to Venice to undergo medical treatment. Returning to Aquileia, he again took up his duties with the San Ellaro choir, and probably also conducted the cathedral choir from time to time until his death on May 3 or 4, 1582.

Four collections of works by Mainerio are known to have been published in his lifetime: a religious choral collection published in Venice in 1574, which includes a *Magnificat* for eight voices and a four-voice *Regina coeli; Choreae variorum nationum,* presumably published in Venice in 1576 (no copy exists, unless it has been confused with the following publication); *Primo libro di balli,* the collection of dances already described in the Listening Outline, published in Venice 1578; and a second sacred collection, published in Venice in 1580, which included a six-voice *Magnificat* and a six-voice motet, *O sacrum convivium*.

Bibliography

Schuler, Manfred. *Musikalische Denkmäler*. Vol. V. Mainz, 1960.

So great is the correspondence between music and the soul that many, seeking out the essence of the latter, have thought it to be full of harmonious accords, to be, indeed, a pure harmony. All nature itself, to speak the truth, is nothing but a perfect music that the Creator causes to resound in the ears of man, to give him pleasure and to draw him gently to Himself.

Jan Pieterszoon Sweelinck

FIFTEEN/
THE BAROQUE ERA

ONE evening in the fall of the year 1600, a composer named Jacopo Peri hid half a dozen musicians behind some scenery on the stage of the theater in a handsome palace in Florence, Italy. These musicians filled the hall with a harmonious web of plucked, strummed, wind, and keyboard sounds. The music was a perfect background for the actors who were singing in one of the world's first operas. The title of the opera was *Euridice,* and it was being staged as part of the ceremonies celebrating the marriage of King Henry IV of France to Maria de' Medici of Florence.

This celebration was one of the harbingers of a new era in music, an era known as the *Baroque.* This was a period of enormous achievements in the arts and sciences. In Italy, Galileo perfected a telescope which he used to discover the mountainous character of the moon's surface. In England, William Harvey made important discoveries about the circulation of blood in the human body. Also in England, John Milton wrote his fantastic story of Satan's rebellion against God, *Paradise Lost.* During this period in Holland, Rembrandt included many outstanding citizens of Amsterdam in his famous painting *The Night Watch.*

The painting, the architecture, and the music of this period were dramatic, elaborate, and highly ornamented. The spirit of the era was truly theatrical. In all fields, artists tried to outdo each other in producing works of grandeur and magnificence.

Many observers considered such works overdone. The swirling forms and vivid colors reminded them of the irregularly shaped, tiny pearls that the Portuguese called *barroco.* For this reason, the seventeenth century came to be called *the Baroque era* by its successors, who considered all this elaborate detail irregular and grotesque.

In music, it is generally assumed that the Baroque era started around the year 1600 with the birth of opera, and lasted until around 1750, the year of Johann Sebastian Bach's death. It is impossible to hold to these dates exactly, however, for both the beginning and ending of the era were gradual.

No other age has turned out such a vast quantity of good—and often the greatest—music. Such a wealth of creativity was to be expected of a period that was literally bursting with music on almost all social levels. Composers of the Baroque were almost all very prolific; all turned out at least *some* truly inspired music. And most were known and respected in their own time.

The Baroque movement began in Italy as part of the Counter-Reformation, and from there spread northward. Although the Thirty Years' War—that great struggle between Roman Catholicism and Protestantism—delayed the development of Baroque music in the German lands for a generation, the Baroque spirit spread north from Italy and became every bit as much a part of the Protestant Reformation as of the Catholic Counter-Reformation.

While much religious music was composed in the Baroque era for liturgical purposes, especially in the Lutheran Church, an increasing amount of instrumental music was written for nonliturgical purposes: background music for weddings, the elevation of a civil or religious official to office, the dedication of a new building, preludes, and postludes.

Peter Spring, Inner Principal
Group, High Altar, Augustin
Church of Freibourg, Switzerland.

Music for private entertainment flourished in the households of the nobility and the wealthy, the composers writing music for dancing, to accompany the evening meal, or simply to entertain after supper. A considerable amount of music was written for amateur performers, too.

In the large, wealthy courts, opera and ballet flourished. Produced as a form of entertainment for very special occasions, these forms developed popularity and soon spread far beyond the lands of their origin—Italy for opera and France for ballet. Instrumental music in all forms became more important as the musical instruments themselves were more highly developed.

The early Baroque composers began to write in a homophonic texture, using one principal melody accompanied by chords. The *a cappella* style of polyphonic, unaccompanied vocal music disappeared. (Later in the era, polyphonic writing returned to join such homophonic writing as equally acceptable.)

One of the most important aspects of Baroque music had to do with contrasts of sound, the *stile concertante.* Composers would contrast the sound of a solo voice against that of a chorus, or that of voices against instruments, or that of a small group of instruments against that of a large group.

The Baroque era was also very conscious of structure. Many musical forms developed. *Opera* was the cornerstone of the period, and its development of the *recitativo* or *recitative* affected all vocal forms. The Baroque composer Giulio Caccini spoke of recitativo as "speaking in music," and Jacopo Peri said it was "to imitate a speaking person in song." In addition to opera, other monumental forms of the era included, in the field of vocal music, the *oratorio* (of which Handel's *Messiah,* p. 63, is an excellent example); the *cantata;* and the *Passion* (on which Penderecki's twentieth-century work, p. 268, is patterned). Instrumental forms included the *solo sonata;* the *fugue* (the Bach *Toccata and Fugue in D Minor,* p. 370, is a good example of this); the *concerto grosso* (such as the Bach *Brandenburg Concerto No. 2,* p. 374); the *solo concerto* (after which the *Concerto No. 1 in D for Guitar and Orchestra* by Castelnuovo-Tedesco, p. 91, is patterned); and the *suite* (such as Handel's *Water Music,* p. 379).

As is evident from the number of these forms, a unique development in the Baroque era was the trend toward different styles of writing for instruments and for voices. Whereas instruments and singing voices were interchangeable in the music of the Renaissance, the Baroque composers developed techniques of writing for instruments and voices that were characteristic of the individual timbres of each.

Another important achievement of the Baroque era was the abandonment of the concept of *tactus,* the regular flow of beats that had been a pervasive part of Renaissance music. Composers in the *stile moderno* departed from a strict beat and moved toward rhythmic extremes, sometimes discarding the beat altogether in recitative passages, the music being marked *senza battuta,* "without beat."

The characteristic most frequently associated with the Baroque is the affinity between the soprano and bass voices (in both instrumental and vocal music). While most music of the Renaissance was written for four or more voices of equal importance, the music of the Baroque era was written with the melody in the upper or soprano voice and a countermelody of almost equal importance in the bass. This gave rise to the designation of the era by some scholars as the *thorough bass* or *basso continuo* period. This *continuo,* or bass line, was always written out; the cello (or in earlier times, its forerunner, the viola da gamba) played the continuo part as written, while a keyboard instrument (usually the harpsichord for secular works, the organ for sacred) played the given bass line and improvised on chords above it. (On some occasions, these chords were indicated by the composers with a series of numbers that appeared under the bass line. This was then called a *figured bass,* and to play it on a keyboard instrument was called *realizing* the figured bass.)

While early Baroque music lacked tonal direction, the continuo helped lead toward the establishment of chordal progressions. In the Renaissance, this had happened as a result of linear writing rather than of the vertical considerations which emerged in the Baroque era. The newly developing tonality occasioned by the use of chordal progressions excluded most of the earlier modal writing and led to the common use of major and minor scale patterns as we know them.

Above, Peter Paul Rubens, *The Assumption of the Virgin,* 1626 (National Gallery of Art, Washington, D.C.). Below, Gianlorenzo Bernini, *Throne of St. Peter,* 1656–66, detail (St. Peter's Basilica, Rome). Two works epitomizing the Baroque style: dramatic, elaborate, highly ornamented, and full of theatrical grandeur.

Interior of St. Mark's Basilica, with choir stalls at upper left and right.

Sacrae Symphoniae

by **GIOVANNI GABRIELI**

The jewel among Italian cities is the strange and wonderful water world of Venice. In that city there are buildings of delicately carved marble that stand alongside streets of water filled with boats, barges, and gondolas. And Venice has a jewel all its own: St. Mark's Basilica.

During the Middle Ages, when Venice was at the height of its power as a commercial and political city, the law required every captain of a ship to bring something back from his travels to decorate the basilica. As a result, every inch of the building is covered with brilliant mosaics of gold and precious stones, sculptures, bronzes, and jewels. The high altar alone contains 1,300 pearls, 400 garnets, 90 amethysts, 300 sapphires, 30 emeralds, 15 rubies, 4 topazes, and 2 cameos.

In the sixteenth century, all the splendid ceremonies and pageants of public and religious life took place at St. Mark's Basilica. The doges, or mayors, of Venice, dressed in scarlet silk and purple velvet, led huge processions across the square to the church. The richness of all this decoration called for music of equally elaborate style.

For over thirty of these glorious years, Giovanni Gabrieli served as organist at this church (roughly from 1585 until his death in 1612). His compositions occupy a unique place in the history of music, serving well as a bridge from the Renaissance to the Baroque.

In the year 1597, Gabrieli published one of the most important collections of early Baroque music. Titled in Latin *Sacrae Symphoniae* (Sacred Symphonies), it contains forty-five vocal compositions of a religious nature and sixteen works that, according to the musicologist Robert Paul Block, "make up one of the first great monuments of instrumental ensemble music: fourteen canzoni and two sonatas that surpass any of their genre at that time, and that were only rarely matched in the following decades."[1] The significance of these works cannot be overemphasized, for in them Gabrieli was the first composer to contrast polyphonic and homophonic writing and duple and triple meter within the same piece. He also was a pioneer in his use of dynamic markings, suggesting by the use of the words *forte* and *piano* which passages were to be played loudly and which softly. Gabrieli called most of his instrumental works *canzona* or *sonata.* These two terms were, in their original meaning (from the words *cantare,* "to sing," and *sonare,* suggesting instrumental music, "to be played"), opposed to one another, but the forms seemed to converge at the end of the sixteenth century. *Canzona* points to a connection with the French *chanson* (song). Actually, in the second half of the sixteenth century, transcriptions for lute of French chansons under the title *Canzona alla francese* frequently appeared in Italy. Later, however, this designation was applied to all kinds of independent instrumental pieces. At the end of the sixteenth century, during Gabrieli's lifetime, the words *alla francese* disappeared and were replaced by *Canzona per sonare* (meaning roughly "song transcriptions to be played instrumentally").

Canzon duodecimi toni à 8

The *Canzon duodecimi toni à 8* is the fifth of the instrumental works from Gabrieli's *Sacrae Symphoniae* of 1597. While the word *canzon* literally means "song" in Italian, the use in this instance, as we have noted, could be more appropriately translated "instrumental piece."

It was not the custom to indicate precisely the scoring in the instrumental music of this era. In this piece, Giovanni Gabrieli made only a few suggestions for the scoring, but it is certain that all known instrumental families were employed at the performances of his music. In our recording of the *Canzona on the Twelfth Tone,* under the direction of Helga Weber, we hear dulzians, a theorboe, crumhorns, and a harpsichord.

Dulzians are soft-voiced, double-reeded, sixteenth-century forerunners of the modern bassoon. (The dulzian derives its name from the Latin word *dulcia,* meaning "sweet.") The *theorboe* was a sixteenth-century form of double lute with two or more

1. Robert Paul Block, *Giovanni Gabrieli: Symphoniae Sacrae (1597)* (London, 1972), p. 1.

sets of tuning pegs, the lower set carrying the strings that lie over the fingerboard, the upper carrying the longer bass strings that were played open (unstopped). The theorboe was used to accompany ensembles of instruments or singers and was almost never featured as a solo instrument.

The eight voices in the score are divided by the composer into two four-voice choirs, each made up of a soprano and alto crumhorn and a tenor and bass dulzian. The first choir is augmented by a theorboe that reinforces the harmonies, while the second choir is augmented by a harpsichord that serves a similar purpose.

The "twelfth tone" of the title, as mentioned earlier, refers to the twelfth church mode, known as the *hypoionian*—a scalelike pattern equivalent to that of all the white keys on the piano from G to G, but with C used as the tone of greatest emphasis and the final tone.

LISTENING OUTLINE

The *Canzon duodecimi toni à 8* is divided into six sections, some of them quite short. The meter varies between duple and triple, the writing between polyphonic and homophonic. Frequently Gabrieli makes use of antiphonal effects, one choir answering the other.

The first section, in duple meter, is sixteen measures in length and employs only the first choir. It is written in imitative counterpoint (that is, each voice imitating the first voice); the alto voice announces the subject of the first section, the tenor voice enters one measure later with the same melody played a fifth lower.

Example 1

Alto I (Crumhorn)

Tenor I (Dulcian)

The soprano voice then enters with the subject, imitated four measures later by the bass. A final statement of this subject by the alto voice brings this brief section to a close and leads to the next section, in triple meter.

The second section is only nine measures long. Each choir is treated homophonically, although they respond to each other antiphonally (that is, answering back and forth). This section begins:

Example 2

The third section, eleven measures in length, returns to duple meter. Again, each choir is treated homophonically while they answer one another antiphonally. This section begins:

Example 3

The next section is quite extensive and there is no change of meter. The second choir is heard by itself for fourteen measures. The soprano, alto, and bass are scored homophonically; the tenor moves in counterpoint. The ascending melody of the soprano voice begins:

Example 4

The entrance of the first choir briefly overlaps the conclusion of the statement by the second choir. The melody of the first choir is a rhythmic and melodic variation of Example 4.

An antiphonal passage follows. It begins:

Example 5

Accompanied by the first choir as it was the first time, the melody of Example 4 returns in that choir's soprano voice. An extended passage follows in which the melody of Example 4 is heard passing from one voice to another in both choirs.

Choir II drops out as Choir I restates the opening polyphonic passage (Example 1).

The meter returns to $\frac{8}{4}$ as the second section, starting with Example 2, is heard again.

Returning to duple meter, the antiphonal writing of Example 3 is heard again.

The closing section, sixteen measures in length, is antiphonal. It begins:

Example 6

About the Composer

GIOVANNI GABRIELI Born: *c.* 1557
Venice, Italy

Died: August 12, 1612
Venice, Italy

It is a paradox that Giovanni Gabrieli set out to publish all of his famous uncle Andrea's compositions as his main project in life and, by including some of his own compositions at the end of each volume, became more famous than his uncle.

The original creations of Giovanni Gabrieli emphasized the traits of a new era in music. During his days at St. Mark's in Venice, he composed works in the new *concertante* style, scoring his sacred works for several choirs and spatially placing them in various balconies of the basilica. He was one of the first composers to indicate, in several instances, which instruments of the ensemble he wanted to play specific melodic lines. He composed in bold harmonies as well as in the traditional polyphonic style of the earlier era. He made use of dissonances on occasion, and was one of the first to employ his instrumental forces independent of the vocal line.

Very little is known of Gabrieli's life before he arrived at St. Mark's. He undoubtedly received most of his musical education from his uncle, Andrea Gabrieli, a well-known composer in his own right. At eighteen, Giovanni traveled to Munich, where he became a musical assistant to the composer Orlando di Lasso at the court chapel. He remained in the German city for four years, and his first two works, both madrigals, were published there.

Gabrieli returned to Venice and served for a time as a substitute for the first organist at St. Mark's. He was appointed second organist in 1584 at the same time his uncle Andrea was appointed first organist. On his uncle's death in 1585, Giovanni became the first organist, a post he occupied for twenty-six years, until his death in 1612.

Bibliography

Arnold, Denis. "Ceremonial Music in Venice at the Time of the Gabrielis." *Proceedings of the Royal Music Association.* Vol. 82, No. 1 (1955–56). London: Royal Music Association, 1956.

_____. *Giovanni Gabrieli: Opera Omnia.* 5 vols. Rome: Corpus Mensurabilis Musicae, 1971.

Toccata and Fugue in D Minor

by JOHANN SEBASTIAN BACH

Scholars can claim with confidence that the D minor *Toccata* is Bach's best-known organ work; it is also one of his most startlingly dramatic and striking works, and well deservedly, one of his most popular. It is interesting to note that this is an extremely youthful work, probably written when Bach was about twenty-one. The dashing young organist sets out to overwhelm his listeners with dazzling fireworks, intensity, and exuberance, but there is no youthful uncertainty here: the formal construction shows the hand of the master at work!

Though we generally refer to this work as being in two movements—*Toccata* and *Fugue*—the form is, in fact, that of the old North German toccata (Bach entitles this entire work simply *Toccata*), a single-movement piece sometimes in three parts: a fugal section enclosed by opening and closing sections of a highly improvisatory and rhapsodic nature. The fugue in this case is rather loosely structured and serves to relax the incredible tensions that are built up in the opening section and further intensified in the closing section.

The generic form of the *toccata*—which takes its name from the Italian verb *"toccare,"* meaning "to touch"—came into being with the development of keyboard instruments that were capable of virtuoso display. The brilliant passage work, including staccato effects, evolved out of the rapid touching of the keys. Instrumental passages suggestive of vocal recitative occurred. Bach brought to his organ toccatas not only brilliance but also musical worth and a pointed relationship with the fugue that followed.

Toccatas sound at times like free improvisation, a freedom of style resulting from changes of tempo and dynamics and the use of arpeggios and broken chords as well as rapid scale passages.

The word *fugue* comes from the Latin *"fuga,"* meaning "flight," perhaps originally suggesting that in this type of polyphonic work, one voice "flies" right after another. In a form-conscious period such as the Baroque, it was only natural that one form become the cornerstone of the era. The fugue was that form.

Fugues are written for two or more voices—voices that may be either vocal or instrumental. The principal melody or theme in a fugue is called the *subject,* and each voice in turn states it at the beginning. While this might sound as though we were describing a round such as *Three Blind Mice,* the game of "follow the leader" differs somewhat in a fugue. First of all, the second voice in a fugue sings or plays the theme on a different pitch level than that of the first voice. Also, after the second and succeeding voices have finished stating the subject, usually in a tonally adjusted form to allow for the different pitch level, they are no longer obligated to imitate the first voice.

By the time the fugal form had fully developed, the major-minor system of tonality was well established. In fact, one of the important relationships within the fugal form concerns the pitch of the first statements of the principal theme. The first voice to enter (which may be any one) presents the melody in the key of the fugue. In this key it is called the *subject.* When the second voice enters, it is usually in the dominant key (the D Minor *Toccata* is an important exception to this custom). This second statement in the dominant key is termed the *answer* (in the D minor *Toccata,* the answer is in the subdominant key).[2] While the second voice is concerned with the answer, the first voice continues with a secondary theme called the *countersubject.* Episodes, built on fragments of the subject and sequential in nature, separate the entrances of the subject or answer in the different voices.

After all voices have entered with either the subject or the answer, a section follows in which the musical ideas are developed. Fragments of the subject and countersubject move to related keys, and much use is made of such contrapuntal techniques as augmentation (lengthening the value of each note), diminution (shortening the value of each note), inversion (turning the melody upside down), and retrogression (turning the melody around so that the last note is the first, and so on).

The last part of a fugue usually employs *stretto,* a technique wherein the answer is heard shortly after the subject begins, and always before the subject is completed. The effect is one of excitement and climax. In the D minor *Fugue,* Bach chooses to omit the stretto and in its place return to the musical idea of the *Toccata.*

2. For a review of dominant and subdominant and another example of a fugue, see Chapter 4, pp. 61 and 65.

LISTENING OUTLINE

The *Toccata* opens with a short introduction marked *Adagio,* which begins with an important motive (Figure A). The symbol ∿ over the first note is an *ornament*—Baroque music is full of such decorations—called, in this instance, a *mordent.* This means that instead of playing only the *A* pitch indicated, the organist decorates it by playing a two-note trill:

Example 1

Figure A from Example 1 is repeated an octave lower in pitch.

A huge seventh chord then starts to rise slowly from the lower depths of the organ:

Example 2

The tempo changes to *Prestissimo,* and the fingers of the organist literally fly across the keyboard in an extended passage of great virtuosity. From time to time, chords punctuate these florid passages, the entire section sounding improvisational. It begins:

Example 3

After a ritard in which bold chords bring the music to a cadence, conclud-ing the opening *Toccata* section, we are ready for the *Fugue.* The subject of this four-voice fugue (Example 4) is derived directly from the opening flourish (Ex-ample 1) of the *Toccata.* It is important to note the emphasis in this subject of the dominant tone, A. The subject is thirty-two notes long, during the course of which A is repeated seventeen times, while the key tone, or tonic, D, is heard only four times. The subject appears first in the tenor voice:

Example 4

As the alto, or second, voice sounds the answer (the melody of Example 3, now in G minor), the tenor voice takes up the countersubject:

Example 5

After a brief episode, the subject appears in the soprano.

Following a somewhat longer episode, the answer appears in the bass as the deep tones produced by the pipes of the organ's pedalboard.

In the following extended section, episodes made up of scales and arpeg-gios suggest an echo, one figure responding to another. Fragments of the sub-ject appear from time to time.

Eventually the subject returns in the following sequence:

Subject
 bass voice
 alto voice
 tenor voice
  episodic material
 alto voice
  a cadence occurs
 bass voice (unaccompanied)
 tenor voice

Following a lengthy episode, the closing section returns to the spirit of the *Toccata.* Fiery downward and upward sweeps, built out of an inversion of the opening *Toccata* flourish, follow, the left hand alternating with the right hand. This passage is marked *Recitativo* and includes an *accelerando* and *rallentando*.

A measure of slow-moving chords is followed by a measure of pedal solo, concluding with solid chords.

An upward and downward sweep in thirty-second notes—marked *Presto* —leads to the final measures of grandiose chords that return us, in the final one, to D minor.

Brandenburg Concerto No. 2

by JOHANN SEBASTIAN BACH

The *concerto* was the most important ensemble form developed during the Baroque era. The generic name *concerto* evolved from the Latin noun *concertatio,* meaning "contest" or "dispute." In all concertos, there are two different sources of sound that "contest" or "dispute" in presenting the thematic material. These two sources, although always unequal in numbers of players, perform as equals, never as a solo ensemble with an accompaniment.

Two forms of concerto developed during the Baroque era: the *solo concerto* and the *concerto grosso.* In the solo concerto, the sound of a solo instrument is contrasted with that of an orchestra.[3] In a concerto grosso, the most popular form during the Baroque, there exist two instrumental ensembles: a large group (usually all stringed instruments) called the *concerto, tutti,* or *ripieni,* and a small group (usually two violins and continuo —consisting of cello and harpsichord) called the *concertino* or *principale.*

During the fall of 1719, a young Prussian prince, whose hobby was collecting concertos, met Johann Sebastian Bach. Prince Christian Ludwig, Margrave of Brandenburg, was a bachelor who lived alternately in Berlin and on his estate at Malchow. He not only loved music but spent a large part of his income on it. In the process, he acquired a remarkable collection of concertos by famous living composers. When he first met Bach, according to one of Bach's friends, the prince was "struck by [Bach's] musical power," and immediately commissioned the thirty-year-old composer to write some music for his orchestra. The resulting six concerti grossi Bach completed in March of 1721 and dedicated to the prince, works known today as the six *Brandenburg Concertos.*

The original score of the second concerto is entitled *Concerto secondo à Tromba, 1 Flauto, 1 Hautbois* [oboe], *1 Violino concertate, 2 Violini, 1 Viola è Violone in Ripieno col*

---

3. The *Concerto No. 1 for Guitar and Orchestra* by Mario Castelnuovo-Tedesco discussed in Chapter 6 (p. 91) is a modern adaptation of this *solo concerto* form.

Violoncello è Basso per il Cembalo. The concertino thus is comprised of trumpet, flute,[4] oboe, and solo violin; opposed to a tutti of strings (first and second violins, violas, and basso continuo). There are three movements: an *Allegro,* an *Andante,* and a closing *Allegro assai.*

One of Bach's earliest biographers, Philipp Spitta, remarks that we have here

> a true Concerto Grosso, except that the concertino consists of four, all of high register; namely, one string and three winds; so that a departure is made in every way from the custom which decrees that the concertino shall consist of two violins and a cello . . . . On account of its crystal-clear and transparent organism this concerto is a greater favorite than the more closely woven First; the feeling, moreover, is throughout of a kind easily entered into. The marvelously beautiful *Andante* is soft and tenderly simple while the first and last movements rush and riot with all the freshness and vigor of youth.[5]

Third Movement: Allegro assai

LISTENING OUTLINE

Accompanied only by the continuo (cello and harpsichord), the high, piercing sound of the F trumpet (much smaller and far more difficult to play than the traditional A trumpet of the orchestra) is heard introducing the principal melody:

Example 1

The oboe answers Example 1 with a restatement of it in the dominant key (C major). A short episode by the trumpet leads to a repetition of Example 1 in the original key by the solo violin of the concertino. The flute answers with a statement of Example 1 in the dominant key.

---

4. The performance on the recording, by the Württemberg Chamber Orchestra conducted by Jörg Faerber, follows the old Baroque practice of using a recorder. In the Baroque era, the flute we know today was only used when the score specified *transverse flute.*
5. Philipp Spitta, *J. S. Bach: His Work and Influence on the Music of Germany* (New York, 1951).

Short ascending and descending arpeggios echo back and forth between flute, oboe, and violin. The trumpet responds with a variant of Example 1. It then takes up a new melodic figure (Example 2). The ripieno enters for the first time as Example 2 is heard.

Example 2

The solo violin takes up Example 1, which soon gives way to a descending figure followed by scalelike passages in the flute.

The oboe makes a full statement of Example 1; the basso continuo answers with a statement of the opening four-and-one-half measures of it.

A brief figure in the violin and oboe leads to a repetition by the trumpet, joined at first by the flute, of the first half of Example 2. After a short episode, a variant of Figure A from Example 2 is played successively by oboe, flute, violin, and trumpet (at first joined by the oboe), the final trumpet statement leading to an extended variant of the figure.

Soon the oboe repeats Example 1, answered by the flute. The continuo once again takes up Example 1; this statement is answered by the trumpet. A three-measure flute episode leads to a final statement by the trumpet of the opening figure from Example 1.

About the Composer

JOHANN SEBASTIAN BACH   Born: March 21, 1685
        Eisenach, Germany

        Died: July 28, 1750
        Leipzig, Germany

The name of Bach is a legend in the musical annals of Germany, for the known history of the tribe extends over seven generations, and members of it still flourish, though the direct male line of the composer died out in the nineteenth century. The stock was pure German of the sturdiest physical and mental type; and a surprisingly large proportion of it was musically gifted.

Johann Sebastian's father was the town musician of Eisenach, and was also probably the court musician to the duke. Johann Sebastian received his elementary education at the Gymnasium (or school) while he learned the violin and viola from his father. When Johann Sebastian was nine, his mother died. Although his father remarried, he died within a year of the mother. The ten-year-old orphan was sent to Ohrdruf, some thirty miles from Eisenach, to live with his eldest brother, Johann Christoph, who was organist at St. Michael's Church there. From his brother Johann Sebastian received his first keyboard lessons and probably his first lessons on the pipe organ.

When he was fifteen, Johann Sebastian had to find a means of earning his own living. He became a chorister at St. Michael's Church in Lüneburg, some 200 miles from his brother's home. It is likely that he walked the distance to take the position. He spent three years at the Lüneberg church, making several trips to nearby cities to hear more music. He walked thirty miles to Hamburg to hear the famous German organist, Johann Adam Reinken (then eighty years old) play, and also made several trips to Celle, where the court orchestra played music from the French repertory. What schooling Bach had in the formal art of composition he received from the Lüneburg organist, Georg Böhm.

At eighteen, Bach joined the staff of Duke Johann Ernst in Weimar as a string player and organist. After five months in that position, he was appointed organist for St. Boniface's Church in Arnstadt, where a newly completed pipe organ attracted him. He encountered difficulty there with both the ministerial staff and the congregation because of his improvisations and original compositions, which they did not appreciate. He took a leave from that position to travel to Lübeck to hear the famous organist and composer Dietrich Buxtehude play, and failed to return to Arnstadt until commanded to do so.

Resigning his position at Arnstadt, Bach became the organist at Mülhausen, where he stayed for a year. He married during his tenure there and felt the salary was not sufficient to support a family. He next took a position as organist and chamber musician to Duke Wilhelm Ernst of Sachsen-Weimar. During the nine years that he occupied that post, he composed some of his finest organ works and a number of church cantatas. Bach, his wife, and four children then moved to Cöthen, where he served the prince as a musical director for five years.

The sudden death of his wife left him with the added responsibility of rearing and looking after his children, one daughter and four sons (a pair of twins had died shortly after birth). A year and a half later he married the daughter of the court trumpeter, a girl named Anna Magdalena. His household was always a happy one, and Anna Magdalena did much to further her husband's music, even copying parts. In addition to the five surviving children of his first marriage, they raised seven daughters and six sons of their own. Many of Bach's compositions were written as educational pieces for his wife and children.

On February 7, 1723, Bach auditioned for the position that was vacant at the choir school in Leipzig, conducting his recently completed *Cantata No. 22.* He was accepted

Entrance to St. Thomas Church, Leipzig, where Bach served as music director for the last twenty-seven years of his life.

and assumed the duties of caring for the music in both Leipzig churches, St. Thomas and St. Nicholas, in addition to superintending the training and performance of both the vocal and instrumental students associated with the churches. He remained cantor (music director) of St. Thomas Church for the balance of his life.

Bach wrote five sets of sacred compositions for every Sunday and feast day of the year, and at least five Passions. The manuscripts of many of these have been lost, but we still have the music for 190 sacred cantatas, the St. Matthew and St. John *Passions,* and the oratorios for Christmas, Easter, and Ascension. Bach also wrote a quantity of keyboard music, including numerous works for both the pipe organ and the harpsichord. For orchestra, he wrote the six *Brandenburg Concertos,* four orchestral suites, and a number of concertos for harpsichord and solo violin.

Bibliography

Schwendowius, B., and Doemling, W., eds. *Johann Sebastian Bach: Life, Times, Influence.* Kassel: Bärenreiter, 1977.

Spitta, Philipp. *J. S. Bach: His Work and Influence on the Music of Germany.* Translated by Clara Bell and J. A. Fuller-Maitland. 3 vols. London: Novello, 1899. Reprinted, New York: Dover, 1951.

Water Music

by **GEORG FRIEDRICH HANDEL**

One warm summer evening in the year 1717, George I, King of England, decided to go on a pleasure cruise on the river Thames. To provide entertainment as the royal barge skimmed over the surface of the water headed for a kingly banquet in Chelsea, a second barge followed alongside. It was filled with court musicians for whom Georg Friedrich Handel, the official court composer, had written some special music: a suite that he called quite simply, *Water Music.*

On July 19, 1717, the London *Daily Courant* reported the event that had taken place two days earlier:

> On Wednesday Evening, at about 8, the King took the Water at Whitehall in an open Barge . . . and went up the River towards Chelsea. Many other Barges with Persons of Quality attended . . . . A City Company's Barge was employ'd for the Musick, wherein were 50 Instruments of all sorts, who play'd all the way from Lambeth (where the Barges drove with the Tide without rowing, as far as Chelsea) the finest Symphonies, compos'd express for this Occasion, by Mr. Hendel; which his Majesty liked so well, that he caus'd it to be plaid over three times in going and returning. At Eleven his Majesty went a-shore at Chelsea, where a Supper was prepar'd, and then there was another very fine Consort of Musick, which lasted till 2; after which, his Majesty came again into his Barge, and return'd the same way, the Musick continuing to play till he landed.

In a private report Friedrich Bonet, the Prussian Resident in London, added the information that the instruments on the barge included trumpets, horns, bassoon, German flutes (the modern style of transverse orchestral flute), recorders, and strings (including *continuo*); that each performance lasted an hour; that there were two performances before supper and one after; and that the orchestra cost £ 150 (then approximately $750), and was paid for by Baron Kielmansegg. (The Baron's wife, Madame Kielmansegg, was George I's rather elderly mistress.)

The *Water Music* played that summer's evening on the Thames was made up of more than twenty-two different movements, practically all of them—with the exception of the overture—dances. Such a set of dances in the same or related keys was called a *suite,* and was the only meaning this word had during the Baroque era. The individual movements, while based on traditional dance rhythms and forms, were not meant to accompany actual dancing but instead were intended for listening; in other words, written as *concert music.* And as is true of most multimovement works, the dances within a suite would alternate between fast and slow to provide variety and contrast.

Orchestrated for instruments whose tones could be heard outdoors over the surface of the river, *Water Music* is scored for two oboes, bassoon, two French horns, two trumpets, strings, and continuo. Later rescorings by others have frequently added flutes and piccolo to this instrumentation.

Alla hornpipe

The *Alla hornpipe* is one of the best-known movements and is both brisk and lively in spirit and rhythm. The hornpipe had been a popular dance in England since the sixteenth century, one with many characteristic steps and gestures. It was usually performed as a solo dance by sailors; it was danced with arms folded. The Italian word *alla* in the title suggests "in the time," or rhythm, of a *hornpipe*.

Most hornpipes, including Handel's, were in moderate $\frac{3}{2}$ time. Also, like most dances, Handel's *Alla hornpipe* is in ternary form.

Antonio Canale (known as Canaletto), *London: The Thames and the City of London from Richmond House,* c. 1746 (Goodwood House, London). Although the painting dates from several years later, the two barges on the river must be similar to those used when the *Water Music* was first performed.

LISTENING OUTLINE

The violins take up the first melody (Example 1), which is in two parts, indicated by the letters A and B.

Example 1

The trumpets repeat part A of the tune; the horns echo it. The trumpets next play the opening of the B part, only to be echoed by the horns again.

Strings play a variant of the B part of the theme, which is repeated, started by the trumpets and finished by the horns. The trumpets next repeat the opening of the B part, and then bring the first section of this tripartite work to a closing cadence.

The contrasting middle section is softer. The melody of it is given over completely to the violins. It begins:

Example 2

A return is made to the first section. Once again strings announce Example 1 in its entirety.

In turn, trumpets and then horns play the opening half of Example 1, the A section. Trumpets, then horns, play the opening of the B part of Example 1.

Strings play a variant of the B part of the theme that is repeated, started by the trumpets and finished by the horns. The trumpets respond with a passage that leads to the final cadence of the work.

The biographical sketch and bibliography for Handel may be found in Chapter 4, pp. 72–73.

Serenity, repose, grace—the characteristics of the antique works of the Greek
classical era—are also those of Mozart's
school.

Robert Schumann

SIXTEEN/
THE CLASSIC ERA

THERE was a time when people believed that common sense could solve all the riddles of the world. It was a time in history when people placed great faith in human powers of observation and reason; called the *Age of Enlightenment,* this time period lasted for most of the eighteenth century.

This was an age of enlightenment in science: Isaac Newton theorized the law of gravity; Carolus Linnaeus, the Swedish botanist, classified all known forms of animal and plant life. Benjamin Franklin demonstrated the electrical nature of lightning. It was a cosmopolitan age. Foreign-born rulers were to be found throughout Europe: German kings in England, Sweden, and Poland; a Spanish king in Naples; a German princess as Empress of Russia. Artists and writers were associated with capitals far removed from the lands of their birth: the Frenchman Voltaire was at the Prussian court, the Italian poet Metastasio at the Viennese court; Italian opera composers were in residence in Paris and London. It was because of this cosmopolitan atmosphere that the Viennese Haydn was hailed in London, the German Gluck in the capital of France.

While princes and courts were to be found throughout Europe, they were rapidly declining in power and influence. For centuries, feudal landlords and princes had ruled in Europe. Now the common man had begun to assert himself. He wanted something to say about how he was to be governed. It was the eighteenth-century Frenchman Jean Jacques Rousseau who said that the power of the government rests in the consent of the people who are governed.

A bare fourteen years after Rousseau published *The Social Contract,* the American colonies revolted against England. Having fought for and won their independence, the colonies formed the United States of America, a nation where "all men are created equal."

King Louis XVI of France had helped the American rebels win their battle to form a democratic republic. In 1793 he lost his life at the guillotine when his own subjects revolted to form the first democratic republic in Europe.

Out of the chaos and bloodshed of the French Revolution, a "little corporal" named Napoleon Bonaparte rose to power; France became an empire during his reign, and French influence was extended to every country in Europe except England.

While the name *Age of Enlightenment* was given to the social mores, political conditions, and philosophy of this period, the music and architecture of the times was called *Classic.* The term *Classic* was first applied around 1820 to the music of the late eighteenth century to suggest that this music had abandoned the ornateness and over-decoration associated with the earlier Baroque era. It had returned to the ideals of the classical culture of ancient Greece—formal beauty within unity, clarity of purpose, and self-control in expression. It was an intellectual approach rather than an emotional one.

Unfortunately there is no word in music that has more connotations and is more misused than the word *classic.* It has three separate and distinct meanings. To the musician, it refers to music composed in the last part of the eighteenth and the very early part of the nineteenth centuries, the period we have been describing, and this is the sense in which the term has been used throughout this book. By the definition in the

Jacques Germain Soufflot, *Le Panthéon,* Paris, 1755–92. Soufflot modeled the pillars after ancient Roman temples. The sparsely decorated walls are far from the earlier Baroque era's ornateness.

dictionary, it refers to a work of the "first class or rank; a work, especially in literature or art, of the highest class and of acknowledged excellence"; and to the average listener, the term means most symphonic, choral, and ballet music, in contradistinction to the term *popular,* which refers to commercial and dance music.

The composers associated with the Classic era of the late eighteenth century are Gluck, Haydn, Mozart, and the early Beethoven. For many years it was believed that Haydn created some of the forms in use, such as the symphony. More recent research has revealed that the concepts of the Classic era were already in use before the Baroque era was finished. While Johann Sebastian Bach was composing some of the greatest masterpieces in the Baroque idiom, four of his sons were busy developing the forms, including the symphony, that were to be the highlights of the later era.

Around the year 1745, musicians in and around the court at Mannheim, Germany (known as the *Mannheim School* of composers) were establishing the sonata and the symphony as the cornerstones of the new style. Polyphonic writing was no longer supreme; the emphasis was placed on the melody, which was to be accompanied by simple chords. (Rousseau said that music was "the art of pleasing by the succession and combination of agreeable sounds, . . . the art of inventing tunes and accompanying them with suitable harmonies; to sing two melodies at once [as in the polyphonic style of the Baroque] is like making two speeches at once in order to be more forceful.")

The invention of the pianoforte (now commonly known simply as the *piano*) was, by the instrument's very nature and name, to change the style of keyboard composition. Because of its different action, this new instrument could play both soft (*piano*) and loud (*forte*), and all the shades of dynamics between the two, simply by the force used to strike the keys. Gradual dynamic changes within a phrase became possible and were indicated in the later music of the Classic era. The instruments of the orchestra became more standardized as the woodwind instruments were perfected. And as courts disappeared, public concerts started to take place for the first time.

One caution must be mentioned, however. The overgeneralization often made that the music of the Classic era was all form without emotion and the music of the later Romantic era was all emotion without form is completely false. Music of the Classic era was a portrayal of emotion within restricted limits, a controlled expression. Music of the Romantic age expressed emotion much more freely, and liberties were taken with form to serve this purpose, but form was never abandoned.

Jacques Louis David, *The Death of Socrates,* 1787 (Metropolitan Museum of Art, New York). David turned to classical Greece for subject matter, and the figures appear almost like ancient Greek statues.

Main ballroom of the Esterházy Palace, Eisenstadt, where Haydn and his orchestra performed for Prince Nikolaus.

Symphony No. 88 in G Major

by FRANZ JOSEPH HAYDN

Joseph Haydn spent forty-eight years of his long life in the employ of the Esterházy family, the wealthiest princes in the Austro-Hungarian empire of the eighteenth century. During the reign of Prince Nikolaus Esterházy, who dearly loved music, Haydn was requested to provide music almost nightly for the Prince's pleasure. For this purpose Nikolaus had amassed a relatively good-sized orchestra (well trained, too, under Haydn's guidance) for his court at Eisenstadt. It was for this group that Haydn composed over eighty symphonies. His *Symphony No. 88* was not one of them, though.

Whatever caused him to compose one of his most popular, indeed one of his greatest, symphonies for such a shady character as Johann Peter Tost, is difficult to understand. But we have the evidence in Haydn's own letters that he did write what he called his Eighty-eighth "Symphony in G Major" for Tost, a sort of rapscallion violinist, who apparently was a good enough musician to lead the second violin section in Haydn's own orchestra at Eisenstadt for five years, from 1783 to 1788.

In 1788, Tost traveled to Paris, taking along the manuscripts of two Haydn symphonies and six string quartets. Apparently Haydn had given him the rights to these works and expected him to sell them in Paris. But Tost went one step further: he apparently sold Parisian publisher Sieber not two but three "Haydn" symphonies (the third being by the less famous and far less talented Adalbert Gyrowetz) as well as six Haydn sonatas to which he had no right at all. "Thus Herr Tost," Haydn dryly wrote to Sieber, "has swindled you; you can claim your damages with him in Vienna."

Fourth Movement: Allegro con spirito

The *rondo* is one of the most frequently employed forms for the final movement of Classical symphonies. The rondo was originally derived from the *rondel* form in verse and became one of the first established forms in music. It consists of a principal or rondo theme that alternates with several episodes based on secondary themes. The name *rondo* implies at least two such episodes.

In the fourth movement of Haydn's *Symphony No. 88,* there are eight episodes which are based on five secondary themes, the principal theme appearing after each episode. Outlined, the rondo would appear as follows:

Principal theme (repeated)
   Subtheme A
Principal theme
   Subtheme A
Principal theme
   Subtheme B
Principal theme (in a variation)
   Subtheme C
Principal theme
   Subtheme A
Principal theme (in a second variation)
   Subtheme D
Principal theme
   Subtheme A
Principal theme
   Subtheme E (derived from Subtheme C)
Principal theme (incomplete variant)

LISTENING OUTLINE

The Principal Theme is stated by the violins. It is a melody reminiscent of a Viennese folk tune.

Principal Theme

Violins, Bassoons

The Principal Theme is repeated.

The first subtheme is introduced by the violins:

Subtheme A

The Principal Theme is heard again, followed by a repetition of Subtheme A.

The violins, flute, and bassoon repeat the Principal Theme, and then the violins alone introduce the second subtheme:

Subtheme B

A variation of the Principal Theme is followed by the third subtheme:

Subtheme C

The Principal Theme returns and is followed by subtheme A.

A new subtheme is introduced, a theme derived from the Principal Theme and treated in canonic form.

Subtheme D

Principal Theme, Subtheme A, and Principal Theme are heard in succession.

The last subtheme, derived from Subtheme C, is introduced:

Subtheme E

The final statement of the Principal Theme in varied form concludes the fourth movement.

About the Composer

FRANZ JOSEPH HAYDN   Born: March 31, 1732
Rohrau, Austria

Died: May 31, 1809
Vienna, Austria

Joseph Haydn was the second son of a wheelwright, a peasant who had established the family home in Rohrau, a little village about 100 miles southeast of Vienna. Haydn's father was a good amateur musician, and there was always music in the home as the boy was growing up. When Joseph was five, his musical talent was noticed by his cousin, a choir director and schoolteacher. The cousin took the boy home with him and gave him musical instruction in singing, the violin, and other instruments, as well as lessons in Latin. The musical director of St. Stephen's Cathedral in Vienna heard this precocious lad of eight and was so impressed that he found a place for him in the choir at the cathedral.

As was the custom of the time, singing in the choir also provided board and room as well as instruction in music and academic subjects. Haydn's later accounts of life at the cathedral school make several references to the scarcity of both food and a good education, in his case. When Haydn's voice changed, the cathedral no longer had use for his services, so he was released. His only possessions, as he later recalled, were "three poor shirts and a threadbare coat."

A friend provided him with a temporary bed and soon loaned him 150 florins so he could rent a room of his own, one that had a rickety old harpsichord. Haydn supported himself for almost eight years by giving music lessons to children, playing in

Pianoforte, c. 1720.

serenades that were then very popular in Vienna, and serving as an accompanist for an Italian singing teacher.

Haydn's first position of official stature was at the castle of Count Fürnberg, where he played chamber music and composed a number of works. Through von Fürnberg Haydn became acquainted with Count Morzin, who appointed him his music director. In his new position, Haydn wrote his first symphony, in 1759, his twenty-seventh year.

When Count Morzin experienced some financial difficulty and had to dismiss his employees, he saw to it that Haydn was introduced to Prince Paul Anton Esterházy. The Esterházy estate at Eisenstadt had been completed only a few years earlier, a spacious estate built by one of the richest and most influential families in Europe. Haydn became a Kapellmeister there, and received a salary from the estate that lasted until his death forty-eight years later.

The fact that Haydn's status in the household was the equivalent of a servant did not bother him at all, for this was the custom of the time. His duties were many and varied. He handled many administrative matters. He was in charge of both music and instruments, and he had to take care of the personal needs of the musicians employed by the court. He conducted the orchestra, he directed the opera presentations given in the theater of the castle, he took part in chamber music performances, and he was expected to compose new works for all of these court functions. During his association with the Esterházy family, Haydn composed over eighty symphonies, forty-three string quartets, and nearly all of his many operas.

Bibliography

Geiringer, Karl. *Haydn: A Creative Life in Music.* Berkeley: University of California Press, 1968.

Jacob, Heinrich Eduard. *Joseph Haydn: His Art, Times, and Glory.* Translated by Richard and Clara Winston. Reprint of 1950 edition. Westport, Conn.: Greenwood Press; 1971.

Sonata No. 11 in A Major
by WOLFGANG AMADEUS MOZART

The *sonata* was the principal form for solo works used during the Classic era (and also the Romantic era that followed). Most sonatas were written for piano solo or for violin with piano accompaniment and consisted of three contrasting movements.

The *Sonata No. 11 in A Major* (K. 331) for piano is one of Mozart's best known and most beloved works, one full of tenderness, beauty, and drama; yet it was written during one of the most desperate and critical episodes in the composer's career.

Mozart, under his father's tutelage, was a child prodigy. He started keyboard lessons when he was three and composed his first work, a *Minuet,* when he was four; by the time he was six, his father had begun to schedule concert tours all over Europe for him, which in the next four years led young Wolfgang to play before the crowned heads of Austria, France, England, and the Netherlands. When he was fourteen, the Pope presented him with a decoration.

The unfortunate thing about child prodigies, however, is that they grow up. Although Mozart retained all of his skill at the keyboard and certainly developed into a more perceptive composer as the years went by, the public no longer would pay money to see him, for he was no longer a cute little lad of five or six sitting at the harpsichord playing difficult music. At twenty-one, it seemed that Mozart—at least according to his father—was a has-been. No longer was anyone interested in arranging concerts in which the young man could perform, and, try as the family might, no permanent position as a court musician could be found for him.

Finally, on September 23, 1777, Mozart and his mother left their home in Salzburg in a desperate effort to locate a secure job for Wolfgang. After unsuccessful stops in Munich, Augsberg, and Mannheim, the two reached Paris on March 23. Once again disappointment followed. No position could be found for young Mozart in any of the courts of the French capital. Tragedy then followed disappointment. Mozart's mother became fatally ill in Paris, and died in her son's arms on July 3. It was during this disheartening and tragic sojourn in Paris that Mozart composed his delightful, youthful *Sonata No. 11 in A Major.* (He finally left Paris on September 26, 1778, without ever having found a position.)

Rondo alla turca

The *Sonata No. 11* is in three movements, the concluding one being the famous *Rondo alla turca* or "Rondo in Turkish style." This work was designed so that it could be played on the piano of that time, which had a janizary attachment designed to color the instrument's tone with a rattling noise and a tremulous twang.[1] This trick followed the current interest in oriental porcelains, gardens, plays, operas, and architecture.

The *Rondo alla turca* could be outlined as follows:

Principal Theme	A section (repeated)
	B-A section (repeated)
Episode 1	A section (repeated)
	B section (repeated)
	C-B section (repeated)
	A section (repeated)

---

1. *Janizary* refers to the music of the military bodyguard of Turkish sovereigns, music characterized by the sound of large drums, cymbals, triangle, and Turkish crescent. The Turkish crescent was a percussion instrument consisting of a wooden stick surmounted by crescent-shaped crossbars and an ornament shaped like a pavilion or Chinese hat, all with numerous small bells and jingles.

Principal Theme	A section (repeated)
	B section (repeated)
Episode 2	Variant of theme of Episode 1, A section (repeated)
Coda	Variant of Principal Theme

LISTENING OUTLINE

The Principal Theme, as indicated in the outline, is in two parts (A and B), each of which is immediately repeated after its initial statement. (Only the opening measures of the B section are quoted in the following examples.)

Principal Theme (A section)

Principal Theme (Opening of B section)

The first episode is made up of three sections (A, B, and C-B), each of which is repeated immediately after its initial statement. Only the opening four measures of each section are quoted in the following examples.

Episode 1 (A section)

Episode 1 (B section)

Episode 1 (C-B section)

The Principal Theme returns. Both the A and the B-A sections are repeated in turn.

The second episode begins with a variant of the A theme from the first episode.

The variant is repeated in its entirety.

The Coda is based on a variant of the Principal Theme, the first few measures being quoted in the following example. This brings the *Rondo* to a rousing conclusion.

Coda

(octave higher)

Symphony No. 40 in G Minor

by WOLFGANG AMADEUS MOZART

Mozart's last three symphonies (Nos. 39, 40, and 41) were completed in six weeks' time, between June 26 and August 10, 1788. As with the *Sonata No. 11,* one cannot tell from listening to these magnificent works—the crowning achievement of Mozart's symphonic writing—the difficult circumstances under which they were written.

In the first half of 1788, when Mozart was at the height of his creative powers, his everyday circumstances suddenly began to deteriorate. Although he had finally been appointed court composer to the Emperor in Vienna (some eleven years after his unsuccessful trip to Paris), the position paid only 800 gulden (something under $400) a year. And what the emperor desired was light music for the entertainment of the court. (Mozart said, "Too much for what I compose, too little for what I could compose.")

In desperation, Mozart had started inquiring among his friends to see if he could borrow enough money to pay the rent and buy food. To bring in further income, Mozart scheduled a series of concerts for June, but these had to be canceled. Nevertheless, he continued to compose with characteristically incredible speed. Although it is likely that the *Symphony No. 40* was written for the series of concerts that was never given, the work was probably performed at a concert two years later—just eight months before Mozart's death. It was conducted by the Italian composer and conductor Antonio Salieri. This is suggested because Mozart originally scored the work for flute, pairs of oboes, bassoons and horns, and strings, and at some later time added two clarinets and rewrote the oboe parts to accommodate them. It is highly improbable that he would have gone to that trouble unless there was a definite performance in view.

Three of the movements of this symphony are based on the sonata-allegro form—the first, second, and fourth.[2] The third movement is in the minuet and trio form.

First Movement: Allegro molto

LISTENING OUTLINE

The movement opens with the Principal Subject played by the violins, accompanied by lower strings:

Example 1 (Principal Subject)

Example 1 is repeated.

A bridge passage modulates to the relative major key, B-flat. The Second Subject begins in the violins with a little added figure by the clarinet and bassoon:

Example 2 (Second Subject)

Example 2 is repeated. (It is orchestrated differently and lacks the last two measures.)

2. For a review of the sonata-allegro form, see page 126.

The closing portion of the exposition is based on Figure A of Example 1, which is repeated several times by clarinets and bassoons, against an augmentation of it in the strings.

The development treats, basically, only the Principal Subject (Example 1). At first, most of the theme is heard as it moves from one tonality to another; then, only Figure A from it is heard. This section ends as finally only the first three notes of Figure A are heard, sometimes inverted.

In the recapitulation, the bassoon joins in a countermelody as the strings repeat the Principal Subject (Example 1).

The Second Subject (Example 2) appears twice, both times in G minor. The second statement is incomplete.

Figure A of Example 1 is heard again and again as the recapitulation closes.

The opening portion of the Principal Subject (Example 1) is heard four times in the coda. The second violins are heard first with it, and before they finish, the first violins play it in counterpoint to the second violins. It is then taken up by violas, then by woodwinds. A series of final chords concludes the movement.

Second Movement: Andante

LISTENING OUTLINE

Also in sonata-allegro form, the second movement opens with a Principal Subject played softly by the strings; it is then repeated.

Example 3 (Principal Subject)

After a lengthy section in which the music modulates to the dominant key, B-flat major, the Second Subject is introduced by the violins:

Example 4 (Second Subject)

The development is based on Figures A and B from Example 3, each repeated several times in different keys; these figures alternate between the strings and the woodwinds.

The Principal Subject (Example 3) returns to open the recapitulation.

After a rather extended bridge in which fragments of Example 3 are heard, the Second Subject (Example 4) is repeated in E-flat and brings the movement to a close.

Third Movement: Minuet and Trio: Allegretto

The minuet was the only dance form of the Baroque that did not become obsolete at the end of that era. It was regularly employed as the third movement of the Classical symphony. The Classical symphonic minuet in general, and this one in particular, does not really resemble the original dance on which it is based. The minuet in this symphony is more vehement than a dance minuet would have allowed, and it would have been most irregular to have a minuet in a minor key as this one is.

The minuet is in $\frac{3}{4}$ meter and usually a very stately tempo. It is formally divided into three parts, the first and third being the same (hence the overall form is ternary). Each of the three sections is, in itself, binary in form, the second theme of each being derived from the first.

The name of the middle section of the third movement, *trio,* is both confusing and misleading. Its name is a holdover from the Baroque minuet, in which only three instruments played the middle section for contrast. For example, the first trio of the Minuet in Bach's *Brandenburg Concerto No. 1* is scored for two oboes and bassoon. Although the full orchestra participates in the trios of Classical minuets, it is usually thinner in orchestration than the minuet and frequently—like this one—softer and more delicate in texture.

The *minuet and trio* is based on two themes, each of which has an important variant. This form is outlined in the following list. The subscript beside certain letters (A_1 for example) indicates that the theme of that section is a variant of the A theme.

Minuet
  A theme
  A theme repeated
  A_1 theme (usually twice
    the length of A)
  A_1 theme repeated

Trio
  B theme (generally more
    lyrical than the A theme)
  B theme repeated
  B_1 theme (usually twice
    the length of B)
  B_1 theme repeated

Minuet
  A theme
  B theme

LISTENING OUTLINE

The A theme of the minuet is played by the violins:

Example 5 (A theme)

Violins

Example 5, which is thirteen measures long in its entirety, is repeated.

The second part of the minuet is based on a theme derived from Example 5. It is played by the woodwinds:

Example 6 (A₁ theme)

Oboes, Clarinets

The second part of the minuet is twenty-eight measures in length and is repeated.

The trio changes abruptly to the major tonality, G. The first theme is presented by the first violins:

Example 7 (B theme)

Violins

This section of eighteen measures is repeated.

The second part of the trio is based on a theme derived from that of the first section of the trio (Example 7):

Example 8 (B₁ theme)

The French horns are heard prominently in the last portion of this section. This entire section is repeated.

Both parts of the minuet are heard again, although neither section is repeated this time.

Fourth Movement: Finale: Allegro assai

LISTENING OUTLINE

The Principal Subject is introduced immediately. It starts with upward leaps for the strings (sounding the tonic chord), answered by the full orchestra.

Example 9 (Principal Subject)

The Second Subject is less energetic and more lyrical:

Example 10 (Second Subject)

The exposition closes with repetitions of Figure B from Example 9.

Once again, Mozart is concerned only with the Principal Subject in the development section. Figure A from Example 9 appears first in the strings and is then echoed by the woodwinds. Each time this dialogue is repeated, it is done in a different tonality.

After a brief pause, the Principal Subject (Example 9) is recapitulated. The Second Subject, a variant of Example 10, returns in G minor.

Figure B of Example 9 returns in the coda as it did at the end of the exposition, and leads to the final chords of the symphony.

About the Composer

WOLFGANG AMADEUS MOZART   Born: January 27, 1756
Salzburg, Austria

Died: December 5, 1791
Vienna, Austria

A contemporary letter by Friedrich Grimm describes both Mozart's travels and his abilities as a composer:

> We have just now seen Herr Mozart, who during his stay in Paris in 1764, had so great a success. He has been in England eighteen months, and six months in Holland, and has of late [come] back here, on his way to Salzburg. All over, there has been but one opinion. He has astounded all connoisseurs. . . . As early as two years ago, he composed and edited sonatas; and since then, he has had six sonatas printed for the Queen of England; six for the Princess of Nassau-Weilburg; he has composed Symphonies for a large orchestra, that have been performed and were acclaimed with great praise. He has even written several Italian arias, and I am not giving up hope that he will [soon] have written an opera for some Italian theater.

This letter ends with a most revealing fact: "this curious boy is now nine years old!"

Never before or since has there been such a precocious child in the field of music. Of the seven children born to Leopold Mozart and his wife, only two survived: Maria Anna (known to the family as Nannerl) and Wolfgang. Leopold Mozart was an excellent violinist who not only was the assistant concertmaster of the court orchestra at Salzburg but also the court composer and the author of a book on violin technique. Young Wolfgang, in bed for his nap, could hear the piano lessons his sister Nannerl received in the parlor. He was so interested in the keyboard that at three he could pick out many chords and melodies, and with instruction, he could play the piano well by the time he was four.

After the years of traveling all over Europe with his father and sister, giving concerts before the nobility of major kingdoms, Mozart was appointed court and cathedral organist by the Archbishop of Salzburg. Mozart was just twenty-three, and the salary was 450 florins (just a little over $200 in buying power at that time).

It was not long before the archbishop and Mozart quarreled. Mozart, who had been entertained royally by so many kings and queens, felt it degrading to eat with the servants in the archbishop's palace, and when the archbishop added insult to injury by requiring Mozart to ask permission from him to play a benefit concert for orphans, Mozart resigned in a huff.

Wolfgang moved to Vienna. Now twenty-five, he was free of all commitments for the first time in his life. He enjoyed the musical climate in Vienna. He met the famous Haydn, and also participated in a contest with Muzio Clementi, an Italian composer famous for his keyboard sonatinas.

Against his father's wishes, Mozart married. Constanze Weber was a young lady he had met many years before on his travels; her family had recently relocated in Vienna. Although Constanze was a fine singer, her temperament did not make her an ideal wife. The house was frequently in disorder, and she managed money poorly and spent what income her husband made very foolishly, so that Wolfgang never again knew freedom from financial worries.

In spite of his adverse financial condition and unhappy home life, Mozart's creative energies were at their peak. In a short period of time he turned out the opera *The Marriage of Figaro,* which was produced in Vienna in 1786; *Don Giovanni,* an opera about the legendary Don Juan, produced in Prague in 1787; his comic opera *Così fan tutte* (Women are Like That), produced in Vienna in 1790; and *The Magic Flute,* his final opera, produced in Vienna in 1791.

Mozart made a trip to Berlin in 1789, visiting Dresden and Leipzig along the way. He played the organ at Johann Sebastian Bach's church in Leipzig, remarking, "Here is one man from whom we can all learn."

In 1791, the year he worked on his *Requiem,* Mozart's health showed signs of giving way. His final illness has never been diagnosed by the medical profession.

Bibliography

Davenport, Marcia. *Mozart.* New York: Avon, 1979.

Einstein, Alfred. *Mozart: His Character, His Work.* Translated by A. Mendel and N. Broder. New York: Oxford University Press, 1945, 1965.

PICTURE CREDITS

MUSIC CREDITS

Roman numerals denote movements; superscripts indicate credits.

STUDENT RECORDS

Record 1, Side A

1. Benjamin Britten, *The Young Person's Guide to the Orchestra.* Brandon de Wilde, narrator; the Pro Musica Symphony of Vienna, Hans Swarowsky, conductor. Beginning (9'55")[1]

Record 1, Side B

1. *The Young Person's Guide to the Orchestra,* conclusion (7'15")[1]
2. Georges Bizet, *Carmen Suite: Les Toréadors.* The Bamberg Symphony Orchestra, Marcel Couraud, conductor (2'21")[1]

Record 2, Side A

1. Aaron Copland, *Rodeo: Saturday Night Waltz.* The Dallas Symphony Orchestra, Donald Johanos, conductor (4'53")[1]
2. Georg Friedrich Handel, *Messiah: Hallelujah!* The London Philharmonic Choir; The London Philharmonic Orchestra, Sir Adrian Boult, conductor (4'33")[1]

Record 2, Side B

1. Modest Mussorgsky, *Pictures at an Exhibition* (orchestrated by Maurice Ravel): *Bydlo.* The St. Louis Symphony Orchestra, Leonard Slatkin, conductor (2'30")[1] Ⓟ 1976

2. Mario Castelnuovo-Tedesco, *Concerto No. 1 in D Major for Guitar and Orchestra: III. Ritmico e Cavalleresco.* Ernesto Bitetti, guitar; Orquesta de Conciertos de Madrid, José Buenago, conductor (6'18")[2]

Record 3, Side A

1. Antonin Dvořák, *Slavonic Dances,* Opus 46, No. 1: *Presto.* The Bamberg Symphony Orchestra, Antal Dorati, conductor (3'38")[1] Ⓟ 1975
2. Ludwig van Beethoven, *Symphony No. 5: I. Allegro con brio.* The Vienna Symphony Orchestra, Otto Klemperer, conductor (6'22")[1]

Record 3, Side B

1. Robert Schumann, *Die beiden Grenadiere.* Eric Kunz, baritone; The Vienna State Opera Orchestra, Anton Paulik, conductor (3'49")[3]
2. Ottorino Respighi, *The Pines of Rome: Pines of the Appian Way.* The London Symphony Orchestra, Sir Malcolm Sargent, conductor (4'21")[1]

Record 4, Side A

1. Béla Bartók: *Concerto for Orchestra: Giuoco delle coppie.* The Bamberg Symphony Orchestra, Heinrich Hollreiser, conductor (6'52")[1]
2. İlhan Mimaroğlu: *Bowery Bum (Study After Jean Dubuffet)* (2'46")[1]

Record 4, Side B

1. John Coltrane, *Simple Like.* John Coltrane, tenor saxophone; McCoy Tyner, piano; Steve Davis, bass; Billy Higgins, drums (3'46")[4]
2. Johann Sebastian Bach, *Brandenburg Concerto No. 2: III. Allegro assai.* Helmut Schneidewind, trumpet; Hartmut Strebel, flute; Willy Schnell, oboe; Susanne Lautenbacher, violin; Martin Galling, harpsichord; Peter Buck, cello; Würtemberg Chamber Orchestra, Jörg Faerber, conductor (2'55")[1]
3. Wolfgang Amadeus Mozart, *Piano Sonata No. 11 in A Major* (K. 331): *Rondo alla turca.* Walter Klein, piano (3'07")[1]

1 Courtesy of The Moss Music Group, Inc.
2 Courtesy of Musical Heritage Society
3 Courtesy of Vanguard Recording Society, Inc.
4 Courtesy of Springboard International Records, Inc.

INDEX

t

WORKSHEET 1: READING

A. After reading Chapter 1, complete the following sentences by placing the most appropriate word or words in the blank.

1. According to physicists, all sound consists of audible _____ .

2. The term *pitch* refers to how _____ or how _____ a tone may be.

3. The term *dynamics* refers to how _____ or how _____ a tone may be.

4. The four main families of instruments found in a symphony orchestra are _____ , _____ , _____ , and _____ .

5. The four principal instruments found in the string family are, from highest to lowest, the _____ , the _____ , the _____ , and the _____ _____ .

6. The violinist who sits closest to the conductor is head of the string section and is known as the _____ .

7. The _____ is usually the first instrument we hear at a concert, because it plays the pitch A before the program starts to enable the other musicians to tune their instruments.

8. The four members of the brass family are, from highest to lowest, the _____ , the _____ , the _____ , and the _____ .

9. On a brass instrument, the tone is produced by the vibrating _____ of the player.

10. _____ _____ is the composer of *The Young Person's Guide to the Orchestra.*

B. In the following questions, place the letter of the correct choice in the blank.

1. What is the correct source of tone production for each instrument?
   A. Vibrating a single reed   B. Vibrating a double reed   C. Blowing across a mouth hole

   Piccolo _____   Clarinet _____

   Flute _____   Bass clarinet _____

   Oboe _____   Bassoon _____

   English horn _____   Contrabassoon _____

2. What is the correct category for each percussion instrument?
   A. Tuned (pitched)   B. Untuned (unpitched)

   Timpani _____   Bass drum _____

   Snare drum _____   Orchestra bells _____

NAME_____

Chimes _____   Cymbals _____

Gong _____   Castanets _____

C. Decide whether the following statements are true or false and circle the appropriate letter.

1. *Harmonics* refers to the chords that accompany a melody.   T   F
2. The stringed instruments outnumber numerically the other families of instruments found in a symphony orchestra.   T   F
3. There are two sections of violins in a symphony orchestra, the *first violins* and the *second violins*.   T   F
4. The viola is slightly smaller than the violin.   T   F
5. Because of the height of the bass viol, players have to stand to play it, or sit on a high stool.   T   F
6. In a *fugue*, every instrumental voice enters at the same time playing the melody.   T   F

D. In the following examples, circle the letter of the word or phrase that completes each sentence correctly.

1. Music is an art created by organizing
     A. sound   B. forms   C. aesthetics
2. Tone exists
     A. on paper   B. in time   C. in the imagination
3. By *timbre*, we mean
     A. the characteristic quality of tone   B. the duration of a tone   C. the loudness or softness of a tone
4. Compared to the viola, the cello is
     A. twice the size   B. half the size   C. one-seventh larger
5. The harp's ancestry can be traced back
     A. to late-nineteenth-century Europe   B. to the aboriginal music of America
     C. 4,000 years to Mesopotamia

WORKSHEET 1: LISTENING

A. Listen to the recording of *The Young Person's Guide to the Orchestra* by Benjamin Britten on Record 1 (Sides A and B) in this book. After careful study, and with as many additional references to the recording as you may need, respond to the following questions.

 1. In the introduction, Britten uses the four families of instruments found in a symphony orchestra. Identify the order in which you hear them by placing a 1, 2, 3, or 4 beside their names.

   Brass _____   Strings _____

   Percussion _____   Woodwinds _____

 2. In the section devoted to the instruments in the woodwind family, identify the order in which you hear them by placing a 1, 2, 3, or 4 beside their names.

   Bassoons _____   Flutes and piccolo _____

   Clarinets _____   Oboes _____

 3. In the section devoted to the instruments of the string family, identify the order in which you hear them by placing a 1, 2, 3, 4, or 5 beside their names.

   Bass viols (double basses) _____   Violas _____

   Cellos _____   First and second violins _____

   Harp _____

 4. In the section devoted to instruments of the brass family, identify the order in which you hear them by placing a 1, 2, or 3 beside their names.

   French horns (Horns) _____   Trumpets _____

   Trombones and bass tuba _____

 5. In the section devoted to instruments of the percussion family, identify the order in which you hear them by placing a 1, 2, 3, 4, 5, 6, or 7 beside their name.

   Bass drum and cymbals _____   Timpani (kettledrums) _____

   Castanets and gong _____   Whip _____

   Snare (side) drum and Chinese (wood) block _____   Xylophone _____

   Tambourine and triangle _____

B. Listen to the recording of *Saturday Night Waltz* from Aaron Copland's *Rodeo* on Record 2 (Side A) in this book. After careful study, and with as many additional references to the recording as you may need, place the letter of the most nearly correct answer in the blank.

 1. Which family of instruments plays the introduction? _____
    A. brass   B. percussion   C. strings   D. woodwinds

NAME_____

2. Which instrument plays the first solo melody? _____
    A. oboe   B. trumpet   C. violin   D. xylophone
3. When the solo melody is repeated, which instruments play it? _____
    A. oboe   B. trumpet   C. violins   D. xylophone
4. In the slowest section of the waltz—just after a series of repeated unison pitches played by several different instruments, a slow, lyrical melody and its countermelody are played. Which instruments play them? _____
    A. violas and clarinet   B. flutes and piccolo   C. timpani and trumpet   D. trombones and tuba
5. Which instruments play the closing measures of this piece? _____
    A. brass and timpani   B. percussion and flutes   C. strings and horns   D. woodwinds and trumpets

C. Listen to the recording of *Giuoco delle coppie* (*Game of the Couples*) from Béla Bartók's *Concerto for Orchestra* on Record 4 (Side A) in this book. After careful study, and with as many additional references to the recording as you may need, place the letter of the most nearly correct answer in the blank.

1. The rhythmic introduction is played by the _____.
    A. bass drum   B. snare drum (without snares)   C. timpani   D. wood block
2. The first theme or melody is introduced by a pair of _____.
    A. bassoons   B. flutes   C. trumpets   D. violins
3. This is followed (approximately 36 seconds from the beginning) with a melody played by a pair of _____.
    A. harps   B. horns (French horns)   C. oboes   D. violas
4. The next theme (approximately 1 minute, 5 seconds from the beginning) is introduced by a pair of _____.
    A. bass viols   B. bells   C. clarinets   D. trombones
5. The following theme (approximately 1 minute, 28 seconds from the beginning) is played by a pair of _____.
    A. cellos   B. flutes   C. trumpets   D. violins
6. The next theme (approximately 2 minutes, 14 seconds from the beginning) is played by a pair of _____.
    A. muted cellos   B. muted trumpets   C. muted violas   D. muted violins
7. The hymnlike section that follows (approximately 3 minutes, 5 seconds from the beginning) is played by the

_____ family.
    A. brass   B. percussion   C. string   D. woodwind

WORKSHEET 2: READING

A. After reading Chapter 2, complete the following sentences by placing the most appropriate word or words in the blank.

   1. The first beat of any set usually receives a little more stress; we call this the natural _____.

   2. _____ in music is the organization of beats into groups usually marked off by bar lines.

   3. The two basic meters in music are _____ and _____.

   4. All other meters are called _____.

   5. Orchestral compositions (without voices) made up of numerous short but separate related pieces are called

      _____.

B. In the following questions, place the letters of the correct choices in the blank.

   1. A. ♩   B. ♪   C. 𝅝   D. ♩

      Whole note _____   Quarter note _____

      Half note _____   Eighth note _____

   2. A. $\frac{2}{2}$ B. $\frac{3}{2}$ C. $\frac{2}{4}$ D. $\frac{3}{4}$

      Duple meter _____   Triple meter _____

C. Decide whether the following statements are true or false and circle the appropriate letter.

   1. Rhythm is a pervasive part of life.   T   F
   2. A sense of regular pulses, once established, tends to be continued in the listener's mind even when the
      external sound has stopped.   T   F
   3. Both the first and second themes in *Les Dragons d'Alcalà* are accompanied by the same rhythm pattern. T   F

D. Complete the following sentences by placing the letter of the correct word or phrase in the blank.

   1. The word *rhythm* comes from the Greek *rhythmos*, which means _____.
      A. measured motion   B. to flow   C. measured time

   2. The pulse of the music is called _____.
      A. beat   B. measures   C. rhythm

   3. Recognizable, repeated short groupings of sounds and silences are called _____.
      A. melodic fragments   B. syncopated fragments   C. rhythm patterns

NAME_____

4. *Les Dragons d'Alcalà* from the *Carmen Suite* is in _____ meter.
      A. duple   B. triple   C. compound

5. The *Aragonaise* from the *Carmen Suite* is in _____ meter.
      A. duple   B. triple   C. compound

6. The *Carmen Suite* was composed by _____.
      A. Johann Sebastian Bach   B. Georges Bizet   C. Johannes Brahms

E. In the following examples, choose the correct combination of notes and rests needed to complete the second measure and place its letter in the blank.

1. _____

2. _____

3. _____

4. _____

5. _____

WORKSHEET 2: LISTENING

A. Listen to the recording of *Les Toréadors* from the *Carmen Suite* by Georges Bizet on Record 1 (Side B) in this book. After careful study, and with as many additional references to the recording as you may need, place the letter of the most nearly correct answer in the blank.

1. *Les Toréadors* is in _____ meter.
   A. duple   B. triple   C. compound

2. The rhythm pattern of the first theme sounds most nearly like _____ .
   A. dum dee-dee dum dum   B. dum dee-dee DEE-dee-dee-dee   C. dum dum dum-dum-dum

3. Within that first theme (sixteen measures without repeat), this pattern is heard _____ times.
   A. 3   B. 6   C. 11

4. The rhythm pattern of the second theme sounds most nearly like _____ .
   A. dum dee-dee DEE-dee-dee-dee   B. dum dum dum-dum-dum
   C. dum dum dum dum DUM dee-dee dum dum

5. In the second melody, this rhythm pattern is heard essentially _____ times.
   A. two   B. three   C. four

6. In the section in which the famous *Toréador's Song* occurs, the rhythm is in _____ meter.
   A. duple   B. triple   C. compound

7. In that *Toréador* theme, the repeated rhythm pattern most nearly sounds like _____ .
   A. dum dum dee-dee dum   B. DUM dee—da DUM dum   C. dee-dee-dee-dee DUM

8. The rhythm pattern heard in the closing section is identical to that of _____ .
   A. the beginning (the martial melody)   B. the second theme (the woodwind-and-string theme)
   C. the third theme (the *Toréador's Song*)

B. Listen to the recording of *The Young Person's Guide to the Orchestra* by Benjamin Britten on Record 1 (Sides A and B) in this book. After careful study, and with as many additional references to the recording as you may need, place the correct word in the blank.

1. Henry Purcell's theme which is heard at the very beginning, played by the entire orchestra, is in _____ meter.
   duple (either $\frac{2}{4}$ or $\frac{4}{4}$)   triple

2. When that theme is played by the woodwind choir, it is in _____ meter.
   duple (either $\frac{2}{4}$ or $\frac{4}{4}$)   triple

3. When this same theme is played by the brass choir, it is in _____ meter.
   duple (either $\frac{2}{4}$ or $\frac{4}{4}$)   triple

NAME_____

4. Although there are *ritardandos* in it, this same theme is in _____ meter when played by the bassoons.

     duple (either $\frac{2}{4}$ or $\frac{4}{4}$)   triple

5. When the violins take up the theme, it is in _____ meter.

     duple ($\frac{2}{4}$ or $\frac{4}{4}$)   triple

6. The trumpet version of this theme is in _____ meter.

     duple ($\frac{2}{4}$ or $\frac{4}{4}$)   triple

7. The trombones play this theme in _____ meter.

     duple ($\frac{2}{4}$ or $\frac{4}{4}$)   triple

8. When the timpani and other percussion play their variant of Purcell's theme, it is in _____ meter.

     $\frac{6}{8}$ $\frac{9}{8}$

9. The subject of the fugue is in _____ meter.

     duple ($\frac{2}{4}$ or $\frac{4}{4}$)   triple

C. Listen to the recording of the third movement (*Ritmico e Cavalleresco*) from Mario Castelnuovo-Tedesco's *Concerto No. 1 in D for Guitar and Orchestra* on Record 2 (Side B) in this book. After careful study, and with as many additional references to the recording as you may need, place the letter of the most nearly correct answer in the blank.

1. At the beginning of the third movement, the music is in _____ time.

    A. $\frac{2}{8}$ B. $\frac{3}{8}$ C. $\frac{6}{8}$

2. In the slower middle section (just before the long guitar solo) where the guitar is playing a melodic series of chords, the music is in _____ time.

    A. $\frac{3}{4}$ B. $\frac{4}{4}$ C. $\frac{6}{8}$

3. After the long guitar solo, the music changes to _____ time.

    A. $\frac{2}{8}$ B. $\frac{3}{8}$ C. $\frac{6}{8}$

4. The principal melody, heard at the very beginning of the movement, has rhythm patterns that could best be described as combinations of _____ and _____.

    A. DUM dum dum   B. DUM dee-dee   C. DEE-dee-dee-dee dum   D. dum dee-dee DUM

5. In the second theme (the quiet, more lyric theme made up of melodic chords played by the guitar), the characteristic rhythm pattern could be described as _____.

    A. dum dee-dee-dee   B. dum dum da-DEE dum   C. dee-dee-dee-dee dum

WORKSHEET 3: READING

A. After reading Chapter 3, complete the following sentences by placing the appropriate word in the blank.

    1. Melody is, in the most general sense, a succession of musical _____ having some kind of design or musical meaning.

    2. In discussing melody, we must notice that a succession of tones indicates both direction and _____.

    3. When tones in a melody change, they may do so by stepwise or _____ movement.

    4. The tones in a melody may also change by leaps. This we call _____ movement.

    5. A five-tone scale is called a _____ scale.

    6. Short sections of a melody that correspond to the lines of a poem are called _____.

B. In the blank space to the right of each statement, place the letter of the musical example that best represents the statement.

A.

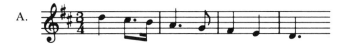

B.

C.

D.

    1. A melody that moves upward by conjunct motion _____

    2. A melody that moves downward by disjunct motion _____

    3. A melody that moves upward by disjunct motion _____

    4. A melody that moves downward by conjunct motion _____

NAME_____

C. Decide whether the following statements are true or false and circle the appropriate letter.

1. Melody represents the horizontal element of music's texture. T   F
2. A melody may be said to be the line or curve of music. T   F
3. The upward or downward direction of a line of melody does not depend upon the relative highness or lowness of its pitches. T   F
4. The relative duration of the tones in a melody determines its rhythm. T   F
5. All melodies must be tuneful. T   F
6. A good melody has a sense of continuity: a beginning, a dramatic or emotional peak, and a definite ending. T   F
7. Most melodies of Western composers are based on modal patterns. T   F
8. The major and minor scale patterns are the most frequently employed in music of recent Western civilization. T   F
9. A cadence is a melodic formula that conveys the imprssion of a momentary or permanent conclusion. T   F

D. In the following examples, circle the letter of the word or phrase that completes each sentence correctly.

1. When tones in a melody change, they may go
     A. up   B. down   C. up *or* down
2. Before major and minor scale patterns came into use around the seventeenth century, the scale-like patterns on which most melodies were based were known as
     A. phrases   B. periods   C. modes
3. Most phrases in vocal music and many in instrumental music end with a
     A. cadence   B. flourish   C. accidental
4. A cadence that suggests only a momentary pause is called
     A. a perfect cadence   B. an imperfect cadence   C. a terminal cadence
5. Most of the tones at the beginning of the second melody in *Buckaroo Holiday* from *Rodeo*
     A. move downward in direction   B. move upward in direction   C. are repeated many times

WORKSHEET 3: LISTENING

A. Listen to the recording of *Saturday Night Waltz* from *Rodeo* by Aaron Copland on Record 2 (Side A) in this book. After careful study, and with as many references to the recording as you may need, respond to the following questions.

   1. In the first melody, when the tones in the melody change, do they move essentially by conjunct or disjunct motion? _____

   2. When the tones of the second melody change, do they move essentially by conjunct or disjunct movement? _____

   3. Which of the two melodies makes use of more repeated tones? _____

   4. Is the meter of *Saturday Night Waltz* duple or triple? _____

   5. The first melody of *Saturday Night Waltz* is played by what instrument? _____

   6. What instruments play the repetition of the first melody? _____

   7. Is there a repeated rhythm pattern within the first melody? _____

   8. Is there a repeated rhythm pattern within the second melody? _____

   9. The *Saturday Night Waltz* ends with which—the first or the second melody? _____

B. Listen to the recording of the first movement (*Allegro con brio*) from Ludwig van Beethoven's *Symphony No. 5* on Record 3 (Side A) in this book. After careful study, and with as many additional references to the recording as necessary, place the letter of the most nearly correct answer in the appropriate blank.

   1. There are _____ repeated tones in the opening four-note motive.
      A. two   B. three   C. four

   2. The opening motive is heard in its original rhythm and tempo (speed) _____ times in succession.
      A. two   B. three   C. four

   3. The melodic direction of this motive is _____ .
      A. upward   B. downward   C. upward and downward

   4. This movement is by _____ motion.
      A. conjunct   B. disjunct   C. conjunct and disjunct

   5. In the faster melody that immediately follows—a melody made out of repetitions of the four-note motive—this motive is heard in its original or in slightly varied form _____ .
      A. once   B. a few times   C. many times

   6. Shortly after this, the violins play an eight-note melody, which is immediately repeated by the clarinet and then by violins and flute. (This melody is approximately 48 seconds from the beginning of the movement.) These repetitions by the clarinet and then the violins and flute are _____ repetitions.
      A. exact   B. slightly varied   C. greatly varied

NAME_____

7. This melody concludes on a pitch that is _____ its starting pitch.
   A. higher than   B. lower than   C. the same as

8. This opening section ends with a violin melody (approximately 1 minute, 7 seconds from the beginning of the movement) that sweeps _____ .
   A. upward   B. downward   C. downward and upward

9. A very quiet solo for unaccompanied oboe occurs about 4 minutes, 31 seconds from the beginning of the movement.
   This short solo moves essentially by _____ motion.
   A. conjunct   B. disjunct   C. repeated tone

10. Toward the end of the movement (approximately 6 minutes, 19 seconds from the beginning), the violins introduce a
    new melody that moves forcefully _____ .
    A. upward   B. downward   C. upward then downward

C. Listen to the recording of *Rondo alla turca* from the *Sonata No. 11 in A for Piano* by Wolfgang Amadeus Mozart on
   Record 4 (Side B) in this book. After careful study, and with as many additional references to the recording as you may
   need, place the letter of the most nearly correct answer in the blank.

   1. The melody at the beginning of the *Rondo alla turca* moves essentially _____ in direction.
      A. upward   B. downward

   2. This melody moves essentially by _____ motion.
      A. conjunct   B. disjunct

   3. The first 6 seconds of his melody (before its repetition) are said to be a _____ .
      A. cadence   B. mode   C. phrase

   4. The second melody, heard approximately 13 seconds from the beginning, moves essentially by _____ motion.
      A. conjunct   B. disjunct

   5. The few notes preceding the slight pause at the end of this section—those notes approximately 37 seconds from the
      beginning—are said to be leading to a _____ .
      A. cadence   B. mode   C. phrase

   6. The first three notes of the new melody introduced at this point move in a(n) _____ direction.
      A. upward   B. downward

   7. They move by _____ motion.
      A. conjunct   B. disjunct

   8. The next new melody introduced, a rather fast-moving one in 16th notes (and approximately 51 seconds from the
      beginning), moves _____ .
      A. downward / upward / downward   B. upward / downward / upward

   9. The tones in it move essentially by _____ motion.
      A. conjunct   B. disjunct

   10. In the last four measures of the composition (approximately 2 minutes, 55 seconds from the beginning), the melodic
       line is said to be approaching a final _____ .
       A. cadence   B. mode   C. phrase

WORKSHEET 4: READING

A. After reading Chapter 4, complete the following sentences by placing the appropriate word or words in the blank.

1. A chord consists of _____ or more different pitches sounded at the same time.

2. Music whose texture consists of a single, unaccompanied melodic line is called _____ music.

3. Music with more than one concurrent melodic line is called _____ music.

4. Music whose texture consists of a single melody accompanied by chords is called _____ music.

5. A logical sequence of chords is called a chord _____ .

6. The three most important chords in any key are based on the scale degrees indicated by the Roman numerals

   _____ , _____ , and _____ .

7. The I chord is called the _____ chord.

8. The IV chord is called the _____ chord.

9. The V chord is called the _____ chord.

10. When a fourth tone (seven tones above the root) is added to the dominant chord, the resulting chord is called a

   _____ _____ chord.

11. A stable or static chord that suggests repose is called a _____ ; a chord which requires resolution is called a

   _____ .

12. *Messiah* is scored for orchestra, _____ soloists, and a _____ -voice chorus.
                                 (number)   (number)

13. The voices in that chorus are, from highest to lowest: _____ , _____ , _____ , and

   _____ .

B. Place whole notes on the staff, one above another, to illustrate the chord indicated.

1. A triad built on G

2. A triad built on F

3. A C chord in first inversion

NAME_____

4. An F chord in first inversion

5. A V^7 chord in the key of C (no sharps or flats in the key signature)

6. A IV chord in the key of F (one flat in the key signature)

7. A IV chord in the key of G (one sharp in the key signature)

C. Decide whether the following statements are true or false and circle the appropriate letter.

1. *Harmony* refers to the structure and function of chords.   T   F
2. Most melodies can be harmonized in only one way.   T   F
3. Some of the same chord patterns used by Bach and Beethoven are still in use today.   T   F
4. Music in which each voice sings or plays its own melodic line is called polyphonic music.   T   F
5. All chords are triads.   T   F
6. All triads are chords.   T   F
7. A major chord consists of the fundamental tone and the two overtones that have the closest physical relationship to it.   T   F
8. Four chords are more important in each key than the other three.   T   F
9. The relationship of the I, IV, and V chords to each other does not change when the key changes.   T   F

WORKSHEET 4: LISTENING

A. Listen to the recording of the *Hallelujah!* chorus from *Messiah* by Georg Friedrich Handel on Record 2 (Side A) in this book. After careful study, and with as many references to the recording as you may need, place the letter of the most nearly correct answer in the blank.

1. At the point at which the voices first enter with the word *Hallelujah!*, the texture is _____.
   A. monophonic   B. polyphonic   C. homophonic
2. At the point where the text *for the Lord God Omnipotent reigneth* occurs for the first time, the texture is

   _____.

   A. monophonic   B. polyphonic   C. homophonic

3. At the point at which the text is *and He shall reign for ever and ever*, the texture is _____.
   A. monophonic   B. polyphonic   C. homophonic
4. The closing section, based on the text *King of Kings and Lord of Lords* is _____.
   A. monophonic   B. polyphonic   C. homophonic
5. At the beginning of the polyphonic section that starts with the basses singing the text *and He shall reign for ever and*

   ever (approximately 1 minute, 54 seconds from the beginning), the basses are imitated, in turn, by the _____,

   the _____ , and finally the _____ .

   A. sopranos   B. altos   C. tenors

6. The *chord progression* of the final statement of the word *Hallelujah!* is known harmonically as a _____.
   A. cadence   B. mode   C. phrase
7. The *Hallelujah!* chorus is scored for orchestra and _____.
   A. four-voice chorus   B. four soloists   C. four soloists and chorus
8. Throughout the *Hallelujah!* chorus the predominant orchestral sound is that of the _____.
   A. brass   B. strings   C. woodwinds
9. The *Hallelujah!* chorus is in _____ meter.
   A. duple ($\frac{2}{4}$ or $\frac{4}{4}$)   B. triple   C. $\frac{6}{8}$
10. In the opening phrase of the *Hallelujah!* chorus, there are _____ different rhythms that are repeated one or more times.
    A. two   B. four   C. six
11. With one major exception, the melodic progression of the first statement of the text *for the Lord God Omnipotent*

    reigneth by the chorus is all _____.

    A. by conjunct motion   B. by disjunct motion   C. in repeated notes

12. The overall movement of this phrase could be described as _____.
    A. upward then downward   B. downward then upward   C. downward throughout

13. The *Hallelujah!* chorus is in the _____ tonality throughout.
    A. major   B. minor   C. modal

NAME_____

B. Listen to the recording of *Simple Like* by John Coltrane on Record 4 (Side B) in this book. After careful study, and with as many references to the recording as you may need, place the letter of the most nearly correct answer in the blank.

1. In the first 32-bar chorus, there are _____ changes of chords.
   A. many   B. very few   C. no

2. In the first chorus, the chords are played by the _____ .
   A. drum set   B. bass viol   C. piano

3. The rhythmic emphasis is essentially provided by the _____ .
   A. drum set   B. bass viol   C. piano

4. The melody of the first three choruses of the 32-bar tune is played by the _____ .
   A. tenor saxophone   B. piano   C. bass viol

5. The melody of the fourth and fifth choruses is played by the _____ .
   A. tenor saxophone   B. piano   C. bass viol

6. The harmonic foundation, or bass line of the harmony, is provided by the _____ .
   A. drum set   B. bass viol   C. saxophone

7. *Simple Like* is in _____ meter.
   A. duple ($\frac{2}{4}$ or $\frac{4}{4}$)   B. triple   C. $\frac{6}{8}$

8. There _____ important rhythm patterns in the opening melody.
   A. are   B. are no

9. The 32-bar melody moves essentially by _____ motion.
   A. conjunct   B. disjunct

10. The overall motion is essentially _____ .
    A. upward   B. downward   C. alternately upward and downward

C. Listen to the recording of *The Young Person's Guide to the Orchestra* on Record 1 (Sides A and B) in this book. After careful study, and with as many references to the recording as you may need, place the letter of the most nearly correct answer in the blank.

1. The opening section for full orchestra is in _____ tonality.
   A. major   B. minor   C. modal

2. The woodwind repetition is in _____ tonality.
   A. major   B. minor   C. modal

3. The texture throughout this opening section for full orchestra, woodwinds, brass, and strings is _____ .
   A. monophonic   B. polyphonic   C. homophonic

4. The harmonic accompaniment in the bass viol variation is provided by _____ .
   A. brass   B. strings   C. woodwinds

5. The harp variation is made up principally of _____ .
   A. cadences   B. chords   C. scales

6. The two trumpets play essentially in _____ with each other.
   A. harmony   B. counterpoint   C. unison

7. The fugal section, starting with the flutes and piccolo playing the Subject, is _____ in texture.
   A. monophonic   B. polyphonic   C. homophonic

8. Eventually we hear Purcell's original theme in _____ with Britten's fugal Subject.
   A. counterpoint   B. harmony   C. unison

9. The short closing section in chordal style (just after a short percussion solo) can be considered _____ .
   A. an indefinite cadence   B. a perfect cadence   C. a phrase

NAME_____

WORKSHEET 5: READING

A. After reading Chapter 5, complete the following sentences by placing the letter or letters of the correct answer in the blank.

1. The three principal elements of music are _____ , _____ , and _____ (any order).
    A. timbre   B. rhythm   C. melody   D. harmony   E. dynamics   F. tempo   G. form or design

2. The three affective elements of music are _____ , _____ , and _____ any order).
    A. timbre   B. rhythm   C. melody   D. harmony   E. dynamics   F. tempo   G. form or design

3. The element that concerns the loudness or softness of music is called _____ .
    A. dynamics   B. tempo   C. timbre

4. When a composer wants the music to grow louder, he indicates this to the performer by the use of the Italian word

    _____ .

    A. *crescendo*   B. *diminuendo*   C. *forte*

5. The expression *sforzando* (*sfz*) means that the note or chord so indicated should be _____ .
    A. heavily accented   B. lightly accented   C. unaccented

B. For each musical expression in the left column, select the best description from the column at right and place its letter in the blank.

forte	_____	A. very soft
cresc.	_____	B. soft
mp	_____	C. medium soft
dim.	_____	D. *sforzando*
fortissimo	_____	E. medium loud
piano	_____	F. growing louder
$>$	_____	G. loud
mezzoforte	_____	H. getting softer
pp	_____	I. very loud
$<$	_____	J. extremely loud
fff	_____	K. *crescendo*
sfz	_____	L. *diminuendo*

NAME_____

C. Decide whether the following statements are true or false and circle the appropriate letter.

1. The three affective elements of music are so called because these elements enhance or change the essential nature of a rhythm, melody, or chord progression.   T   F

2. *Dynamics* refers in music to its "vivacity."   T   F

3. The symbol ⟼ means that the performer should make the music grow louder.   T   F

4. The symbol > over a note or chord means that the note or chord should be accented.   T   F

5. *Cresc.* stands for the Italian word *crescendo* and means that the music should become gradually louder.   T   F

6. *Dim.* or *dimin.* stands for the Italian word *diminuendo* and means that the music should become gradually softer.   T   F

7. *Fortissimo* means "very loud."   T   F

8. *Piano* means "very, very soft."   T   F

9. The Italian word *mezzo* used in conjunction with *forte* or *piano* means "medium" loud or soft.   T   F

10. By the late nineteenth century, composers realized it was no longer desirable to indicate their precise intentions with dynamic markings.   T   F

WORKSHEET 5: LISTENING

A. Listen to the recording of *Bydlo* from *Pictures at an Exhibition* by Modest Mussorgsky on Record 2 (Side B) in this book. After careful study, and with as many references to the recording as you may need, place the letter of the most nearly correct answer in the blank.

1. At the very beginning, the dynamic level is _____.
   A. soft   B. medium   C. loud

2. In the middle, the dynamic level is _____.
   A. soft   B. medium   C. loud

3. At the end, the dynamic level is _____.
   A. soft   B. medium   C. loud

4. To describe the change in dynamic level from the beginning of *Bydlo* to its midpoint, we can use the expression

   _____.
   A. static   B. *crescendo*   C. *diminuendo*

5. To describe the change in dynamic level from the midpoint of *Bydlo* to its conclusion, we can use the expression

   _____.
   A. static   B. *crescendo*   C. *diminuendo*

6. If the opening melody of *Bydlo* is marked to be played very softly (*pp*), then the accompaniment in the low strings

   and woodwinds must be _____.
   A. still softer   B. considerably louder   C. the same dynamic level

7. The opening melody in *Bydlo* is played by a _____.
   A. bassoon   B. bass viol   C. tuba

8. *Bydlo* is in _____ meter.
   A. duple ($\frac{2}{4}$ or $\frac{4}{4}$)   B. triple   C. $\frac{6}{8}$

9. The curve or line of the opening melody is essentially _____.
   A. upward then downward   B. downward then upward   C. continuously upward

10. In the accompaniment at the beginning, the same chord—alternating between root position and first inversion—is

    heard _____ times before it changes.
    A. seven   B. sixteen   C. twenty-three

11. At the dramatic climax of this opening melody, the movement is by _____ motion.
    A. conjunct   B. disjunct

12. The final cadence is played by _____.
    A. muted brass   B. woodwinds *fortissimo*   C. muted strings

NAME_____

B. Listen to the recording of *The Pines of the Appian Way* from Ottorino Respighi's *The Pines of Rome* on Record 3 (Side B) in this book. After careful study, and with as many references to the recording as you may need, place the letter of the most nearly correct answer in the blank.

1. Respighi, like most composers of his era, was very specific about the dynamic effects he wanted, using expression marks from *pppp* to *fff* and frequently including additional directions such as *pppp perdendosi* (becoming lost) and *ppp più possible* (as much as possible). At the beginning of the violin part in *The Pines of the Appian Way*, which of the following would be the appropriate expression mark? _____
   A. *ffff*   B. *mf*   C. *pppp*

2. In the opening horn call for four French horns, five measures from the beginning, which of the following would be the appropriate expression mark? _____
   A. *mf*   B. *ppp*   C. *fff*

3. At the approximate midpoint of the movement, the music is _____.
   A. loud   B. soft   C. extremely soft

4. At the final cadence, the most appropriate marking would be _____.
   A. *fff*   B. *mp*   C. *ppp*

5. The overall effect from beginning to end of this movement is of one long _____.
   A. *crescendo*   B. *diminuendo*   C. *fortissimo*

6. The low-pitched melodic fragment, about 7 seconds from the beginning, is played by the _____.
   A. bass clarinet   B. trumpet   C. xylophone

7. The lengthy modal melody heard approximately 1 minute, 3 seconds from the beginning is played by the _____.
   A. bass viol   B. English horn   C. French horn

8. The *Pines of the Appian Way* is in _____ meter.
   A. duple ($\frac{2}{4}$ or $\frac{4}{4}$)   B. triple   C. $\frac{6}{8}$

9. The accompanying rhythm at the beginning sounds like that of a _____.
   A. march   B. polka   C. waltz

10. The military fanfare that starts in the French horns approximately 1 minute, 56 seconds from the beginning (the horns soon being joined by the trumpets) moves essentially by _____ motion.
    A. conjunct   B. disjunct   C. static

11. This fanfare figure always seems to be _____ in pitch.
    A. moving higher   B. moving lower   C. remaining static

12. By listening to the timpani and bass viols at the beginning, we hear a pedal point—a repeated pitch—that does not change for approximately _____.
    A. 10 seconds   B. 35 seconds   C. 2 minutes

13. When this repeated pedal point changes, it moves higher in pitch by _____.
    A. a very large interval   B. a somewhat large interval   C. an extremely small interval.

14. The final cadence is played by _____.
    A. the full orchestra   B. the strings only   C. the woodwinds only

C. Listen to the recording of the *Allegro assai* from Johann Sebastian Bach's *Brandenburg Concerto No. 2* on Record 4 (Side B) in this book. After careful study, and with as many references to the recording as you may need, place the letter of the most nearly correct answer in the blank.

1. Bach, like most composers of his era, used very few expression marks in his compositions. In the *Allegro assai* there is not a single expression mark by him. At the beginning of the piece, the dynamic level seems to be about

    _____ .
       A. *fortississimo*   B. *forte*   C. *pianississimo*

2. When the flute (recorder) repeats the first melody, about 30 seconds from the beginning of the movement, the

    dynamic level seems to be _____ .
       A. *fortissimo*   B. between *mezzoforte* and *mezzopiano*   C. *pianissimo*

3. In the section that begins with a flute and violin duet (about 1 minute, 7 seconds from the beginning), the dynamic

    level seems to be _____ .
       A. *fortissimo*   B. *forte*   C. *piano*

4. The final cadence seems to be about _____ dynamic level.
       A. *fortissimo*   B. *mezzopiano*   C. *piano*

5. The *Allegro assai* is in _____ meter.
       A. duple ($\frac{2}{4}$ or $\frac{4}{4}$)   B. triple   C. $\frac{6}{8}$

6. The movement in the opening trumpet melody is _____ .
       A. entirely by conjunct motion   B. entirely by disjunct motion   C. by both conjunct and disjunct motion

7. The *Allegro assai* is essentially _____ in texture.
       A. monophonic   B. polyphonic   C. homophonic

8. The tonality of the *Allegro assai* is _____ .
       A. major   B. minor   C. modal

NAME_____

WORKSHEET 6: READING

A. After reading Chapter 6, complete the following sentences by placing the appropriate word in the blank.

1. The speed of the basic pulse in music is called its _____ .

2. It is the _____ who makes the final, critical choice of tempo in playing a piece of music.

3. During the fifteenth and sixteenth centuries, *tactus* meant about _____ beat(s) per second.

4. A mechanical, clocklike device for establishing a given tempo is called a _____ .

5. Tempo markings in music are generally stated in the _____ language.

6. In a three-movement concerto, the _____ movement is usually the slow movement.

B. In the following questions, place the letter of the correct choice in the blank spaces.

1. For each tempo indication in Italian in the left column, select the most appropriate English translation from the right-hand column.

   Adagio _____   A. Brisk (cheerful)

   Allegro _____   B. Broad (very slow)

                          C. Lively (quite fast)

   Andante _____   D. Moderate

   Grave _____   E. Slow (quite slow)

                          F. Solemn (very, very slow)

   Largo _____   G. Very fast

   Moderato _____   H. Very, very fast

   Prestissimo _____   I. A walking pace

   Presto _____

   Vivace _____

2. For each Italian word in the left column, select the most appropriate English translation from the right-hand column.

   meno _____   A. less

   molto _____   B. little

   non troppo _____   C. little by little

   poco _____   D. not too much

   poco a poco _____   E. very

NAME_____

3. For every tempo sign or symbol in the left column, select the appropriate meaning from the right-hand column.

a tempo _____	A. *fermata*
accel. _____	B. freedom of tempo
⌢ _____	C. gradually getting faster
	D. gradually getting slower
rall. or *rit.* _____	E. in tempo
rubato _____	F. original tempo or speed
Tempo I _____	

C. Decide whether the following statements are true or false and circle the appropriate letter.

1. Tempo and rhythm are the same thing.   T   F
2. The choice of tempo is one of the most important acts of any performing musician.   T   F
3. Italian expression marks found on most music indicate more than just tempo; most indicate mood or spirit as well.   T   F
4. Mozart was the first composer to put metronome markings on some of his music.   T   F
5. As music approaches a cadence, the tempo usually becomes slower.   T   F
6. When the music is *correctly* played, it is impossible to have variations in tempo within a measure.   T   F
7. In almost all multimovement works—compositions consisting of two or more separate movements—each movement has a different tempo.   T   F

WORKSHEET 6: LISTENING

A. Listen to the recording of the Finale, *Ritmico e Cavalleresco*, from Mario Castelnuovo-Tedesco's *Concerto No. 1 in D for Guitar and Orchestra* on Record 2 (Side A) in this book. After careful study, and with as many references to the recording as you may need, place the letter of the most nearly correct answer in the blank.

1. The tempo at the very beginning of the Finale is _____.
   A. very, very slow   B. slow   C. fast

2. As the music approaches the cadenza (the guitar solo approximately 2 minutes, 45 seconds from the beginning to about 3 minutes, 30 seconds), the tempo _____.
   A. becomes much faster   B. remains steady   C. slows down

3. In the cadenza, when the guitar plays the principal theme of the Finale, the tempo _____.
   A. becomes faster   B. remains the same   C. becomes slower

4. In the cadenza, when the guitar plays the series of repeated notes, the tempo _____.
   A. becomes faster   B. remains the same   C. becomes slower

5. When the orchestra reenters after the cadenza, the tempo—compared to that when the orchestra played at the beginning—is _____.
   A. faster   B. the same   C. slower

6. As the final cadence is approached (the last 15 or 20 seconds of the movement), the tempo _____.
   A. becomes faster   B. remains the same   C. becomes slower

7. The beginning of the Finale is in _____ meter.
   A. duple ($\frac{2}{4}$ or $\frac{4}{4}$)   B. triple   C. $\frac{6}{8}$

8. In the slower middle section (just before the long guitar solo) at the point where the guitar is playing a melodic series of chords, the music is in _____ meter.
   A. duple ($\frac{2}{4}$ or $\frac{4}{4}$)   B. triple   C. $\frac{6}{8}$

9. After the long guitar solo, the music is in _____.
   A. duple ($\frac{2}{4}$ or $\frac{4}{4}$)   B. triple   C. $\frac{6}{8}$

10. The melodic movement of the opening theme played by the full orchestra is by _____ motion.
    A. conjunct   B. disjunct   C. conjunct and disjunct

11. The texture of the opening section is _____.
    A. monophonic   B. polyphonic   C. homophonic

12. The tonality at the opening of the movement is _____.
    A. major   B. minor   C. modal

13. The tonality at the final cadence is _____.
    A. major   B. minor   C. modal

NAME_____

14. The dynamic level at the opening could best be described as _____.
   A. very soft   B. loud   C. extremely loud and blatant

15. In the middle section in which the guitar introduces the second theme (playing chords to accompany the melody)

   the dynamic level could be described as _____.
   A. soft   B. loud   C. extremely loud

B. Listen to the recording of *Giuoco delle coppie* (*Game of the Couples*) from Béla Bartók's *Concerto for Orchestra* on Record 4 (Side A) in this book. After careful study, and with as many references to the recording as you may need, place the letter of the most nearly correct answer in the blank.

   1. The tempo at the beginning, as the snare drum plays the introduction, is _____.
      A. extremely fast   B. moderate   C. extremely slow   D. irregular

   2. When the pair of bassoons enters, the tempo _____.
      A. becomes much faster   B. remains approximately the same   C. becomes much slower

   3. When the pair of clarinets enters, the tempo _____.
      A. becomes much faster   B. remains approximately the same   C. becomes much slower

   4. In the middle of the section for two flutes, the composer marked the score *poco rallent.* In the performance on this

      record, the composer's directions are _____.
      A. easily perceived   B. barely perceived   C. completely ignored   D. of no importance

   5. After muted trumpets have played, there is a hymnlike section played by the brass. It is marked by the composer
      lo stesso tempo. In the performance on this recording, the conductor responds to the marking by playing the music

      _____.
      A. much slower   B. the same tempo   C. much faster

   6. In the closing measures of the hymnlike section we hear, over the sustained tones of the horns, first flute and oboe,

      then three bassoons. At this point the tempo _____.
      A. becomes faster   B. becomes slower   C. remains the same   D. becomes erratic

   7. From this point to the end of the movement there are _____ changes of tempo.
      A. many   B. very few   C. no   D. many erratic

C. Listen to the recording of *The Young Person's Guide to the Orchestra* by Benjamin Britten on Record 1 (Sides A and B) in this book. After careful study, and with as many references to the recording as you may need, place the letter of the most nearly correct answer in the blank.

   1. At the very beginning, the tempo could be described as _____.
      A. fast and lively   B. extremely fast   C. slow and majestic

   2. In the woodwind variation, the tempo _____.
      A. becomes very fast   B. does not change   C. becomes extremely slow

   3. The tempo of the clarinet variation is _____.
      A. extremely fast   B. moderate   C. extremely slow

4. In the clarinet variation, there are _____ .
    A. *accelerandos*   B. *ritards*   C. no deviations in tempo

5. In the bassoon variation there are _____ .
    A. several *accelerandos*   B. some *rubatos* and a *ritard*   C. no tempo changes

6. Benjamin Britten uses one of the following tempo indications for the violin variation. Which do you think is the

    most appropriate for what you hear? _____
    A. *Brillante—alla polacca* (like a polonaise)   B. *Tempo di marcia* (march tempo)
    C. *Largo e maestoso* (slow and majestic)

7. At the beginning of the bass viol variation, the tempo becomes _____ .
    A. increasingly slower   B. increasingly faster   C. very steady in pulse

8. Britten uses one of the following tempo indications for the trumpet variation. Which do you think is most

    appropriate for what you hear? _____
    A. *Largo*   B. *Andante espressivo*   C. *Vivace*

9. Britten uses one of the following tempo indications for the trombone variation. Which do you think is most

    appropriate for what you hear? _____
    A. *Allegro pomposa* (pompous *Allegro*)   B. *Lento moderato* (moderately slow)
    C. *Presto e vivace* (fast and lively)

10. The concluding fugal section is in a _____ tempo.
    A. slow and stately   B. moderate   C. lively

NAME_____

WORKSHEET 7: READING

A. After reading Chapter 7, complete the following sentences by placing the most appropriate word or words in the blank.

   1. _____ is concerned with the proportion of the parts or sections to each other and to the whole.

   2. The symbols 𝄆 𝄇 are known as _____ signs.

   3. When the first and last sections of a three-part work are similar, the work is said to be in _____ form.

   4. When a melody or motive is immediately repeated, but on a different pitch level, it is called a melodic _____ .

   5. The process concerned with a motive or short theme that serves as a seed out of which larger and more complicated passages can grow is known as _____ .

B. For every concept listed in the left column, choose the musical example that best illustrates that concept in staff notation and place its letter in the blank.

contrast _____

melodic sequence _____

repetition _____

variation _____

(Lullaby) A.

(Heaven, Heaven) B.

(Sailing) C.

(For He's a Jolly Good Fellow) D.

C. Decide whether the following statements are true or false and circle the appropriate letter.

   1. Repetition, especially immediate repetition, is the easiest design element in music to recognize aurally.　T　F

   2. All melodic repetitions must be exact.　T　F

   3. Sometimes a variation occurs when one or more elements change and others remain unchanged.　T　F

   4. Contrast is a pervasive part of musical composition.　T　F

NAME_____

5. Balance is concerned with the use of melody, rhythm, and harmony to produce an aesthetically pleasing or harmoniously integrated whole.   T   F
6. Form or design is of relatively little importance in creating an aesthetically rewarding musical composition.   T   F
7. The organization of the elements of music in a composition creates its design.   T   F
8. When one or more of the elements of music is repeated identically, unity cannot be achieved in the composition.   T   F

WORKSHEET 7: LISTENING

A. Listen to the recording of Antonin Dvořák's *Slavonic Dance* Opus 46, No. 1, on Record 3 (Side A) in this book. After careful study, and with as many references to the recording as you may need, complete the following sentences by placing the most appropriate word in the blank.

  1. A melodic sequence is heard at the very beginning of the dance _____ times in immediate succession.

  2. The melodic sequence that occurs in the second theme (played softly by oboe and flute) is heard _____ times in the statement of the theme and its repetition.

  3. The opening phrase of the theme of the middle section (played by flute and oboe) is repeated almost exactly

     _____ times in its initial statement with its repetition.

  4. After the second theme in the middle section (played by the flute and oboe) is heard, we return to the melody of

     the _____ theme of the middle section.

  5. This is followed by a repetition of the _____ theme of the dance.

  6. The last theme heard in the Coda, just before the final chord, is the _____ theme of the dance.

  7. The *Slavonic Dance No. 1* is in _____ meter.

  8. Its tempo is _____ .

  9. It is in a _____ tonality.

  10. Its texture is basically _____ .

  11. The dynamic level at the beginning is _____ .

  12. The dynamic level of the second section is relatively _____ .

  13. When the first theme is repeated in its entirety by the full orchestra, the dynamic level is _____ .

  14. The dynamic level at the end is _____ .

B. Listen to the recording of the *Rondo alla turca* from Wolfgang Amadeus Mozart's *Sonata No. 11 in A for Piano* on Record 4 (Side B) in this book. After careful study, and with as many references to the recording as you may need, place the letter of the most nearly correct answer in the blank.

  1. In the first theme and its repeat, how many times is the opening melodic figure heard, in its original form or a

     variant? _____

     A. 2   B. 8   C. 12

NAME_____

2. In the second section and its repeat, how many times is the second melodic figure heard, in its original form or a variant? _____

    A. 2   B. 8   C. 12

3. In the first episode (eight measures) and its repeat, how many times is the third melodic figure heard, in its original form or a close variant? _____

    A. 2   B. 8   C. 12

4. The *Rondo alla Turca* is in _____ meter.
   A. duple ($\frac{2}{4}$ or $\frac{4}{4}$)   B. triple   C. $\frac{6}{8}$

5. The tempo of the *Rondo* is moderately _____.
   A. slow   B. fast

6. The dynamic level at the beginning is moderately _____.
   A. soft   B. loud

7. The *Rondo* begins in the _____ tonality.
   A. major   B. minor

8. The *Rondo* ends in the _____ tonality.
   A. major   B. minor

9. The texture of the *Rondo* is essentially _____.
   A. monophonic   B. polyphonic   C. homophonic

C. Listen to the recording of John Coltrane's *Simple Like* on Record 4 (Side B) in this book. After careful study, and with as many references to the recording as you may need, place the letter of the most nearly correct answer in the blank.

1. How many times is the first three-note melodic figure heard in the opening phrase? _____
   A. once   B. 3 times   C. 6 times

2. The second phrase is _____ the first.
   A. in contrast to   B. exactly the same as   C. a variant of

3. The opening melodic figure is _____ in the opening section.
   A. featured prominently   B. seldom heard   C. heard once

4. At the beginning of the piano chorus, the three-note repeated melodic figure is _____.
   A. heard frequently   B. heard only once   C. not heard at all

5. The overall design of *Simple Like* could be outlined: _____.
   A. A–A–B–B   B. A-B-A   C. A-B-A-C-A

6. The meter of *Simple Like* is _____.
   A. duple ($\frac{2}{4}$ or $\frac{4}{4}$)   B. triple   C. $\frac{6}{8}$

7. The tempo is _____ .
    A. extremely fast   B. moderate   C. extremely slow

8. The texture of *Simple Like* is essentially _____ .
    A. monophonic   B. polyphonic   C. homophonic

NAME_____

WORKSHEET 8: READING

Part I (Romanticism: Beethoven)

A. After reading the first part of Chapter 8 (to p. 132), complete the following sentences by placing the letter of the most nearly correct answer in the blank.

1. There are _____ movements in most symphonies.
   A. two   B. three   C. four

2. Beethoven _____ the scope of the symphonic form.
   A. condensed   B. enlarged   C. left unchanged

3. Beethoven made the third movement of his *Eroica Symphony* a _____.
   A. march   B. scherzo   C. minuet

4. Each movement of a symphony takes its name from the _____ marking assigned by the composer.
   A. dynamic   B. meter signature   C. tempo

5. The sonata-allegro form of the first movement is traditionally based on _____ themes.
   A. two   B. three   C. four

6. The three principal sections in the sonata-allegro form are, in sequence, _____, _____, and

   _____.
   A. introduction   B. coda   C. recapitulation   D. development   E. exposition

7. The two themes heard at the beginning of the exposition in a sonata-allegro are in _____ keys or tonalities.
   A. the same   B. different

8. The finale, or fourth movement, of Beethoven's *Symphony No 5* is in _____ form.
   A. rondo   B. sonata-allegro   C. scherzo

B. Decide whether the following statements are true or false and circle the appropriate letter.

1. The Romantic era in music occupied most of the nineteenth century.   T   F
2. In its earlier stages, the Romantic movement was led mostly by older men.   T   F
3. In old French, *romant* means an imaginative story, as opposed to a plain retelling of the facts.   T   F
4. Romantic artists and writers were fascinated by tales of chivalrous love.   T   F
5. There was little interest during the Romantic era in folklore and the picturesque.   T   F
6. In all the arts, Romanticism brought out imagination and emotion.   T   F
7. Painters of the Romantic era were enraptured by nature.   T   F
8. The Industrial Revolution made a better way of life for everyone in the last half of the nineteenth
   century.   T   F
9. Beethoven was greatly fascinated by Napoleon and by the French Revolution, with its battle cry of
   "liberty, equality, and fraternity" for all.   T   F

NAME_____

WORKSHEET 8: LISTENING

Part I (*Symphony No. 5* by Ludwig van Beethoven)

A. Listen to the recording of the *Allegro con brio* from Ludwig van Beethoven's *Symphony No. 5* on Record 3 (Side A) in this book. After careful study, and with as many additional references to the recording and the text as necessary, place the letter of the most nearly correct answer in the blank.

1. At the beginning of the movement, the basic rhythm pattern (dee-dee-dee DUM) is heard in its original slow and majestic form _____ .
    A. once   B. twice   C. six times

2. After this rhythm pattern has been used to form the Principal Theme, which is heard at a faster tempo, it is heard _____ times in succession before the pause.
    A. 2   B. 11   C. 22

3. The tempo of the first movement could be described as _____ .
    A. brisk   B. relatively slow   C. very slow and majestic

4. The first movement is in _____ meter.
    A. duple ($\frac{2}{4}$ or $\frac{4}{4}$)   B. triple   C. $\frac{6}{8}$

5. The Principal Theme is played by members of the _____ section.
    A. brass   B. string   C. woodwind

6. The Second Theme is introduced by the _____ .
    A. clarinet   B. trumpet   C. violins

7. This theme is immediately repeated by _____ .
    A. clarinet and flute   B. clarinet and timpani   C. cellos and bass viols

8. We can distinguish the beginning of the development from the repetition of the exposition because at the beginning of the development the rhythmic-melodic motive changes _____ .
    A. meter   B. tempo   C. tonality (key)

9. The tempo of this movement is _____ .
    A. *Allegro con brio*   B. *Andante cantabile*   C. *Molto vivace*

10. The dynamic level at the very beginning is _____ .
    A. loud   B. moderate   C. soft

11. The dynamic level of the Principal Theme, compared to the opening motive, is _____ .
    A. softer   B. the same   C. louder

12. The *Allegro con brio* is generally _____ in texture.
    A. monophonic   B. polyphonic   C. homophonic

READING: Part II (Chopin, Schubert, Schumann, Strauss)

A. After reading the second part of Chapter 8 (pp. 133–52), respond to the following questions by circling the letter of the word or phrase that completes each sentence correctly.

1. Character pieces are

   A. short piano works   B. songs about colorful individuals   C. long works for orchestra

2. Chopin composed almost exclusively for

   A. the violin   B. the human voice   C. the piano

3. *Nocturne* means

   A. morning music   B. afternoon music   C. night music

4. The greatest composer of art songs was

   A. Schubert   B. Beethoven   C. Chopin

5. German songs of the nineteenth and early twentieth centuries that blend poetry, voice, and piano into a unified whole are called

   A. tone poems   B. song cycles   C. lieder

6. In a strophic song, each stanza is set

   A. to the same music   B. to completely different music   C. to a combination of the same and new music

7. In *Erlkönig*, the galloping of horses is suggested by

   A. the text   B. a sound-effect record   C. a repeated figure in the piano

8. In the Schumann song *Die beiden Grenadiere*, to suggest the country of origin of the grenadiers, the composer uses the national anthem of

   A. Germany   B. France   C. Italy

9. The rhythm at the beginning of *Die beiden Grenadiere* suggests a

   A. march   B. waltz   C. polka

10. Schumann originally wanted to become a

    A. composer   B. pianist   C. conductor

B. Decide whether the following statements are true or false and circle the appropriate letter.

1. The piano became the most important solo instrument during the Romantic era.   T   F
2. The piano in the nineteenth century was quite a different instrument from the one known in the eighteenth century.   T   F
3. The piano of the nineteenth century was closely akin to the piano we know today.   T   F
4. Folk songs first developed during the Romantic era.   T   F
5. All folk songs were considered *lieder* in the new nineteenth-century use of the word.   T   F
6. In *lieder*, the piano is of equal importance with the voice.   T   F
7. *Die beiden Grenadiere* tells the tale of two of Napoleon's soldiers returning from Russia.   T   F
8. Richard Strauss was among the last of the major German composers of art songs.   T   F

NAME_____

LISTENING: Part II (*Die beiden Grenadiere* **by Robert Schumann**)

A. Listen to the recording of Robert Schumann's song *Die beiden Grenadiere* on Record 3 (Side B) in this book. After careful listening, and with as many references to the recording and to the text as necessary, complete the following statements by placing the letter of the most nearly correct answer in the blank.

1. At the beginning, the rhythm suggests a _____ .
     A. waltz   B. march   C. polka

2. On the phrase *und der Kaiser, der Kaiser gefangen!* ("And the Emperor, the Emperor taken prisoner!") the tempo
   _____ .
     A. slows down slightly   B. accelerates   C. doubles in time value

3. Melodically, the section beginning with the text *Da weinten zusammen die Grenadier* ("Those two soldiers then
   wept") is _____ .
     A. similar to the first section   B. unlike any other section   C. identical to the last section

4. The melody of the passage *So will ich liegen und horchen still* ("So shall I lie there, listening") is derived from
   _____ .
     A. *God Save the Queen*   B. *The Maple Leaf Forever*   C. *The Marseillaise*

5. The dramatic climax of the song occurs _____ .
     A. at the beginning   B. toward the middle   C. at the end

6. The song is sung by _____ .
     A. a soprano   B. an alto   C. a baritone

7. The meter at the beginning of the song is _____
     A. duple ($\frac{2}{4}$ or $\frac{4}{4}$)   B. triple   C. $\frac{6}{8}$

8. The song maintains this meter _____ .
     A. for the first section only   B. for the first and last sections only   C. throughout

9. The overall tempo of *Die beiden Grenadiere* could be described as _____ .
     A. very fast   B. moderate   C. very slow

10. *Die beiden Grenadiere* is essentially _____ in texture.
     A. monophonic   B. polyphonic   C. homophonic

READING: Part III (Wagner, Puccini, Brahms, Tchaikovsky, Mahler)

A. After reading the last part of Chapter 8 (pp. 153–87), respond to the following statements by placing the letter of the correct choice in the blank.

1. The poet-musicians of the Middle Ages were called _____ in southern France.
   A. Meistersinger   B. troubadours   C. minstrels

2. Members of the German singing guild were called _____.
   A. Meistersinger   B. troubadours   C. minstrels

3. Wagner's opera based on the German singing guilds was named _____.
   A. *Tannhauser*   B. *Parsifal*   C. *Die Meistersinger von Nürnberg*

4. Toward the end of the Overture, Wagner combines, polyphonically, _____ different melodies in a remarkable passage.
   A. two   B. three   C. four

5. One of the greatest of the nineteenth-century Italian opera composers was _____.
   A. Georges Bizet   B. Giacomo Puccini   C. Richard Wagner

6. *Verismo* operas deal with scenes of _____.
   A. historical pageantry   B. mythological subjects   C. everyday life

7. Johannes Brahms is known by the concert-going public primarily as a composer of _____.
   A. orchestral music   B. operas   C. ballets

8. During the nineteenth century, Italian composers were interested primarily in composing _____.
   A. ballets   B. operas   C. symphonies

9. During the nineteenth century, the German and Austrian composers were most concerned with composing

   _____.

   A. ballets   B. operas   C. symphonies

10. During the nineteenth century, the French composers were most interested in composing _____.
    A. ballets   B. symphonies   C. tone poems

11. Ballet originated at the courts of _____.
    A. England and Scotland   B. France and Burgundy   C. Germany and Austria

12. Ballet includes only _____.
    A. dance and pantomime   B. spoken dialogue   C. sung dialogue

13. Mahler's symphonies were conceived for orchestras that were _____ the early nineteenth-century orchestra.
    A. the same size as   B. smaller than   C. larger than

NAME_____

B. Decide whether the following statements are true or false and circle the appropriate letter.

1. The German poet-musicians called their guild the *Meistersinger*—the "mastersingers." T F
2. For his opera *Die Meistersinger von Nürnberg*, Wagner chose as one of the central characters an actual historical personage, one of the greatest of early German poets, Hans Sachs. T F
3. Opera was the principal vocal form of the Romantic era. T F
4. Operas are made up of a few songs and much spoken dialogue. T F
5. Many operas include both dancers and choruses in the setting. T F
6. *Recitative* is a type of song-speech. T F
7. *La Bohème* is an example of *verismo* opera. T F
8. Most Puccini operas have overtures. T F
9. Johannes Brahms used the folk poetry of Russia and Poland for his *Liebeslieder Walzer*. T F
10. The *Liebeslieder Walzer* were never intended by the composer to be performed with only a two-piano accompaniment. T F
11. Tchaikovsky first encountered ballet as an art form in France. T F
12. There is no spoken dialogue in ballet; the text is sung throughout. T F
13. Gustav Mahler was one of the last of the great nineteenth-century Romantic composers of symphonies. T F
14. By Mahler's time, the symphony orchestra had grown to its largest size. T F
15. Most Mahler symphonies are gargantuan in length and structure. T F
16. Mahler always believed that the public should know the program he had in mind when composing his symphonies. T F
17. Mahler's *Symphony No. 5* has essentially five movements. T F

LISTENING: Part III (*Carmen Suite* by Georges Bizet)

A. Listen to the recording of *Les Toréadors*, from the *Carmen Suite* by the late nineteenth-century French Romantic composer Georges Bizet, on Record 1 (Side B) in this book. (It should be recalled that *Les Toréadors* serves as the orchestral introduction to Act I of the opera *Carmen* and is based on certain motives and themes heard later in the opera.) After careful study, and with as many additional references to the recording as necessary, place the letter of the most nearly correct answer in the blank.

1. The opening phrase is scored for _____.
   A. brass   B. full orchestra   C. woodwinds

2. The opening section is in _____ meter.
   A. duple ($\frac{2}{4}$ or $\frac{4}{4}$)   B. triple   C. $\frac{6}{8}$

3. *Les Toréadors* opens with a rhythm pattern that is prominent in the opening theme. That rhythm pattern could be notated as _____.

   A.

   DUM dee-dee DEE-dee-dee-dee

   B.

   DEE-dee-dee-dee DEE-dee-dum

   C.

   DUM-dee-dee DUM-dee-dee

4. The dynamic level at the beginning is _____.
   A. soft   B. moderate   C. loud

5. The texture of the opening section is _____.
   A. monophonic   B. polyphonic   C. homophonic

6. The second theme is played by _____.
   A. upper woodwinds and strings   B. brass   C. low woodwinds and brass

7. The dynamic level of this second theme is _____ the first theme.
   A. softer than   B. the same as   C. louder than

8. This second theme is in _____ meter.
   A. duple ($\frac{2}{4}$ or $\frac{4}{4}$)   B. triple   C. $\frac{6}{8}$

NAME_____

9. The third theme (sung in the opera by the Toréador and thus called *The Toréador's Song*) is played by _____.
   A. brass   B. strings   C. woodwinds

10. The accompaniment to the tune, including a brief four-measure introduction, is played by the _____.
    A. brass   B. strings   C. woodwinds

11. The texture is strictly _____.
    A. monophonic   B. polyphonic   C. homophonic

12. The most characteristic rhythm pattern of this theme is _____.

    A.

    DUM dee-dee dum dum

    B.

    dum dee—da DUM dum

    C.

    dee-dee dum dum dum

13. The movement of the first phrase of the melody is mostly by _____ motion.
    A. conjunct   B. disjunct   C. static

14. The movement of the last phrase of the melody is mostly by _____ motion.
    A. conjunct   B. disjunct   C. static

15. A _____ soon follows and the music becomes much louder.
    A. *crescendo*   B. *diminuendo*   C. *rallentando*

16. The overall form of *Les Toréadors* could be outlined: _____.
    A. A-B   B. A-B-A   C. A-B-A-C-A

WORKSHEET 9: READING

A. After reading Chapter 9, respond to the following questions by placing the letter of the correct choice in the blank.

1. An awareness of Nationalism in its broadest sense was awakened by the start of the _____.
    A. Franco-Prussian War   B. French Revolution   C. First World War

2. The Mighty Five were a group of five composers from _____.
    A. France   B. Norway   C. Russia

3. One of the leaders of the Nationalistic school in Bohemia was _____.
    A. Edvard Grieg   B. Jean Sibelius   C. Bedřich Smetana

4. All but two of Rimsky-Korsakov's operas are based upon _____.
    A. national subjects, historical or legendary   B. plays by the German poet Goethe
    C. stories of his own creation

5. One of Rimsky-Korsakov's well-known operas is _____.
    A. *Le Coq d'or*   B. *The Nutcracker*   C. *Sleeping Beauty*

6. One of Alexander Borodin's three incomplete operas is titled _____.
    A. *Alexander Nevsky*   B. *Boris Godunov*   C. *Prince Igor*

7. The most familiar dance music from *Prince Igor* is known as _____.
    A. *Dance of the Mirlitons*   B. *Polka*   C. *The Polovetsian Dances*
8. The Nationalistic movement in Bohemia was an attempt by the Czechs to free themselves from the language and

    rule of the _____.
    A. French   B. Germans   C. Italians

9. Bedřich Smetana composed a number of operas, the best known of which is _____.
    A. *The Bartered Bride*   B. *La Bohème*   C. *Carmen*

B. For each composer in the left column, find the composition in the column at right and place its letter in the blank.

Dvořák	_____	A. *The Bartered Bride*
Glinka	_____	B. *Finlandia*
Grieg	_____	C. *A Life for the Czar*
Mussorgsky	_____	D. *Norwegian Dances*
Rimsky-Korsakov	_____	E. *Boris Godunov*
Sibelius	_____	F. *Russian Easter Overture*
Smetana	_____	G. *Slavonic Dances*

NAME_____

C. Decide whether the following statements are true or false and circle the appropriate letter.

1. Nationalism grew out of the mainstream of Romanticism in the last half of the nineteenth century. T F
2. As a movement, Nationalism was never self-conscious or aggressive. T F
3. None of the group of Russian composers known as The Mighty Five had any formal training in composition during their formative years. T F
4. Rimsky-Korsakov was greatly attracted to the folk tales and legends of his native Russia. T F
5. Many of the melodies of *Le Coq d'or*, if not actual Russian folk songs, are folklike in nature. T F
6. Many Russian folk melodies are based on the old church modes rather than on modern major and minor scale patterns. T F
7. Alexander Borodin worked on his opera *Prince Igor* for eighteen years and never completed it. T F
8. Borodin did much research into history, archaeology, and folk music while working on *Prince Igor*. T F
9. Bohemian music has never been influenced by German culture. T F
10. The Czech National Theater was built in 1862 for the exclusive purpose of presenting operas in the native Czech language. T F

WORKSHEET 9: LISTENING

A. Listen to the recording of *Bydlo* from *Pictures at an Exhibition* by Modest Mussorgsky on Record 2 (Side B) in this book. (It should be noted that in 1874, the year Mussorgsky originally composed *Pictures at an Exhibition*, Poland had been under Russian rule for almost eighty years, and thus such Polish subjects as peasant life, including oxcarts on the farms, were appropriate for the Russian Nationalists.) After careful study, and with as many references to the recording and the text of Chapters 5 and 9 as necessary, place the letter of the most nearly correct answer in the blank.

1. Modest Mussorgsky was _____ by birth.
    A. German   B. French   C. Russian

2. Mussorgsky was one of a group of composers known as _____.
    A. The Mighty Five   B. The Six   C. The Suprematists

3. *Pictures at an Exhibition* was inspired by an actual exhibit of sketches, watercolors, and architectural designs of

    works by Victor Hartmann held in _____.
    A. St. Augustine, Florida   B. St. Petersburg, Russia   C. St. Paul, Minnesota

4. Although the word *Bydlo* means "cattle" in Polish, Mussorgsky used the word in the title to suggest _____.
    A. a cattleman   B. a crude oxcart   C. a peasant

5. Marked by Mussorgsky *Sempre moderato pesante* (A clumsy, moderate tempo, always), *Bydlo* is in _____ meter.
    A. duple ($\frac{2}{4}$ or $\frac{4}{4}$)   B. triple   C. $\frac{6}{8}$

6. The clumsy rhythm of the rolling, stolid wooden wheels is suggested by _____.
    A. high woodwinds   B. loud brass and timpani   C. low strings and woodwinds

7. The overall dynamic level could best be outlined: _____.

    A. soft $<$ loud $>$ soft   B. loud $>$ soft $<$ loud

    C. soft ⊏ loud

8. The overall dynamic pattern might suggest, programmatically, _____.
    A. the oxcart approaching the listener, then disappearing in the distance
    B. the oxcart leaving, and then returning again   C. the oxcart getting ever closer to the listener

9. The opening theme of *Bydlo* is played by a _____.
    A. flute   B. violin   C. tuba

10. The curve of the first two phrases of the melody could be described as _____.
    A. moving continuously downward   B. moving upward, then downward   C. moving downward then upward

11. The movement in these two phrases is by _____.
    A. conjunct   B. disjunct   C. both conjunct and disjunct

12. The texture throughout *Bydlo* is _____.
    A. monophonic   B. polyphonic   C. homophonic

NAME_____

WORKSHEET 10: READING

A. After reading Chapter 10, respond to the following questions by placing the letter of the correct choice in the blank.

1. In music, the Impressionist movement centered largely in _____.
   A. London   B. Paris   C. Berlin

2. In addition to the traditional major and minor scale patterns, Debussy also made use of melodies built out of _____ and _____ scales.
   A. symbolistic   B. dodecaphonic   C. modal   D. twelve-tone   E. whole-tone

3. Maurice Ravel was less a true Impressionist than Debussy because Ravel relied more on _____ and _____.
   A. clear metrical rhythms   B. sliding chords   C. strong cadences   D. chromaticism
   E. ill-defined forms

4. Maurice Ravel's *Daphnis et Chloé* is _____.
   A. a ballet   B. an opera   C. a symphony

5. The story of *Daphnis et Chloé* was derived from _____.
   A. a painting by Manet   B. a legend by Longus   C. a poem by Mallarmé

6. Ottorino Respighi called his three major orchestral works (*The Pines of Rome, The Fountains of Rome,* and *Roman Festivals*) _____.
   A. ballets   B. symphonic poems   C. string quartets

B. For each composer listed in the left column, find the country of his birth in the column at right and place that letter in that blank.

John Alden Carpenter	_____	A. England
Manuel de Falla	_____	B. France
Claude Debussy	_____	C. Germany
Frederick Delius	_____	D. Italy
Charles Tomlinson Griffes	_____	E. Spain
Jacques Ibert	_____	F. United States
Maurice Ravel	_____	
Ottorino Respighi	_____	
Albert Roussel	_____	
Cyril Scott	_____	

NAME_____

C. Decide whether the following statements are true or false and circle the appropriate letter.

1. *Impressionism* is a term music borrowed from a style of French painting.   T   F
2. Impressionism in art was a revolt against the "realism" of nineteenth-century painting.   T   F
3. The Impressionist painters worked in Paris during the first half of the nineteenth century.   T   F
4. The Symbolist poets attempted to suggest a fantasy of imagination rather than describe in detail.   T   F
5. Claude Debussy was the leading exponent of Impressionism in music.   T   F
6. Debussy himself adopted the word *impressionism* to apply to his new style of composition.   T   F
7. In Debussy's Impressionistic works, a succession of orchestral colors takes the place of dynamic development.   T   F
8. In Impressionistic music, themes and musical subjects were no longer of conventional length and symmetry.   T   F
9. New chordal combinations and chords with unresolved dissonances were widely used by the Impressionist composers.   T   F
10. There is an ethereal quality to much Impressionistic music.   T   F
11. A triptych entitled *Nocturnes* is the work that firmly established Debussy as a composer to be regarded with respect. T   F
12. Debussy intended his *Nocturnes* to assume the generic form of all nocturnes.   T   F
13. In *The Pines of Rome*, Ottorino Respighi used nature as a point of departure in order to recall memories and visions. T   F

WORKSHEET 10: LISTENING

A. Listen to the recording of *The Pines of the Appian Way* from Ottorino Respighi's symphonic poem *The Pines of Rome* on Record 3 (Side B) in this book. After careful study, and with as many references to the recording and to the text as necessary, place the letter of the most nearly correct answer in the blank.

1. The pulsating beat heard immediately at the beginning of *The Pines of the Appian Way* is played most prominently

   by the _____ .
      A. tuba   B. xylophone   C. timpani

2. This pulsating beat stops _____ .
      A. just before the end of the composition   B. on the last chord of the composition
      C. at the end of measure 16 (approximately 15 seconds)

3. The first melodic motive that is heard, arising from the bass voice of the orchestra, is played by a _____ .
      A. tuba   B. bass clarinet   C. timpani

4. When the violins and violas first enter (the score is marked by the composer "like a lament"), the harmonies they

   play could be described as _____ .
      A. dissonant   B. soothing   C. ethereal

5. Over the strings, we hear a chordal passage played by three _____ .
      A. violins   B. French horns   C. flutes

6. A rather long modal melody is heard about 1 minute, 3 seconds from the beginning. It is played by _____ .
      A. a flute   B. a harp   C. an English horn

7. Toward the end of this solo, we hear melodic fragments played by bassoons and clarinets in a passage whose texture

   could be described as _____ .
      A. monophonic   B. polyphonic   C. homophonic

8. The military fanfare that starts in the French horns (approximately 1 minute, 56 seconds from the beginning) with

   other brass soon joining in moves essentially by _____ .
      A. conjunct motion   B. disjunct motion   C. conjunct and disjunct motion

9. This fanfare figure always seems to keep moving _____ in pitch.
      A. upward   B. downward   C. up and down

10. At the beginning of *The Pines of the Appian Way*, the dynamic level is _____ .
       A. extremely soft   B. moderate   C. extremely loud

11. As the music progresses, there is a _____ in the dynamic level.
       A. gradual *diminuendo*   B. gradual *crescendo*   C. static quality

12. At the dynamic climax of the music, the instruments of the _____ family are heard most prominently.
       A. brass   B. string   C. woodwind

13. The rhythm throughout the composition could best be described as that of a _____ .
       A. waltz   B. ancient minuet   C. march

NAME_____

14. The tempo could best be described as _____.
    A. extremely fast   B. moderate   C. extremely slow

15. With few exceptions, the texture could be described as _____.
    A. monophonic   B. polyphonic   C. homophonic

16. At the first dramatic climax, the tonality is _____.
    A. a cross between minor and modal tonalities   B. major   C. the whole-tone scale

17. The final cadence is played by the _____.
    A. full orchestra   B. strings only   C. woodwinds only

WORKSHEET 11: READING

A. After reading Chapter 11, respond to the following statements by placing the letter of the correct choice in the blank.

1. Many twentieth-century composers have reacted against the _____ music of the German Romantic composers of the nineteenth century.
   A. atonal   B. tonal   C. nontonal

2. *Polytonality* refers to more than one _____.
   A. tonal center   B. rhythm   C. style

3. One of the first well-known works to make use of polytonality was _____.
   A. *Concerto for Orchestra* by Béla Bartók   B. *Estancia* by Alberto Ginastera
   C. *Petrouchka* by Igor Stravinsky

4. The "method of composing with twelve tones which are related only to one another" was the creation of _____.
   A. Béla Bartók   B. Arnold Schoenberg   C. Igor Stravinsky

5. Dodecaphonic music is _____ music.
   A. atonal   B. tonal   C. rhapsodic

6. The rhythmic freedom of twentieth-century music means that _____.
   A. melodies do not have to be of symmetrical form   B. bar lines are not always required to maintain the meter
   C. there can be frequent changes of meter signature   D. all of the above are true
   E. none of the above is true

7. Music in which chance is an element is known as _____ music.
   A. aleatoric   B. atonal   C. atrophied

8. In addition to polytonal music, Charles Ives also composed works that were _____.
   A. atonal   B. polyrhythmic   C. polyharmonic   D. all of the above   E. none of the above

9. Béla Bartók is a composer of _____ origin.
   A. American   B. Argentinian   C. Hungarian

10. Bartók's *Concerto for Orchestra* makes frequent use of such intervals as _____.
    A. thirds   B. sixths   C. sevenths   D. all of the above   E. none of the above

11. Igor Stravinsky was born in _____.
    A. France   B. United States   C. Russia

12. Igor Stravinsky composed three famous ballets for the impressario Diaghilev: _____, _____, and

    _____.

      A. *Swan Lake*   B. *Petrouchka*   C. *The Firebird*   D. *The Rite of Spring*   E. *The Stone Flower*

13. During the first performance, the opening measures of *The Rite of Spring* brought _____.
    A. loud cheers   B. derisive laughter   C. complete indifference

14. The opening solo for _____ in Stravinsky's *The Rite of Spring* is scored very high in its register.
    A. bassoon   B. clarinet   C. saxophone

NAME_____

15. George Gershwin called his first concert-jazz piece a rhapsody because it was _____.
    A. rigidly classical in structure   B. completely free in structure   C. in binary form

16. The title of Ginastera's *Estancia* could be translated as _____.
    A. estate   B. crude peasant dance   C. folk dance

17. The *malambo* is a vigorous and typical dance of the _____.
    A. Brazilians   B. gauchos   C. Mexicans

18. Alberto Ginastera is a composer of _____ origin.
    A. American   B. Argentinian   C. Italian

19. Krzysztof Penderecki is a composer of _____ origin.
    A. Argentinian   B. Italian   C. Polish

20. The text of Penderecki's *Passio et Mors Domini Nostri Iesu Christi secundum Lucam* is taken from the book of _____ in the Bible.
    A. St. Matthew   B. St. Luke   C. the Psalms of David

21. Carman Moore is a composer of _____ origin.
    A. American   B. Argentinian   C. Polish

22. In his *Four Movements for a Fashionable Five-Toed Dragon*, Carman Moore uses such nontraditional instruments as _____.

    A. pi'pa   B. synthesizer   C. harpsichord   D. A, B, and C   E. neither A, B, nor C

B. For each composition in the left column, find the composer in the column on the right and place that letter in the blank.

Amahl and the Night Visitors	_____	A. Béla Bartók
An American in Paris	_____	B. John Cage
		C. George Gershwin
Concerto for Orchestra	_____	D. Alberto Ginastera
Estancia	_____	E. Charles Ives
		F. Gian-Carlo Menotti
The Firebird	_____	G. Carman Moore
4' 33"	_____	H. Krzysztof Penderecki
		I. Igor Stravinsky
Four Movements for a Fashionable Five-Toed Dragon	_____	J. Edgard Varèse
The Holidays Symphony	_____	
Ionisation	_____	
Passio et Mors Domini Nostri Iesu Christi secundum Lucam	_____	
Petrouchka	_____	
Porgy and Bess	_____	
Ragtime for Eleven Instruments	_____	

Rhapsody in Blue _____

The Rite of Spring _____

Swanee _____

*Threnody for the Victims
of Hiroshima* _____

C. Decide whether the following statements are true or false and circle the appropriate letter.

1. The universally accepted term for the music of our time is *Twentieth-Century Music*. T F
2. Twentieth-century music represents a revolt against German Romanticism of the nineteenth century. T F
3. The composers of the twentieth century have been a busy group, lashing out in many different directions. T F
4. No single style of composition has become representative of the contemporary era. T F
5. Jazz has had little influence on the compositional style of twentieth-century composers. T F
6. Compositions by Charles Ives antedated the polytonal work of Igor Stravinsky. T F
7. Atonal music means music without a tonal center. T F
8. Rhythm has been an extremely important element in twentieth-century music. T F
9. Composers of the twentieth century have written for larger numbers of percussion than any of the earlier composers. T F
10. Charles Ives quotes many American melodies in his orchestral work *The Fourth of July*. T F
11. *The Fourth of July*, performed when Ives was still very young, launched him on his career as one of America's best-known composers of the 1910s. T F
12. The *Concerto for Orchestra* is perhaps the most frequently performed of Béla Bartók's orchestral compositions. T F
13. The story of Stravinsky's *The Rite of Spring* is based on a vision of pagan Russia. T F
14. Accents play an important part in the structure of the *Dance of the Adolescents* from Stravinsky's *The Rite of Spring*. T F
15. George Gershwin was neither the first nor the last composer to adapt the jazz idiom to concert music. T F
16. Gershwin's *Concerto in F* was his first attempt to blend the jazz idiom with the symphonic tradition. T F
17. At first, clarinetists said that the opening clarinet glissando in the *Rhapsody in Blue* was unplayable. T F
18. A *malambo* is an agile, footstamping dance. T F
19. The Polish composer Krzysztof Penderecki has written many large works for chorus, orchestra, and soloists. T F
20. Penderecki believes one must be a practicing churchgoer in order to compose religious music. T F
21. *Stabat Mater* by Penderecki ends on a polytonal chord. T F
22. Carman Moore, in his orchestral works, makes use of such diverse idioms as rock, jazz, and the symphonic tradition. T F
23. The pi'pa is a guitarlike instrument of Chinese origin. T F

NAME_____

WORKSHEET 11: LISTENING

A. Listen to the recording of *Giuoco delle coppie* from Béla Bartók's *Concerto for Orchestra* on Record 4 (Side A) in this book. After careful study, and with as many references to the recording and the text as necessary, place the letter of the most nearly correct answer in the blank.

1. *Giuoco delle coppie* is essentially in _____ meter.
     A. duple ($\frac{2}{4}$ or $\frac{4}{4}$)   B. triple   C. $\frac{6}{8}$

2. There are _____ changes from this underlying metrical structure.
     A. many   B. relatively few   C. no

3. The overall effect of the rhythm is one of _____.
     A. relatively little syncopation   B. syncopation throughout   C. absolutely no syncopation

4. The opening solo for snare drum involves _____.
     A. polyrhythms   B. syncopation   C. polytonality

5. In the theme for clarinets, Bartók occasionally achieves a varied rhythmical division of the measure by grouping

   sixteenth notes into sets of _____.
     A. 2 and 4   B. 3 and 5   C. 4 and 6

6. *Giuoco delle coppie* is essentially _____.
     A. atonal   B. tonal   C. monophonic

7. The movement within the several melodies of *Giuoco delle coppie* is essentially by _____.
     A. conjunct motion   B. disjunct motion

8. The texture of the movement is essentially _____.
     A. monophonic   B. polyphonic   C. homophonic

9. The trio for brass could be considered harmonically _____.
     A. pleasing and traditional   B. harsh and very dissonant

10. The opening of the movement is unusual in that the first eight measures are a solo for an unaccompanied

    _____.
     A. bassoon   B. tuba   C. snare drum

11. Most of the duets and melodic passages in the movement are scored for _____.
     A. percussion   B. winds   C. strings

12. The tempo of the movement could be described as _____.
     A. very fast   B. moderate   C. very slow

13. The trio is marked by the composer "at the same tempo." In the performance on this recording, the conductor

    _____.
     A. follows the composer's request   B. selects a faster tempo   C. selects a slower tempo

NAME_____

14. Although the trumpets are normally the loudest of the wind instruments that Bartók uses in his "pairs," the trumpet duet is the softest passage because _____ .
    A. the trumpets are muted   B. the trumpets are placed offstage   C. the other instruments all play so loudly

15. Throughout the trio section, the dynamic level _____ .
    A. becomes intensely loud   B. varies greatly from soft to loud   C. remains essentially the same

B. Listen to the recording of *Saturday Night Waltz* from *Rodeo* by Aaron Copland on Record 2 (Side A) in this book. After careful study, and with as many references to the recording and the text as necessary, place the letter of the most nearly correct answer in the blank.

1. *Saturday Night Waltz* is in _____ meter.
    A. duple ($\frac{2}{4}$ or $\frac{4}{4}$)   B. triple   C. $\frac{6}{8}$

2. There are _____ changes in meter.
    A. many   B. relatively few   C. no

3. The overall effect of the rhythm is one of _____ .
    A. relatively little syncopation   B. syncopation throughout   C. no syncopation

4. In the opening, introductory section, the strings _____ .
    A. sound as if they were tuning   B. are played *pizzicato*   C. play a tuneful American folk melody

5. *Saturday Night Waltz* is essentially _____ .
    A. atonal   B. tonal   C. monophonic

6. In the first melody, when the tones of the melody change, they move by _____ motion.
    A. conjunct   B. disjunct   C. both conjunct and disjunct

7. When the tones of the second melody change, they move essentially by _____ motion.
    A. conjunct   B. disjunct

8. The range of the first melody is _____ than that of the second.
    A. greater   B. less

9. The _____ makes more use of repeated tones.
    A. first melody   B. second melody

10. The first melody of *Saturday Night Waltz* is played by _____ .
    A. a clarinet   B. an oboe   C. a bassoon

11. The repetition of the first melody is played by _____ .
    A. violins   B. clarinets   C. trumpets

12. Within the first melody there is _____ .
    A. changing of tonality   B. atonalism   C. a repeated rhythm pattern

13. The *Saturday Night Waltz* ends with the _____ melody.
    A. first   B. second   C. third

14. With the exception of the introduction, the dynamic level of *Saturday Night Waltz* is essentially _____ .
    A. soft   B. loud

15. The tempo of the *Saturday Night Waltz* _____ .
    A. varies very little   B. varies greatly from slow to fast

16. The texture of *Saturday Night Waltz* is essentially _____ .
    A. monophonic   B. polyphonic   C. homophonic

NAME_____

WORKSHEET 12: READING

A. After reading Chapter 12, respond to the following statements by placing the letter of the correct choice in the blank.

   1. The tape composer has access to approximately _____ precisely calculated dynamic levels.
       A. fewer than 10   B. 40 or more   C. more than 100

   2. The tape composer has access to _____ of durational values.
       A. a limited number   B. an unlimited number

   3. *Musique concrète* refers to music created on tape from _____ sound sources.
       A. electronic   B. natural

   4. The first synthesizer, or device for creating musical tones by purely electronic means, was _____ .
       A. the Hammond organ in 1935   B. the Moog synthesizer in 1953   C. The Dynamophone of 1906

   5. The big interest and growth in electronic music had to wait until the development of the _____ made it practical.
       A. synthesizer   B. tape recorder   C. vacuum tube

   6. The first tape music was heard in the United States in _____ .
       A. 1930   B. 1941   C. 1952

   7. The pitch of a sound is produced by the synthesizer's _____ .
       A. filters   B. oscillators   C. amplitude shapers

   8. The timbre of a sound is controlled by the synthesizer's _____ .
       A. filters   B. potentiometers   C. amplitude shapers

   9. The loudness of a sound is determined by the _____ .
       A. filter   B. oscillator   C. amplitude shaper

10. The oscillators produce the exact _____ of a tone.
       A. loudness   B. pitch   C. decay

11. The amplitude shaper on a synthesizer controls the _____ .
       A. timbre   B. pitch   C. loudness

12. One of the first things to listen for in a piece of electronic music is the _____ .
       A. dynamic level   B. overall structure   C. sound source

NAME_____

B. For each of the following instruments, find the inventor or developer in the left column and place that letter in the first blank. Then choose the correct date of the invention or development from the right-hand column and place it in the second blank.

A. Thaddeus Cahill   Around the turn of the century
B. Laurens Hammond   1920
C. Maurice Martenot   1928
D. Robert A. Moog   1935
E. RCA   1957
F. Leon Theremin   1960

Dynamophone _____ _____

Hammond organ _____ _____

Mark II synthesizer _____ _____

Moog synthesizer _____ _____

Ondes martenot _____ _____

Theremin _____ _____

C. Decide whether the following statements are true or false and circle the appropriate letter.

1. Electronic music was devised to replace all forms of traditional music.   T   F
2. There are no performers involved in tape music.   T   F
3. The electronic composer is not limited to the seventy to eighty pitch levels at the disposal of traditional composers.   T   F
4. All natural musical tones consist of a fundamental tone and a series of overtones.   T   F
5. Experimentation in the field of electronic music started about 1950.   T   F
6. Pierre Schaeffer created the first music made completely by electrical-mechanical means shortly after the Second World War.   T   F
7. Today's performance synthesizer can produce more than one tone at a time.   T   F
8. Synthesizers are limited in the types of sound they can produce.   T   F
9. Each property of a sound is determined by a specific synthesizer function.   T   F
10. Listening to a piece of electronic music is quite unlike listening to a work composed in the more traditional idioms.   T   F
11. All sounds in Luciano Berio's *Thema (Omaggio a Joyce)* are derived from the sound of the human voice.   T   F
12. All sounds in İlhan Mimaroğlu's *Intermezzo* were created by electrical means.   T   F

WORKSHEET 12: LISTENING

A. Listen to the recording of *Bowery Bum (Study After Jean Dubuffet)* by İlhan Mimaroğlu on Record 4 (Side A) in this book. After careful study, and with as many references to the recording and to the text as necessary, place the letter of the most nearly correct answer in the blank.

1. *Bowery Bum* is _____.
   A. in strongly marked duple meter   B. in strongly marked triple meter
   C. almost without apparent regular, measurable pulse

2. Most melodic movement in *Bowery Bum* is _____.
   A. upward   B. downward   C. static

3. Most such melodic movements are by _____ motion.
   A. conjunct   B. disjunct

4. The texture of *Bowery Bum* is essentially _____.
   A. monophonic   B. polyphonic   C. homophonic

5. The tempo of *Bowery Bum* is basically _____.
   A. quite fast   B. moderate   C. quite slow

6. The overall dynamic level of *Bowery Bum* is _____.
   A. extremely loud   B. moderate   C. very soft

7. The composer achieves higher pitches from the initial sound source of the rubber band by _____ the tape.
   A. slowing down   B. reversing   C. speeding up

8. One of the design elements of *Bowery Bum* is concerned with _____ as melodic fragments bounce back and forth between right and left channels.
   A. sound superimposition   B. sound transformation   C. sound synthesis

9. The only sound source for the music of *Bowery Bum* is that of a _____.
   A. synthesizer   B. sine-wave generator   C. single rubber band

NAME_____

WORKSHEET 13: READING

A. After reading Chapter 13, complete the following sentences by placing the appropriate word or words in the blank.

    1. The front line of early New Orleans-style jazz ensembles usually included

        A. _____   C. _____

        B. _____

    2. The rhythm section of early New Orleans-style jazz ensembles usually included

        A. _____   C. _____

        B. _____   D. _____

    3. A drum set usually consists of

        A. _____   D. _____

        B. _____   E. _____

        C. _____

    4. Today we find the instrumentation of most jazz ensembles includes such instruments as

        Brass: A. _____

                B. _____

        Woodwinds: A. _____

                B. _____ (alto, tenor, or baritone)

                C. _____

        Rhythm: A. _____ (electric or acoustic)

                B. _____ (electric or acoustic)

                C. _____

                D. _____

B. In the following questions, place the letter of the correct choice in the blank spaces.

    1. For each jazz technique listed in the left column, find the correct definition in the column on the right and place that letter in the blank.

        bend   _____   A. use of a metal or plastic device to change or deaden the tone of a brass instrument

        fall   _____   B. similar to *flutter tonguing*, achieved by rolling an *r* while playing

        flutter   _____

NAME_____

glissando   _____

growl   _____

mute   _____

smear   _____

vibrato   _____

C. growling at the back of the throat while playing a note

D. the weaving above and below the exact pitch (much slower than *vibrato*)

E. the reverse of a smear; player sounds correct pitch, then falls off rapidly to an indeterminant, much lower tone

F. approaching a note from slightly below its exact pitch, holding this out-of-tune effect for desired time, then sliding up to correct pitch

G. sliding from one pitch to another

H. slight undulation or variance in pitch, weaving back and forth a little above and below note itself

2. Match each type of mute listed in the left column with its picture in the column on the right and place that letter in the blank.

cup mute   _____

derby   _____

straight mute   _____

wha-wha   _____

A.

B.

C.

D.

3. For each period of jazz history listed in the left column, find the correct pair of dates from the list at the right and place that letter in the blank.

Bebop _____

New York, Chicago, and Kansas City _____

Cool Jazz _____

New Orleans or Dixieland _____

New Wave or Free Form _____

New York and Swing _____

Present and Future _____

A. 1900–1920
B. 1920–1935
C. 1932–1942
D. 1940–1950
E. 1949–1955
F. 1957–
G. 1980–

C. Decide whether the following statements are true or false and circle the appropriate letter.

1. Jazz emerged around the turn of the century.	T	F
2. The exact date and birthplace of jazz are unknown.	T	F
3. Jazz is an art with few or no cultural ties to Africa.	T	F
4. Jazz is never concerned with melodic or rhythmic embellishments.	T	F
5. Blues and ragtime are the sad music of America's blacks.	T	F
6. The syncopated effect of ragtime later became one of the chief characteristics of jazz.	T	F
7. In jazz rhythm, all notes are played for the exact value indicated in the notated music.	T	F
8. The blues scale in jazz probably developed around the time the early black jazz musicians tried to work with the seven-tone major and minor scale patterns.	T	F
9. The blue notes in a blues scale are the third and seventh tones of the scale.	T	F
10. All instruments are capable of playing the blues scale.	T	F
11. The harmonic structure became the basis of improvisation in early jazz.	T	F
12. As jazz became more sophisticated, chords more complex than the tonic, subdominant, and dominant were used.	T	F
13. Saxophones did not become part of most jazz ensembles until the 1920s.	T	F
14. During the big band era of the 1930s, as many as thirty musicians could be found in some jazz bands.	T	F
15. Stringed instruments are never used in jazz ensembles.	T	F
16. Most jazz can be considered cast in the theme-with-variation form.	T	F
17. In the original New Orleans type of band, written or printed music was never used.	T	F
18. Boogie-woogie was principally a pianistic style of jazz.	T	F
19. The Swing era derived its name from Duke Ellington's tune *It Don't Mean a Thing If It Ain't Got That Swing.*	T	F
20. Swing musicians used a hotter tone than their predecessors.	T	F

NAME_____

D. For each of the following statements, place the letter of the correct choice in the blank.

1. Two of the most obvious characteristics of jazz are _____ and _____ .
    A. polyphony   B. improvisation   C. syncopation   D. isolation   E. monophony

2. Jazz originally had _____ beats, or pulses, to a bar.
    A. two   B. three   C. six

3. The syncopated nature of jazz probably evolved from the _____ with which the black creators of jazz were familiar.
    A. marches   B. children's songs   C. spirituals

4. The custom of not playing jazz rhythms exactly the way they are notated has been called, by some scholars,

    _____ .
    A. delayed syncopation   B. anticipated rhythm   C. tactus

5. The special scale usually associated with most jazz tunes is called the _____ scale.
    A. pentatonic   B. whole-tone   C. blues

6. The traditional harmonic pattern in blues and much jazz is _____ bars in length.
    A. 8   B. 12   C. 16

7. When everyone in a jazz ensemble improvises simultaneously, it is called a _____ .
    A. jam session   B. break   C. riff

8. Sometimes a small cadenza occurs at the end of a phrase with a long note or rest; this is a chance for the soloist to

    show off and is called a _____ .
    A. jam session   B. break   C. riff

9. A _____ is a short phrase, usually of two to four bars, repeated many times over the changing harmonies of a theme.
    A. jam session   B. break   C. riff

10. In jazz, the composer is the person who creates the original tune; the _____ is the one who develops the variations and writes them out.
    A. conductor   B. impressario   C. arranger   D. expediter

WORKSHEET 13: LISTENING

A. Listen to the recording of *Simple Like* by John Coltrane on Record 4 (Side B) in this book. After careful study, and with as many references to the recording and the text as necessary, place the letter of the most nearly correct answer in the blank.

1. *Simple Like* is in _____ meter.
   A. duple ($\frac{2}{4}$ or $\frac{4}{4}$)   B. triple   C. $\frac{6}{8}$

2. The tempo of *Simple Like* is _____.
   A. moderately slow and leisurely   B. moderately fast and agitated

3. Most of the melodic material in *Simple Like* is presented by the _____.
   A. drum set   B. bass   C. saxophone

4. That special timbre known as _____ in jazz is evident in the tone of John Coltrane's performance.
   A. bending   B. vibrato   C. fluttering

5. The solo line of the saxophone includes many _____ and _____.
   A. repeated melodic motives   B. wide-spaced jumps and leaps   C. quotations from well-known jazz tunes
   D. melodic sequences

6. The harmonic background provided by the piano makes use, essentially, of _____.
   A. simple, triadic chords   B. more complex chords

7. The _____ is featured in the fourth and fifth chorus of *Simple Like*.
   A. saxophone   B. piano   C. bass

8. The rhythm section in *Simple Like* includes: _____.
   A. piano, drum set, bass   B. synthesizer, drum set, electric guitar   C. vibes, drum set, bass

9. The overall form of *Simple Like* is essentially _____.
   A. two-part (binary)   B. three-part (ternary)   C. through-composed

NAME_____

WORKSHEET 14: READING

A. After reading Chapter 14, respond to the following statements by placing the letter of the correct word or phrase in the blank.

1. The Renaissance lasted, roughly, from _____.
   A. 1100 to 1250   B. 1450 to 1650   C. 1600 to 1750

2. The Renaissance is set off from the Middle Ages by the advent of _____, _____, and

   _____.

   A. the Crusades   B. gunpowder   C. the compass   D. the discovery of China
   E. moveable type   F. the steam engine

3. *A cappella* singing refers to vocal music without _____.
   A. instrumental accompaniment   B. a fixed rhythm   C. harmony

4. *Frottole* made use of _____ texts.
   A. sacred   B. amorous   C. humorous

5. Most frottole are _____.
   A. stanzaic or strophic   B. through-composed

6. Motets are _____ in nature.
   A. humorous   B. amorous   C. sacred

7. English madrigals are generally either _____ or _____.
   A. light and happy   B. sacred   C. filled with remorse and sadness   D. religious

B. For each of the following Renaissance figures, indicate the field of each one's principal contribution by placing the appropriate letter in the blank.

   A. artist (painter, sculptor, architect)
   M. musician (composer, theorist)
   W. writer (poet, dramatist, writer of prose)

   Orlando Gibbons _____   Thomas Morley   _____

   Josquin des Prez _____   Shakespeare   _____

   Leonardo da Vinci _____   Thomás Luis de Victoria _____

   Michelangelo   _____

NAME_____

C. Decide whether the following statements are true or false and circle the appropriate letter.

1. With the growth of trade and industry during the Renaissance, merchant princes became fabulously wealthy. T F
2. The Renaissance person looked at life from a religious point of view rather than in a secular manner. T F
3. Music during the Renaissance became involved in secular as well as religious forms. T F
4. The melodies of popular songs of the Renaissance were sometimes used as the melodic material for settings of the Mass. T F
5. During the Renaissance, a counterpointing of rhythm between voices became as important as the melodic counterpoint between them. T F
6. Renaissance art and the humanistic movement began and developed in Italy before moving northward. T F
7. The Flemish composers imitated in style the earlier Italian composers of the Renaissance. T F
8. Word painting in music is an attempt to represent musically specific poetic images. T F
9. Imitative counterpoint means that each voice or part imitates its predecessors. T F
10. Like their earlier Italian models, English madrigals tended to become highly contrapuntal. T F
11. In contrast to the highly chromatic harmony of the earlier Italian madrigals, the harmonic structure of English madrigals was quite direct and simple. T F
12. A lute ayer (or air) is a song for solo voice and lute accompaniment. T F
13. Crumhorns are an ancient oboe type of instrument, made in a variety of sizes. T F

Note: Due to space limitations in placing the Renaissance music selections on the student records, there is no listening worksheet for Chapter 14.

WORKSHEET 15: READING

A. After reading Chapter 15, respond to the following by placing the letter of the correct word or phrase in the blank.

1. The birth of _____ around the year 1600 ushered in the new Baroque era.
   A. the symphony   B. opera   C. the concerto

2. The Baroque era probably assumed its name from the Portuguese word *barroco*, which originally referred to

   _____ .
   A. a pearl of irregular and imperfect shape   B. ornately designed walls   C. large instrumental ensembles

3. The death of _____ in 1750 is frequently used as the terminal date of the Baroque era in music.
   A. Georg Friedrich Handel   B. Giovanni Gabrieli   C. Johann Sebastian Bach

4. *A cappella* singing refers to _____ choral singing.
   A. unaccompanied   B. accompanied   C. monophonic

5. The Baroque movement began in Italy as part of the _____ .
   A. Resorgimento   B. Reformation   C. Counter-Reformation

6. The development of Baroque music in the German lands was delayed by _____ .
   A. the Napoleonic wars   B. the Thirty Years' War   C. the Franco-Prussian War

7. The early Baroque composers started to write in a _____ texture.
   A. monophonic   B. polyphonic   C. homophonic

8. Later in the era, _____ writing returned to join homophonic writing as equally acceptable.
   A. monophonic   B. polyphonic   C. homophonic

9. *Stile concertante* refers to a style based on _____ .
   A. contrasts of sound   B. use of polyphonic textures   C. use of homophonic textures

10. The basso continuo is usually performed by two instruments, a _____ and _____ .
    A. first violin   B. harpsichord   C. cello   D. second violin   E. flute (recorder)

11. The term *figured bass* refers to numbers that appear under the bass line in printed music, informing the keyboard

    player what _____ to play.
    A. chords   B. melody   C. rhythm

12. The word *canzona* in the title of Gabrieli's *Canzona on the Twelfth Tone* points to a connection to French _____ .
    A. dance patterns   B. liturgical music   C. chansons (songs)

13. Dulzians are soft-voiced, double-reeded, sixteenth-century forerunners of the modern _____ .
    A. flute   B. oboe   C. bassoon

14. A toccata usually is a keyboard work full of _____ .
    A. brilliant passage work   B. chromatic alterations   C. ambiguities of rhythm

15. The principal melody or theme in a fugue is called the _____ .
    A. Principal Melody   B. Subject   C. Tune

NAME_____

16. Georg Friedrich Handel was, for the latter part of his life, court composer to the king of _____.
    A. England   B. Italy   C. Germany

17. During the Baroque era, the generic form of the _____ referred to a set of dances in the same or related keys that were grouped together for performance purposes.
    A. toccata   B. suite   C. concerto grosso

B. Decide whether the following statements are true or false and circle the appropriate letter.

 1. The birth of opera around the year 1600 marked the beginning of the Baroque era in music.   T   F
 2. The Baroque was a period of limited achievement in the arts and sciences.   T   F
 3. The spirit of the Baroque was truly theatrical.   T   F
 4. Many artists of later epochs thought Baroque works overdone in reference to ornament and detail.   T   F
 5. It has been said that no other age has turned out such a vast quantity of good—and often the greatest—music.   T   F
 6. Composers of the Baroque were almost all very prolific.   T   F
 7. Much instrumental music was written for nonliturgical purposes.   T   F
 8. Very little music was written for amateur performers, especially those in the households of the nobility and wealthy.   T   F
 9. During the Baroque era, there was no appreciable difference in the style of writing for voices and for instruments.   T   F
10. Baroque composers frequently discarded the underlying pulse or beat in passages of recitative.   T   F
11. The characteristic most frequently associated with the Baroque era is the affinity between soprano and bass voices.   T   F
12. The *D Minor Toccata* of Johann Sebastian Bach is one of his lesser-known masterpieces.   T   F
13. In a fugue, once the second voice has entered with the Answer, the first voice continues with a secondary theme called the Countersubject.   T   F
14. In stretto, the polyphonic entrances overlap.   T   F

WORKSHEET 15: LISTENING

A. Listen to the recording of the third movement (*Allegro assai*) from the *Brandenburg Concerto No. 2* by Johann Sebastian Bach on Record 4 (Side B) in this book. After careful study, and with as many references to the recording and the text as necessary, respond to the following statements by placing the most nearly correct word or words in the blanks.

   1. The third movement (*Allegro assai*) from Bach's *Brandenburg Concerto No. 2* is scored for a *tutti* or *ripieni* of strings and continuo, and a *concertino* that consists of _____, _____, _____, and _____.

   2. The *continuo* consists of _____ and _____.

   3. The *Allegro assai* is in _____ meter.

   4. At the beginning, only the sounds of the _____ and continuo are heard.

   5. The _____ enters next in imitative counterpoint.

   6. The third entrance is by the _____, and the fourth by the _____.

B. For each of the following statements, place letter of the most nearly correct answer in the blank.

   1. As *Allegro assai* indicates, the tempo is quite _____.
      A. slow   B. fast

   2. The *Allegro assai* is in the _____ mode.
      A. major   B. minor   C. major, then the minor

   3. The *ripieno* enters for the first time when _____.
      A. the principal melody is heard the first time   B. the principal melody is heard the second time
      C. the second melody is heard the first time   D. the second melody is heard the second time

   4. The principal melody involves a _____ figure.
      A. homophonic   B. sequential   C. recitative

   5. The second melody moves primarily by _____ motion.
      A. conjunct   B. disjunct

   6. The *Allegro assai* is essentially _____ in texture.
      A. monophonic   B. polyphonic   C. homophonic

C. Listen to the recording of the *Hallelujah!* chorus from *Messiah* by Georg Friedrich Handel on Record 2 (Side A) in this book. After careful study, and with as many references to the recording as you may need, place the letter of the most nearly correct answer in the blank.

   1. At the point at which the voices first enter with the word *Hallelujah!*, the texture is _____.
      A. monophonic   B. polyphonic   C. homophonic

NAME_____

2. At the point where the text *for the Lord God Omnipotent reigneth* occurs for the first time, the texture is

    _____ .

    A. monophonic   B. polyphonic   C. homophonic

3. At the point at which the text is *and He shall reign for ever and ever*, the texture is _____ .
    A. monophonic   B. polyphonic   C. homophonic

4. The closing section, based on the text *King of Kings and Lord of Lords* is _____ in texture.
    A. monophonic   B. polyphonic   C. homophonic

5. The *Hallelujah!* chorus contrasts a body of _____ sound with that of vocal sounds.
    A. instrumental   B. vocal   C. guitar

6. Throughout the *Hallelujah!* chorus, the predominant orchestral sound is that of the _____ .
    A. brass   B. strings   C. woodwinds

7. The *Hallelujah!* chorus is in _____ meter.
    A. duple ($\frac{2}{4}$ or $\frac{4}{4}$)   B. triple   C. $\frac{6}{8}$

8. In the opening phrase of the *Hallelujah!* chorus, there are _____ different rhythm patterns that are repeated one or more times.
    A. two   B. four   C. six

9. The *Hallelujah!* chorus is in the _____ mode.
    A. major   B. minor   C. major, then minor

10. The *Hallelujah!* chorus is performed at a _____ tempo.
    A. very slow   B. moderately fast   C. extremely fast

WORKSHEET 16: READING

A. After reading Chapter 16, respond to the following statements by placing the letter of the correct word or phrase in the blank.

1. The eighteenth century was sometimes referred to as _____.
   A. the Humanistic Era   B. the Age of Enlightenment   C. the Opulent Era

2. The word *classic* was used to describe the music of the eighteenth century because it seemed to suggest _____.
   A. the highest class of acknowledged excellence   B. the opposite of what we term "popular" music
   C. a return to the ideals of the classic structure of ancient Greece

3. The Mannheim School of composers helped establish the _____ and _____ as the cornerstones of the new style.
   A. opera   B. symphony   C. cantata   D. oratorio   E. sonata

4. The _____ form is one of the most frequently employed forms for the finales of symphonies.
   A. minuet   B. theme with variations   C. rondo

5. The sonata-allegro form is based on _____ themes.
   A. two   B. three   C. four

6. The three sections of the sonata-allegro form are: _____, _____, and _____.
   A. trio   B. exposition   C. development   D. minuet   E. rondo   F. recapitulation

B. Decide whether the following statements are true or false and circle the appropriate letter.

1. The eighteenth-century—the Classic era—was a cosmopolitan age.   T   F
2. During this period, princes and courts were gaining in strength, power, and influence.   T   F
3. Music of the Classic era turned away from the overdecoration of the earlier Baroque era.   T   F
4. Music of the Classic era sought beauty, clarity, and self-control in expression.   T   F
5. The invention and development of the piano changed the style of keyboard composition.   T   F
6. It has been truly said that music of the Classic era is all form without emotion.   T   F
7. In a rondo, a principal theme alternates with several episodes based on secondary themes.   T   F
8. A minuet and trio is based on two themes, each of which has an important variant.   T   F
9. The trio is always performed at a higher dynamic level (louder) than the minuet.   T   F

NAME_____

WORKSHEET 16: LISTENING

A. Listen to the recording of the final movement (*Rondo alla turca*) from the *Sonata No. 11 in A for Piano* by Wolfgang Amadeus Mozart on Record 4 (Side B) in this book. After careful study, and with as many references to the recording and the text as necessary, place the letter of the most nearly correct answer in the blank.

1. The *Rondo alla turca* is in _____ meter.
   A. duple ($\frac{2}{4}$ or $\frac{4}{4}$)   B. triple   C. $\frac{6}{8}$

2. The tempo of the *Rondo alla turca* could be described as _____.
   A. slow   B. moderate   C. brisk

3. Most of the melodies in the *Rondo alla turca* move principally by _____ motion.
   A. conjunct   B. disjunct

4. The Principal Theme opens with a _____.
   A. fanfare   B. sequence   C. fugal section

5. The texture of the *Rondo alla turca* is _____.
   A. monophonic   B. polyphonic   C. homophonic

6. The A section of the Principal Theme in the *Rondo alla turca* is in the _____ mode.
   A. major   B. minor

7. The first episode is in the _____ mode.
   A. major   B. minor

8. There are _____ episodes in the *Rondo alla turca*.
   A. two   B. three   C. four

A B C D E F G H I J 0 1 2 3 4 5 6 7 8

NAME_____